December 2006

Dear Hannah,
   I love this book
never read it from u
Since I have two, I'm giving

Battlefield of the Mind

you one and Keeping the
other for me. Hope it's
helpful for you too!
            Love,
            Aunt Bobbie

Battlefield of the Mind

Winning the Battle in Your Mind

by
Joyce Meyer

WARNER
Faith®

NEW YORK   BOSTON   NASHVILLE

Unless otherwise indicated, all Scripture quotations are taken from *The Amplified Bible* (AMP). *The Amplified Bible, Old Testament,* copyright © 1965, 1987 by the Zondervan Corporation. *The Amplified New Testament,* copyright © 1954, 1958,1987 by The Lockman Foundation. Used by permission.

Scripture quotations marked NKJV are taken from *The New King James Version* of the Bible. Copyright © 1979, 1980, 1982 by Thomas Nelson, Inc., Publishers. Used by permission.

Scripture quotations marked KJV are taken from the *King James Version* of the Bible.

Warner Books Edition

Warner Faith

Time Warner Book Group
1271 Avenue of the Americas, New York, NY 10020
Visit our Web site at www.twbookmark.com.

Warner Faith® and the Warner Faith name and logo are trademarks of Time Warner Book Group Inc.

Printed in the United States of America

First Warner Faith Edition: October 2002
10 9

ISBN: 0-446-69214-X (Special Sales Edition)
LCCN: 2002110910

Dedication

I would like to dedicate *Battlefield of the Mind* to my oldest son, David.

I know your personality is enough like mine that you have had your share of struggles in the mental realm. I see you growing continually, and I know that you are experiencing the victories that come from the renewal of the mind.

I love you, David, and I am proud of you. Keep pressing on!

Contents

PART 1:

The Importance of the Mind

Introduction

How can we express the importance of our thoughts sufficiently in order to convey the true meaning of Proverbs 23:7: **For as he** [a person] **thinks in his heart, so is he...?**

The longer I serve God and study His Word, the more I realize the importance of thoughts and words. On a fairly regular basis, I find the Holy Spirit leading me to study in these areas.

I have said, and I believe it is true, that as long as we are on this earth we will need to study in the areas of thoughts and words. No matter how much we know in any area, there are always new things to learn, and things we have previously learned that we need to be refreshed in.

For the weapons of our warfare are not physical [weapons of flesh and blood], but they are mighty before God for the overthrow and destruction of strongholds,

[Inasmuch as we] refute arguments and theories and reasonings and every proud and lofty thing that sets itself up against the [true] knowledge of God; and we lead every thought and purpose away captive into the obedience of Christ (the Messiah, the Anointed One).

2 CORINTHIANS 10:4,5

What does Proverbs 23:7 really mean? The *King James Version* says, ...**As he** [a man] **thinketh in his heart, so is he....** Another translation states, "As a man thinks in his heart, so does he become."

The mind is the leader or forerunner of all actions. Romans 8:5 makes it clear: **For those who are according to the flesh and are controlled by its unholy desires set their minds on and pursue those things which gratify the flesh, but those who are according to the Spirit and are controlled by the desires of the Spirit set their minds on and seek those things which gratify the [Holy] Spirit.**

Our actions are a direct result of our thoughts. If we have a negative mind, we will have a negative life. If, on the other hand, we renew our mind according to God's Word, we will, as Romans 12:2 promises, prove out in our experience "the good and acceptable and perfect will of God" for our lives.

I have divided this book into three main parts. This first part deals with the importance of thoughts. I want to establish firmly in your heart forever that you need to begin to think about what you are thinking about.

So many people's problems are rooted in thinking patterns that actually produce the problems they experience in their lives. Satan offers wrong thinking to everyone, but we do not have to accept his offer. Learn what types of thinking are acceptable to the Holy Spirit and what types are not acceptable.

Second Corinthians 10:4,5 clearly indicates that we must know the Word of God well enough to be able to compare what is in our mind with what is in the mind of God; any thought that attempts to exalt itself above the Word of God we are to cast down and bring into captivity to Jesus Christ.

I pray that this book will help you to do that.

The mind is the battlefield. It is a vital necessity that we line up our thoughts with God's thoughts. This is a process that will take time and study.

Don't ever give up, because little by little you are changing. The more you change your mind for the better, the more your life will also change for the better. When you begin to see God's good plan for you in your thinking, you will begin to walk in it.

Chapter

1

*The Mind
Is the Battlefield*

The Mind Is the Battlefield

From this Scripture we see that we are in a war. A careful study of this verse informs us that our warfare is not with other human beings but with the devil and his demons. Our enemy, Satan, attempts to defeat us with strategy and deceit, through well-laid plans and deliberate deception.

For we are not wrestling with flesh and blood [contending only with physical opponents], but against the despotisms, against the powers, against [the master spirits who are] the world rulers of this present darkness, against the spirit forces of wickedness in the heavenly (supernatural) sphere.

EPHESIANS 6:12

The devil is a liar. Jesus called him **...the father of lies and of all that is false** (John 8:44.) He lies to you and me. He tells us things about ourselves, about other people and about circumstances that are just not true. He does not, however, tell us the entire lie all at one time.

He begins by bombarding our mind with a cleverly devised pattern of little nagging thoughts, suspicions, doubts, fears, wonderings, reasonings and theories. He moves slowly and cautiously (after all, well-laid plans take time). Remember, he has a strategy for his warfare. He has studied us for a long time.

He knows what we like and what we don't like. He knows our insecurities, our weaknesses and our fears. He knows what bothers us most. He is willing to invest any amount of time it takes to defeat us. One of the devil's strong points is patience.

TEARING DOWN STRONGHOLDS

For the weapons of our warfare are not physical [weapons of flesh and blood], but they are mighty before God for the overthrow and destruction of strongholds,

[Inasmuch as we] refute arguments and theories and reasonings and every proud and lofty thing that sets itself up against the [true] knowledge of God; and we lead every thought and purpose away captive into the obedience of Christ (the Messiah, the Anointed One).

2 Corinthians 10:4,5

Through careful strategy and cunning deceit, Satan attempts to set up "strongholds" in our mind. A stronghold is an area in which we are held in bondage (in prison) due to a certain way of thinking.

In this passage, the Apostle Paul tells us that we have the weapons we need to overcome Satan's strongholds. We will learn more about these weapons later, but right now, please notice that once again we see that we are engaged in warfare, spiritual warfare. Verse 5 shows us clearly the location of the battlefield on which this warfare is waged.

The Amplified Bible translation of this verse says that we are to take these weapons and refute arguments. The devil argues with us; he offers us theories and reasonings. All of this activity goes on in the mind.

The mind is the battlefield.

SUMMARY OF THE SITUATION

Thus, so far we have seen that:

1. We are engaged in a war.
2. Our enemy is Satan.
3. The mind is the battlefield.
4. The devil works diligently to set up strongholds in our mind.
5. He does it through strategy and deceit (through well-laid plans and deliberate deception).
6. He is in no hurry; he takes his time to work out his plan.

Let's examine his plan more clearly through a parable.

MARY'S SIDE

Mary and her husband, John, are not enjoying a happy marriage. There is strife between them all the time. They are both angry, bitter and resentful. They have two children who are being affected by the problems in the home. The strife is showing up in their school work and behavior. One of the children is having stomach problems caused by nerves.

Mary's problem is that she doesn't know how to let John be the head of their home. She is bossy — she wants to make all the decisions, handle the finances and discipline the children. She wants to work so she will have her "own" money. She is independent, loud, demanding and a nag.

About now you may be thinking, "I've got her answer. She needs to know Jesus."

She does know Him! Mary received Jesus as her Savior five years ago — three years after she and John were married.

"Do you mean there hasn't been a change in Mary since receiving Jesus as Savior?"

Yes, there has been change. She believes she is going to heaven even though her bad behavior causes her to feel constant condemnation. She has hope now. Before she met Jesus, she was miserable and hopeless; now she is just miserable.

Mary knows that her attitude is wrong. She wants to change. She has received counseling from two people, and she gets in almost every prayer line asking for victory over anger, rebellion, unforgiveness, resentment and bitterness. Why hasn't she seen more improvement?

The answer is found in Romans 12:2: **Do not be conformed to this world (this age), [fashioned after and adapted to its external, superficial customs], but be transformed (changed) by the [entire] renewal of your mind [by its new ideals and its new attitude], so** that you may prove [for yourselves] what is the good and acceptable and perfect will of God, even the thing which is good and acceptable and perfect [in His sight for you].

Mary has strongholds in her mind. They have been there for years. She doesn't even understand how they got there. She knows she shouldn't be rebellious, bossy, nagging, etc., but she doesn't know what to do to change her nature. It seems that she simply reacts in certain situations in an unseemly way because she can't control her actions.

Mary can't control her actions because she doesn't control her thoughts. She doesn't control her thoughts because there are strongholds in her mind that the devil set up early in her life.

Satan begins to initiate his well-laid plans and to sow his deliberate deception at a very young age. In Mary's case, her problems started long ago, in childhood.

As a child Mary had an extremely domineering father who often spanked her just because he was in a bad mood. If she made one wrong move, he would vent his anger on her. For years, she suffered helplessly as her father mistreated her and her mother. He was disrespectful in all his ways toward his wife and daughter. Mary's brother, however, could do no wrong. It seemed as if he was favored just because he was a boy.

By the time she was sixteen, Mary had been brain-washed for years by Satan who had told her lies that went something like this: "Men really think they are something. They are all alike; you can't trust them. They will hurt you and take advantage of you. If you're a man, you've got it made in life. You can do anything you want. You can order people around, be the boss, treat people any way you please and nobody (especially not wives or daughters) can do anything about it."

As a result, Mary's mind was resolved: "When I get away from here, nobody is ever going to push me around again!"

Satan was already waging war on the battlefield of her mind. Play those thoughts over and over in your head a hundred thousand times or more over a period of ten years, and see if you're ready to get married and become a sweet, submissive, adoring wife. Even if by some miracle you should want to be, you won't know how. This is the kind of mess in which Mary finds herself today. What can she do? What can any of us do in such a situation?

THE WEAPONS OF THE WORD

...If you abide in My word [hold fast to My teachings and live in accordance with them], you are truly My disciples.

And you will know the Truth, and the Truth will set you free.

John 8:31,32

Here Jesus tells us how we are to win the victory over the lies of Satan. We must get the knowledge of God's truth in us, renew our minds with His Word, then use the weapons of 2 Corinthians 10:4,5 to tear down strongholds and every high and lofty thing that exalts itself against the knowledge of God.

These "weapons" are the Word received through preaching, teaching, books, tapes, seminars and private Bible study. But we must "abide" (continue) in the Word until it becomes revelation given by inspiration of the Holy Spirit. Continuing is important. In Mark 4:24 Jesus says, ...**The measure [of thought and study] you give [to the truth you hear] will be the measure [of virtue and knowledge] that comes back to you....** I repeat, we must *continue* using the weapon of the Word.

Two other spiritual weapons available to us are praise and prayer. Praise defeats the devil quicker than any other battle plan, but it must be genuine heart praise, not just lip service or a method being tried to see if it works. Also, praise and prayer both involve the Word. We praise God according to His Word and His goodness.

Prayer is relationship with the Godhead. It is coming and asking for help or talking to God about something that bothers us.

If you want to have an effective prayer life, develop a good personal relationship with the Father. Know that He loves you, that He is full of mercy, that He will help you. Get to know Jesus. He is your Friend. He died for you. Get to know the Holy Spirit. He is with you all the time as your Helper. Let Him help you.

Learn to fill your prayers with the Word of God. God's Word and our need is the basis on which we come to Him.

So, our weapons are the Word used in various ways. As Paul tells us in 2 Corinthians, our weapons are not carnal (fleshly) weapons; they are spiritual. We need spiritual weapons because we are fighting master spirits, yes, even the devil himself. Even Jesus used the weapon of the Word in the wilderness to defeat the devil. (Luke 4:1-13.) Each time the devil lied to Him, Jesus responded with, "It is written," and quoted him the Word.

As Mary learns to use her weapons, she will begin to tear down the strongholds that have been built in her mind. She will know the truth that will set her free. She will see that not all men are like her earthly father. Some are, but many are not. Her husband, John, is not. John loves Mary very much.

JOHN'S SIDE

The other side of the story involves John. He, too, has problems that are a contributing factor to the situation he and Mary face in their marriage, home and family.

John should be taking his position as head of the family. God intends for him to be the priest of his home. John is also born again and knows the proper order for family life. He knows that he should not allow his wife to run the household, the finances, the children and him. He knows all this, but he doesn't do anything about it except feel defeated and retreat into TV and sports.

John is hiding from his responsibility because he hates confrontation. He prefers to take a passive attitude, thinking, "Well, if I just leave this situation alone, perhaps it will work itself out." Or, he excuses himself from taking real action by saying, "I'll pray about it." Of course, prayer is good, but not if it is merely a way of avoiding responsibility.

Let me clarify what I mean when I say that John should assume his God-given position in the home. I don't mean that he should come on like "Mr. Macho," ranting and raving about his authority. Ephesians 5:25 teaches that a man should love his wife as Christ loved the Church. John needs to take responsibility, and with responsibility comes authority. He should be firm with his wife — loving but firm. He should reassure Mary that even though she was hurt as a child, as she releases herself to God through trusting Him, she will gain confidence that not all men are like her father was.

John should be doing a lot of things; but like Mary, he also has "mindsets" that open the door for the devil to hold him captive. There is also a battle going on in John's mind. Like Mary, he was verbally abused in childhood. His domineering mother had a sharp tongue and frequently said hurtful things to him, things like: "John, you're such a mess; you'll never amount to anything."

John tried hard to please his mother because he craved her approval (as all children do); but the harder he tried, the more mistakes he made. He had a habit of being clumsy, so his mother told him all the time what a "klutz" he was. Of course, he dropped things because he was trying so hard to please that it made him nervous, and so he defeated his purpose.

He also experienced some unfortunate rejection from children with whom he desired to be friends. This type of thing happens to most of us at some time in our lives, but it devastated John because he already felt rejected by his mother.

And there was a girl whom he really liked in his early high school years who rejected him for another boy. By the time all of these things had tallied up in John's life, and the devil had worked on him, building strongholds in his mind for years and years, John simply had no courage to be anything but quiet, shy and withdrawn.

John is a low-key type person who simply chooses not to make waves. For years he has been having thoughts directed into him that go something like this: "There is no point in telling anyone what you think; they won't listen anyway. If you want people to accept you, you just need to go along with whatever they want."

The few times he tried to stand his ground on an issue, it seemed that he always ended up losing, so he finally decided that confrontation wasn't worth the effort.

"I'm going to lose anyway in the end," he reasoned, "so why even start anything?"

WHAT IS THE ANSWER?

The Spirit of the Lord [is] upon Me, because He has anointed Me [the Anointed One, the Messiah] to preach the good news (the Gospel) to the poor; He has sent Me to announce release to the captives and recovery of sight to the blind, to send forth as delivered those who are oppressed [who are downtrodden, bruised, crushed, and broken down by calamity],

To proclaim the accepted and acceptable year of the Lord [the day when salvation and the free favors of God profusely abound].

Luke 4:18,19

With John and Mary's conflicting problems, it is not too hard to imagine what their home life is like. Remember, I said there was a lot of strife in it. Strife isn't always open warfare. Many times, strife is an angry undercurrent in the home that everyone knows is there, but nobody deals with. The atmosphere in their home is terrible, and the devil loves it!

What will happen to John and Mary and their children? Will they make it? They are Christians — it would be a shame to see their marriage fail and their family ruined. Actually, though, it is up to them. John 8:31,32 will be a key Scripture passage in their decision. If they continue to study God's Word, they will know the truth, and acting on the truth will set them free. *But* they must each face the truth about themselves and their past as God reveals it to them.

The truth is always revealed through the Word; but sadly, people don't always accept it. It is a painful process to face our faults and deal with them. Generally speaking, people justify misbehavior. They allow their past and how they were raised to negatively affect the rest of their lives.

Our past may explain why we're suffering, but we must not use it as an excuse to stay in bondage.

Everyone is without excuse because Jesus always stands ready to fulfill His promise to set the captives free. He will walk us across the finish line of victory in any area if we are willing to go all the way through it with Him.

THE WAY OUT

For no temptation (no trial regarded as enticing to sin, no matter how it comes or where it leads) has overtaken you and laid hold on you that is not common to man [that is, no temptation or trial has come to you that is beyond human resistance and that is not adjusted and adapted and belonging to human experience, and such as man can bear]. But God is faithful [to His Word and to His compassionate nature], and He [can be trusted] not to let you be tempted and tried and assayed beyond your ability and strength of resistance and power to endure, but with the temptation He will [always] also provide the way out (the means of escape to a landing place), that you may be capable and strong and powerful to bear up under it patiently.

1 Corinthians 10:13

I hope you see from this parable-type example how Satan takes our circumstances and builds strongholds in our lives — how he wages war on the battlefield of the mind. But, thank God, we have weapons to tear down the strongholds. God doesn't abandon us and leave us helpless. First Corinthians 10:13 promises us that God will not allow us to be tempted beyond what we can bear, but with every temptation He will also provide the way out, the escape.

Any one of us may be Mary or John. I am sure that most of us relate in some way to the scenario. Their problems are internal — in their thoughts and attitudes. Their outward behavior is only a result of their inner life. Satan knows well that if he can control our thoughts, he can control our actions.

You may have some major strongholds in your life that need to be broken. Let me encourage you by saying, "God is on your side." There is a war going on, and your mind is the battlefield. But the good news is that God is fighting on your side.

Chapter

2

A Vital Necessity

A Vital Necessity

This one Scripture alone lets us know how very important it is that we think properly. Thoughts are powerful, and according to the writer of the book of Proverbs, they have creative ability. If our thoughts are going to affect what we become, then it should certainly be a priority that we think right thoughts.

For as he thinks in his heart, so is he....

PROVERBS 23:7

I want to impress on you the absolute necessity of getting your thinking in line with God's Word.

You cannot have a positive life and a negative mind.

THE MIND OF THE FLESH

VERSUS THE MIND OF THE SPIRIT

For those who are according to the flesh and are controlled by its unholy desires set their minds on and pursue those things which gratify the flesh, but those who are according to the Spirit and are controlled by the desires of the Spirit set their minds on and seek those things which gratify the [Holy] Spirit.

Romans 8:5

In the *King James Version* the eighth chapter of Romans teaches us that if we "mind" the things of the flesh, we will walk in the flesh; but if we "mind" the things of the Spirit, we will walk in the Spirit.

Let me put it another way: If we think fleshly thoughts, wrong thoughts, negative thoughts, we cannot walk in the Spirit. It seems as if renewed, God-like thinking is a vital necessity to a successful Christian life.

There are times when we humans will be lazy about something if we don't realize how important it is to pay attention to it. But, when we realize it is a matter that will cause great problems if we let it go, then we get in gear and take care of it because we realize it is so important.

Let us say, for example, that the bank calls and tells you that your account is overdrawn by $850. You immediately look for the problem. Perhaps in your search you discover that you failed to make a deposit that you thought you had made. You rush to the bank right away with the deposit, so you won't have any further problems.

I would like for you to consider this matter of getting the mind renewed in the same manner.

Your life may be in a state of chaos because of years of wrong thinking. If so, it is important for you to come to grips with the fact that *your life will not get straightened out until your mind does.* You should consider this area one of *vital necessity.* Be serious about tearing down the strongholds Satan has built in your mind. Use your weapons of the Word, praise and prayer.

BY THE SPIRIT

...Not by might, nor by power, but by My Spirit...says the Lord of hosts.

Zechariah 4:6

One of the best aids to freedom is asking God for a lot of help — and asking often.

One of your weapons is prayer (asking). You can't overcome your situation by determination alone. You do need to be determined, but determined in the Holy Spirit, not in the effort of your own flesh. The Holy Spirit is your Helper — seek His help. Lean on Him. You can't make it alone.

A VITAL NECESSITY

For the believer, right thinking is a vital necessity. A vital necessity is something that is so important that one simply cannot live without it — like a heart beat is vital, or blood pressure is vital. These are things without which there is no life.

The Lord impressed this truth on me years ago concerning personal fellowship with Him in prayer and the Word. I was having a terrible time disciplining myself to do these things until He showed me that they are a vital necessity. Just as my physical life is dependent upon my vital signs, so my spiritual life is dependent upon spending regular, quality time with God. Once I learned that fellowship with Him is vital, I gave it priority in my life.

In the same way, once I realized that right thinking is vital to victorious living, I got more serious about thinking about what I was thinking about, and choosing my thoughts carefully.

As You Think, So Are You

Either make the tree sound (healthy and good), and its fruit sound (healthy and good), or make the tree rotten (diseased and bad), and its fruit rotten (diseased and bad); for the tree is known and recognized and judged by its fruit.

Matthew 12:33

The Bible says that a tree is known by its fruit.

The same is true in our lives. Thoughts bear fruit. Think good thoughts, and the fruit in your life will be good. Think bad thoughts, and the fruit in your life will be bad.

Actually, you can look at a person's attitude and know what kind of thinking is prevalent in his life. A sweet, kind person does not have mean, vindictive thoughts. By the same token, a truly evil person does not have good, loving thoughts.

Remember Proverbs 23:7 and allow it to have an impact on your life: for as you think in your heart, so are you.

Chapter
3

Don't Give Up!

Don't Give Up!

No matter how bad the condition of your life and your mind, don't give up! Regain the territory the devil has stolen from you. If necessary, regain it one inch at a time, always leaning on God's grace and not on your own ability to get the desired results.

And let us not lose heart and grow weary and faint in acting nobly and doing right, for in due time and at the appointed season we shall reap, if we do not loosen and relax our courage and faint.

GALATIANS 6:9

In Galatians 6:9 the Apostle Paul simply encourages us to keep on keeping on! Don't be a quitter! Don't have that old "give-up" spirit. God is looking for people who will go all the way through with Him.

GO THROUGH

When you pass through the waters, I will be with you, and through the rivers, they will not overwhelm you. When you walk through the fire, you will not be burned or scorched, nor will the flame kindle upon you.

Isaiah 43:2

Whatever you may be facing or experiencing right now in your life, I am encouraging you to go through it and not give up!

Habakkuk 3:19 says that the way we develop hind's feet (a hind is an animal that can climb mountains swiftly) is ...**to walk [not to stand still in terror, but to walk] and make [spiritual] progress upon my high places [of trouble, suffering, or responsibility]**!

The way God helps us make spiritual progress is by being with us to strengthen and encourage us to "keep on keeping on" in rough times.

It's easy to quit; it takes faith to go through.

THE CHOICE IS YOURS!

I call heaven and earth to witness this day against you that I have set before you life and death, the blessings and the curses; therefore choose life, that you and your descendants may live.

Deuteronomy 30:19

There are thousands upon thousands of thoughts presented to us every day. The mind has to be renewed to follow after the Spirit and not the flesh. Our carnal (worldly, fleshly) minds have had so much practice operating freely that we surely don't have to use any effort to think wrong thoughts.

On the other hand, we have to purposely choose right thinking. After we have finally decided to be like-minded with God, then we will need to *choose* and to *continue to choose* right thoughts.

When we begin to feel that the battle of the mind is just too difficult and that we aren't going to make it, then we must be able to cast down that kind of thinking and choose to think that we are going to make it! Not only must we choose to think that we are going to make it, but we must also decide not to quit. Bombarded with doubts and fears, we must take a stand and say: "I will never give up! God is on my side, He loves me, and He is helping me!"

You and I will have many choices to make throughout our lives. In Deuteronomy 30:19 the Lord told His people that He had set before them life and death and urged them to choose life. And in Proverbs 18:21 we are told, **Death and life are in the power of the tongue, and they who indulge in it shall eat the fruit of it....**

Our thoughts become our words. Therefore, it is vitally important that we *choose* life-generating thoughts. When we do, right words will follow.

DON'T GIVE UP!

When the battle seems endless and you think you'll never make it, remember that you are reprogramming a very carnal, fleshly, worldly mind to think as God thinks.

Impossible? *No!*

Difficult? *Yes!*

But, just think, you have God on your team. I believe He is the best "computer programmer" around. (Your mind is like a computer that has had a lifetime of garbage programmed into it.) God is working even on you; at least, He is if you have invited Him to have control of your thoughts. He is reprogramming your mind. Just keep cooperating with Him — *and don't give up!*

It will definitely take time, and it won't all be easy, but you are going in the right direction if you choose God's way of thinking. You will spend your time doing something, so it may as well be going forward and not staying in the same mess for the rest of your life.

TURN AND TAKE POSSESSION!

The Lord our God said to us in Horeb, You have dwelt long enough on this mountain.

Turn and take up your journey and go to the hill country of the Amorites....

Behold, I have set the land before you; go in and take possession of the land which the Lord swore to your fathers, to Abraham, to Isaac, and to Jacob, to give to them and to their descendants after them.

Deuteronomy 1:6-8

In Deuteronomy 1:2, Moses pointed out to the Israelites that it was only an eleven-day journey to the border of Canaan (the Promised Land), yet it had taken them forty years to get there. Then in verse 6, he told them, "The Lord God says to us, 'You have dwelt long enough on this mountain.'"

Have you dwelt long enough on the same mountain? Have you spent forty years trying to make an eleven-day trip?

In my own life, I finally had to wake up and realize that I was going nowhere. I *was a Christian without victory.* Like Mary and John, I had many wrong mindsets and many mental strong-holds that had been built up over years and years. The devil had lied to me, and I had believed him. Therefore, I had been living in deception.

I had been at the same mountain long enough. I had spent forty years making what could have been a much shorter journey had I known the truth of God's Word.

God showed me that the Israelites stayed in the wilderness because they had a "wilderness mentality" —certain types of wrong thinking that kept them in bondage. We will deal with this subject in a future chapter, but for now, let me urge you to make a quality decision that you are going to get your mind renewed and learn to choose your thoughts carefully. Make up your mind that you will not quit and give up until victory is complete and you have taken possession of your rightful inheritance.

Chapter
4

Little by Little

Little by Little

The renewing of your mind will take place *little by little*, so don't be discouraged if progress seems slow.

Just before they entered the Promised Land, the Lord told the Israelites that He would drive out their enemies before them little by little lest "the beasts of the field" increase among them.

And the Lord your God will clear out those nations before you, little by little; you may not consume them quickly, lest the beasts of the field increase among you.

DEUTERONOMY 7:22

I believe pride is the "beast" that will consume us if we receive too much freedom too quickly. It is actually better to be set at liberty in one area at a time. That way, we appreciate our freedom more; we realize it is truly a gift from God and not something we can make happen in our own strength.

SUFFERING PRECEDES LIBERATION

And after you have suffered a little while, the God of all grace [Who imparts all blessing and favor], Who has called you to His [own] eternal glory in Christ Jesus, will Himself complete and make you what you ought to be, establish and ground you securely, and strengthen, and settle you.

1 Peter 5:10

Why do we need to suffer "a little while"? I believe that from the time we actually realize we have a problem until Jesus delivers us, we endure a type of suffering, but we rejoice even more when freedom comes. When we try to do something on our own, fail and then realize that we must wait on Him, our hearts overflow with thanksgiving and praise as He rises up and does what we cannot do ourselves.

NO CONDEMNATION

Therefore, [there is] now no condemnation...for those who are in Christ Jesus, who live [and] walk not after the dictates of the flesh, but after the dictates of the Spirit.

Romans 8:1

Don't receive condemnation when you have setbacks or bad days. Just get back up, dust yourself off and start again. When a baby is learning to walk, he falls many, many times before he enjoys confidence in walking. However, one thing in a baby's favor is the fact that, even though he may cry a while after he has fallen, he always gets right back up and tries again.

The devil will try his hardest to stop you in this area of renewing the mind. He knows that his control over you is finished once you have learned to choose right thoughts and reject wrong ones. He will attempt to stop you through discouragement and condemnation.

When condemnation comes, use your "Word weapon." Quote Romans 8:1, reminding Satan and yourself that you do not walk after the flesh but after the Spirit. Walking after the flesh is depending on yourself; walking after the Spirit is depending on God.

When you fail (which you will), that doesn't mean that you are a failure. It simply means that you don't do everything right. We all have to accept the fact that along with strengths we also have weaknesses. Just let Christ be strong in your weaknesses; let Him be your strength on your weak days.

I repeat: *don't receive condemnation.* Your total victory will come, but it will take time because it will come "little by little."

DON'T GET DISCOURAGED

Why are you cast down, O my inner self? And why should you moan over me and be disquieted within me? Hope in God and wait expectantly for Him, for I shall yet praise Him, my Help and My God.

Psalm 42:5

Discouragement destroys hope, so naturally the devil always tries to discourage us. Without hope we give up, which is what the devil wants us to do. The Bible repeatedly tells us not to be discouraged or dismayed. God knows that we will not come through to victory if we get discouraged, so He always encourages us as we start out on a project by saying to us, "Don't get discouraged." God wants us to be encouraged, not *discouraged.*

When discouragement or condemnation tries to overtake you, examine your thought life. What kind of thoughts have you been thinking? Have they sounded something like this?

"I'm not going to make it; this is too hard. I always fail, it has always been the same, nothing ever changes. I'm sure other people don't have this much trouble getting their minds renewed. I may as well give up. I'm tired of trying. I pray, but it seems as if God doesn't hear. He probably doesn't answer my prayers because He is so disappointed in the way I act."

If this example represents your thoughts, it is no wonder you get discouraged or come under condemnation. Remember, you become what you think. Think discouraging thoughts, and you'll get discouraged. Think condemning thoughts, and you'll come under condemnation. Change your thinking and be set free!

Instead of thinking negatively, think like this:

"Well, things are going a little slow; but, thank God, I'm making some progress. I'm sure glad I'm on the right path that will lead me to freedom. I had a rough day yesterday. I chose wrong thinking all day long. Father, forgive me, and help me to 'keep on keeping on.' I made a mistake, but at least that is one mistake I won't have to make again. This is a new day. You love me, Lord. Your mercy is new every morning.

"I refuse to be discouraged. I refuse to be condemned. Father, the Bible says that You don't condemn me. You sent Jesus to die for me. I'll be fine — today will be a great day. You help me choose right thoughts today."

I'm sure you can already feel the victory in this type of cheerful, positive, God-like thinking.

We like everything instantaneous. We have the fruit of patience inside, but it is being worked to the outside. Sometimes

God takes His time about bringing us our full deliverance. He uses the difficult period of waiting to stretch our faith and to let patience have her perfect work. (James 1:4 KJV.) God's timing is perfect. He is never late.

Here is another good thought to think: "I believe God. I believe He is working in me no matter what I may feel or how the situation may look. The Lord has begun a good work in me, and He will bring it to full completion." (Philippians 1:6; 2:13.)

It is in this manner that you can effectively use your weapon of the Word to tear down strongholds. I recommend that you not only purposely think right thoughts, but that you go the extra mile and speak them aloud as your confession.

Remember, God is delivering you, *little by little,* so don't be discouraged and don't feel condemned if you make a mistake.

Be patient with yourself!

Chapter
5

Be Positive

Be Positive

*P*ositive minds produce positive lives. Negative minds produce negative lives. Positive thoughts are always full of faith and hope. Negative thoughts are always full of fear and doubt.

...it shall be done for you as you have believed....

MATTHEW 8:13

Some people are afraid to hope because they have been hurt so much in life. They have had so many disappointments, they don't think they can face the pain of another one. Therefore, they refuse to hope so they won't be disappointed.

This avoidance of hope is a type of protection against being hurt. Disappointment hurts! So rather than be hurt again, many people simply refuse to hope or to believe that anything good will ever happen to them. This type of behavior sets up a negative lifestyle. Everything becomes negative because the thoughts are negative. Remember Proverbs 23:7: **For as he** (a person) **thinks in his heart, so is he....**

Many years ago, I was extremely negative. I always say that if I thought two positive thoughts in a row my mind would get in a cramp. My whole philosophy was this: "If you don't expect anything good to happen, then you won't be disappointed when it doesn't."

I had encountered so many disappointments in life — so many devastating things had happened to me — that I was afraid to believe that anything good might happen. I had a terribly negative outlook on everything. Since my thoughts were all negative, so was my mouth; therefore, so was my life.

When I really began to study the Word and to trust God to restore me, one of the first things I realized was that the negativism had to go.

In Matthew 8:13 Jesus tells us that it will be done for us as we have believed. The *King James Version* says, **...as thou hast believed, so be it done unto thee....** Everything I believed was negative, so naturally many negative things happened to me.

This doesn't mean that you and I can get anything we want by just thinking about it. God has a perfect plan for each of us, and we can't control Him with our thoughts and words. But, we must think and speak in agreement with His will and plan for us.

If you don't have any idea what God's will is for you at this point, at least begin by thinking, "Well, I don't know God's plan, but I know He loves me. Whatever He does will be good, and I'll be blessed."

Begin to think positively about your life.

Practice being positive in each situation that arises. Even if whatever is taking place in your life at the moment is not so good, expect God to bring good out of it, as He has promised in His Word.

ALL THINGS WORK FOR GOOD

We are assured and know that [God being a partner in their labor] all things work together and are [fitting into a plan] for good to and for those who love God and are called according to [His] design and purpose.

Romans 8:28

This Scripture does not say that all things are good, but it does say that all things *work together for good.*

Let's say you're planning to go shopping. You get in the car, and it won't start. There are two ways you can look at this situation. You can say, "I knew it! It never fails. Every time I want to do something, it gets all messed up. I figured this shopping trip would end up a flop; my plans always do." Or you can say, "Well, I wanted to go shopping, but it looks like I can't go right now. I'll go later when the car is fixed. In the meantime, I believe this change in plans is going to work out for my good. There is probably some reason I need to be at home today, so I'm going to enjoy my time there."

In Romans 12:16 the Apostle Paul tells us to readily adjust ourselves to people and things. The idea is that we must learn to become the kind of person who plans things but who doesn't fall apart if that plan doesn't work out.

Recently I had an excellent opportunity to practice this principle. Dave and I were in Lake Worth, Florida. We had been ministering there for three days, and we were packing and getting ready to go to the airport to go home. I had planned to wear slacks and a blouse with flat shoes, so I could be comfortable during the return trip.

I started getting dressed and couldn't find my slacks. We looked all over the place and finally found them in the bottom of the closet. They had slipped off the hanger and were terribly wrinkled. We take a portable clothes steamer with us, and I tried to steam out the wrinkles. I put on the outfit and saw that it was just not going to look right. My only other choice was a dress and high heels.

I could feel my emotions getting upset with the situation. You see, any time we don't get what we want, our feelings will rise up and try to get us into self-pity and a negative attitude. I recognized immediately that I had a choice to make. I could be irritable because things hadn't worked out the way I wanted them to, or I could adjust myself to the situation and go ahead and enjoy the trip home.

Even a person who is really positive won't have everything work out the way he would like it to all the time. But the positive person can go ahead and decide to enjoy himself no matter what happens. The negative person never enjoys anything.

A negative person is no fun to be with. He brings a gloomy overcast to every project. There is a "heaviness" about him. He is a complainer, a murmurer and a faultfinder. No matter how many good things are going on, he always seems to spot the one thing that could be a potential problem.

When I was in my days of extreme negativism, I could walk into someone's home that had been newly decorated, and rather than seeing and commenting on all the lovely surroundings, I would spot a corner of wallpaper that was loose or a smudge on the window. I am so glad Jesus has set me free to enjoy the good things in life! I am free to believe that with faith and hope in Him, the bad things can be turned around for good.

If you are a negative person, *don't feel condemned!* Condemnation is negative. I'm sharing these things so you can recognize your problem with being negative and begin to trust God to restore you, not to get you to become negative about your negativism.

The pathway to freedom begins when we face the problem without making excuses for it. I'm sure that if you are a negative person there is a reason for it — there always is. But remember, as a Christian, according to the Bible, you are a new person now.

A New Day!

Therefore if any person is [ingrafted] in Christ (the Messiah) he is a new creation (a new creature altogether); the old [previous moral and spiritual condition] has passed away. Behold, the fresh and new has come!

2 Corinthians 5:17

As "a new creation," you don't have to allow the old things that happened to you to keep affecting your new life in Christ. You're a new creature with a new life in Christ. You can have your mind renewed according to the Word of God. Good things are going to happen to you.

Rejoice! It's a new day!

The Work of the Holy Spirit

However, I am telling you nothing but the truth when I say it is profitable (good, expedient, advantageous) for you that I go away.

Because if I do not go away, the Comforter (Counselor, Helper, Advocate, Intercessor, Strengthener, Standby) will not come to you [into close fellowship with you]; but if I go away, I will send Him to you [to be in close fellowship with you].

And when He comes, He will convict and convince the world and bring demonstration to it about sin and about righteousness (uprightness of heart and right standing with God) and about judgment.

John 16:7,8

The hardest part of being set free from negativism is facing the truth and saying, "I'm a negative person, and I want to change. I can't change myself, but I believe God will change me as I trust Him. I know it will take time, and I'm not going to get discouraged with myself. *God has begun a good work in me, and He is well able to bring it to full completion.*" (Philippians 1:6.)

Ask the Holy Spirit to convict you each time you start to get negative. That is part of His job. John 16:7,8 teaches us that the Holy Spirit will convict us of sin and convince us of righteousness. When the conviction comes, ask God to help you. Don't think you can handle this yourself. Lean on Him.

Even though I was extremely negative, God let me know that if I would trust Him, He would cause me to be very positive. I was having a hard time trying to keep my mind in a positive pattern. Now, I can't stand negativism. It's like a person who smokes. Many times, a smoker who has quit smoking has no tolerance for cigarettes. I'm that way. I smoked for many years, but after I quit, I couldn't even stand the smell of smoke.

I'm the same way about being negative. I was a very negative person. Now, I can't stand negativism at all; it is almost offensive to me. I guess I've seen so many good changes in my life since I've been delivered from a negative mind that now I'm opposed to anything negative.

I face reality, and I encourage you to do the same. If you are sick, don't say, "I'm not sick," because that's just not true; but you can say, "I believe God is healing me." You don't have to say, "I'll probably get worse and end up in the hospital"; instead, you can say, "God's healing power is working in me right now; I believe I'll be all right."

Everything must be balanced. That doesn't mean tempering your positivism with a little negativism, but it does mean having a "ready mind" to deal with whatever happens to you, whether it is positive or negative.

A READY MIND

These were more noble than those in Thessalonica, in that they received the word with all readiness of mind, and searched the scriptures daily, whether those things were so.

Acts 17:11 KJV

The Bible says that we are to have a ready mind. That means that we are to have minds that are open to the will of God for us, whatever that will may be.

For example, recently a young lady whom I know experienced the sorrow of a broken engagement. She and the young man were praying about whether or not the Lord would have them continue dating, even though they had decided not to get married at that time. The young lady wanted the relationship to continue and was thinking, hoping and believing that her former fiance would call and feel the same way.

I advised her to have a "ready mind" in case things didn't work out that way. She said, "Well, isn't that being negative?"

No, it isn't!

Negativism would be to think, "My life is over; no one will ever want me. I have failed, so now I'll be miserable forever!"

Being positive would be to say: "I'm really sad this thing has happened, but I'm going to trust God. I hope my boyfriend and I can still date. I'm going to ask and believe for our relationship to be restored; but more than anything, I want God's perfect will. If things don't turn out the way I want them to, *I'll survive,* because

Jesus lives in me. It may be hard for a while, but I trust the Lord. I believe that in the end everything will work out for the best."

This is facing facts, having a ready mind and still being positive.

This is balance.

THE FORCE OF HOPE

[For Abraham, human reason for] hope being gone, hoped in faith that he should become the father of many nations, as he had been promised, So [numberless] shall your descendants be.

He did not weaken in faith when he considered the [utter] impotence of his own body, which was as good as dead because he was about a hundred years old, or [when he considered] the barrenness of Sarah's [deadened] womb.

No unbelief or distrust made him waver (doubtingly question) concerning the promise of God, but he grew strong and was empowered by faith as he gave praise and glory to God.

Romans 4:18-20

Dave and I believe that our ministry in the Body of Christ will grow each year. We always want to help more people. But we also realize that if God has a different plan, and if we end up at the end of a year with no growth (everything the same as when we started), we cannot let that situation control our joy.

We believe *for* many things, but beyond them all, we believe *in* Someone. That Someone is Jesus. We don't always know what is going to happen. We just know it will always work out for our good!

The more positive you and I become, the more we will be in the flow of God. God is certainly positive, and to flow with Him, we must also be positive.

You may have really adverse circumstances. You may be thinking, "Joyce, if you knew my situation, you wouldn't even expect me to be positive."

I encourage you to reread Romans 4:18-20 in which it is reported that Abraham, after sizing up his situation (he didn't ignore the facts), considered (thought about briefly) the utter impotence of his own body and the barrenness of Sarah's dead womb. Although all human reason for hope was gone, he hoped in faith.

Abraham was very positive about a very negative situation!

Hebrews 6:19 tells us that hope is the anchor of the soul. Hope is the force that keeps us steady in a time of trial. Don't ever stop hoping. If you do, you're going to have a miserable life. If you are already having a miserable life because you have no hope, start hoping. Don't be afraid. I can't promise you that things will always turn out exactly the way you want them to. I can't promise you that you'll never be disappointed. But, even in disappointing times, if they do come, you can hope and be positive. Put yourself in God's miracle-working realm.

Expect a miracle in your life.

Expect good things!

EXPECT TO RECEIVE!

TO RECEIVE, EXPECT!

And therefore the Lord [earnestly] waits [expecting, looking, and longing] to be gracious to you; and therefore He lifts Himself up, that He may have mercy on you and show loving-kindness to you. For the Lord is a God of justice. Blessed (happy, fortunate, to be envied) are all those who [earnestly] wait for Him, who expect and look and long for Him [for His victory, His favor, His love, His peace, His joy, and His matchless, unbroken companionship]!

Isaiah 30:18

This passage has become one of my favorite Scriptures. If you will meditate on it, it will begin to bring great hope. In it, God is saying that He is looking for someone to be gracious (good) to, but it cannot be someone with a sour attitude and a negative mind. It must be someone who is expecting (looking and longing for God to be good to him or her).

EVIL FOREBODINGS

What are "evil forebodings"?

Shortly after I began to study God's Word, I was combing my hair one morning in the bathroom when I realized that in the atmosphere around me was a vague, threatening feeling that something bad was going to happen. I became aware that I had actually had that feeling with me most of the time.

I asked the Lord, "What is this feeling I always have?"

"Evil forebodings," He answered.

I did not know what that meant, nor had I ever heard of it. Shortly thereafter, I found the phrase in Proverbs 15:15: **All the days of the desponding and afflicted are made evil [by anxious thoughts and forebodings], but he who has a glad heart has a continual feast [regardless of circumstances].**

I realized at that time that most of my life had been made miserable by evil thoughts and forebodings. Yes, I had circumstances that were very difficult, but even when I didn't, I was still miserable because my thoughts were poisoning my outlook and robbing me of ability to enjoy life and see good days.

KEEP YOUR TONGUE FROM EVIL!

For let him who wants to enjoy life and see good days [good — whether apparent or not] keep his tongue free from evil and his lips from guile (treachery, deceit).

1 Peter 3:10

This verse plainly tells us that enjoying life and seeing good days, and having a positive mind and mouth, are linked together.

No matter how negative you are or how long you have been that way, I know you can change because I did. It took time and "heaping helpings" of the Holy Spirit, but it was worth it.

It will be worth it to you too.

Whatever happens, trust in the Lord — and be positive!

Chapter
6

Mind-Binding Spirits

Mind-Binding Spirits

I once reached a place in my walk with God where I was having a hard time believing certain things that I had previously believed. I didn't understand what was wrong with me, and as a result, I got confused. The longer the predicament went on, the more confused I became. The unbelief seemed to be growing by leaps and bounds. I began to question my call; I thought I was losing the vision God had given me for the ministry. I was miserable (unbelief always produces misery).

Be careful for nothing; but in every thing by prayer and supplication with thanksgiving let your requests be made known unto God.

And the peace of God, which passeth all understanding, shall keep your hearts and minds through Christ Jesus.

PHILIPPIANS 4:6,7 KJV

Two days in a row I heard this phrase coming up out of my spirit: *"mind-binding spirits."* The first day I didn't think much about it. However, the second day, as I began a time of intercession, I heard it again for about the fourth or fifth time: *"mind-binding spirits."*

I knew from all the people to whom I had ministered that multitudes of believers have trouble with their minds. I thought the Holy Spirit was leading me to pray for the Body of Christ against a spirit called "Mind Binding." So I began to pray and come against mind-binding spirits in Jesus' name. After only a couple of minutes of praying, I felt a tremendous deliverance come to my own mind. It was quite dramatic.

DELIVERED FROM MIND-BINDING SPIRITS

Nearly every deliverance God has brought to me has been progressive and has come about by believing and confessing the

Word of God. John 8:31,32 and Psalm 107:20 are my testimony. In John 8:31,32 Jesus says, ...**If you abide** (continue) **in My word,...you are truly My disciples. And you will know the Truth, and the Truth will set you free.** Psalm 107:20 says of the Lord, **He sends forth His word and heals them and rescues them from the pit and destruction.**

But this time I felt and knew immediately that something had happened in my mind. Within minutes I was able to believe again in areas I had been struggling with just prior to my time of prayer.

I'll give you an example. Before being attacked by the mind-binding demons, I believed that according to the Word of God, the fact that I was a woman from Fenton, Missouri, whom no one knew, wouldn't make any difference in my life or ministry. (Galatians 3:28.) When God was ready, *He* would open doors that no one could close (Revelation 3:8), and I would preach all over the world the practical, liberating messages He had given me.

I believed I would have the privilege of sharing the Gospel throughout the nation by radio (not because of me, but in spite of me). I knew that, according to the Scriptures, God chooses weak and foolish things to confound the wise. (1 Corinthians 1:27.) I believed that the Lord was going to use me to heal the sick. I believed that our children would be used in ministry. I believed all sorts of wonderful things that God had placed in my heart.

However, when the mind-binding spirits attacked me, I couldn't seem to believe much of anything. I thought things like, "Well, I probably just made all that up. I just believed it because I wanted to, but it probably won't ever happen." But when the spirits left, the ability to believe came rushing back.

DECIDE TO BELIEVE

So too the [Holy] Spirit comes to our aid and bears us up in our weakness; for we do not know what prayer to offer nor how to offer it worthily as we ought, but the Spirit Himself goes to meet

our supplication and pleads in our behalf with unspeakable yearn-
ings and groanings too deep for utterance.

Romans 8:26

As Christians, we need to learn to *decide* to believe. God often
gives us faith (a product of the Spirit) for things that our minds
just can't always seem to come into agreement with. The mind
wants to understand everything — the why, the when and the
how of it all. Often, when that understanding is not given by God,
the mind refuses to believe what it cannot understand.

It frequently happens that a believer *knows* something in his
heart (his inner man), but his mind wars against it.

I had decided long before to believe what the Word says, and
to believe the *rhema* (the revealed Word) that God gave me (the
things He spoke to me or the promises He gave me personally),
even if I didn't understand why, when or how it would come to
pass in my life.

But this thing I had been battling was different; it was beyond
decision. I was bound by these mind-binding spirits and just
couldn't bring myself to believe.

Thank God that through the Holy Spirit He showed me how
to pray, and His power prevailed even though I didn't know I was
praying for myself when I started.

I'm sure that you are reading this book right now because you
were led to it. You too may be having problems in this area. If so,
I encourage you to pray in Jesus' name. By the power of His blood,
come against "mind-binding spirits." Pray this way not just one
time but any time you experience difficulty in this area.

The devil never runs out of fiery darts to throw against us
when we are trying to go forward. Lift up your shield of faith and
remember James 1:2-8 which teaches us that we can ask God for
wisdom in trials and He will give it to us and will show us what
to do.

I had a problem, a fiery dart I had not encountered before. But God showed me how to pray, and I was set free.

You will be too.

Chapter

7

*Think About
What You're Thinking About*

Think About What You're Thinking About

The Word of God teaches us what we should spend our time thinking about.

I will meditate on Your precepts and have respect to Your ways [the paths of life marked out by Your law].

PSALM 119:15

The psalmist said that he thought about or meditated on the precepts of God. That means that he spent a lot of time pondering and thinking on the ways of God, His instructions and His teachings. Psalm 1:3 says that the person who does this ...**shall be like a tree firmly planted [and tended] by the streams of water, ready to bring forth its fruit in its season; its leaf also shall not fade or wither; and everything he does shall prosper [and come to maturity].**

It is very beneficial to think about God's Word. The more time a person spends meditating on the Word, the more he will reap from the Word.

BE CAREFUL WHAT YOU THINK!

...**Be careful what you are hearing. The measure [of thought and study] you give [to the truth you hear] will be the measure [of virtue and knowledge] that comes back to you — and more [besides] will be given to you who hear.**

Mark 4:24

What a great Scripture! It tells us that the more time we spend thinking about the Word we read and hear, the more power and ability we will have to do it — the more revelation knowledge we will have about what we have read or heard. Basically this tells us that we will get from the Word of God what we put into it.

Notice especially the promise that the amount of thought and study we devote to the Word will determine the amount of virtue and knowledge that will come back to us.

Vine's *An Expository Dictionary of New Testament Words* says that in certain Scriptures of the *King James Version* the Greek word *dunamis* meaning "power" is translated "virtue."[1] According to *The New Strong's Exhaustive Concordance of the Bible,* another translation of *dunamis* is "ability."[2] Most people do not delve into the Word of God very deeply. As a result, they get confused about why they are not powerful Christians living victorious lives.

The truth is that most of them really don't put much effort of their own into the study of the Word. They may go out and hear others teach and preach the Word. They may listen to sermon tapes or read the Bible occasionally, but they are not really dedicated to making the Word a major part of their lives, including spending time thinking about it.

The flesh is basically lazy, and many people want to get something for nothing (with no effort on their part); however, that really is not the way it works. I will say it again, *a person will get out of the Word what he is willing to put into it.*

MEDITATE ON THE WORD

Blessed (happy, fortunate, prosperous, and enviable) is the man who walks and lives not in the counsel of the ungodly [following their advice, their plans and purposes], nor stands [submissive and inactive] in the path where sinners walk, nor sits down [to relax and rest] where the scornful [and the mockers] gather.

But his delight and desire are in the law of the Lord, and on His law (the precepts, the instructions, the teachings of God) he habitually meditates (ponders and studies) by day and by night.

Psalm 1:1,2

According to Webster, the word *meditate* means "1. To reflect on: PONDER. 2. To plan or intend in the mind...To engage in contemplation."[3] Vine's *An Expository Dictionary of New Testament Words* says that *meditate* means "...primarily, to care for,...to attend to, practise,...be diligent in,...to practise is the prevalent sense of the word,...to ponder, imagine,... to premeditate."[4]

Proverbs 4:20 says, **My son, attend to my words; consent and submit to my sayings.** If we put Proverbs 4:20 together with these definitions of the word "meditate," we see that we attend to God's Word by meditating on it, by pondering on it, by contemplating it, by rehearsing or practicing it in our thinking. The basic idea is that if we want to do what the Word of God says, we must spend time thinking about it.

Remember the old saying, "Practice makes perfect"? We really do not expect to be experts at anything in life without a lot of practice, so why would we expect Christianity to be any different?

MEDITATION PRODUCES SUCCESS

This Book of the Law shall not depart out of your mouth, but you shall meditate on it day and night, that you may observe and do according to all that is written in it. For then you shall make your way prosperous, and then you shall deal wisely and have good success.

Joshua 1:8

If you want to be a success and prosper in all your dealings, the Bible says you must meditate on the Word of God day and night.

How much time do you spend thinking about the Word of God? If you are having problems in any area of your life, an honest answer to this question may disclose the reason why.

For most of my life, I didn't think about what I was thinking about. I simply thought whatever fell into my head. I had no revelation that Satan could inject thoughts into my mind. Much of what was in my head was either lies that Satan was telling me or just plain nonsense — things that really were not worth spending my time thinking about. The devil was controlling my life because he was controlling my thoughts.

THINK ABOUT WHAT YOU'RE THINKING ABOUT!

Among these we as well as you once lived and conducted ourselves in the passions of our flesh [our behavior governed by our

corrupt and sensual nature], obeying the impulses of the flesh and
the thoughts of the mind....

Ephesians 2:3

Paul warns us here that we are not to be governed by our sensual nature or to obey the impulses of our flesh, the thoughts of
our carnal mind.

Although I was a Christian, I was having trouble because I had
not learned to control my thoughts. I thought about things that
kept my mind busy but were not productive in a positive way.

I needed to change my thinking!

One thing the Lord told me when He began to teach me about
the battlefield of the mind became a major turning point for me.
He said, "Think about what you're thinking about." As I began to
do so, it was not long before I began to see why I was having so
much trouble in my life.

My mind was a mess!

I was thinking all the wrong things.

I went to church, and had done so for years, but I never actually thought about what I heard. It went in one ear and out the
other, so to speak. I read some Scriptures in the Bible every day, but
never thought about what I was reading. I was not *attending* to the
Word. I was not giving any thought and study to what I was hearing. Therefore, no virtue or knowledge was coming back to me.

MEDITATE ON THE WORKS OF GOD

We have thought of Your steadfast love, O God, in the midst of
Your temple.

Psalm 48:9

The psalmist David talked frequently about meditating on all
the wonderful works of the Lord — the mighty acts of God. He
said that he thought on the name of the Lord, the mercy of God
and many other such things.

When he was feeling depressed, he wrote in Psalm 143:4,5: **Therefore is my spirit overwhelmed and faints within me [wrapped in gloom]; my heart within my bosom grows numb. I remember the days of old; I meditate on all Your doings; I ponder the work of Your hands.**

We see from this passage that David's response to his feelings of depression and gloom was not to meditate on the problem. Instead, he literally came against the problem by *choosing* to remember the good times of past days — pondering the doings of God and the works of His hands. In other words, he thought on something good, and it helped him overcome depression.

Never forget this: *your mind plays an important role in your victory.*

I know that it is the power of the Holy Spirit working through the Word of God that brings victory into our lives. But a large part of the work that needs to be done is for us to line up our thinking with God and His Word. If we refuse to do this or choose to think it is unimportant, we will never experience victory.

BE TRANSFORMED BY RENEWING YOUR MIND

Do not be conformed to this world (this age), [fashioned after and adapted to its external, superficial customs], but be transformed (changed) by the [entire] renewal of your mind [by its new ideals and its new attitude], so that you may prove [for yourselves] what is the good and acceptable and perfect will of God, even the thing which is good and acceptable and perfect [in His sight for you].

Romans 12:2

In this passage the Apostle Paul is saying that if we want to see God's good and perfect will proven out in our lives, we can — *if* we have our minds renewed. Renewed to what? Renewed to God's way of thinking. By this process of new thinking we will be changed or transformed into what God intends for us to be. Jesus has made this transformation possible by His death and resurrection. It becomes a reality in our lives by this process of the renewal of the mind.

Let me say at this point, to avoid any confusion, that right thinking has *nothing* to do with salvation. Salvation is based solely on the blood of Jesus, His death on the cross and His resurrection. Many people will be in heaven because they truly accepted Jesus as their Savior, but many of these same people will never have walked in victory or enjoyed the good plan God had for their lives because they did not get their mind renewed according to His Word.

For years, I was one of those people. I was born again. I was going to heaven. I went to church and followed a form of religion, but I really had no victory in my life. The reason is because I was thinking on the wrong things.

THINK ON THESE THINGS

For the rest, brethren, whatever is true, whatever is worthy of reverence and is honorable and seemly, whatever is just, whatever is pure, whatever is lovely and lovable, whatever is kind and winsome and gracious, if there is any virtue and excellence, if there is anything worthy of praise, think on and weigh and take account of these things [fix your minds on them].

Philippians 4:8

The Bible presents a lot of detailed instruction on what kinds of things we are to think about. I am sure that you can see from these various Scriptures that we are instructed to think on good things, things that will build us up and not tear us down.

Our thoughts certainly affect our attitudes and moods. Everything the Lord tells us is for our own good. He knows what will make us happy and what will make us miserable. When a person is full of wrong thoughts he is miserable, and I have learned from personal experience that when someone is miserable, he usually ends up making others miserable also.

You should take inventory on a regular basis and ask yourself, "What have I been thinking about?" Spend some time examining your thought life.

Thinking about what you're thinking about is very valuable because Satan usually deceives people into thinking that the source of their misery or trouble is something other than what it really is. He wants them to think they are unhappy due to what is going on around them (their circumstances), but the misery is actually due to what is going on *inside* them (their thoughts).

For many years I really believed that I was unhappy because of things others were doing or not doing. I blamed my misery on my husband and my children. If they would be different, if they would be more attentive to my needs, if they would help around the house more, then, I thought, I would be happy. It was one thing and then another for years. I finally faced the truth, which was that none of these things had to make me unhappy if I chose to have the right attitude. My thoughts were what was making me miserable.

Let me say it one final time: *Think about what you are thinking about.* You may locate some of your problems and be on your way to freedom very quickly.

PART 2:

Conditions of the Mind

Introduction

*I*n what condition is your mind?

Have you noticed that the condition of your mind changes? One time you may be calm and peaceful, and another time anxious and worried. Or you may make a decision and be sure about it, then later find your mind in a confused condition concerning the very thing you were previously so clear and certain about.

...But we have the mind of Christ (the Messiah) and do hold the thoughts (feelings and purposes) of His heart.

1 CORINTHIANS 2:16

There have been times in my own life when I have experienced these things, as well as others. There have been times when I seemed to be able to believe God without any trouble, and then there have other times when doubt and unbelief haunted me mercilessly.

Because it seems that the mind can be in so many different conditions, I began to wonder, when is my mind normal? I wanted to know what normal was so I could learn to deal with the abnormal thinking patterns immediately upon their arrival.

For example, a critical, judgmental and suspicious mind should be considered abnormal for a believer. However, for a major portion of my life, it was normal for me — although it should not have been. It was what I was used to, and even though my thinking was very wrong and was causing a lot of problems in my life, I did not know that there was anything wrong with what I was thinking.

I did not know that I could do anything about my thought life. I was a believer, and had been for years, but I had no teaching at all about my thought life or about the proper condition for a believer's mind to be in.

Our minds are not born again with the New Birth experience — they have to be renewed. (Romans 12:2.) As I have said several times, the renewal of the mind is a process that requires time. Do not be devastated, even if you read the next part of this book and discover that most of the time your mind is in a condition that is abnormal for someone claiming Christ as Savior. Recognizing the problem is the first step toward recovery.

In my own case, I began to get a lot more serious about my relationship with the Lord several years ago, and it was at that time that He began revealing to me that many of my problems were rooted in wrong thinking. My mind was in a mess! I doubt that it was ever in the condition it should have been — and if it was, it did not last long.

I felt overwhelmed when I began to see how much wrong thinking I was addicted to. I would try to cast down the wrong thoughts that came into my mind, and they would come right back. But, little by little, freedom and deliverance did come.

Satan will aggressively fight against the renewal of your mind, but it is vital that you press on and continue to pray and study in this area until you gain measurable victory.

When is your mind normal? Is it supposed to wander all over the place, or should you be able to keep it focused on what you're doing? Should you be upset and confused, or should you be peaceful and reasonably sure of the direction you should be taking in life? Should your mind be full of doubt and unbelief, should you be anxious and worried, tormented by fear? Or is it the privilege of the child of God to cast all his care upon Him? (1 Peter 5:7.)

The Word of God teaches us that we have the mind of Christ. What do you think His mind was like when He lived on the earth — not only as the Son of God but also as the Son of Man?

Prayerfully proceed into the next part of *Battlefield of the Mind*. I believe it will open your eyes to normal and abnormal mindsets for the person who is a disciple of Jesus and who has determined to walk in victory.

Chapter

8

When Is My Mind Normal?

When Is My Mind Normal?

Notice that Paul prays that you and I will gain wisdom by having "the eyes of (our) heart" enlightened. Based on several things I have studied, I describe "the eyes of the heart" as the mind.

[For I always pray to] the God of our Lord Jesus Christ, the Father of glory, that He may grant you a spirit of wisdom and revelation [of insight into mysteries and secrets] in the [deep and intimate] knowledge of Him,

As a Christian, in what condition should our mind be? In other words, what should be the normal state of the mind of the believer? In order to answer that question, we must look at the different functions of the mind and the spirit.

By having the eyes of your heart flooded with light, so that you can know and understand the hope to which He has called you, and how rich is His glorious inheritance in the saints (His set-apart ones).

EPHESIANS 1:17,18

According to the Word of God, the mind and the spirit work together: this is what I call the principle of "the mind aiding the spirit."

To better understand this principle, let's see how it works in the life of the believer.

THE MIND-SPIRIT PRINCIPLE

For what person perceives (knows and understands) what passes through a man's thoughts except the man's own spirit within him? Just so no one discerns (comes to know and comprehend) the thoughts of God except the Spirit of God.

1 Corinthians 2:11

When a person receives Christ as His personal Savior, the Holy Spirit comes to dwell in him. The Bible teaches us that the Holy Spirit knows the mind of God. Just as a person's own spirit within him is the only one who knows his thoughts, so the Spirit of God is the only One Who knows the mind of God.

Since the Holy Spirit dwells in us, and since He knows the mind of God, one of His purposes is to reveal to us God's wisdom and revelation. That wisdom and revelation is imparted to our spirit, and our spirit then enlightens the eyes of our heart, which is our mind. The Holy Spirit does this so we can understand on a practical level what is being ministered to us spiritually.

NORMAL OR ABNORMAL?

As believers, we are spiritual, and we are also natural. The natural does not always understand the spiritual; therefore, it is vitally necessary for our minds to be enlightened concerning what is going on in our spirits. The Holy Spirit desires to bring us this enlightenment, but *the mind often misses what the spirit is attempting to reveal because it is too busy.* A mind that is too busy is abnormal. The mind is normal when it is at rest — not blank, but at rest.

The mind should not be filled with reasoning, worry, anxiety, fear and the like. It should be calm, quiet and serene. As we proceed into this second section of the book you will observe several abnormal conditions of the mind and possibly recognize them as frequent conditions of your own mind.

It is important to understand that the mind needs to be kept in the "normal" condition described in this chapter. Compare it with the usual condition of our minds and you will see why we frequently have very little revealed to us by the Holy Spirit, and why far too often we feel ourselves lacking in wisdom and revelation.

Remember, the Holy Spirit attempts to enlighten the mind of the believer. The Holy Spirit gives information from God to the person's spirit, and if his spirit and mind are aiding one another, then he can walk in divine wisdom and revelation. But if his mind is too busy, it will miss what the Lord is attempting to reveal to him through his spirit.

THE STILL SMALL VOICE

And he said, Go forth, and stand upon the mount before the Lord. And, behold, the Lord passed by, and a great and strong wind rent the mountains, and brake in pieces the rocks before the Lord; but the Lord was not in the wind: and after the wind an earthquake; but the Lord was not in the earthquake:

And after the earthquake a fire; but the Lord was not in the fire: and after the fire a still small voice.

1 Kings 19:11,12 KJV

For years I prayed for revelation, asking God to reveal things to me by His Spirit Who lived within me. I knew that request was scriptural. I believed the Word and felt sure I should be asking and receiving. Yet, much of the time I felt like what I called a "spiritual dunce." Then I learned that I was not receiving much of what the Holy Spirit wanted to reveal to me simply because my mind was so wild and busy that it was missing the information being offered.

Imagine two people in a room together. One is trying to whisper a secret to the other. If the room is filled with a loud noise, even though the message is being communicated, the one waiting for the secret information will miss it simply because the room is so noisy he can't hear. Unless he is paying close attention, he may not even realize that he is being spoken to.

That's the way it is with communication between God's Spirit and our spirit. The ways of the Holy Spirit are gentle; most of the time He speaks to us as He did to the prophet in this passage — in "a still small voice." It is therefore vital that we learn to keep ourselves in a condition conducive to hearing.

THE SPIRIT AND THE MIND

Then what am I to do? I will pray with my spirit [by the Holy Spirit that is within me], but I will also pray [intelligently] with my mind and understanding....

1 Corinthians 14:15

Perhaps a better way to understand this principle of "mind aiding spirit" is to think of prayer. In this verse the Apostle Paul said that he prayed both with his spirit and with his mind.

I understand what Paul is talking about because I do the same thing. I frequently pray in the spirit (in an unknown tongue); after I have prayed that way for a while, often something will come to my mind to pray in English (my known tongue). I believe in this way the mind aids the spirit. They work together to get the knowledge and wisdom of God to me in a way that I can understand it.

This also works in the reverse. There are times when I want to pray, so I make myself available to God for prayer. If there is no particular stirring in my spirit, I simply begin to pray out of my mind. I pray about issues or situations that I am aware of. Sometimes these prayers seem really flat — there is no help coming from my spirit. I seem to be struggling, so I go on to something else that I already know about.

I continue in this fashion until the Holy Spirit within me takes hold with me on some issue. When He does, then I know I have hit on something that He wants to pray about, not just something I am trying to pray about. In this way my mind and my spirit are working together, aiding one another in accomplishing the will of God.

TONGUES AND INTERPRETATION

Therefore, the person who speaks in an [unknown] tongue should pray [for the power] to interpret and explain what he says.

For if I pray in an [unknown] tongue, my spirit [by the Holy Spirit within me] prays, but my mind is unproductive [it bears no fruit and helps nobody].

1 Corinthians 14:13,14

Another example of the way the spirit and the mind work together is the gift of tongues with interpretation.

When I speak in tongues, my mind is unfruitful until God gives either me or someone else the understanding of what I am saying; then my mind becomes fruitful.

Please keep in mind that the gifts are not tongues and translation. Translation is an exact word-for-word account of the message, whereas in interpretation one person gives an understanding of what another has said, but in the interpreter's own style as expressed through his own particular personality.

Let me give you an example: Sister Smith may stand up in church and give a message in an unknown tongue. It has come from her spirit, and neither she nor anyone else knows what she has said. God may cause me to understand what the message was, but perhaps in a general way. As I step out in faith, and begin to interpret what was spoken, I make the message understandable to all. But it comes through me in my own unique way of expression.

Praying in the spirit (in an unknown tongue), and interpretation (of that unknown tongue) is a marvelous way to understand the principle of "mind aiding spirit." The spirit is speaking something, and the mind is given understanding.

Now just think about this: if Sister Smith speaks in an unknown tongue, and God is looking for someone to give forth the interpretation, He will have to pass me by if my mind is too wild and busy to listen. Even if He tries to give the interpretation to me, I will not receive it.

When I was young in the Lord and learning about spiritual gifts, I prayed almost exclusively in tongues. After quite some time had passed, I began to feel bored with my prayer life. As I talked to the Lord about it, He let me know that I was bored because I had no understanding of what I was praying about. Although I realize that I do not *always* have to understand what I am saying when I pray in the spirit, I have learned that this type of prayer is out of balance and not the most fruitful if I *never* have any understanding.

PEACEFUL, ALERT MIND

You will guard him and keep him in perfect and constant peace whose mind [both its inclination and its character] is stayed on

You, because he commits himself to You, leans on You, and hopes confidently in You.

Isaiah 26:3

I hope you can readily see from these examples that your mind and your spirit certainly do work together. *Therefore, it is of utmost importance that your mind be maintained in a normal condition.* Otherwise, it cannot aid your spirit.

Satan, of course, knows this fact, so he attacks your mind, waging war against you on the battlefield of your mind. He wants to overload and overwork your mind by filling it with every kind of wrong thought so it cannot be free and available to the Holy Spirit working through your own human spirit.

The mind should be kept peaceful. As the prophet Isaiah tells us, when the mind is stayed on the right things, it will be at rest.

Yet the mind should also be alert. This becomes impossible when it is loaded down with things it was never intended to carry.

Think it over: how much of the time is your mind normal?

Chapter

9

A Wandering, Wondering Mind

A Wandering, Wondering Mind

In the previous chapter we stated that a mind too busy is abnormal. Another condition of the mind that is abnormal is for it to be wandering all over the place. An inability to concentrate indicates mental attack from the devil.

Wherefore gird up the loins of your mind....

1 PETER 1:13 KJV

Many people have spent years allowing their minds to wander because they have never applied principles of discipline to their thought life.

Quite often people who cannot seem to concentrate think they are mentally deficient. However, an inability to concentrate can be the result of years of letting the mind do whatever it wants to do, whenever it wants to do it. A lack of concentration can also be a symptom of vitamin deficiency. Certain B-vitamins enhance concentration, therefore, if you have an inability to concentrate, ask yourself if you're eating right and are nutritionally sound.

Extreme fatigue can also affect concentration. I have found that when I am excessively tired Satan will try to attack my mind because he knows it is more difficult to resist him during these times. The devil wants you and me to think that we are mentally deficient so we will not attempt to do anything to cause him problems. He wants us to passively accept whatever lies he tells us.

One of our daughters had difficulty concentrating during her childhood years. Reading was difficult for her because concentration and comprehension go hand in hand. Many children and even some adults don't comprehend what they read. Their eyes scan the words on the page, but their minds do not really understand what is being read.

Often a lack of comprehension is the result of a lack of concentration. I know that, for myself, I can read a chapter in the

Bible or a book and all of a sudden realize that I do not know what I have read at all. I can go back and read it again, and it all seems new to me because, even though my eyes were scanning the words on the page, my mind had wandered off somewhere else. Because I did not stay focused on what I was doing, I failed to comprehend what I was reading.

Often the real problem behind a lack of comprehension is a lack of attention caused by a wandering mind.

A WANDERING MIND

Keep your foot [give your mind to what you are doing]....
Ecclesiastes 5:1

I believe the expression "keep your foot" means "don't lose your balance or get off track." The amplification of this phrase indicates that one stays on track by keeping his mind on what he is doing.

I had a wandering mind and had to train it by discipline. It was not easy, and sometimes I still have a relapse. While trying to complete some project, I will suddenly realize that my mind has just wandered off onto something else that has nothing to do with the issue at hand. I have not yet arrived at a place of perfect concentration, but at least I understand how important it is not to allow my mind to go wherever it wishes, whenever it desires.

Webster's dictionary defines the word *wander* as: "1. To move about aimlessly: ROAM. 2. To go by an indirect route or at no set pace: AMBLE. 3. To proceed in an irregular course or action: MEANDER...5. To think or express oneself unclearly or incoherently."[1]

If you are like me, you can be sitting in a church service listening to the speaker, really enjoying and benefiting from what is being said, when suddenly your mind begins to wander. After a while you "wake up" to find that you don't remember a thing that has been going on. Even though your body stayed in church, your mind has been at the shopping center browsing through the stores or home in the kitchen cooking dinner.

Remember, in spiritual warfare the mind is the battlefield. That is where the enemy makes his attack. He knows very well that even though a person attends church, if he can't keep his mind on what is being taught, he will gain absolutely nothing by being there. The devil knows that a person cannot discipline himself to complete a project if he cannot discipline his mind and keep it on what he is doing.

This mind-wandering phenomenon also occurs during conversation. There are times when my husband, Dave, is talking to me and I listen for a while; then all of a sudden I realize that I have not heard a thing he has been saying. Why? Because I allowed my mind to wander off on something else. My body was standing there appearing to listen, yet in my mind I heard nothing.

For many years, when this sort of thing happened, I would pretend that I knew exactly what Dave was saying. Now I stop and say, "Can you back up and repeat that? I let my mind wander off, and I did not hear a thing you said."

In this way, I feel that at least I am dealing with the problem. Confronting issues is the only way to get on the victorious side of them!

I have decided that if the devil went to the trouble to attack me with a wandering mind, then perhaps something was being said that I needed to hear.

One way to combat the enemy in this area is by taking advantage of the cassette tapes provided by most churches. If you haven't yet learned to discipline your mind to keep it on what is being said in church, then buy a tape of the sermon each week and listen to it as many times as you need in order to get the message.

The devil will give up when he sees that you are not going to give in.

Remember, Satan wants you to think that you are mentally deficient — that something is wrong with you. But the truth is, you just need to begin disciplining your mind. Don't let it run all over town, doing whatever it pleases. Begin today to "keep your foot," to keep your mind on what you're doing. You will need to practice for a while. Breaking old habits and forming new ones always takes time, but it is worth it in the end.

A WONDERING MIND

Truly I tell you, whoever says to this mountain, Be lifted up and thrown into the sea! and does not doubt at all in his heart but believes that what he says will take place, it will be done for him.

For this reason I am telling you, whatever you ask for in prayer, believe (trust and be confident) that it is granted to you, and you will [get it].

Mark 11:23,24

Faced with one thing or another, I frequently began to hear myself say, "I wonder." For example:

"I wonder what the weather will be like tomorrow."

"I wonder what I should wear to the party."

"I wonder what kind of grades Danny (my son) will get on his report card."

"I wonder how many people will show up at the seminar."

The dictionary partially defines the word *wonder* in the noun form as "a feeling of puzzlement or doubt" and in the verb form as "to be filled with curiosity or doubt."[2]

I have come to learn that I am much better off to do something positive than to just wonder all the time about everything imaginable. Instead of wondering what kind of grades Danny will get, I can believe that he will make good grades. Rather than wondering what I should wear to the party, I can decide what to wear. Instead of wondering about the weather or about how many people will attend one of my meetings, I can just turn the matter over to the Lord, trusting Him to work out all things for good regardless of what happens.

Wondering leaves a person in indecision, and indecision causes confusion. Wondering, indecision and confusion prevent an individual from receiving from God, by faith, the answer to his prayer or need.

Notice that in Mark 11:23,24 Jesus did not say, "Whatever you ask for in prayer, *wonder* if you will get it." Instead, He said, "Whatever you ask for in prayer, *believe* that you will receive it — and you will!"

As Christians, as *believers*, we are to believe — not doubt!

Chapter
10

A Confused Mind

A Confused Mind

Chapter

10

We have discovered that wondering and confusion are relatives. Wondering, rather than being definite in thought, can and does cause doubt and confusion.

James 1:5-8 are excellent Scriptures that help us understand how to overcome wondering, doubt and confusion and to receive what we need from God. To me, the "man of two minds" (the *King James Version* calls him "a double-minded man") is the picture of confusion as he constantly goes back and forth, back and forth, never deciding on anything. As soon as he thinks he has made a decision, here comes wondering, doubt and confusion to get him operating once again in two minds. He is uncertain about everything.

I lived much of my life like that, not realizing that the devil had declared war against me and that my mind was the battlefield. I was totally confused about everything, and didn't understand why.

If any of you is deficient in wisdom, let him ask of the giving God [Who gives] to everyone liberally and ungrudgingly, without reproaching or faultfinding, and it will be given him.

Only it must be in faith that he asks with no wavering (no hesitating, no doubting). For the one who wavers (hesitates, doubts) is like the billowing surge out at sea that is blown hither and thither and tossed by the wind.

For truly, let not such a person imagine that he will receive anything [he asks for] from the Lord.

[For being as he is] a man of two minds (hesitating, dubious, irresolute), [he is] unstable and unreliable and uncertain about everything [he thinks, feels, decides].

JAMES 1:5-8

REASONING LEADS TO CONFUSION

...O ye of little faith, why reason ye among yourselves?....
Matthew 16:8 KJV

95

Thus far, we have talked about wondering and we will talk more about doubt in the next chapter. Right now I would like to elaborate a little more on confusion.

A large percentage of God's people are admittedly confused. Why? As we have seen, one reason is wondering. Another is reasoning. The dictionary partially defines the word *reason* in the noun form as an "underlying fact or motive that provides logical sense for a premise or occurrence" and in the verb form as "to use the faculty of reason: think logically."[1]

A simple way to say it is, reasoning occurs when a person tries to figure out the "why" behind something. Reasoning causes the mind to revolve around and around a situation, issue or event attempting to understand all its intricate component parts. We are reasoning when we dissect a statement or teaching to see if it is logical, and disregard it if it is not.

Satan frequently steals the will of God from us due to reasoning. The Lord may direct us to do a certain thing, but if it does not make sense — if it is not logical — we may be tempted to disregard it. What God leads a person to do does not always make logical sense to his mind. His spirit may affirm it and His mind reject it, especially if it would be out of the ordinary or unpleasant or if it would require personal sacrifice or discomfort.

DON'T REASON IN THE MIND,

JUST OBEY IN THE SPIRIT

But the natural man receiveth not the things of the Spirit of God: for they are foolishness unto him: neither can he know them, because they are spiritually discerned.

1 Corinthians 2:14 KJV

Here is a practical, personal illustration that I hope will help bring more understanding on this issue of reasoning in the mind versus obedience in the spirit.

One morning as I was getting dressed to minister in a weekly meeting that I conducted near my hometown, I started thinking about the woman who ran our ministry of helps there and how faithful she had been. A desire rose up in my heart to do something to bless her in some way.

"Father, Ruth Ann has been such a blessing to us all these years," I prayed, "what can I do to bless her?"

Immediately, my eyes fell on a new red dress that was hanging in my closet, and I knew in my heart the Lord was prompting me to give that dress to Ruth Ann. Although I'd bought it three months earlier, I had never worn it. As a matter of fact, it was still hanging under the plastic bag I'd brought it home in. I really liked it, but every time I thought about wearing it, for some reason I just had no desire to put it on.

Remember, I said that when my eyes fell on the red dress, I *knew* I should give it to Ruth Ann. However, I really did not *want* to give it up, so I immediately began to reason in my mind that God could not be telling me to give her the red dress because it was brand new, never worn, rather expensive — and I had even purchased red and silver earrings to match it!

Had I kept my carnal mind out of the situation and continued to be sensitive to God in my spirit, everything would have gone nicely, but we humans have an ability to deceive ourselves through reasoning when we really don't want to do what God is saying. Within a couple of minutes I had forgotten the whole thing and had gone on about my business. The bottom line was that I did not want to give the dress away because it was new and I liked it. My mind reasoned that the desire I felt could not be God, but that the devil was trying to take from me something I enjoyed.

Some weeks later I was getting ready for another meeting at the same location, just as before, when once again Ruth Ann's name came up in my heart. I began to pray for her. I repeated the whole scene again, saying, "Father, Ruth Ann has been such a blessing to us, what can I do to bless her?" Immediately, I saw the red dress again and I got a sinking feeling in my flesh because I now remembered the other incident (which I had quickly and totally forgotten).

This time there was no squirming out of it; either I had to face the fact that God was showing me what to do and do it, or I simply had to say, "I know what You are showing me, Lord, but I am just not going to do it." I love the Lord too much to willfully, knowingly disobey Him, so I began to talk to Him about the red dress.

Within minutes I realized that on the previous occasion I had reasoned my way right out of the will of God, and it had taken only a moment to do it. I had thought that I couldn't be hearing from the Lord because the dress was new. Yet now I realized that the Bible says nothing about giving away only old things! It would be more of a sacrifice for me to give the dress away because it was new, but it would also be more of a blessing to Ruth Ann.

As I opened up my heart to God, He began to show me that I had purchased the dress for Ruth Ann to begin with; that was the reason I could never bring myself to wear it. The Lord had intended to use me as His agent to bless her all the time. But I'd had my own idea about the dress and, until I was willing to lay down my idea, I could not be led by the Spirit.

This particular incident taught me a lot. The realization of how easily we can be led by our heads and allow reasoning to keep us out of God's will provoked in me a "reverential" fear of reasoning.

Remember, according to 1 Corinthians 2:14, the natural man does not understand the spiritual man. My carnal mind (my natural man) did not understand giving away a new dress I had never worn, but my spirit (my spiritual man) understood it well.

I hope this example will bring more understanding to you in this area and help you walk in the will of God more than ever before.

(By the way, I know you're probably wondering if I ever gave Ruth Ann the red dress. Yes, I did, and now she works in our office full time and still wears the red dress to work occasionally.)

BE A DOER OF THE WORD!

But be doers of the Word [obey the message], and not merely listeners to it, betraying yourselves [into deception by reasoning contrary to the Truth].

James 1:22

Any time we see what the Word says and refuse to do it, reasoning has somehow gotten involved and deceived us into believing something other than the truth. We cannot spend excessive time trying to understand (mentally) everything the Word says. If we bear witness in the spirit, we can move ahead and do it.

I have found out that God wants me to obey Him, whether or not I feel like it, want to or think it is a good idea.

When God speaks, through His Word or in our inner man, we are not to reason, debate or ask ourselves if what He has said is logical.

When God speaks, we are to mobilize – not rationalize.

TRUST GOD, NOT HUMAN REASON

Lean on, trust in, and be confident in the Lord with all your heart and mind and do not rely on your own insight or understanding.
Proverbs 3:5

In other words, do not rely on reasoning. Reasoning opens the door for deception and brings much confusion.

I once asked the Lord why so many people are confused and He said to me, "Tell them to stop trying to figure everything out, and they will stop being confused." I have found it to be absolutely true. Reasoning and confusion go together.

You and I can ponder a thing in our heart, we can hold it before the Lord and see if He desires to give us understanding, but the minute we start feeling confused, we have gone too far.

Reasoning is dangerous for many reasons, but one of them is this: we can reason and figure something out that seems to make sense to us. But what we have reasoned to be correct may still be incorrect.

The human mind likes logic and order and reason. It likes to deal with what it understands. Therefore, we have a tendency to put things into neat little bins in the compartments of our mind, thinking, "This must be the way it is because it fits so nicely here." We can find something our minds are comfortable with and still be totally wrong.

The Apostle Paul said in Romans 9:1, **I am speaking the truth in Christ. I am not lying; my conscience [enlightened and prompted] by the Holy Spirit bearing witness with me.** Paul knew he was doing the right thing, not because his reasoning said it was right, but because it bore witness in his spirit.

As we have seen, the mind does, at times, aid the spirit. The mind and the spirit do work together, but the spirit is the more noble organ and should always be honored above the mind.

If we know in our spirit that a thing is wrong, we should not allow reasoning to talk us into doing it. Also, if we know something is right, we must not allow reasoning to talk us out of doing it.

God gives us understanding on many issues, but we do not have to understand everything to walk with the Lord and in obedience to His will. There are times when God leaves huge question marks as tools in our lives to stretch our faith. Unanswered questions crucify the flesh life. It is difficult for human beings to give up reasoning and simply trust God, but once the process is accomplished, the mind enters into a place of rest.

Reasoning is one of the "busy activities" in which the mind engages that prevents discernment and revelation knowledge. There is a big difference in head knowledge and revelation knowledge.

I don't know about you, but I want God to reveal things to me in such a way that I *know* in my spirit that what has been revealed to my mind is correct. I don't want to reason, to figure and to be logical, rotating my mind around and around an issue until I am worn out and confused. I want to experience the peace of mind and heart that comes from trusting in God, not in my own human insight and understanding.

You and I must grow to the place where we are satisfied to know the One Who knows, even if we ourselves do not know.

Resolve to Know Nothing but Christ

As for myself, brethren, when I came to you, I did not come proclaiming to you the testimony and evidence or mystery and secret of God [concerning what He has done through Christ for the salvation of men] in lofty words of eloquence or human philosophy and wisdom;

For I resolved to know nothing (to be acquainted with nothing, to make a display of the knowledge of nothing, and to be conscious of nothing) among you except Jesus Christ (the Messiah) and Him crucified.

1 Corinthians 2:1,2

This was Paul's approach to knowledge and reasoning, and I have come to understand and appreciate it. It took a long time, but I finally realized that in many instances, the less I know the happier I am. Sometimes we find out so much it makes us quite miserable.

I was always a very curious, inquisitive person. I had to have everything figured out in order to be satisfied. God began to show me that my constant reasoning was the basis of my confusion and that it was preventing me from receiving what He wanted to give me. He said, "Joyce, you must lay aside carnal reasoning if you ever expect to have discernment."

I realize now that I felt more secure if I had things figured out. I did not want any loose ends in my life. I wanted to be in control — and when I did not understand things, I felt out of control — frightened. But I was lacking something. I had no peace of mind and was physically worn out from reasoning.

This type of continual wrong mental activity will even make your physical body tired. It can leave you exhausted!

God required me to give it up, and I strongly suggest the same thing for anyone who is addicted to reasoning. Yes, I said addicted to reasoning. We can become addicted to wrong mental activity just as someone else can get addicted to drugs or alcohol or nicotine. I was *addicted* to reasoning and when I gave it up I had withdrawal symptoms. I felt lost and frightened because I did not know what was going on. I even felt bored.

I had spent so much of my mental time reasoning that when I gave it up, I had to become accustomed to my mind being so peaceful. For a while it seemed boring, but now I love it. While I used to run my mind all the time on everything, now I can't tolerate the pain and labor of reasoning.

Reasoning is not the normal condition in which God wants our mind to reside.

Be aware that when the mind is filled with reasoning, it is not normal. At least not for the Christian who intends to be victorious — the believer who intends to win the war that is fought on the battlefield of the mind.

Chapter
11

*A Doubtful
and Unbelieving Mind*

A Doubtful and Unbelieving Mind

We usually talk about doubt and unbelief together as if they are one and the same. Actually although they can be connected, the two are very different things.

...O you of little faith, why did you doubt?

MATTHEW 14:31

And He marveled because of their unbelief....

MARK 6:6

Vine's *An Expository Dictionary of New Testament Words* partially defines *doubt* in the verb form as "...to stand in two ways...implying uncertainty which way to take,...said of believers whose faith is small....being anxious, through a distracted state of mind, of wavering between hope and fear...."[1]

The same dictionary notes that one of the two Greek words translated as *unbelief* "is always rendered 'disobedience' in the R.V." (the Revised Version of the King James translation).[2]

As we look then at these two powerful tools of the enemy, we see that doubt causes a person to waver between two opinions, whereas unbelief leads to disobedience.

I think it is going to be helpful to be able to recognize exactly what the devil is trying to attack us with. Are we dealing with doubt or with unbelief?

DOUBT

...How long will you halt and limp between two opinions?....

1 Kings 18:21

I heard a story that will shed light on doubt.

There was a man who was sick and who was confessing the Word over his body, quoting healing Scriptures and believing for his healing to manifest. While doing so, he was intermittently attacked with thoughts of doubt.

After he had gone through a hard time and was beginning to get discouraged, God opened his eyes to the spirit world. This is what he saw: a demon speaking lies to him, telling him that he was not going to get healed and that confessing the Word was not going to work. But he also saw that each time he confessed the Word, light would come out of his mouth like a sword, and the demon would cower and fall backward.

As God showed him this vision, the man then understood why it was so important to keep speaking the Word. He saw that he did have faith, which is why the demon was attacking him with doubt.

Doubt is not something God puts in us. The Bible says that God gives every man a ...**measure of faith** (Romans 12:3 KJV). God has placed faith in our heart, but the devil tries to negate our faith by attacking us with doubt.

Doubt comes in the form of thoughts that are in opposition to the Word of God. This is why it is so important for us to know the Word of God. If we know the Word, then we can recognize when the devil is lying to us. Be assured that he lies to us in order to steal what Jesus purchased for us through His death and resurrection.

DOUBT AND UNBELIEF

[For Abraham, human reason for] hope being gone, hoped in faith that he should become the father of many nations, as he had been promised, So [numberless] shall your descendants be.

He did not weaken in faith when he considered the [utter] impotence of his own body, which was as good as dead because he was about a hundred years old, or [when he considered] the barrenness of Sarah's [deadened] womb.

No unbelief or distrust made him waver (doubtingly question) concerning the promise of God, but he grew strong and was empowered by faith as he gave praise and glory to God,

Fully satisfied and assured that God was able and mighty to keep His word and to do what He had promised.
Romans 4:18-21

When I am in a battle, knowing what God has promised and yet being attacked with doubt and unbelief, I like to read or meditate on this passage.

Abraham had been given a promise by God that He would cause him to have an heir from his own body. Many years had come and gone and still there was no child as a result of Abraham and Sarah's relationship. Abraham was still standing in faith, believing what God had said would come to pass. As he stood, he was being attacked with thoughts of doubt, and the spirit of unbelief was pressing him to disobey God.

Disobedience in a situation like this can simply be to give up when God is prompting us to press on. Disobedience is disregarding the voice of the Lord, or whatever God is speaking to us personally, not just transgressing the Ten Commandments.

Abraham continued to be steadfast. He kept praising and giving glory to God. The Bible states that as he did so, he grew strong in faith.

You see, when God tells us something or asks us to do something, the faith to believe it or to do it comes with the word from God. It would be ridiculous for God to expect us to do something and not give us the ability to believe that we can do it. Satan knows how dangerous we will be with a heart full of faith, so he attacks us with doubt and unbelief.

It is not that we don't have faith, it is just that Satan is trying to destroy our faith with lies.

Let me give you an example. It concerns the time when I received my call to the ministry. It was an ordinary morning like any other, except that I had been filled with the Holy Spirit three weeks earlier. I had just finished listening to my first teaching tape. It was a message by minister Ray Mossholder titled "Cross Over to the Other Side." I was stirred in my heart and amazed that anyone could teach for one whole hour from one Scripture and that all of his teaching would be interesting.

As I was making my bed, I suddenly felt an intense desire well up in me to teach God's Word. Then the voice of the Lord came to me saying, "You will go all over the place and teach My Word, and you will have a large teaching tape ministry."

There would have been no natural reason at all for me to believe that God had actually spoken to me, or that I could or ever would do what I thought I had just heard. I had many problems within myself. I would not have appeared to be "ministry material," but God chooses the weak and foolish things of the world to confound the wise. (1 Corinthians 1:27 KJV.) He looks on the heart of man and not the flesh. (1 Samuel 16:7.) If the heart is right, God can change the flesh.

Although there was nothing in the natural to indicate that I should believe, when the desire came over me, I was filled with faith that I could do what the Lord wanted me to do. When God calls, He gives desire, faith and ability to do the job. But, I also want to tell you that during the years I spent in training and waiting, the devil regularly attacked me with doubt and unbelief.

God places dreams and visions in the hearts of His people; they begin as little "seeds." Just as a woman has a seed planted into her womb when she becomes pregnant, so we become "pregnant," so to speak, with the things God speaks and promises. During the "pregnancy," Satan works hard to try and get us to "abort" our dreams. One of the tools he uses is doubt; another is unbelief. Both of these work against the mind.

Faith is a product of the spirit; it is a spiritual force. The enemy doesn't want you and me to get our mind in agreement with our spirit. He knows that if God places faith in us to do a thing, and we get positive and start consistently believing that we can actually do it, then we will do considerable damage to his kingdom.

KEEP WALKING ON THE WATER!

But the boat was by this time out on the sea, many furlongs [a furlong is one-eighth of a mile] distant from the land, beaten and tossed by the waves, for the wind was against them.

And in the fourth watch [between 3:00-6:00 a.m.] of the night, Jesus came to them, walking on the sea.

And when the disciples saw Him walking on the sea, they were terrified and said, It is a ghost! And they screamed out with fright.

But instantly He spoke to them, saying, Take courage! I AM! Stop being afraid!

And Peter answered Him, Lord, if it is You, command me to come to You on the water.

He said, Come! So Peter got out of the boat and walked on the water, and he came toward Jesus.

But when he perceived and felt the strong wind, he was frightened, and as he began to sink, he cried out, Lord, save me [from death]!

Instantly Jesus reached out His hand and caught and held him, saying to him, O you of little faith, why did you doubt?

And when they got into the boat, the wind ceased.

Matthew 14:24-32

I emphasized the last verse because I want to call your attention to the program the enemy lined out in this passage. Peter stepped out at the command of Jesus to do something he had never done before. As a matter of fact, no one had ever done it except Jesus.

It required faith!

Peter made a mistake; he spent too much time looking at the storm. He became frightened. Doubt and unbelief pressed in on him, and he began to sink. He cried out to Jesus to save him, and He did. But notice that the storm ceased as soon as *Peter got back into the boat!*

Remember in Romans 4:18-21 where Abraham did not waver when he considered his impossible situation? Abraham knew the conditions, but unlike Peter, I don't think he thought about them or talked about them all the time. You and I can be aware of our circumstances and yet, purposely, keep our mind on something that will build us up and edify our faith.

That is why Abraham stayed busy giving praise and glory to God. We glorify God when we continue to do what we know is right even in adverse circumstances. Ephesians 6:14 teaches us that in times of spiritual warfare, we are to tighten the belt of truth around us.

When the storm comes in your life, dig in both heels, set your face like flint and be determined in the Holy Spirit to stay out of the boat! Very often the storm ceases as soon as you quit and crawl back into a place of safety and security.

The devil brings storms into your life to intimidate you. During a storm, remember that the mind is the battlefield. Don't make your decisions based on your thoughts or feelings, but check with your spirit. When you do, you will find the same vision that was there in the beginning.

No Wavering Allowed!

If any of you is deficient in wisdom, let him ask of the giving God [Who gives] to everyone liberally and ungrudgingly, without reproaching or faultfinding, and it will be given him.

Only it must be in faith that he asks with no wavering (no hesitating, no doubting). For the one who wavers (hesitates, doubts) is like the billowing surge out at sea that is blown hither and thither and tossed by the wind.

For truly, let not such a person imagine that he will receive anything [he asks for] from the Lord.

James 1:5-7

My pastor, Rick Shelton, tells a story about how confused he became trying to decide what to do when he graduated from Bible college. God had placed it strongly in his heart to return to St. Louis, Missouri, and start a local church after graduation, which he intended to do. However, when it was time to go, he had approximately fifty dollars in his pocket, a wife, one child and another on the way. Obviously, his circumstances were not very good.

In the midst of trying to make his decision, he received two very good offers to join the staff of other large, well-established ministries. His salary would have been good. The ministry opportunities were attractive and, if nothing else, just the honor of working for either of these ministries would have bolstered his ego. The longer he deliberated, the more confused he became. (It sounds like Mr. Doubt was visiting him, doesn't it?)

At one time he had known exactly what he wanted to do, and now he was *wavering* between options. Since his circumstances did not favor going back to St. Louis, it was tempting to accept one of the other offers, but he could not get peaceful about either course of action. He finally asked the advice of one of the pastors who had offered him a job, and the man wisely said, "Go somewhere, get quiet and still, then turn your head off. Look into your heart, see what is there, and do it!"

When he followed the pastor's advice, he quickly found that in his heart was the church in St. Louis. He did not know how he could do it with what he had in hand, but he went forth obediently, and the results were wonderful.

Today, Rick Shelton is the founder and senior pastor of Life Christian Center in St. Louis, Missouri. Currently, Life Christian Center is a church of approximately three thousand people with a worldwide outreach. Thousands of lives have been blessed and transformed over the years through its ministry. I was an associate pastor there for five years, and my ministry, Life In The Word, was birthed during that time. Just think how much the devil would have stolen through doubt and unbelief if Pastor Shelton had been led by his head instead of his heart.

DOUBT IS A CHOICE

In the early dawn the next morning, as He was coming back to the city, He was hungry.

And as He saw one single leafy fig tree above the roadside, He went to it but He found nothing but leaves on it [seeing that in the fig tree the fruit appears at the same time as the leaves]. And He said to it, Never again shall fruit grow on you! And the fig tree withered up at once.

When the disciples saw it, they marveled greatly and asked, How is it that the fig tree has withered away all at once?

And Jesus answered them, Truly I say to you, if you have faith (a firm relying trust) and do not doubt, you will not only do what has been done to the fig tree, but even if you say to this mountain, Be taken up and cast into the sea, it will be done.

And whatever you ask for in prayer, having faith and [really] believing, you will receive.

Matthew 21:18-22

When His disciples marveled and asked Jesus how He was able to destroy the fig tree with just a word, He said to them in essence, *"If you have faith and do not doubt,* you can do the same thing that I have done to the fig tree — and even greater things than this." (John 14:12.)

We have already established that faith is the gift of God, so we know that we have faith. (Romans 12:3.) But doubt is a choice. It is the devil's warfare tactic against our minds.

Since you can choose your own thoughts, when doubt comes you should learn to recognize it for what it is, say "No, thank you" — and keep on believing!

The *choice* is yours!

Unbelief Is Disobedience

And when they were come to the multitude, there came to him a certain man, kneeling down to him, and saying,

Lord, have mercy on my son: for he is lunatick, and sore vexed: for ofttimes he falleth into the fire, and oft into the water.

And I brought him to thy disciples, and they could not cure him.

Then Jesus answered and said, O faithless and perverse generation, how long shall I be with you? how long shall I suffer you?

bring him hither to me.

And Jesus rebuked the devil; and he departed out of him: and the child was cured from that very hour.

Then came the disciples to Jesus apart, and said, Why could not we cast him out?

And Jesus said unto them, Because of your unbelief....

Matthew 17:14-20 KJV

Remember that unbelief leads to disobedience.

Perhaps Jesus had taught His disciples certain things to do in these cases, and their unbelief caused them to disobey Him; therefore, they were unsuccessful.

In any case, the point is that unbelief, like doubt, will keep us from doing what God has called and anointed us to accomplish in life. It will also keep us from experiencing the sense of peace that He wants us to enjoy as we find rest for our souls in Him. (Matthew 11:28,29 KJV.)

A Sabbath Rest

Let us therefore be zealous and exert ourselves and strive diligently to enter that rest [of God, to know and experience it for ourselves], that no one may fall or perish by the same kind of unbelief and disobedience [into which those in the wilderness fell].

Hebrews 4:11

If you read the entire fourth chapter of the book of Hebrews, you will find it speaking about a sabbath rest that is available to God's people. Under the Old Covenant, the Sabbath was observed as a day of rest. Under the New Covenant, this sabbath rest spoken of is a spiritual place of rest. It is the privilege of every believer to refuse to worry or have anxiety. As believers, you and I can enter the rest of God.

Careful observation of Hebrews 4:11 reveals that we will never enter that rest except through believing, and we will forfeit it through unbelief and disobedience. Unbelief will keep us in "wilderness living," but Jesus has provided a permanent place of rest, one that can be inhabited only through living by faith.

LIVING FROM FAITH TO FAITH

For therein is the righteousness of God revealed from faith to faith: as it is written, The just shall live by faith.

Romans 1:17 KJV

I remember an incident that may drive this point home very clearly. One evening I was walking around my house trying to do some household things, and I was so miserable. I did not have any joy — there was no peace in my heart. I kept asking the Lord, "What's wrong with me?" I often felt that way, and I sincerely wanted to know what my problem was. I was trying to follow all the things I was learning in my walk with Jesus, but something surely seemed to be missing.

About that time the phone rang and, while I was talking, I thumbed through a box of Scripture cards someone had sent me. I wasn't really looking at any of them, just flipping them around while I was on the phone. When I hung up, I decided to choose one at random and see if I could get any encouragement from it.

I pulled out Romans 15:13, **May the God of your hope so fill you with all joy and peace in believing [through the experience of your faith] that by the power of the Holy Spirit you may abound and be overflowing (bubbling over) with hope.**

I saw it!

My whole problem was doubt and unbelief. I was making myself unhappy by believing the devil's lies. I was being negative. I could not have joy and peace because I was not believing. It is impossible to have joy and peace and live in unbelief.

Make a decision to believe God and not the devil!

Learn to live from faith to faith. According to Romans 1:17, that is the way the righteousness of God is revealed. The Lord had to reveal to me that instead of living from faith to faith I would often live from faith to doubt to unbelief. Then I would go back to faith for a while, and later, return to doubt and unbelief. Back and forth I would go from one to the other. That's why I was having so much trouble and misery in my life.

Remember, according to James 1:7,8 (KJV), the double-minded man is unstable in all his ways and never receives what he wants from the Lord. Make up your mind that you will not be double-minded; don't live in doubt!

God has a great life planned for you. Don't let the devil steal it from you through lies! Instead, ...refute arguments and theories and reasonings and every proud and lofty thing that sets itself up against the [true] knowledge of God; and...lead every thought and purpose away captive into the obedience of Christ (the Messiah, the Anointed One) (2 Corinthians 10:5).

Chapter
12

An Anxious
and Worried Mind

An Anxious and Worried Mind

Anxiety and worry are both attacks on the mind intended to distract us from serving the Lord. The enemy also uses both of these torments to press our faith down, so it cannot rise up and help us live in victory.

...fret not thyself in any wise....

PSALM 37:8 KJV

Some people have such a problem with worry that it might even be said that they are addicted to worrying. If they do not have something of their own to worry about, they will worry over someone else's situation. I had this problem, so I am well qualified to describe the condition.

Because I was constantly worrying about something, I never enjoyed the peace that Jesus died for me to have.

It is absolutely impossible to worry and live in peace at the same time.

Peace is not something that can be put on a person; it is a fruit of the Spirit (Galatians 5:22), and fruit is the result of abiding in the vine. (John 15:4 KJV.) Abiding relates to entering the "rest of God" spoken of in the fourth chapter of Hebrews as well as other places in the Word of God.

There are several words in the Bible that refer to worry, depending on what translation is being read. The *King James Version* does not use the word "worry." In addition to "fret not" (Psalm 37:8), other sample phrases used to warn against worry are "take no thought," (Matthew 6:25), "be careful for nothing" (Philippians 4:6) and "casting...all your care" (1 Peter 5:7). I generally use *The Amplified Bible,* which includes several different translations of these and other phrases relating to the subject. In order to simplify the teaching in the rest of this chapter, I will refer to the condition as "worry."

WORRY DEFINED

Webster defines the word *worry* as follows: "—vi. 1. To feel uneasy or troubled....—vt. 1. To cause to feel anxious, distressed, or troubled....—n....2. A source of nagging concern."[1] I have also heard it defined as to torment oneself with disturbing thoughts.

When I saw the part about tormenting oneself with disturbing thoughts, I decided right then and there that I am smarter than that. I believe every Christian is. I think believers have more wisdom than to sit around and torment themselves.

Worry certainly never makes anything better, so why not give it up?

Another part of the definition also enlightened me: "To seize by the throat with teeth and shake or mangle, as one animal does another, or to harass by repeated biting and snapping."[2]

Pondering this definition, I made the following correlation — the devil uses worry to do to us precisely what is described above. When we have had a bout with worry for even a few hours, that is exactly how we feel — as if someone has had us by the throat and shaken us until we are totally worn out and mangled. The repetition of thoughts that comes and won't let up is like the repeated biting and snapping described in this definition.

Worry is definitely an attack from Satan upon the mind. There are certain things the believer is instructed to do with his mind, and the enemy wants to make sure that they are never done. So the devil attempts to keep the mental arena busy enough with the wrong kinds of thinking so that the mind never gets around to being used for the purpose for which God designed it.

We will be discussing the right things to do with the mind in a later chapter, but for now let's continue our study of worry until we get a full revelation on just how useless it really is.

Matthew 6:25-34 are excellent Scriptures to read when we feel a "worry attack" coming on. Let's look at each of these verses separately to see what the Lord is saying to us about this vital subject.

IS NOT LIFE GREATER THAN THINGS?

Therefore I tell you, stop being perpetually uneasy (anxious and worried) about your life, what you shall eat or what you shall drink; or about your body, what you shall put on. Is not life greater [in quality] than food, and the body [far above and more excellent] than clothing?

Matthew 6:25

Life is intended to be of such high quality that we enjoy it immensely. In John 10:10, Jesus said, **The thief comes only in order to steal and kill and destroy. I came that they may have and enjoy life, and have it in abundance (to the full, till it overflows).** Satan attempts to steal that life from us in many ways — one of them being worry.

In Matthew 6:25 we are being taught that there is nothing in life that we are to worry about — not any aspect of it! The quality of life that God has provided for us is great enough to include all those other things, but if we worry about the things, then we lose them as well as the life He intended us to have.

AREN'T YOU MORE VALUABLE THAN A BIRD?

Look at the birds of the air; they neither sow nor reap nor gather into barns, and yet your heavenly Father keeps feeding them. Are you not worth much more than they?

Matthew 6:26

It might do all of us good to spend some time watching birds. That's what our Lord told us to do.

If not every day, then at least every now and then we need to take the time to observe and remind ourselves how well our feathered friends are cared for. They literally do not know where their next meal is coming from; yet, I have personally never seen a bird sitting on a tree branch having a nervous breakdown due to worry.

The Master's point here is really very simple, *"Are you not worth more than a bird?"*

Even though you may be wrestling with a poor self-image, surely you can believe that you are more valuable than a bird, and look how well your heavenly Father takes care of them.

What Do You Gain by Worrying?

And who of you by worrying and being anxious can add one unit of measure (cubit) to his stature or to the span of his life?
Matthew 6:27

The point is quickly made that worry is useless. It does not accomplish any good thing. If that is so, then why worry, why be so anxious?

Why Be So Anxious?

And why should you be anxious about clothes? Consider the lilies of the field and learn thoroughly how they grow; they neither toil nor spin.

Yet I tell you, even Solomon in all his magnificence (excellence, dignity, and grace) was not arrayed like one of these.

But if God so clothes the grass of the field, which today is alive and green and tomorrow is tossed into the furnace, will He not much more surely clothe you, O you of little faith?
Matthew 6:28-30

Using the illustration of one of His creations, the Lord makes the point that if a flower, which does nothing, can be so well taken care of and look so good that it outshines even Solomon in all his majesty, then surely we can believe that we will be taken care of and provided for.

THEREFORE, DON'T WORRY OR BE ANXIOUS!

Therefore do not worry and be anxious, saying, What are we going to have to eat? or, What are we going to have to drink? or, What are we going to have to wear?

Matthew 6:31

I like to amplify this verse a bit and include one more question, "What are we going to do?"

I think Satan sends out demons whose job it is to do nothing but repeat that phrase in the believer's ear all day long. They fire off difficult questions, and the believer wastes his precious time attempting to come up with an answer. The devil is constantly waging war on the battlefield of the mind, hoping to engage the Christian in long, drawn-out, costly combat.

Notice that part of verse 31 in which the Lord instructs us not to worry or be anxious. Remember that out of the abundance of the heart the mouth speaks. (Matthew 12:34 KJV.) The enemy knows that if he can get enough of the wrong things going on in our mind, they will eventually begin to come out of our mouth. Our words are very important because they confirm our faith — or in some instances our lack of faith.

SEEK GOD, NOT GIFTS

For the Gentiles (heathen) wish for and crave and diligently seek all these things, and your heavenly Father knows well that you need them all.

But seek (aim at and strive after) first of all His kingdom and His righteousness (His way of doing and being right), and then all these things taken together will be given you besides.

Matthew 6:32,33

It is clear that God's children are not to be like the world! The world seeks after things, but we are to seek the Lord. He has promised that if we will do that, He will add to us all these things He knows we need.

We must learn to seek God's face and not His hand!

Our heavenly Father delights in giving His children good things, but only if we are not seeking after them.

God knows what we need before we ask. If we will simply make our requests known to Him (Philippians 4:6 KJV), He will bring them to pass in His own good timing. Worry will not help our cause at all. It will, in fact, hinder our progress.

TAKE ONE DAY AT A TIME

So do not worry or be anxious about tomorrow, for tomorrow will have worries and anxieties of its own. Sufficient for each day is its own trouble.

Matthew 6:34

I like to describe worry or anxiety as spending today trying to figure out tomorrow. Let's learn to use the time God has given to us for what He intended.

Life is to be lived – here and now!

Sadly, very few people know how to live each day to the fullest. But you can be one of them. Jesus said that Satan, the enemy, comes to steal your life. (John 10:10.) Don't allow him to do it any longer! Don't spend today worrying about tomorrow. You have enough things going on today; it needs all of your attention. God's grace is on you to handle whatever you need for today, but tomorrow's grace will not come until tomorrow comes — so don't waste today!

DON'T FRET OR HAVE ANXIETY

Do not fret or have any anxiety about anything, but in every circumstance and in everything, by prayer and petition (definite requests), with thanksgiving, continue to make your wants known to God.

Philippians 4:6

This is another good Scripture to consider when a "worry attack" comes.

I highly recommend speaking the Word of God out of the mouth. It is the two-edged sword that must be wielded against the enemy. (Hebrews 4:12; Ephesians 6:17 KJV.) A sword in its sheath won't do any good during an attack.

God has given us His Word, *use it!* Learn Scriptures like this one and when the enemy attacks, counter his attack with the same weapon that Jesus used: *the Word!*

CAST DOWN IMAGINATIONS

...refute arguments and theories and reasonings and every proud and lofty thing that sets itself up against the [true] knowledge of God; and...lead every thought and purpose away captive into the obedience of Christ (the Messiah, the Anointed One).

2 Corinthians 10:5

When the thoughts being offered you do not agree with God's Word, the best way to shut the devil up is to speak the Word.

The Word coming forth out of a believer's mouth, with faith to back it up, is the single most effective weapon that can be used to win the war against worry and anxiety.

CAST YOUR CARES UPON GOD

Therefore humble yourselves [demote, lower yourselves in your own estimation] under the mighty hand of God, that in due time He may exalt you,

Casting the whole of your care [all your anxieties, all your worries, all your concerns, once and for all] on Him, for He cares for you affectionately and cares about you watchfully.

1 Peter 5:6,7

When the enemy tries to give us a problem, we have the privilege of casting it upon God. The word "cast" actually means to pitch or throw. You and I can pitch or throw our problems to God and, believe me, He can catch them. He knows what to do with them.

This passage lets us know that to humble ourselves is not to worry. A person who worries still thinks that in some way he can solve his own problem. Worry is the mind racing around trying to find a solution to its situation. The proud man is full of himself, while the humble man is full of God. The proud man worries; the humble man waits.

Only God can deliver us, and He wants us to know that, so that in every situation our first response is to lean on Him and to enter His rest.

THE REST OF GOD

O our God, will You not exercise judgment upon them? For we have no might to stand against this great company that is coming against us. We do not know what to do, but our eyes are upon You.

2 Chronicles 20:12

I love this verse! The people in it had come to the place of realizing three things for certain:

1. They had no might against their enemies.

2. They did not know what to do.

3. They needed to have their eyes focused on God.

In verses 15 and 17 of that same passage, we see what the Lord said to them once they came to this realization and freely acknowledged it to Him:

...Be not afraid or dismayed at this great multitude; for the battle is not yours, but God's....

You shall not need to fight in this battle; take your positions, stand still, and see the deliverance of the Lord....

What is our position? It is one of abiding in Jesus and entering the rest of God. It is one of waiting on the Lord continually with our eyes focused upon Him, doing what He directs us to do and otherwise having a "reverential fear" of moving in the flesh.

Concerning entering God's rest I would like to say this: there is no such thing as "the rest of God" without opposition.

To illustrate, let me share a story I once heard involving two artists who were asked to paint pictures of peace as they perceived it. One painted a quiet, still lake, far back in the mountains. The other painted a raging, rushing waterfall which had a birch tree leaning out over it with a bird resting in a nest on one of the branches.

Which one truly depicts peace? The second one does, because there is no such thing as peace without opposition. The first painting represents stagnation. The scene it sets forth may be serene; a person might be motivated to want to go there to recuperate. It may offer a pretty picture, but it does not depict "the rest of God."

Jesus said, **Peace I leave with you; My [own] peace I now give and bequeath to you. Not as the world gives do I give to you...** (John 14:27). His peace is a spiritual peace, and His rest is one that operates in the midst of the storm — not in its absence. Jesus did not come to remove all opposition from our lives, but rather to give us a different approach to the storms of life. We are to take His yoke upon us and learn of Him. (Matthew 11:29). That means that we are to learn His ways, to approach life in the same way He did.

Jesus did not worry, and we do not have to worry either!

If you are waiting to have nothing to worry about before you stop worrying, then I probably should tell you that you will have to wait a long time, because that time may *never* come. I am not being negative. I am being honest!

Matthew 6:34 suggested that we not worry about tomorrow because each day will have sufficient trouble of its own. Jesus Himself said that, and He certainly was not negative. Being at peace, enjoying the rest of God in the midst of the storm, gives much glory to the Lord because it proves that His ways work.

WORRY, WORRY, WORRY!

I wasted many years of my life worrying about things that I could do nothing about. I would like to have those years back and be able to approach them in a different way. However, once you have spent the time God has given you, it is impossible to get it back and do things another way.

My husband, on the other hand, never worried. There was a time when I would get angry at him because he would not worry with me — and join me in talking about all the gloomy possibilities if God did not come through and meet our needs. I would sit in the kitchen, for example, and pore over the bills and checkbook, getting more upset by the moment, because the bills were more than the money. Dave would be in the next room playing with the children, watching television while they jumped up and down on his back and put rollers in his hair.

I can remember saying to him in an unpleasant tone, "Why don't you come out here and do something instead of playing while I try to figure this mess out!" When he responded with, "What would you like me to do?" I could never think of anything; it just made me angry that he would dare to enjoy himself while we were facing such a desperate financial situation.

Dave would calm me down by reminding me that God had always met our needs, that we were doing our part (which was tithing, giving offerings, praying and trusting) and that the Lord would continue to do His part. (I should clarify that Dave was trusting while I was worrying). I would go in the room with him and the children and a short while later the thoughts would creep back into my mind, "But what are we going to do? How are we going to pay these bills? What if..."

And then I would see all these disasters on the movie screen of my imagination — foreclosure of the mortgage, repossession of the car, embarrassment in front of relatives and friends if we had to ask for financial help and on and on. Have you ever been to that "movie" or had those kinds of thoughts run through your mind constantly? Of course you have, otherwise you probably would not be reading this book.

After entertaining the thoughts the devil was offering me for a while, I would wander back out into the kitchen, get out all the bills, the calculator and the checkbook and start going over the whole mess again. The more I would do so, the more upset I would become. Then we would repeat the same scene! I would yell at Dave and the children for having a good time while I was taking all the "responsibility"!

Actually what I was experiencing was not responsibility, it was care — something God had specifically told me to cast on Him.

I look back now and realize that I wasted all those evenings that God gave me in my early married life. The time He gives us is a precious gift. But I gave it to the devil. Your time is your own. Use it wisely; you won't pass this way again.

God met all our needs, and He did it in a variety of ways. He never let us down — not one time. God is faithful!

DON'T WORRY — TRUST GOD

Let your character or moral disposition be free from love of money [including greed, avarice, lust, and craving for earthly possessions] and be satisfied with your present [circumstances and with what you have]; for He [God] Himself has said, I will not in any way fail you nor give you up nor leave you without support. [I will] not, [I will] not, [I will] not in any degree leave you helpless nor forsake nor let [you] down (relax My hold on you)! [Assuredly not!]

Hebrews 13:5

This is an excellent Scripture to use to encourage yourself when you have concern about whether or not God will come through and meet your needs.

In this passage, the Lord is letting us know that we do not need to have our minds set on money, wondering how we are going to take care of ourselves, because He will take care of these things for us. He has promised never to fail us or forsake us.

Do your part, but do not try to do God's part. The load is too heavy to bear — and if you're not careful, you will break under the weight of it.

Don't worry. **Trust (lean on, rely on, and be confident) in the Lord and do good; so shall you dwell in the land and feed surely on His faithfulness, and truly you shall be fed** (Psalm 37:3).

That's a promise!

Chapter

13

A Judgmental, Critical and Suspicious Mind

A Judgmental, Critical and Suspicious Mind

Much torment comes to people's lives because of judgmental attitudes, criticism and suspicion. Multitudes of relationships are destroyed by these enemies. Once again, the mind is the battlefield.

Judge not, that ye be not judged.

MATTHEW 7:1 KJV

Thoughts — just "I think" — can be the tool the devil uses to keep a person lonely. People do not enjoy being around anyone who needs to voice an opinion about everything.

To illustrate, I once knew a woman whose husband was a very wealthy businessman. He was generally very quiet, and she wanted him to talk more. He knew a great deal about a lot of things. She would get angry at him when they were in a group of people and someone would start a conversation on a subject about which her husband could have knowledgeably contributed much insight. He could have told them everything he knew, but he wouldn't.

One evening after he and his wife had returned home from a party, she chastised him, saying, "Why didn't you speak up and tell those people what you knew about what they were talking about? You just sat there and acted as if you didn't know anything at all!"

"I already know what I know," he replied. "I try to be quiet and listen so I can find out what others know."

I would imagine that this was precisely why he was wealthy. He was also wise! Few people gain wealth without wisdom. And few people have friends without using wisdom in relationships.

Being judgmental, opinionated and critical are three sure ways to see relationships dissolve. Satan, of course, wants you and me to be lonely and rejected, so he attacks our minds in these areas. This chapter, hopefully, will help us recognize wrong thought patterns as well as learn how to deal with suspicion.

Judging Defined

In Vine's *An Expository Dictionary of New Testament Words,* one of the Greek words translated *judgment* is partially defined as "a decision passed on the faults of others" and is cross-referenced to the word "condemnation."[1] According to this same source, one of the Greek words translated *judge* is partially defined as "to form an opinion" and is cross-referenced to the word "sentence."[2]

God is the only One Who has the right to condemn or sentence, therefore, when we pass judgment on another, we are, in a certain sense, setting ourselves up as God in his life.

I don't know about you, but that puts a little "godly fear" in me. I have a lot of nerve, but I am not interested in trying to be God! These areas were once a major problem in my personality, and I believe I will be able to share some things God has taught me that will help you.

Criticism, opinions and judgment all seem to be relatives, so we will discuss them together as one giant problem.

I was critical because I always seemed to see what was wrong instead of what was right. Some personalities are more given to this fault than others. Some of the more jovial personality types do not want to see anything but the "happy or fun" things in life, so they really don't pay much attention to the things that could spoil their enjoyment. The more melancholy personality or the controlling personality often sees what is wrong first; generally, people with this type personality are generous in sharing their negative opinions and outlook with others.

We must realize that we have our own way of seeing things. We like to tell people what we think, and that is exactly the point — what I think may be right for me, but not necessarily right for you, and vice versa. We all know, of course, that "Thou shalt not steal" is right for everyone, but I am speaking here of the thousands of things we encounter every day that are neither right nor wrong necessarily but are simply personal choices. I might add that these are choices that people have a right to make on their own without outside interference.

My husband and I are extremely different in our approach to many things. How to decorate a house would be one of those things. It isn't that we don't like anything the other one chooses, but if we go out to shop for household things together, it seems Dave always likes one thing and I like something else. Why? Simply because we are two different people. His opinion is just a good as mine, and mine is just as good as his; they are simply different.

It took me years to understand that there wasn't something wrong with Dave just because he did not agree with me. And, of course, I usually let him know that I thought there was something wrong with him because he did not share my opinion. Obviously, my attitude caused much friction between us and hurt our relationship.

Pride: An "I" Problem

...I warn everyone among you not to estimate and think of himself more highly than he ought [not to have an exaggerated opinion of his own importance], but to rate his ability with sober judgment, each according to the degree of faith apportioned by God to him.

Romans 12:3

Judgment and criticism are fruit of a deeper problem — pride. When the "I" in us is bigger than it should be, it will always cause the kinds of problems we are discussing. The Bible repeatedly warns us about being high-minded.

Whenever we excel in an area, it is only because God has given us a gift of grace for it. If we are high-minded or have an exaggerated opinion of ourselves, then it causes us to look down on others and value them as "less than" we are. This type of attitude or thinking is extremely detestable to the Lord, and it opens many doors for the enemy in our lives.

HOLY FEAR

Brethren, if any person is overtaken in misconduct or sin of any sort, you who are spiritual [who are responsive to and controlled by the Spirit] should set him right and restore and reinstate him, without any sense of superiority and with all gentleness, keeping an attentive eye on yourself, lest you should be tempted also.

Bear (endure, carry) one another's burdens and troublesome moral faults, and in this way fulfill and observe perfectly the law of Christ (the Messiah) and complete what is lacking [in your obedience to it].

For if any person thinks himself to be somebody [too important to condescend to shoulder another's load] when he is nobody [of superiority except in his own estimation], he deceives and deludes and cheats himself.

Galatians 6:1-3

Careful examination of these Scriptures quickly reveals to us how we are to respond to the weakness we observe in others. It sets forth the mental attitude we are to maintain within ourselves. We must have a "holy fear" of pride and be very careful of judging others or of being critical of them.

WHO ARE WE TO PASS JUDGMENT?

Who are you to pass judgment on and censure another's household servant? It is before his own master that he stands or falls. And he shall stand and be upheld, for the Master (the Lord) is mighty to support him and make him stand.

Romans 14:4

Think of it this way: let's say your neighbor came to your door and began instructing you on what your children should wear to school and what subjects she felt they should take. How would you respond? Or, suppose your neighbor stopped in to tell you that she didn't like the way your maid (with whom you were quite satisfied) cleaned your home. What would you say to your neighbor?

This is exactly the point this Scripture is making. Each of us belongs to God, and even if we have weaknesses, He is able to make us stand and to justify us. We answer to God, not to each other; therefore, we are not to judge one another in a critical way.

The devil stays very busy assigning demons to place judgmental, critical thoughts in people's minds. I can remember when it was entertaining for me to sit in the park or the shopping mall and simply watch all the people go by as I formed a mental opinion of each of them: their clothing, hairstyles, companions, etc. Now, we cannot always prevent ourselves from having opinions, but we do not have to express them. I believe we can even grow to the point where we do not have so many opinions, and those we do have are not of a critical nature.

I frequently tell myself, "Joyce, it's none of your business." A major problem is brewing in your mind when you ponder your opinion until it becomes a judgment. The problem grows bigger the more you think about it until you begin to express it to others, or even to the one you're judging. It has then become explosive and has the ability to do a great deal of harm in the realm of relationship as well as in the spiritual realm. You may be able to save yourself future problems by simply learning to say, "This is none of my business."

Judgment and criticism were rampant in my family, so I "grew up with them," so to speak. When that is the case — as it may be for you — it is like trying to play ball with a broken leg. I was trying to "play ball" with God; I wanted to do things His way, to think and act His way, but I couldn't. It took many years of misery before I learned about the strongholds in my mind that had to be dealt with before my behavior could change.

Remember, your actions won't change until your mind does.

Matthew 7:1-6 are some of the classic Scriptures on the subject of judgment and criticism. When you are having trouble with your mind in this area, read these and other Scriptures. Read them, then read them over aloud, and use them as weapons against the devil who is attempting to build a stronghold in your mind. He may be operating out of a stronghold that has already been there for many years.

Let's take a look at this passage and I will comment on each part of it as we go through it.

SOWING AND REAPING JUDGMENT

Do not judge and criticize and condemn others, so that you may not be judged and criticized and condemned yourselves.

For just as you judge and criticize and condemn others, you will be judged and criticized and condemned, and in accordance with the measure you [use to] deal out to others, it will be dealt out again to you.

Matthew 7:1,2

These Scriptures plainly tell us that we will reap what we sow. (Galatians 6:7.) Sowing and reaping do not apply only to the agricultural and financial realms, they also apply to the mental realm. We can sow and reap an attitude as well as a crop or an investment.

One pastor I know often says that when he hears that someone has been talking about him in an unkind or judgmental way, he asks himself, "Are they sowing, or am I reaping?" Many times we are reaping in our lives what we have previously sown into the life of another.

PHYSICIAN, HEAL THYSELF!

Why do you stare from without at the very small particle that is in your brother's eye but do not become aware of and consider the beam of timber that is in your own eye?

Or how can you say to your brother, Let me get the tiny particle out of your eye, when there is the beam of timber in your own eye?

You hypocrite, first get the beam of timber out of your own eye, and then you will see clearly to take the tiny particle out of your brother's eye.

Matthew 7:3-5

The devil loves to keep us busy, mentally judging the faults of others. That way, we never see or deal with what is wrong with us!

We cannot change others; only God can. We cannot change ourselves either, but we can cooperate with the Holy Spirit and allow Him to do the work. Step One to any freedom, however, is to face the truth the Lord is trying to show us.

When we have our thoughts and conversation on what is wrong with everyone else, we are usually being deceived about our own conduct. Therefore, Jesus commanded that we not concern ourselves with what is wrong with others when we have so much wrong with ourselves. Allow God to deal with you first, and then you will learn the scriptural way of helping your brother grow in His Christian walk.

LOVE ONE ANOTHER

Do not give that which is holy (the sacred thing) to the dogs, and do not throw your pearls before hogs, lest they trample upon them with their feet and turn and tear you in pieces.

Matthew 7:6

I believe this Scripture is referring to our God-given ability to love each other.

If you and I have an ability and a command from God to love others, but instead of doing that, we judge and criticize them, we have taken the holy thing (love) and cast it before dogs and hogs (demon spirits). We have opened a door for them to trample on holy things and turn and tear us to pieces.

We need to see that "the love walk" is protection for us against demonic attack. I do not believe the devil can do much harm to someone who really walks in love.

When I became pregnant with our fourth child, I was a Christian, baptized in the Holy Spirit, called into ministry and a diligent Bible student. I had learned about exercising my faith for healing. Yet, during the first three months of the pregnancy, I was very, very sick. I lost weight and energy. I spent most of my time lying on the couch, nauseated and so tired I could barely move.

This situation was really confusing to me since I had felt wonderful during my other three pregnancies. I hadn't known much of God's Word then, even though I was in church, and did not actively use my faith for anything. Now, I was very familiar with God's promises, yet I was sick — and no amount of prayer to God or rebuking the devil was removing the problem!

One day as I lay in bed listening to my husband and children having a good time in the backyard, I aggressively asked God, "What in the world is wrong with me? Why am I so sick? And why am I not getting well?"

The Holy Spirit prompted me to read Matthew 7. I asked the Lord what that passage had to do with me and my health. I kept feeling that I should read it again and again. Finally, God opened my remembrance to an event that had taken place a couple of years earlier.

I had led and taught a home Bible study to which a young lady came whom we will call Jane. Jane attended the course faithfully until she became pregnant, but then it became very difficult for her to join us regularly because she was always tired and feeling bad.

As I lay in my bed that day, I recalled that another "Christian sister" and I had talked about, judged and criticized Jane because she "just would not press through" her circumstances and be diligent in coming to Bible study. We never offered to help her in any way. We just formed an opinion that she was a weakling and was using her pregnancy as an excuse to be lazy and self-indulgent.

Now, I was in the same set of circumstances that Jane had been two years earlier. God showed me that although I had been healthy during my first three pregnancies, I had opened a huge door for the devil by my judgment and criticism. I had taken my pearls, the holy thing (my ability to love Jane), thrown it before the dogs and hogs, and now they had turned and were tearing me to pieces. I can tell you, I was quick to repent. As soon as I did, my health was restored, and I was fine throughout the remainder of my pregnancy.

From this incident I learned an important lesson about the dangers of judging and criticizing others. I would like to be able to say that after that experience I never made another mistake of that nature, but I am sorry to say that I have made many such mistakes since then. Each time, God has had to deal with me, for which I am grateful.

We *all* make mistakes. We *all* have weaknesses. The Bible says that we are not to have a hard-hearted, critical spirit toward each other, but instead to forgive one another and to show mercy to one another just as God for Christ's sake has done for us. (Ephesians 4:32.)

JUDGING BRINGS CONDEMNATION

Therefore you have no excuse or defense or justification, O man, whoever you are who judges and condemns another. For in posing as judge and passing sentence on another, you condemn yourself, because you who judge are habitually practicing the very same things [that you censure and denounce].

Romans 2:1

In other words, the very same things that we judge others for, we do ourselves.

The Lord gave me a very good example once to help me understand this principle. I was pondering why we would do something ourselves and think it was perfectly all right, but judge someone else who does it. He said, "Joyce, you look at yourself through rose-colored glasses, but you look at everyone else through a magnifying glass."

We make excuses for our own behavior, but when someone else does the same thing we do, we are often merciless. Doing unto others as we want them to do to us (Matthew 7:12) is a good life principle that will prevent a lot of judgment and criticism, if followed.

A judgmental mind is an offshoot of a negative mind — thinking about what is wrong with an individual instead of what is right.

Be positive and not negative!

Others will benefit, but you will benefit more than anyone.

GUARD YOUR HEART

Keep and guard your heart with all vigilance and above all that you guard, for out of it flow the springs of life.

Proverbs 4:23

If you want to have life flowing to you and from you, guard your heart.

Certain types of thoughts are "unthinkable" for a believer — judgment and criticism among them. All the things that God tries to teach us are for our own good and happiness. Following His way brings fruitfulness; following the devil's way brings rottenness.

BE SUSPICIOUS OF SUSPICION

Love bears up under anything and everything that comes, is ever ready to believe the best of every person....

1 Corinthians 13:7

I can honestly say that obedience to this Scripture has always been a challenge for me. I was brought up to be suspicious. I was actually taught to distrust everyone, especially if they pretended to be nice, because they must want something.

In addition to being taught to be suspicious of others and their motives, I had several very disappointing experiences with people, not only before I became an active Christian, but afterward as well. Meditating on the components of love and realizing that love always believes the best has helped me greatly to develop a new mindset.

When your mind has been poisoned, or when Satan has gained strongholds in your mind, it has to be renewed according to God's Word. This is done by learning the Word and meditating (pondering, muttering to yourself, thinking on) it.

We have the wonderful Holy Spirit in us to remind us when our thoughts are going in the wrong direction. God does this for me when I am having suspicious thoughts instead of loving thoughts. The natural man thinks, "If I trust people, I'll be taken advantage of." Perhaps, but the benefits will far outweigh any negative experiences.

Trust and faith bring joy to life and help relationships grow to their maximum potential.

Suspicion cripples an entire relationship and usually destroys it.

The bottom line is this — God's ways work; man's ways don't. God condemns judgment, criticism and suspicion, and so should we. Love what God loves and hate what He hates. Allow what He allows and disallow what He disallows.

A balanced attitude is always the best policy. That doesn't mean that we are not to use wisdom and discernment in our dealings with others. We don't have to throw open our life to everyone we meet, giving every person we encounter a chance to crush us. On the other hand, we don't have to look at everyone with a negative, suspicious eye, always expecting to be taken advantage of by others.

TRUST GOD COMPLETELY AND MAN DISCREETLY

But when He was in Jerusalem during the Passover Feast, many believed in His name [identified themselves with His party] after seeing His signs (wonders, miracles) which He was doing.

But Jesus [for His part] did not trust Himself to them, because He knew all [men];

143

And He did not need anyone to bear witness concerning man [needed no evidence from anyone about men], for He Himself knew what was in human nature. [He could read men's hearts.]

John 2:23-25

One time after I had been involved in a disappointing church situation, God brought John 2:23-25 to my attention.

This passage is speaking of Jesus' relationship with His disciples. It plainly says that He did not trust Himself to them. It does not say that He was suspicious of them or that He had no trust in them; it just explains that because He understood human nature (which we all have), He did not trust Himself to them in an unbalanced way.

I learned a good lesson. I had been hurt badly in the situation at church because I had become too involved with a group of ladies and had got out of balance. Every time we get out of balance, we open a door for the devil.

First Peter 5:8 says, **Be well balanced (temperate, sober of mind), be vigilant and cautious at all times; for that enemy of yours, the devil, roams around like a lion roaring [in fierce hunger], seeking someone to seize upon and devour.**

I learned that I had been leaning on the ladies in this group and placing in them a trust that belongs only to God. We can go only so far in any human relationship. If we go beyond wisdom, trouble will brew, and we will be hurt.

Always place your ultimate trust in the Lord. Doing so will open the door for the Holy Spirit to let you know when you're crossing over the line of balance.

Some people think they have discernment when actually they are just suspicious. There is a true gift of the Spirit called the discerning of spirits. (1 Corinthians 12:10 KJV.) It discerns good and bad, not just bad. Suspicion comes out of the unrenewed mind; discernment comes out of the renewed spirit.

Pray for true gifts — not flesh that masquerades as gifts of the Spirit. True spiritual discernment will provoke prayer, not gossip. If a genuine problem is being discerned by a genuine gift, it will follow the scriptural pattern for dealing with it, not fleshly ways that only spread and compound the problem.

Pleasant Words Are Sweet and Healing

The mind of the wise instructs his mouth, and adds learning and persuasiveness to his lips.

Pleasant words are as a honeycomb, sweet to the mind and healing to the body.

Proverbs 16:23,24

Words and thoughts are like bone and marrow — so close, it is hard to divide them. (Hebrews 4:12.)

Our thoughts are silent words that only we and the Lord hear, but those words affect our inner man, our health, our joy and our attitude. The things we think on often come out of our mouth. And, sad to say, sometimes they make us look foolish. Judgment, criticism and suspicion never bring joy.

Jesus said that He came in order that we might have and enjoy life. (John 10:10.) Begin to operate in the mind of Christ, and you will step into a whole new realm of living.

Chapter
14

A Passive Mind

A Passive Mind

*T*his statement is certainly true concerning the area of passivity. Most Christians are not even familiar with the term, nor do they know how to recognize the symptoms.

My people are destroyed for lack of knowledge....

HOSEA 4:6

Passivity is the opposite of activity. It is a dangerous problem because the Word of God clearly teaches that we must be alert, cautious and active (1 Peter 5:8) — that we are to fan the flame and stir up the gift within us. (2 Timothy 1:6.)

I have read various definitions of the word "passivity," and I describe it as a lack of feeling, a lack of desire, general apathy, luke-warmness and laziness. Evil spirits are behind passivity. The devil knows that inactivity, failure to exercise the will, will spell the believer's ultimate defeat. As long as a person is moving against the devil by using his will to resist him, the enemy will not win the war. However, if he enters into a state of passivity, he is in serious trouble.

So many believers are emotionally ruled that an absence of feeling is all that is needed to stop them from doing what they have been taught to do. They praise if they feel like it, give if they feel like it, keep their word if they feel like it — and if they don't feel like it, they don't.

EMPTY SPACE IS A PLACE!

Neither give place to the devil.

Ephesians 4:27 KJV

The place we give Satan is often empty space. An empty, passive mind can be easily filled with all kinds of wrong thoughts.

A believer who has a passive mind and who does not resist these wrong thoughts often takes them as his own thoughts. He doesn't realize that the evil spirit has injected them into his mind because there was empty space there to fill.

One way to keep wrong thoughts out of your mind is to keep your mind full of right thoughts. The devil can be cast out, but he goes and wanders in dry places for a season. When he returns to his old home and finds it empty, the Bible says in Luke 11:24-26 that he comes back, brings others with him and the person's last condition is worse than his first. For this reason we never attempt to cast out an evil spirit from an individual unless that person has been instructed in how to "fill up the empty place."

I am not saying that every person who has an evil thought has an evil spirit. But an evil spirit is often behind evil thoughts. An individual can cast down imaginations repeatedly, but they will always come right back until he learns to fill up the empty space with right thinking. When the enemy returns, he will then find no place in that person.

There are aggressive sins, or sins of commission, and there are passive sins, which are sins of omission. In other words, there are wrong things that we do, and there are right things that we don't do. For example, a relationship can be destroyed by speaking thoughtless words, but it can also be destroyed by the omission of kind words of appreciation that should have been spoken but never were.

A passive person thinks he is doing nothing wrong because he is doing nothing. Confronted with his error, he will say, "I didn't do anything!" His analysis is correct, but his behavior is not. The problem arose precisely because he did nothing.

Overcoming Passivity

My husband Dave had some problems years ago with passivity. There were certain things that he was active in. He went to work every day, played golf on Saturday and watched football on Sunday. Beyond that, it was very hard to motivate him to do anything else. If I needed a picture hung on the wall, it might take him three or four weeks to get it done. This caused great friction between us. It seemed to me that he did what he wanted to, and beyond that he did nothing.

Dave loved the Lord and as he sought Him about this problem, God directed him to some information about passivity and its dangers. He found that evil spirits were behind his non-action. There were certain areas in which he had no problems because he had maintained his will in those areas, but in other areas he had basically, through non-activity, given his will over to the enemy. He was oppressed in those areas and had moved into a place where he had no desire, no "want to," no motivation at all to help him accomplish certain tasks.

Study of the Word of God and prayer were two other areas where he was passive. Since I knew that he was not seeking God for direction, it was hard for me to listen to him. I had a problem with rebellion anyway, and you can see how the devil used our weaknesses against each other. Many people are divorced over just such problems. They really don't understand what is wrong.

I was actually too aggressive. I was always running out ahead of God, in the flesh, "doing my own thing" and expecting the Lord to bless it. Dave did not do much of anything except wait on God, which severely irritated me. We laugh now when we think of how we both used to be, but it was not funny then and had God not gotten our attention, we might have been one of those divorce statistics.

Dave would tell me that I was always out ahead of God, and I would respond by saying that he was ten miles behind God. I was too aggressive, and Dave was too passive.

When a believer is inactive in any area in which he has capability or talent, that particular area begins to atrophy or become immobilized. The longer he does nothing, the less he wants to do anything. One of the best examples is physical exercise.

I am currently on a good exercise program, and the more I exercise, the easier it gets. When I first started, it was very hard. It hurt each time I followed the program, because I had been inactive and passive concerning exercise for a long time. The longer I did nothing, the worse my physical condition became. I was getting weaker and weaker due to non-use of my muscles.

Dave began to see what his problem was! He was dealing with evil spirits that were oppressing him because of long-term inactivity. As the Holy Spirit revealed this truth to him, Dave determined that he would once again be active and aggressive, not lazy or procrastinating.

Making the decision was the easy part; putting it into action was the hard part. It was hard because each of the areas in which he had been passive now had to be "exercised" until it was strong again.

He began to get up at 5:00 a.m. to read the Word and pray before he went to work. *The battle was on!* The devil does not want to give up ground that he has gained, and he won't give it up without a fight. Dave would get up to spend time with God and would fall asleep on the couch. Even though there were mornings when he fell asleep, he was still making progress simply because he was getting up out of bed and attempting to build a prayer life.

There were times when he was bored. There were days when he felt that he was making no progress, that he was not understanding what he was reading anyway or that his prayers were not getting through. But he persisted because of the Holy Spirit's revelation about this condition called "passivity."

I began to notice that when I needed Dave to hang a picture or fix something around the house, he responded immediately. He was beginning to do his own thinking again and make his own decisions. Many times he did not feel like doing it or even want to do it in the natural. But he went beyond his feelings and fleshly desires. The more he took action based on what he knew to be right, the more freedom he enjoyed.

I will be honest and tell you that it was not easy for him. He was not free in a few days or even a few weeks. Passivity is one of the most difficult conditions to overcome because, as I have mentioned, there are no feelings to lend support.

Dave persisted with God's help, and now he is not passive at all. He is the administrator for Life In The Word, oversees all of our radio and television outreach and has responsibility for all the financial aspects of the ministry. He travels full time with me and makes the decisions concerning our travel schedule. He is also an excellent family man. He prays and spends time regularly in God's Word. In short, he is a man to be respected and admired.

He still plays golf and watches sports, but he also does the other things he is supposed to do. Knowing him now and seeing all that he accomplishes, no one would think that he was ever as passive as he once was.

The condition of passivity can be overcome. But the first step to overcoming passivity in actions is to overcome passivity in the mind. Dave could not make progress until he made a decision and changed his way of thinking.

RIGHT ACTION FOLLOWS RIGHT THINKING

Do not be conformed to this world (this age), [fashioned after and adapted to its external, superficial customs], but be transformed (changed) by the [entire] renewal of your mind [by its new ideals and its new attitude]....

Romans 12:2

There is a dynamic principle shown throughout God's Word, and no person will ever walk in victory unless he understands and operates in it: *right action follows right thinking.*

Let me put it another way: *you will not change your behavior until you change your thoughts.*

In God's order of things, right thinking comes first, and right action follows. I believe that right action or correct behavior is a "fruit" of right thinking. Most believers struggle trying to do right, but fruit is not the product of struggle. Fruit comes as a result of abiding in the vine. (John 15:4 KJV.) And abiding in the vine involves being obedient. (John 15:10 KJV.)

I always use Ephesians 4:22-24 when teaching on this principle. Verse 22 says, **Strip yourselves of your former nature [put off and discard your old unrenewed self] which characterized your previous manner of life and becomes corrupt through lusts and desires that spring from delusion.**

Verse 24 continues the thought by saying, **And put on the new nature (the regenerate self) created in God's image, [Godlike] in true righteousness and holiness.**

So we see that verse 22 basically tells us to stop acting improperly, and verse 24 tells us to begin acting properly. But verse 23 is what I call "the bridge Scripture." It tells us how to get from verse 22 (acting improperly) to verse 24 (acting properly): **And be constantly renewed in the spirit of your mind [having a fresh mental and spiritual attitude].**

It is impossible to get from wrong behavior to right behavior without *first* changing thoughts. A passive person may want to do the right thing, but he never will do so unless he purposely activates his mind and lines it up with God's Word and will.

An example that comes to mind involves a man who once got into the prayer line at one of my seminars. He had a problem with lust. He really loved his wife and did not want their marriage to be destroyed, but his problem needed to be solved or he would surely ruin his marriage.

"Joyce, I have a problem with lust," he said. "I just cannot seem to stay away from other women. Will you pray for my deliverance? I have been prayed for many times, but I never seem to make any progress."

This is what the Holy Spirit prompted me to tell him, "Yes, I will pray for you, but you must be accountable for what you are allowing to show on the picture screen of your mind. You cannot visualize pornographic pictures in your thinking, or imagine yourself with these other women, if you ever want to enjoy freedom."

Like this man, others have come to realize, on the spot, why they are not experiencing a breakthrough even though they want to be free: *they want to change their behavior – but not their thinking.*

The mind is often an area where people "play around with sin." Jesus said in Matthew 5:27,28, **You have heard that it was said, You shall not commit adultery. But I say to you that everyone who so much as looks at a woman with evil desire for her has already committed adultery with her in his heart.** The way for sinful action is paved through sinful thinking.

A woman who attended my first home Bible study had committed her life to the Lord and wanted her home and marriage to be straightened out. Everything in her life was a mess — home, children, marriage, finances, physical condition, etc. She openly said that she did not love her husband; in fact, she actually despised him. Knowing that her attitude was not godly, she was willing to love him, but she just could not seem to tolerate being around him.

We prayed, she prayed, everyone prayed! We shared Scripture with her and gave her tapes to listen to. We did everything we knew to do and even though she was seemingly following our advice, she made no progress. *What was wrong?* During a counseling session, it was revealed that she had been a daydreamer all of her life. She was always imagining a fairy tale existence in which she was the princess and Prince Charming came home from work with flowers and candy, sweeping her off her feet with his devotion to her.

She spent her days thinking like this, and when her tired, overweight, sweaty, dirty husband came home from work (with one tooth missing), she despised him.

Think about this situation for a moment. The woman was born again, and yet her life was a mess. She wanted to obey God and live for Him, and she also wanted to love her husband because she knew it was God's will. She was willing to have victory in her life and marriage, but her mind was defeating her. There was no way she could overcome her disgust for her husband until she began to operate out of a "sound mind."

She was mentally living in a world that did not exist and never would. Therefore, she was totally unprepared to deal with reality. She had a passive mind, and since she was not choosing her own thinking according to the Word of God, the evil spirits injected thoughts into her mind.

As long as she thought they were her own thoughts and enjoyed them, she would never experience victory. She changed her thinking, and her life began to change. She changed her mental attitude toward her husband, and he began to change his appearance and his behavior toward her.

SET YOUR MIND ON WHAT IS ABOVE

If then you have been raised with Christ [to a new life, thus sharing His resurrection from the dead], aim at and seek the [rich, eternal treasures] that are above, where Christ is, seated at the right hand of God.

And set your minds and keep them set on what is above (the higher things), not on the things that are on the earth.

Colossians 3:1,2

Once again we see the same principle: if you want to live the resurrection life that Jesus has provided, then seek that new, powerful life by setting your mind and keeping it set on things above, not on things on the earth.

The Apostle Paul is simply saying that if you and I want the good life, then we must keep our mind on good things.

Many believers want the good life, but they are passively sitting around wishing that something good would happen to them.

Often, they are jealous of others who are living in victory and are resentful that their own lives are so difficult.

If you desire victory over your problems, if you truly want to live the resurrection life, *you must have backbone and not just wishbone!* You must be active — not passive. Right action begins with right thinking. Don't be passive in your mind. Start today choosing right thoughts.

Chapter
15

The Mind of Christ

The Mind of Christ

I believe that you have now made a firm decision to choose right thoughts, so let's look at the types of thinking that would be considered right according to the Lord. There are certainly many types of thoughts that would have been considered unthinkable to Jesus when He was on the earth. If we want to follow in His footsteps, then we must begin to think as He did.

For who has known or understood the mind (the counsels and purposes) of the Lord so as to guide and instruct Him and give Him knowledge? But we have the mind of Christ (the Messiah) and do hold the thoughts (feelings and purposes) of His heart.

1 Corinthians 2:16

Right away you're probably thinking, "That's impossible, Joyce, Jesus was perfect. I may be able to improve my thinking, but I will never be able to think as He did."

Well, the Bible tells us that we have the mind of Christ — and a new heart and spirit.

A New Heart and Spirit

A new heart will I give you and a new spirit will I put within you, and I will take away the stony heart out of your flesh and give you a heart of flesh.

And I will put my Spirit within you and cause you to walk in My statutes, and you shall heed My ordinances and do them.

Ezekiel 36:26,27

As Christians, you and I have a new nature, which is actually the nature of God deposited in us at the New Birth.

We can see from this Scripture that God knew if we were to heed His ordinances and walk in His statutes that He would have to give us His Spirit and a new heart (and mind). Romans 8:6 speaks of the mind of the flesh and the mind of the Spirit and tells us that death is the result of following the mind of the flesh, and life is the result of following the mind of the Spirit.

We would make tremendous progress simply by learning how to discern life and death.

If something is ministering death to you, don't do it any longer. When certain lines of thought fill you full of death, you know immediately that it is not the mind of the Spirit.

To illustrate, let's say I'm thinking about an injustice I suffered because of another person, and I begin to get angry. I start thinking about how much I dislike that individual. If I am discerning, I will notice that I am being filled with death. I am getting upset, tense, stressed out — I may even be experiencing physical discomfort. Headache, stomach pain or undue fatigue may be the fruit of my wrong thinking. On the other hand, if I am thinking how blessed I am and how good God has been to me, I will also discern that I am being filled with life.

It is very helpful to a believer to learn to discern life and death within himself. Jesus has made arrangements for us to be filled with life by putting His own mind in us. We can choose to flow in the mind of Christ.

In the following pages of this chapter is a list of things to do in order to flow in the mind of Christ.

1.   *Think positive thoughts.*

> Do two walk together except they make an appointment and have agreed?
>
> Amos 3:3

If a person is thinking according to the mind of Christ, what will his thoughts be like? They will be positive, that's for sure. In an earlier chapter we have already discussed the absolute necessity of positive thinking. You may even want to go back to Chapter 5 at this point and refresh your memory on the importance of being positive. I just went back and read it and got blessed myself even though I wrote it.

Enough can never be said about the power of being positive. God is positive, and if you and I want to flow with Him, we must get on the same wave length and begin to think positively. I am not talking about exercising mind control, but simply about being an all-around, positive person.

Have a positive outlook and attitude. Maintain positive thoughts and expectations. Engage in positive conversation.

Jesus certainly displayed a positive outlook and attitude. He endured many difficulties including personal attacks — being lied about, being deserted by His disciples when He needed them most, being made fun of, being lonely, misunderstood, and a host of other discouraging things. Yet in the midst of all these negatives He remained positive. He always had an uplifting comment, an encouraging word; He always gave hope to all those He came near.

The mind of Christ in us is positive; therefore, any time we get negative, we are not operating with the mind of Christ. Millions of people suffer from depression, and I do not think it is possible to be depressed without being negative — unless the cause is medical. Even in that case, being negative will only increase the problem and its symptoms.

According to Psalm 3:3, God is our glory and the lifter of our heads. He wants to lift everything: our hopes, our attitudes, our moods, our head, hands and heart — our whole life. He is our divine Lifter!

God wants to lift us up, and the devil wants to press us down. Satan uses the negative events and situations of our life to depress us. The dictionary definition of the word *depress* is "to lower in spirits: SADDEN."[1] According to Webster, something that is *depressed* is "sunk below the surrounding region: HOLLOW."[2] *Depress* means to sink, to press down or to hold below ground level. We regularly have the opportunity to think negative thoughts, but they will only press us down further. Being negative won't solve our problems; it will only add to them.

OVERCOME DEPRESSION

Psalm 143:3-10 gives a description of depression and how to overcome it. Let's look at this passage in detail to see the steps we can take to overcome this attack of the enemy:

1. Identify the nature and cause of the problem.

For the enemy has pursued and persecuted my soul, he has crushed my life down to the ground; he has made me to dwell in dark places as those who have been long dead.

Psalm 143:3

"Dwelling in dark places as one who is long dead," certainly sounds to me like a description of someone who is depressed.

Notice that the cause or source of this depression, this attack upon the soul, is Satan.

2. Recognize that depression steals life and light.

Therefore is my spirit overwhelmed and faints within me [wrapped in gloom]; my heart within my bosom grows numb.

Psalm 143:4

Depression oppresses a person's spiritual freedom and power.

Our spirit (empowered and encouraged by God's Spirit) is powerful and free. Therefore, Satan seeks to oppress its power and liberty by filling our mind with darkness and gloom. Please realize that it is vital to resist the feeling called "depression" immediately upon sensing its arrival. The longer it is allowed to remain, the harder it becomes to resist.

3. Remember the good times.

I remember the days of old; I meditate on all Your doings; I ponder the work of Your hands.

Psalm 143:5

In this verse we see the psalmist's response to his condition. Remembering, meditating and pondering are all functions of the mind. He obviously knows that his thoughts will affect his feelings, so he gets busy thinking about the kind of things that will help him overcome the attack upon his mind.

4.   Praise the Lord in the midst of the problem.

I spread forth my hands to You; my soul thirsts after You like a thirsty land [for water]. Selah [pause, and calmly think of that]!

Psalm 143:6

The psalmist knows the importance of praise; he lifts his hands in worship. He declares what his need truly is — he needs God. Only the Lord can cause him to feel satisfied.

Far too often when people get depressed, it is because they are in need of something, and they seek it in the wrong place, which only adds to their problems.

In Jeremiah 2:13 the Lord said, **For My people have committed two evils: they have forsaken Me, the Fountain of living waters, and they have hewn for themselves cisterns, broken cisterns which cannot hold water.**

God alone can water a thirsty soul. Don't be deceived into thinking that anything else can satisfy you fully and completely. Chasing after the wrong thing will always leave you disappointed, and disappointment opens the door for depression.

5.   Ask for God's help.

Answer me speedily, O Lord, for my spirit fails; hide not Your face from me, lest I become like those who go down into the pit (the grave).

Psalm 143:7

The psalmist asks for help. He is basically saying, "Hurry up, God, because I am not going to be able to hold on very much longer without You."

6.   Listen to the Lord.

Cause me to hear Your lovingkindness in the morning, for on You do I lean and in You do I trust. Cause me to know the way wherein I should walk, for I lift up my inner self to You.

Psalm 143:8

The psalmist knows that he needs to hear from God. He needs to be assured of God's love and kindness. He needs God's attention and direction.

7. Pray for deliverance.

Deliver me, O Lord, from my enemies; I flee to You to hide me.
Psalm 143:9

Once again the psalmist is declaring that it is only God Who can help him.

Please notice that throughout this discourse he is keeping his mind on God and not on the problem.

8. Seek God's wisdom, knowledge and leadership.

Teach me to do Your will, for You are my God; let Your good Spirit lead me into a level country and into the land of uprightness.
Psalm 143:10

Perhaps the psalmist is indicating that he has gotten out of the will of God and thus opened the door for the attack on his soul. He wants to be in God's will for he now realizes that it is the only safe place to be.

Then he requests that God help him to be stable. I believe his phrase, "Lead me into a level country," refers to his unsettled emotions. He wants to be level — not up and down.

Use Your Weapons

For the weapons of our warfare are not physical [weapons of flesh and blood], but they are mighty before God for the overthrow and destruction of strongholds,

[Inasmuch as we] refute arguments and theories and reasonings and every proud and lofty thing that sets itself up against the [true] knowledge of God; and we lead every thought and purpose away captive into the obedience of Christ (the Messiah, the Anointed One).
2 Corinthians 10:4,5

Satan uses depression to drag millions into the pit of darkness and despair. Suicide is often the result of depression. A suicidal person is usually one who has become so negative that he sees absolutely no hope for the future.

Remember: *negative feelings come from negative thoughts.*

The mind is the battlefield, the place where the battle is won or lost. Choose today to be positive — casting down every negative imagination — and bringing your thoughts into the obedience of Jesus Christ. (2 Corinthians 10:5 KJV.)

2. *Be God-minded.*

> You will guard him and keep him in perfect and constant peace whose mind [both its inclination and its character] is stayed on You, because he commits himself to You, leans on You, and hopes confidently in You.
>
> Isaiah 26:3

Jesus had a continual fellowship with His heavenly Father. It is impossible to have full fellowship with anyone without having your mind on that individual. If my husband and I are in the car together, and he is talking to me, but I have my mind on something else, we are not really fellowshipping because I am not giving him my full attention. Therefore, I believe we can safely say that the thoughts of a person functioning in the mind of Christ would be on God and on all His mighty work.

MEDITATE ON GOD AND HIS WORKS

> My whole being shall be satisfied as with marrow and fatness; and my mouth shall praise You with joyful lips
>
> When I remember You upon my bed and meditate on You in the night watches.
>
> Psalm 63:5,6

> I will meditate also upon all Your works and consider all Your [mighty] deeds.
>
> Psalm 77:12

> I will meditate on Your precepts and have respect to Your ways [the paths of life marked out by Your law].
>
> Psalm 119:15

> I remember the days of old; I meditate on all Your doings; I ponder the work of Your hands.
>
> Psalm 143:5

The psalmist David spoke frequently about meditating on God, His goodness and His works and ways. It is tremendously uplifting to think on the goodness of God and all the marvelous works of His hands.

I enjoy watching television shows about nature, animals, ocean life, etc., because they depict the greatness, the awesomeness of God, His infinite creativity and how He is upholding all things by the might of His power. (Hebrews 1:3.)

Meditating on God and His ways and works will need to become a regular part of your thought life if you want to experience victory.

One of my favorite verses of Scripture is Psalm 17:15 in which the psalmist says of the Lord, ...**I shall be fully satisfied, when I awake [to find myself] beholding Your form [and having sweet communion with You].**

I spent a lot of unhappy days because I started thinking about all the wrong things the minute I awoke each morning. I can truly say that I have been fully satisfied since the Holy Spirit has helped me operate out of the mind of Christ (the mind of the Spirit) that is within me. Fellowshipping with God early in the morning is one sure way to begin enjoying life.

FELLOWSHIP WITH THE LORD

> ...If I do not go away, the Comforter (Counselor, Helper, Advocate, Intercessor, Strengthener, Standby) will not come to you [into close fellowship with you]; but if I go away, I will send Him to you [to be in close fellowship with you].
>
> John 16:7

These words were spoken by Jesus just before He departed into heaven where He is seated at the right hand of the Father in glory. It is obvious from this Scripture that it is God's will that we be in close fellowship with Him.

Nothing is closer to us than our own thoughts. Therefore, if we will fill our mind with the Lord, it will bring Him into our consciousness and we will begin to enjoy a fellowship with Him that will bring joy, peace and victory to our everyday life.

He is always with us just as He promised He would be. (Matthew 28:20; Hebrews 13:5.) But we will not be conscious of His Presence unless we think about Him. I can be in a room with someone and if I have my mind on lots of other things, I can leave and never even know that person was there. This is the way it is with our fellowship privileges with the Lord. He is always with us, but we need to think on Him and be aware of His presence.

3. Be "God-Loves-Me" Minded.

And we know (understand, recognize, are conscious of, by observation and by experience) and believe (adhere to and put faith in and rely on) the love God cherishes for us. God is love, and he who dwells and continues in love dwells and continues in God, and God dwells and continues in him.

1 John 4:16

I have learned that the same thing is true of God's love that is true of His presence. If we never meditate on His love for us, we will not experience it.

Paul prayed in Ephesians 3 that the people would experience the love of God for themselves. The Bible says that He loves us. But how many of God's children still lack a revelation concerning God's love?

I remember when I began Life In The Word Ministries. The first week I was to conduct a meeting, I asked the Lord what He wanted me to teach and He responded, "Tell My people that I love them."

"They know that," I said. "I want to teach them something really powerful, not a Sunday school lesson out of John 3:16."

The Lord said to me, "Very few of my people really know how much I love them. If they did, they would act differently."

As I began to study the subject of receiving God's love, I realized that I was in desperate need myself. The Lord led me in my study to 1 John 4:16 which states that we should be conscious of God's love. That means it should be something we are actively aware of.

I had an unconscious, vague sort of understanding that God loved me, but the love of God is meant to be a powerful force in our lives, one that will take us through even the most difficult trials into victory.

In Romans 8:35 the Apostle Paul exhorts us, **Who shall ever separate us from Christ's love? Shall suffering and affliction and tribulation? Or calamity and distress? Or persecution or hunger or destitution or peril or sword?** Then in verse 37 he goes on to say, **Yet amid all these things we are more than conquerors and gain a surpassing victory through Him Who loved us.**

I studied in this area for a long time, and I became conscious and aware of God's love for me through thinking about His love and by confessing it out loud. I learned Scriptures about the love of God, and I meditated on them and confessed them out of my mouth. I did this over and over for months, and all the time the revelation of His unconditional love for me was becoming more and more of a reality to me.

Now, His love is so real to me that even in hard times, I am comforted by the "conscious knowing" that He loves me and that I no longer have to live in fear.

FEAR NOT

There is no fear in love; but perfect love casteth out fear....

1 John 4:18 KJV

God loves us perfectly, just as we are. Romans 5:8 (KJV) tells us that ...**God commendeth his love toward us, in that, while we were yet sinners, Christ died for us.**

Believers operating out of the mind of Christ are not going to think about how terrible they are. They will have righteousness-based thoughts. You should have a righteousness-consciousness, meditating regularly on who you are "in Christ."

BE RIGHTEOUSNESS-CONSCIOUS, NOT SIN-CONSCIOUS

For our sake He made Christ [virtually] to be sin Who knew no sin, so that in and through Him we might become [endued with, viewed as being in, and examples of] the righteousness of God [what we ought to be, approved and acceptable and in right relationship with Him, by His goodness].

2 Corinthians 5:21

A large number of believers are tormented by negative thinking about themselves. Thoughts about how God must be so displeased with them because of all their weaknesses and failures.

How much time do you waste living under guilt and condemnation? Notice I said how much time do you waste, because that is exactly what all that kind of thinking is, a waste of time!

Don't think about how terrible you were before you came to Christ. Instead, think about how you have been made the righteousness of God in Him. Remember: *thoughts turn into actions.* If you ever want to behave any better, you have to change your thinking first. Keep thinking about how terrible you are, and you will only act worse. Every time a negative, condemning thought comes to your mind, remind yourself that God loves you, that you have been made the righteousness of God in Christ.

You are changing for the better all the time. Every day you're growing spiritually. God has a glorious plan for your life. These are the truths you must think on.

This is what you are supposed to be doing with your mind!

Think deliberately according to the Word of God; don't just think whatever falls into your head, receiving it as your own thought.

Rebuke the devil and start going forward by thinking right thoughts.

4. *Have an exhortative mind.*

He who exhorts (encourages), to his exhortation....

Romans 12:8

The person with the mind of Christ thinks positive, uplifting, edifying thoughts about other people as well as about himself and his own circumstances.

The ministry of exhortation is greatly needed in the world today. You will never exhort anyone with your words if you have not first had kind thoughts about that individual. Remember that whatever is in your heart will come out of your mouth. Do some "love thinking" on purpose.

Send thoughts of love toward other people. Speak words of encouragement to them.

Vine's *An Expository Dictionary of New Testament Words* defines the Greek word *parakaleo*, which is translated *exhort*, as "primarily, to call to a person (*para* to the side, *kaleo*, to call)...to admonish, exhort, to urge one to pursue some course of conduct...."[3] I interpret this definition to mean coming alongside a person and urging him to press forward in pursuing a course of action. The ministry gift of exhortation spoken of in Romans 12:8 can readily be seen in those who have it. They are always saying something encouraging or uplifting to everyone — something that makes others feel better and encourages them to press on.

We may not all have the ministry gift of exhortation, but anyone can learn to be encouraging. The simple rule is: if it's not good, then don't think it or say it.

Everyone has enough problems already, we don't need to add to their troubles by tearing them down. We should build up one another in love. (Ephesians 4:29.) Don't forget: love always believes the best of everyone. (1 Corinthians 13:7.)

As you begin to think lovely thoughts about people, you will find them behaving in a more lovely manner. Thoughts and words are containers or weapons for carrying creative or destructive power. They can be used against Satan and his works or they can actually help him in his plan of destruction.

Let's say you have a child who has some behavior problems and definitely needs to change. You pray for him and ask God to work in his life, making whatever changes are necessary. Now what do you do with your thoughts and words concerning him during the waiting period? Many people never see the answer to their prayers because they negate what they have asked for with their own thoughts and words before God ever gets a chance to work in their behalf.

Do you pray for your child to change and then entertain all kinds of negative thoughts about him? Or, perhaps pray for change and then think and even say to others, "This kid will never change!" To live in victory, you must begin by lining up your thoughts with God's Word.

We are not walking in the Word if our thoughts are opposite of what it says. We are not walking in the Word if we are not thinking in the Word.

When you pray for someone, line up your thoughts and words with what you have prayed and you will begin to see a breakthrough.

I am not suggesting that you get out of balance. If your child has a behavior problem in school, and a friend asks how he is doing, what should you do if, in reality, no change has manifested? You can say, "Well, we have not seen the breakthrough yet, but I believe God is working and that this child is a powerhouse for the Lord. We will see him change from glory to glory, little by little, day after day."

5. *Develop a thankful mind.*

> Enter into His gates with thanksgiving and a thank offering and into His courts with praise! Be thankful and say so to Him, bless and affectionately praise His name!
>
> Psalm 100:4

A person flowing in the mind of Christ will find his thoughts filled with praise and thanksgiving.

Many doors are opened to the enemy through complaining. Some people are physically ill and live weak, powerless lives due to this disease called complaining that attacks the thoughts and conversations of people.

A powerful life cannot be lived without thanksgiving. The Bible instructs us over and over in the principle of thanksgiving. Complaining in thought or word is a death principle, but being thankful and saying so is a life principle.

If a person does not have a thankful heart (mind), thanksgiving will not come out of his mouth. When we are thankful, we will say so.

BE THANKFUL AT ALL TIMES

> Through Him, therefore, let us constantly and at all times offer up to God a sacrifice of praise, which is the fruit of lips that thankfully acknowledge and confess and glorify His name.
>
> Hebrews 13:15

When do we offer thanksgiving? At all times — in every situation, in all things — and by so doing we enter into the victorious life where the devil cannot control us.

How can he control us if we are going to be joyful and thankful no matter what our circumstances are? Admittedly, this kind of lifestyle sometimes requires a sacrifice of praise or thanksgiving, but I would rather sacrifice my thanksgiving to God than sacrifice my joy to Satan. I have learned (the hard way) that if I get grumpy and refuse to give thanks, then I will end up giving up my joy. In other words, I will lose it to the spirit of complaining.

In Psalm 34:1 the psalmist says, **I will bless the Lord at all times; His praise shall continually be in my mouth.** How can we be a blessing to the Lord? By letting His praise *continually* be in our thoughts and mouths.

Be a grateful person — one filled with gratitude not only toward God, but also toward people. When someone does something nice for you, let him know that you appreciate it.

Show appreciation in your family among the various members. So often, we take for granted the things that God has blessed us with. A sure way to lose something is not to appreciate it.

I appreciate my husband; we have been married a long time but I still tell him that I appreciate him. He is a very patient man in many ways and has a lot of other really good qualities. I know that it helps build and maintain good relationships to let people know that we appreciate them, even mentioning certain things specifically that we are thankful for.

I deal with many people, and it continues to amaze me how some people are so thankful for every little thing that is done for them, while others are never satisfied no matter how much is done on their behalf. I believe pride has something to do with this problem. Some people are so full of themselves that no matter what others do for them, they think they deserve not only that, but more! They seldom express appreciation.

Expressing appreciation is not only good for the other person, but it is good for us, because it releases joy in us.

Meditate daily on all the things you have to be thankful for. Rehearse them to the Lord in prayer, and as you do you will find your heart filling up with life and light.

OFFER THANKS ALWAYS FOR EVERYTHING

And do not get drunk with wine, for that is debauchery; but ever be filled and stimulated with the [Holy] Spirit.

Speak out to one another (the *King James Version* says "speaking to yourselves") in psalms and hymns and spiritual songs, offering praise with voices [and instruments] and making melody with all your heart to the Lord,

At all times and for everything giving thanks in the name of our Lord Jesus Christ to God the Father.

Ephesians 5:18-20

What a powerful group of Scriptures!

How can you and I stay ever filled with the Holy Spirit? By speaking to ourselves (through our thoughts) or to others (through our words) in psalms and hymns and spiritual songs. In other words, by keeping our thoughts and words on, and full of, the Word of God; by offering *praise at all times and for everything, giving thanks.*

6. *Be Word-minded.*

And you have not His word (His thought) living in your hearts, because you do not believe and adhere to and trust in and rely on Him Whom He has sent. [That is why you do not keep His message living in you, because you do not believe in the Messenger Whom He has sent.]

John 5:38

God's Word is His thoughts written down on paper for our study and consideration. His Word is how He thinks about every situation and subject.

In John 5:38 Jesus was chastising some unbelievers. We see from this translation that God's Word is a written expression of His thoughts and that people who want to believe and experience all the good results of believing must allow His Word to be a living message in their hearts. This is accomplished by meditating on the Word of God. This is how His thoughts can become our thoughts — the only way to develop the mind of Christ in us.

The Bible in John 1:14 says that Jesus was the Word made flesh. That would not have been possible had His mind not been filled with the Word of God continually.

Meditating on the Word of God is one of the most important life principles that we can learn. Vine's *An Expository Dictionary of New Testament Words* defines the two Greek words translated *meditate* as follows: "...to care for," "to attend to, practise," to "be diligent in," "to practise is the prevalent sense of the word," "to ponder, imagine," "to premeditate....."[4] Another resource adds "to murmur" or "to mutter" to the definition.[5]

I can't emphasize strongly enough how important this principle is. I call it a life principle because meditating on the Word of God will minister life to you and ultimately to those around you.

Many Christians have become fearful of the word "meditate" due to the meditation practices of pagan and occult religions. But I urge you to remember that Satan has really never had an original idea. He takes what belongs to the Kingdom of Light and perverts it for the kingdom of darkness. We must be wise enough to realize that if meditation produces such power for the side of evil, that it will also produce power for the cause of good. The principle of meditation comes straight out of the Word of God; let's take a look at what the Bible has to say about it.

MEDITATE AND PROSPER

This Book of the Law shall not depart out of your mouth, but you shall meditate on it day and night, that you may observe and do according to all that is written in it. For then you shall make your way prosperous, and then you shall deal wisely and have good success.

Joshua 1:8

In this verse, the Lord is telling us plainly that we will never put the Word into practice physically if we don't first practice it mentally.

Psalm 1:2,3 speaks of the godly man and says: **But his delight and desire are in the law of the Lord, and on His law (the precepts, the instructions, the teachings of God) he habitually meditates (ponders and studies) by day and by night. And he shall be like a tree firmly planted [and tended] by the streams of water, ready to bring forth its fruit in its season; its leaf also shall not fade or wither; and everything he does shall prosper [and come to maturity].**

Meditate and Be Healed

My son, attend to my words; consent and submit to my sayings.

Let them not depart from your sight; keep them in the center of your heart.

For they are life to those who find them, healing and health to all their flesh.

Proverbs 4:20-22

Remembering that one of the defining words for "meditate" is to attend, consider this passage of Scripture which says that the words of the Lord are a source of health and healing to the flesh.

Meditating (pondering, thinking about) the Word of God in our mind will actually affect our physical body. My appearance has been changed during the past eighteen years. People tell me that I actually look at least fifteen years younger today than I did when I first began to diligently study the Word and make it the central focus of my entire life.

Hear and Harvest

And He said to them, Be careful what you are hearing. The measure [of thought and study] you give [to the truth you hear] will be the measure [of virtue and knowledge] that comes back to you — and more [besides] will be given to you who hear.

Mark 4:24

This is like the principle of sowing and reaping. The more we sow, the more we will reap at harvest time. The Lord is saying in Mark 4:24 that the greater the amount of time you and I personally put into thinking about and studying the Word we hear, the more we will get out of it.

READ AND REAP

[Things are hidden temporarily only as a means to revelation.] For there is nothing hidden except to be revealed, nor is anything [temporarily] kept secret except in order that it may be made known.

Mark 4:22

These two verses together are surely telling us that the Word has hidden in it tremendous treasures, powerful life-giving secrets that God wants to reveal to us. They are manifested to those who meditate on, ponder, study, think about, practice mentally and mutter the Word of God.

I know personally, as a teacher of God's Word, the truth of this principle. It seems there is no end to what God can show me out of one verse of Scripture. I will study it one time and get one thing, and another time see something new that I did not even notice before.

The Lord keeps revealing His secrets to those who are diligent about the Word. Don't be the kind of person who always wants to live off of someone else's revelation. Study the Word yourself and allow the Holy Spirit to bless your life with truth.

I could go on and on about the subject of meditating on God's Word. As I have said, it is one of the most important things that you and I can learn to do. All day long, as you go about your daily affairs, ask the Holy Spirit to remind you of certain Scriptures so you can meditate on them. You will be amazed at how much power will be released into your life from this practice. The more you meditate on the Word of God, the more you will be able to readily draw upon its strength in times of trouble. Remember: *the power to do the Word comes from the practice of meditating on it.*

RECEIVE AND WELCOME THE WORD

So get rid of all uncleanness and the rampant outgrowth of
wickedness, and in a humble (gentle, modest) spirit receive and
welcome the Word which implanted and rooted [in your hearts]
contains the power to save your souls.

James 1:21

We see from this Scripture that the Word has the power to
save us from a life of sin, but only as it is received, welcomed and
implanted and rooted in our hearts (minds). This implanting and
rooting takes place through attending to God's Word — by having
it on our mind more than anything else.

If you and I meditate on our problems all the time, we will
become more deeply rooted in them. If we meditate on what is
wrong with ourselves or others, we will become more deeply convinced of the problem and never see the solution. It is as if there
is an ocean full of life available to us, and the instrument we are
given to draw it forth is diligent study and meditation of the Word
of God.

Our ministry is called Life In The Word, and I can say from
experience that there truly *is* life in the Word of God.

CHOOSE LIFE!

Now the mind of the flesh [which is sense and reason without the
Holy Spirit] is death [death that comprises all the miseries arising
from sin, both here and hereafter]. But the mind of the [Holy]
Spirit is life and [soul] peace [both now and forever].

Romans 8:6

Calling your attention again to Philippians 4:8 seems to be a
good way to close this section of the book: ...whatever is true,
whatever is worthy of reverence and is honorable and seemly,
whatever is just, whatever is pure, whatever is lovely and lovable, whatever is kind and winsome and gracious, if there is any
virtue and excellence, if there is anything worthy of praise,
think on and weigh and take account of these things [fix your
minds on them].

The condition your mind should be in is described in this Scripture. You have the mind of Christ, begin to use it. If He wouldn't think it, you shouldn't think it either.

It is by this continual "watching over" your thoughts that you begin to take every thought captive unto the obedience of Jesus Christ. (2 Corinthians 10:5 KJV.)

The Holy Spirit is quick to remind you if your mind is beginning to take you in a wrong direction, then the decision becomes yours. Will you flow in the mind of the flesh or in the mind of the Spirit? One leads to death, the other to life. The choice is yours.

Choose life!

PART 3:

Wilderness Mentalities

Introduction

The people of the nation of Israel wandered around in the wilderness for forty years making what was actually an eleven-day journey. Why? Was it their enemies, their circumstances, the trials along the way or something entirely different that prevented them from arriving at their destination?

It is [only] eleven days' journey from Horeb by the way of Mount Seir to Kadesh-barnea [on Canaan's border; yet Israel took forty years to get beyond it].

DEUTERONOMY 1:2

As I was pondering this situation, God gave me a powerful revelation that has helped me personally as well as thousands of others. The Lord said to me, "The Children of Israel spent forty years in the wilderness making an eleven-day trip because they had a 'wilderness mentality.'"

YOU HAVE STAYED HERE LONG ENOUGH

The Lord our God said to us in Horeb, You have dwelt long enough on this mountain.

Deuteronomy 1:6

We really shouldn't look at the Israelites with such astonishment because most of us do the same thing they did. We keep going around and around the same mountains instead of making progress. The result is, it takes us years to experience victory over something that could have and should have been dealt with quickly.

I think the Lord is saying the same thing to you and me today that He said to the Children of Israel in their day:

"You have dwelt long enough on the same mountain; it is time to move on."

Set Your Mind and Keep It Set

And set your minds and keep them set on what is above (the higher things), not on the things that are on the earth.

Colossians 3:2

God showed me ten "wilderness mentalities" that the Israelites had that kept them in the wilderness. A wilderness mentality is a wrong mindset.

We can have right or wrong mindsets. The right ones benefit us, and the wrong ones hurt us and hinder our progress. Colossians 3:2 teaches us to set our minds and keep them set. We need our minds set in the right direction. Wrong mindsets not only affect our circumstances, but they also affect our inner life.

Some people *live* in a wilderness, while others are a wilderness.

There was a time when my circumstances were not really bad, but I could not enjoy anything in my life because I was a "wilderness" inside. Dave and I had a nice home, three lovely children, good jobs and enough money to live comfortably. I could not enjoy our blessings because I had several wilderness mentalities. My life appeared to me to be a wilderness because that is the way I saw everything.

Some people see things negatively because they have experienced unhappy circumstances all their lives and can't imagine anything getting any better. Then there are some people who see everything as bad and negative simply because that is the way they are on the inside. Whatever its cause, a negative outlook leaves a person miserable and unlikely of making any progress toward the Promised Land.

God had called the Children of Israel out of bondage in Egypt to go to the land He had promised to give them as a perpetual inheritance — a land that flowed with milk and honey and every good thing that they could imagine — a land in which there would be no shortage of anything they needed — a land of prosperity in every realm of their existence.

Most of the generation that the Lord called out of Egypt never entered into the Promised Land; instead, they died in the wilderness. To me, this is one of the saddest things that can happen to a child of God — to have so much available and yet never be able to enjoy any of it.

I was one of those people for many years of my Christian life. I was on my way to the Promised Land (heaven), but I was not enjoying the trip. I was dying in the wilderness. But, thank God for His mercy, a light shone in my darkness, and He led me out.

I pray that this section of the book will be a light to you and prepare you to walk out of your wilderness into the glorious light of God's marvelous Kingdom.

Chapter
16

*"My future is determined
by my past and my present."*

Wilderness Mentality #1

"My future is determined by my past and my present."

Wilderness Mentality #1

The Israelites had no positive vision for their lives — no dreams. They knew where they came from, but they did not know where they were going. Everything was based on what they had seen and could see. They did not know how to see with "the eye of faith."

Where there is no vision, the people perish....
PROVERBS 29:18 KJV

ANOINTED TO BRING DELIVERANCE

The Spirit of the Lord is upon me, because he hath anointed me to preach the gospel to the poor; he hath sent me to heal the brokenhearted, to preach deliverance to the captives, and recovering of sight to the blind, to set at liberty them that are bruised.

To preach the acceptable year of the Lord.

Luke 4:18,19 KJV

I come from a background of abuse; I was raised in a dysfunctional home. My childhood was filled with fear and torment. The experts say that a child's personality is formed within the first five years of his life. My personality was a mess! I lived in pretense behind walls of protection that I had built to keep people from hurting me. I was locking others out, but I was also locking myself in. I was a controller, so filled with fear that the only way I could face life was to feel that I was in control, and then no one could hurt me.

As a young adult trying to live for Christ and follow the Christian lifestyle, I knew where I had come from, but I did not know where I was going. I felt that my future would always be marred by my past. I thought, "How could anyone who has the kind of past I do ever be really all right? It's impossible!" However, Jesus said that He came to make well those who were sick, brokenhearted, wounded and bruised, those broken down by calamity.

Jesus came to open the prison doors and set the captives free. I did not make any progress until I started to believe that I could be set free. I had to have a positive vision for my life; I had to believe that my future was not determined by my past or even my present.

You may have had a miserable past, you may even be in current circumstances that are very negative and depressing. You may be facing situations that are so bad it seems you have no real reason to hope. But I say to you boldly, *your future is not determined by your past or your present!*

Get a new mindset. Believe that with God all things are possible (Luke 18:27); with man some things may be impossible, but we serve a God Who created everything we see out of nothing. (Hebrews 11:3.) Give Him your nothingness and watch Him go to work. All He needs is your faith in Him. He needs for you to believe, and He will do the rest.

EYES TO SEE, EARS TO HEAR

And there shall come forth a rod out of the stem of Jesse, and a Branch shall grow out of his roots:

And the spirit of the Lord shall rest upon him, the spirit of wisdom and understanding, the spirit of counsel and might, the spirit of knowledge and of the fear of the Lord;

And shall make him of quick understanding in the fear of the Lord: and he shall not judge after the sight of his eyes, neither reprove after the hearing of his ears.

Isaiah 11:1-3 KJV

We cannot judge things accurately by the sight of our natural eyes. We must have spiritual "eyes to see" and "ears to hear." We need to hear what the Spirit says, not what the world says. Let God speak to you about your future — not everyone else.

The Israelites continually looked at and talked about the way things were. God brought them out of Egypt by the hand of Moses, talking to them through him about the Promised Land. He wanted them to keep their eyes on where they were going — and off of where they had been. Let's look at a few Scriptures that clearly depict their wrong attitude.

WHAT IS THE PROBLEM?

All the Israelites grumbled and deplored their situation, accusing Moses and Aaron, to whom the whole congregation said, Would that we had died in Egypt! Or that we had died in this wilderness!

Why does the Lord bring us to this land to fall by the sword? Our wives and little ones will be a prey. Is it not better for us to return to Egypt?

Numbers 14:2,3

I encourage you to look over this passage carefully. Notice how negative these people were — complaining, ready to give up easily, preferring to go back to bondage rather than press through the wilderness into the Promised Land.

Actually, they did not have a problem, they were the problem!

BAD THOUGHTS PRODUCE BAD ATTITUDES

Now there was no water for the congregation, and they assembled together against Moses and Aaron.

And the people contended with Moses, and said, Would that we had died when our brethren died [in the plague] before the Lord!

And why have you brought up the congregation of the Lord into this wilderness, that we should die here, we and our livestock?

Numbers 20:2-4

It is easy to see from their own words that the Israelites were not trusting God at all. They had a negative, failure attitude. They decided they would fail before they ever really got started, simply because every circumstance was not perfect. They displayed an attitude that came from a wrong mindset.

Bad attitudes are the fruit of bad thoughts.

A Lack of an Attitude of Gratitude

And they journeyed from Mount Hor by the way to the Red Sea, to go around the land of Edom, and the people became impatient (depressed, much discouraged), because [of the trials] of the way.

And the people spoke against God and against Moses, Why have you brought us out of Egypt to die in the wilderness? For there is no bread, neither is there any water, and we loathe this light (contemptible, unsubstantial) manna.

Numbers 21:4,5

Along with all the other bad attitudes we have already seen in the previous Scriptures, in this passage we see evidence in the Israelites of a tremendous lack of gratitude. The Children of Israel simply could not quit thinking about where they had come from and where they were long enough to get where they were going.

It would have helped them to consider their forefather Abraham. He went through some disappointing experiences in his life, but he did not allow them to negatively affect his future.

No Life with Strife

And there was strife between the herdsmen of Abram's cattle and the herdsmen of Lot's cattle. And the Canaanite and the Perizzite were dwelling then in the land [making fodder more difficult to obtain].

So Abram said to Lot, Let there be no strife, I beg of you, between you and me, or between your herdsmen and my herdsmen, for we are relatives.

Is not the whole land before you? Separate yourself, I beg of you, from me. If you take the left hand, then I will go to the right; or if you choose the right hand, then I will go to the left.

And Lot looked and saw that everywhere the Jordan Valley was well watered. Before the Lord destroyed Sodom and Gomorrah, it was all like the garden of the Lord, like the land of Egypt, as you go to Zoar.

Then Lot chose for himself all the Jordan Valley and [he] traveled east. So they separated.

Genesis 13:7-11

Abraham knew the dangers of living in strife; therefore, he told Lot that they needed to separate. In order to walk in love, and to ensure that there would be no strife between them in the future, Abraham allowed his nephew to choose which valley he wanted first. Lot chose the best one — the Jordan Valley — and they separated.

We must remember that Lot had nothing until Abraham blessed him. Think of the attitude that Abraham could have had, but chose not to! He knew that if he acted properly God would take care of him.

LIFT UP YOUR EYES AND LOOK

The Lord said to Abram after Lot had left him, Lift up now your eyes and look from the place where you are, northward and southward and eastward and westward;

For all the land which you see I will give to you and to your posterity forever.

Genesis 13:14,15

This passage clearly reveals that even though Abraham found himself in less desirable circumstances after his separation from his nephew, God wanted him to "look up" from the place where he was to the place that He wanted to take him.

Abraham had a good attitude about his situation, and as a result the devil could not keep the blessings of God from him. God gave him even more possessions than he had enjoyed before the separation, and blessed him mightily in every way.

I encourage you to take a positive look at the possibilities of the future and begin to "calleth those things that be not as though they were." (Romans 4:17 KJV.) Think and speak about your future in a positive way, according to what God has placed in your heart, and not according to what you have seen in the past or are seeing even now in the present.

Chapter
17

"Someone do it for me;
I don't want to take the responsibility."

Wilderness Mentality #2

"Someone do it for me; I don't want to take the responsibility."

Wilderness Mentality #2

Responsibility is often defined as our response to God's ability. To be responsible is to respond to the opportunities that God has placed in front of us.

God gave Abram's father a responsibility, a chance to respond to His ability. He placed before him the opportunity to go to Canaan. But instead of going all the way with the Lord, he chose to stop and settle in Haran.

> *And Terah took Abram his son, Lot the son of Haran, his grandson, and Sarai his daughter-in-law, his son Abram's wife, and they went forth together to go from Ur of the Chaldees into the land of Canaan; but when they came to Haran, they settled there.*
>
> GENESIS 11:31

It is fairly easy to be excited when God first speaks to us and gives us an opportunity to do something. But, like Terah, many times we never finish what we start because we get into it and realize there is more involved than goosebumps and excitement.

Most new ventures are exciting simply because they are new. Excitement will carry a person along for a while, but it will not take him across the finish line.

Many believers do what the Bible says Terah did. They start out for one place and settle somewhere else along the way. They get tired or weary; they would like to finish their course, but they really don't want all the responsibility that goes with it. If someone else would do it for them, they would love to reap the glory, but it just does not work that way.

PERSONAL RESPONSIBILITY CAN'T BE DELEGATED

The next day Moses said to the people, You have sinned a great sin. And now I will go up to the Lord; perhaps I can make atonement for your sin.

> So Moses returned to the Lord, and said, Oh, these people have sinned a great sin and have made themselves gods of gold!
> Yet now, if You will forgive their sin — and if not, blot me, I pray You, out of Your book which You have written!
>
> Exodus 32:30-32

In my reading and study, I noticed that the Israelites did not want to take responsibility for anything. Moses did their praying; he sought God for them, he even did their repenting when they got themselves in trouble. (Exodus 32:1-14).

A baby has no responsibility at all, but as the child grows up, he is expected to take more and more responsibility. One of the main roles of a parent is to teach their children to accept responsibility. God desires to teach His children the same thing.

The Lord gave me an opportunity to be in full-time ministry — to teach His Word on national radio and television — to preach the Gospel all over the United States and in other nations. But I can assure you that there is a responsibility side to that call that many know nothing of. A lot of people say they want to be in ministry because they think it is a continual spiritual event.

Many times people apply for a job in our organization thinking that the greatest thing that could ever happen to them would be to become a part of a Christian ministry. Later, they discover that they have to work there the same as any other place; they have to get up and get there on time, come under authority, follow a daily routine, etc. When people say they want to come to work for us, I tell them that we don't float around on a cloud all day singing "The Hallelujah Chorus" — we work, and we work hard. We walk in integrity and do what we do with excellence.

Of course, it is a privilege to work in ministry, but I try to make the point to new applicants that when the goosebumps and excitement have subsided, they will find us expecting high levels of responsibility from them.

GO TO THE ANT!

Go to the ant, you sluggard; consider her ways and be wise!—

Which, having no chief, overseer, or ruler,

Provides her food in the summer and gathers her supplies in the harvest.

How long will you sleep, O sluggard? When will you arise out of your sleep?

Yet a little sleep, a little slumber, a little folding of the hands to lie down and sleep —

So will your poverty come like a robber or one who travels [with slowly but surely approaching steps] and your want like an armed man [making you helpless].

Proverbs 6:6-11

This lazy mindset that the Israelites had was one of the things that kept them in the wilderness forty years making an eleven-day trip.

I like to read this passage in Proverbs in which our attention is called to the ant, who without having any supervisor or taskmaster provides for herself and her family.

People who must always have someone else pushing them will never really do anything great. Those who only do what is right when someone is looking won't get very far either. We must be motivated from within, not from without. We must live our lives before God, knowing that He sees all and that our reward will come from Him if we persist in doing what He has asked us to do.

MANY CALLED, FEW CHOSEN

...For many are called, but few chosen.

Matthew 20:16

I once heard a Bible teacher say that this verse means that many are called or given an opportunity to do something for the Lord, but very few are willing to take the responsibility to answer that call.

As I mentioned in a previous chapter, a lot of people have wishbone but no backbone. People with a "wilderness mentality" want to have everything and do nothing.

GET UP AND GO!

After the death of Moses the servant of the Lord, the Lord said to Joshua son of Nun, Moses' minister,

Moses My servant is dead. So now arise [take his place], go over this Jordan, you and all this people, into the land which I am giving to them, the Israelites.

Every place upon which the sole of your foot shall tread, that have I given to you, as I promised Moses.

Joshua 1:1-3

When God told Joshua that Moses was dead and he was to take his place and lead the people across the Jordan into the Promised Land, it meant a lot of new responsibility for Joshua.

The same is true for us as we go forth to claim our spiritual inheritance. You and I will never have the privilege of standing and ministering under God's anointing if we are not willing to take our responsibility seriously.

BEHOLD, NOW IS THE FAVORABLE TIME!

He who observes the wind [and waits for all conditions to be favorable] will not sow, and he who regards the clouds will not reap.

Ecclesiastes 11:4

In 1993, when God showed Dave and me that He wanted us to go on TV, He said, "I am giving you an opportunity to go on television; but if you don't take the opportunity now, it will never pass by you again." Perhaps if God had not let us know that the opportunity was for that particular moment only, we might have procrastinated. After all, we were finally in a position where we could be comfortable.

For nine years, we had been in the process of "birthing" Life In The Word Ministries. Now suddenly God was giving us an opportunity to reach more people, which we wanted to do with all of our heart. However, in order to do it, we would need to leave our comfortable position and take on new responsibility.

When the Lord asks His people to do something, there is a temptation to wait for "a convenient season." (Acts 24:25 KJV.) There is always the tendency to hold back until it won't cost anything or be so difficult.

I encourage you to be a person who is not afraid of responsibility. In meeting resistance you will build your strength. If you only do what is easy, you will always remain weak.

God expects you and me to be responsible and to take care of everything He gives us — to do something with it that will produce good fruit. If we do not use the gifts and talents that He has given us, then we are not being responsible over what He has entrusted to us.

BE PREPARED!

Watch therefore [give strict attention and be cautious and active], for you know neither the day nor the hour when the Son of Man will come.

Matthew 25:13

Matthew 25 is a chapter in the Bible that teaches us what we are to be doing while we are waiting for the Master's return.

The first twelve verses show us ten virgins, five who were foolish and five who were wise. The foolish did not want to do anything extra to be sure they were prepared to meet Him when He returned. They did the bare minimum they could get by with; they did not want to go the extra mile so they took only the amount of oil they needed for their lamps. The wise virgins, however, went beyond what they absolutely had to do. They took extra oil to be sure they were prepared for a long wait.

When the bridegroom came, the foolish found their lamps going out and they, of course, wanted the wise virgins to give them some of their oil. This is usually the case. People who are lazy and procrastinating always want those who work hard and take responsibility to do for them what they should have been doing for themselves.

Use What You've Been Given

...You wicked and lazy and idle servant!....

                                                    Matthew 25:26

Matthew 25 then records a parable that Jesus told about three servants who were given talents that belonged to their master. The master then went away into a far country, expecting his servants to take good care of his goods while he was away.

The man given five talents used them. He invested them and gained five more besides. The man given two talents did the same. But the man given one talent buried it in the ground because he was full of fear. He was scared to step out and do anything. He was afraid of responsibility.

When the master returned, he commended the two servants who had taken what he had given them and had done something with it. But to the man who buried his talent and had done nothing with it, he said, "You wicked and lazy and idle servant!" He then ordered that the one talent be taken from him and given to the man with the ten talents and that the lazy, idle servant be severely punished.

I encourage you to respond to the ability that God has placed in you by doing all that you can with it, so that when the Master returns, you can not only give Him what He has given you, but more besides.

The Bible clearly shows us that it is God's will for us to bear good fruit. (John 15:16.)

Casting Care, Not Responsibility

Humble yourselves therefore under the mighty hand of God, that he may exalt you in due time:

Casting all your care upon him; for he careth for you.

                                                    1 Peter 5:6,7 KJV

Don't be afraid of responsibility. Learn to cast your care, but not your responsibility. Some people learn not to worry about anything; becoming experts at "casting their care," they get so comfortable that they also cast their responsibility.

Set your mind to do what is in front of you and not to run from anything just because it looks challenging.

Always remember that if God gives you whatever you ask Him for, there is a responsibility that goes along with the blessing. If you own a home or a car, God expects you to take care of it. Lazy demons may attack your mind and your feelings, but you have the mind of Christ. You certainly can recognize the devil's deception and press past your feelings and do what you know is right. Asking for something is easy...being responsible for it is the part that develops character.

I recall a time when I kept trying to talk my husband into buying a lake house — a place where we could go to rest, pray and study. A place to "get away from it all." I told him how wonderful it would be, how our children and grandchildren could enjoy it and even how we could take our leadership there and have business meetings and glorious times in prayer together.

It all sounded good, and it felt good to my emotions, but Dave kept telling me everything we would have to do to take care of it. He reminded me of how busy we already were and that we did not have time to be responsible for another home. He told me about the lawn care, the upkeep, the payments, etc. He said we would be better off to rent a place when we needed to get away and not take on the responsibility of owning one.

I was looking at the emotional side of the issue, and he was looking at the practical side. Any time we make a decision, we should look at both sides — not just what will be enjoyable, but the responsibility it will require. A lake home is perfectly fine for those who have the time to put into it, but we really didn't. Deep down I knew that, but on and off for a year I tried to talk Dave into buying one.

I'm glad he stayed firm. If he hadn't, I am sure we would have bought the place, kept it for a while and probably ended up selling it because it was too much work. As it turned out, friends of ours bought a lake home and let us use it as our schedule and theirs permit.

If you use wisdom, you will find God meeting your needs. Anyone operating in the mind of Christ will walk in wisdom — not emotions.

Be responsible!

Chapter
18

*"Please make everything easy;
I can't take it if things are too hard!"*

Wilderness Mentality #3

"Please make everything easy;
I can't take it if things are too hard!"

Wilderness Mentality #3

T his wrong mindset is similar to the one we have just discussed, but enough of a problem among God's people that I believe it is worthy of a chapter in this book.

For this commandment which I command you this day is not too difficult for you, nor is it far off.

DEUTERONOMY 30:11

It is one of the most commonly expressed excuses I hear from people in prayer lines. So often, someone will come to me for advice and prayer, and when I tell them what the Word of God says, or what I think the Holy Spirit is saying, their response is, "I know that's right; God has been showing me the same thing. But Joyce, *it's just too hard.*"

God has shown me that the enemy tries to inject this phrase into people's minds to get them to give up. A few years ago when God revealed this truth to me, He instructed me to stop saying how hard everything was, assuring me that if I did, things would get easier.

Even when we are determined to press through and do something, we spend so much time thinking and talking about "how hard it is" that the project ends up being much more difficult than it would have been had we been positive instead of negative.

When I initially began to see from the Word of God how I was supposed to live and behave, and compared it to where I was, I was always saying, "I want to do things Your way, God, but it is so hard." The Lord led me to Deuteronomy 30:11 in which He says that His commandments are not too difficult or too far away.

The reason our Lord's commands are not too difficult for us is because He gives us His Spirit to work in us powerfully and to help us in all He has asked of us.

THE HELPER

And I will ask the Father, and He will give you another Comforter (Counselor, Helper, Intercessor, Advocate, Strengthener, and Standby), that He may remain with you forever....

John 14:16

Things get hard when we are trying to do them independently without leaning on and relying on God's grace. If everything in life were easy, we would not even need the power of the Holy Spirit to help us. The Bible refers to Him as "the Helper." He is in us and with us all the time to *help* us, to enable us to do what we cannot do — and, I might add, to do with ease what would be hard without Him.

THE EASY WAY AND THE HARD WAY

When Pharaoh let the people go, God led them not by way of the land of the Philistines, although that was nearer; for God said, Lest the people change their purpose when they see war and return to Egypt.

Exodus 13:17

You can be sure that anywhere God leads you, He is able to keep you. He never allows more to come on us than we can bear. (1 Corinthians 10:13.) Whatever He orders, He pays for. We do not have to live in a constant struggle if we learn to lean on Him continually for the strength we need.

If you know God has asked you to do something, don't back down just because it gets hard. When things get hard, spend more time with Him, lean more on Him and receive more grace from Him. (Hebrews 4:16.)

Grace is the power of God coming to you at no cost to you, to do through you what you cannot do by yourself. Beware of thoughts that say, "I can't do this; it's just too hard."

Sometimes God leads us the hard way instead of the easy way, because He is doing a work in us. How will we ever learn to lean on Him, if everything in our lives is so easy that we can handle it by ourselves?

God led the Children of Israel the long, hard way because they were still cowards, and He had to do a work in them to prepare them for the battles they would face in the Promised Land.

Most people think that entering the Promised Land means no more battles, but that is incorrect. If you read the accounts of what took place after the Israelites crossed the Jordan River and went in to possess the land of promise, you will see that they fought one battle after another. But they won all those battles fought in God's strength and under His direction.

God led them the longer, harder route even though there was a shorter, easier one because He knew they were not ready for the battles they would face in possessing the land. He was concerned that when they saw the enemy, they might run back to Egypt, so He took them the harder way to teach them Who He was and that they could not depend on themselves.

When a person is going through a hard time, his mind wants to give up. Satan knows that if he can defeat us in our mind, he can defeat us in our experience. That's why it is so important that we not lose heart, grow weary and faint.

HANG TOUGH!

And let us not lose heart and grow weary and faint in acting nobly and doing right, for in due time and at the appointed season we shall reap, if we do not loosen and relax our courage and faint.
Galatians 6:9

Losing heart and fainting refer to giving up in the mind. The Holy Spirit tells us not to give up in our mind, because if we hold on, we will eventually reap.

Think about Jesus. Immediately after being baptized and filled with the Holy Ghost, He was led by the Spirit into the wilderness to be tested and tried by the devil. He did not complain and become discouraged and depressed. He did not think or speak

211

negatively. He did not become confused trying to figure out why this had to happen! He went through each test victoriously.

In the midst of His trial and temptation, our Lord did not wander around the wilderness forty days and nights talking about how hard it was. He drew strength from His heavenly Father and came out in victory. (Luke 4:1-13.)

Can you imagine Jesus traveling around the country with His disciples talking about how hard everything was? Can you picture Him discussing how difficult going to the cross was going to be...or how He dreaded the things ahead...or how frustrating it was to live under the conditions of their daily lives: roaming the countryside with no place to call home, no roof over their head, no bed to sleep in at night.

In my own situation as I travel from place to place all over the land preaching the Gospel, I have had to learn not to talk about the hardships involved in my kind of ministry. I have had to learn not to complain about how hard it is to stay in a strange hotel each time, eat out constantly, sleep in a different bed every weekend, be away from home, meet new people and grow comfortable with them just in time to move on.

You and I have the mind of Christ, and we can handle things the way He did: by being mentally prepared through "victory thinking" — not "give up thinking."

SUCCESS FOLLOWS SUFFERING

So, since Christ suffered in the flesh for us, for you, arm yourselves with the same thought and purpose [patiently to suffer rather than fail to please God]. For whoever has suffered in the flesh [having the mind of Christ] is done with [intentional] sin [has stopped pleasing himself and the world, and pleases God],

So that he can no longer spend the rest of his natural life living by [his] human appetites and desires, but [he lives] for what God wills.

1 Peter 4:1,2

This passage teaches us a secret concerning how to make it through difficult things and times. Here is my rendition of these two Scriptures:

"Think about everything Jesus went through and how He endured suffering in His flesh, and it will help you make it through your difficulties. Arm yourselves for battle; prepare yourselves to win by thinking as Jesus did...'I will patiently suffer rather than fail to please God...' For if I suffer, having the mind of Christ toward it, I will no longer be living just to please myself, doing whatever is easy and running from all that is hard. But I will be able to live for what God wills and not by my feelings and carnal thoughts."

There is a suffering "in the flesh" that we will have to endure in order to do God's will.

My flesh is not always comfortable with the traveling ministry lifestyle, but I know it is the will of God for me to follow it. Therefore, I have to arm myself with right thinking about it; otherwise, I am defeated before I ever really get started.

There may be an individual in your life who is very difficult to be around, and yet you know that God wants you to stick with the relationship and not run away from it. Your flesh suffers, in that it is not easy to be around that person, but you can prepare yourself by thinking properly about the situation.

SELF-SUFFICIENT IN CHRIST'S SUFFICIENCY

I know how to be abased and live humbly in straitened circumstances, and I know also how to enjoy plenty and live in abundance. I have learned in any and all circumstances the secret of facing every situation, whether well-fed or going hungry, having a sufficiency and enough to spare or going without and being in want.

I have strength for all things in Christ Who empowers me [I am ready for anything and equal to anything through Him Who infuses inner strength into me; I am self-sufficient in Christ's sufficiency].

Philippians 4:12,13

Right thinking "arms" us for battle. Going into battle with wrong thinking is like going to the front lines in a war without a weapon. If we do that, we won't last long.

The Israelites were "whiners," which was one reason why they wandered around forty years, making an eleven-day trip. They whined about every difficulty and complained about each new challenge — always talking about how hard everything was. Their mentality was, "Please make everything easy; I can't take it if things are too hard!"

I realized recently that many believers are Sunday warriors and Monday whiners. They talk a good talk on Sunday — in church with all their friends — but on Monday, when it's time to "walk the talk" and there is nobody around to impress, they faint at the slightest test.

If you are a whiner and a complainer, get a new mindset that says, **I can do all things through Christ who strengthens me** (Philippians 4:13 NKJV).

"I can't help it; I'm just addicted to grumbling, faultfinding and complaining."

Wilderness Mentality #4

"I can't help it; I'm just addicted to grumbling, faultfinding and complaining."

Wilderness Mentality #4

Until we learn to glorify God by our attitude during hard times, we won't get delivered. It is not suffering that glorifies God, but a godly attitude in suffering that pleases Him and brings glory to Him.

If you and I are going to receive from these verses what God wants us to have, we will have to read them slowly and digest each phrase and sentence thoroughly. I will admit that I studied them for years trying to understand why it pleased God so much to see me suffer when the Bible plainly states that Jesus bore my suffering and pains of punishment. (Isaiah 53:3-6.)

For one is regarded favorably (is approved, acceptable, and thankworthy) if, as in the sight of God, he endures the pain of unjust suffering.

[After all] what kind of glory [is there in it] if, when you do wrong and are punished for it, you take it patiently? But if you bear patiently with suffering [which results] when you do right and that is undeserved, it is acceptable and pleasing to God.

1 PETER 2:19,20

It was many years before I realized that the focal point of these verses in 1 Peter is not the suffering but the attitude one should have in suffering.

Notice the word "patiently" being used in this passage, which says that if someone treats us wrong and we handle it patiently, it is pleasing to God. The thing that pleases Him is our patient attitude — not our suffering. To encourage us in our suffering, we are exhorted to look at how Jesus handled the unjust attacks made on Him.

JESUS AS OUR EXAMPLE

For even to this were you called [it is inseparable from your vocation]. For Christ also suffered for you, leaving you [His personal] example, so that you should follow in His footsteps.

He was guilty of no sin, neither was deceit (guile) ever found on His lips.

When He was reviled and insulted, He did not revile or offer insult in return; [when] He was abused and suffered, He made no threats [of vengeance]; but He trusted [Himself and everything] to Him Who judges fairly.

1 Peter 2:21-23

Jesus suffered gloriously! Silently, without complaint, trusting God no matter how things looked, He remained the same in every situation. He did not respond patiently when things were easy and impatiently when they were hard or unjust.

The above Scriptures let us know that Jesus is our example and that He came to show us how to live. How we handle ourselves in front of other people shows them how they should live. We teach our children more by example than by words. We are to be living epistles read of all men (2 Corinthians 3:2,3 KJV) — lights shining out brightly in a dark world. (Philippians 2:15.)

CALLED TO HUMILITY, MEEKNESS AND PATIENCE

I therefore, the prisoner for the Lord, appeal to and beg you to walk (lead a life) worthy of the [divine] calling to which you have been called [with behavior that is a credit to the summons to God's service,

Living as becomes you] with complete lowliness of mind (humility) and meekness (unselfishness, gentleness, mildness), with patience, bearing with one another and making allowances because you love one another.

Ephesians 4:1,2

Some time ago in our family life there was a situation that serves as an excellent example of my point about suffering humbly, meekly and patiently.

Our son, Daniel, had just returned from a missions trip to the Dominican Republic. He came back with a severe rash on his arms and several open sores. He had been told that it was the Dominican Republic version of poison ivy. It looked so bad we felt we needed to confirm what it was. Our family doctor was off that day so we made an appointment with the doctor taking his calls.

Our daughter, Sandra, called and made the appointment, told them how old Daniel was, and that she was his sister and would be bringing him in. We were all very busy that day, including Sandra. After a forty-five-minute drive, she arrived at the doctor's office only to be told, "Oh, I'm sorry, but it is our policy not to treat minors unaccompanied by a parent."

Sandra explained that when she called, she had specifically said she would be bringing her brother in — that she frequently took him to the doctor for us because of our travels. The nurse stood firm that he had to have a parent with him.

Sandra had an opportunity to get upset. She had pushed herself to add this errand to her already overloaded schedule only to learn that her planning and efforts were all in vain. She had another forty-five-minute drive home facing her, and the whole thing seemed like such a waste of time.

God helped her remain calm and loving. She called her dad, who was visiting his mother, and he said he would come and take care of the situation. Dave had felt led that morning to go by our offices and pick up some of my books and tapes, not even really knowing what he was going to do with them. He just felt he was to go get them.

When he got to the doctor's building, the woman registering patients and helping with paperwork asked Dave if he was a minister and if he was married to Joyce Meyer. He told her he was, and she said that she had been seeing me on television and had heard enough of our family names to wonder if it might be the same person. Dave talked with her a while and gave her one of my books on emotional healing.

My point in telling you this story is this: What if Sandra had lost her temper and been impatient? Her witness would have been damaged, if not ruined. Actually, it could have done spiritual harm to the woman who sees me on television, and then observes my family behaving badly.

Many people in the world are trying to find God, and what we show them is much more important than what we tell them. It is, of course, important that we verbally share the Gospel, but to do so and negate what we have said with our own behavior is worse than to say nothing.

Sandra bore her suffering patiently in this situation, and the Word of God states that we are called to this kind of behavior and attitude.

THE PATIENT SUFFERING OF JOSEPH

He sent a man before them, even Joseph, who was sold as a servant.

His feet they hurt with fetters; he was laid in chains of iron and his soul entered into the iron,

Until his word [to his cruel brothers] came true, until the word of the Lord tried and tested him.

Psalm 105:17-19

As an Old Testament example, think about Joseph who was unjustly mistreated by his brothers. They sold him into slavery and told his father that he had been killed by a wild animal. Meanwhile, he was purchased by a wealthy man named Potiphar, who took him into his home as a slave. God gave Joseph favor everywhere he went, and soon he had favor with his new master.

Joseph kept getting promoted, but another unjust thing happened to him. Potiphar's wife tried to entice him into having an affair, but because he was a man of integrity he would have nothing to do with her. Lying to her husband, she said that Joseph had attacked her, which caused him to be imprisoned for something he hadn't done!

Joseph tried to help others the entire time he was in prison. He never complained, and because he had a proper attitude in suffering, God eventually delivered and promoted him. He ultimately had so much authority in Egypt that no one else in the entire land was above him except Pharaoh himself.

God also vindicated Joseph concerning the situation with his brothers, in that they had to come to Joseph for food when the whole land was in a state of famine. Once again, Joseph displayed a godly attitude by not mistreating them even though they deserved it. He told them what they had meant for his harm, God had worked out for his good — that they were in God's hands, not his, and that he had no right to do anything but bless them. (See Genesis, Chapters 39-50.)

THE DANGERS OF COMPLAINING

We should not tempt the Lord [try His patience, become a trial to Him, critically appraise Him, and exploit His goodness] as some of them did — and were killed by poisonous serpents;

Nor discontentedly complain as some of them did — and were put out of the way entirely by the destroyer (death).

Now these things befell them by way of a figure [as an example and warning to us]; they were written to admonish and fit us for right action by good instruction, we in whose days the ages have reached their climax (their consummation and concluding period).

1 Corinthians 10:9-11

From these passages, we can quickly see the difference between Joseph and the Israelites. He did not complain at all, and all they did was complain about every little thing that did not go their way. The Bible is very specific about the dangers of grumbling, faultfinding and complaining.

The message is quite plain. The complaining of the Israelites opened a door for the enemy who came in and destroyed them. They should have appreciated God's goodness — but they didn't — so they paid the price.

We are told that the entire account of their suffering and death was written down to show us what will happen if we behave the way they did.

You and I do not complain with our mouth unless we have first complained in our thoughts. Complaining is definitely a wilderness mentality that will prevent us from crossing over into the Promised Land.

Jesus is our example, and we should do what He did.

The Israelites *complained and remained* in the wilderness.

Jesus *praised and was raised* from the dead.

In this contrast, we can see the power of praise and thanksgiving and also the power of complaining. Yes, complaining, grumbling, murmuring and faultfinding have power — but it is negative power. Each time we give our minds and mouths over to any of it, we are giving Satan a power over us that God has not authorized him to have.

DON'T GRUMBLE, FIND FAULT OR COMPLAIN

Do all things without grumbling and faultfinding and complaining [against God] and questioning and doubting [among yourselves],

That you may show yourselves to be blameless and guileless, innocent and uncontaminated, children of God without blemish (faultless, unrebukable) in the midst of a crooked and wicked generation [spiritually perverted and perverse], among whom you are seen as bright lights (stars or beacons shining out clearly) in the [dark] world.

Philippians 2:14,15

Sometimes it seems that the whole world is complaining. There is so much grumbling and murmuring and so little gratitude and appreciation. People complain about their job and their boss when they should be thankful to have regular work and appreciate the fact that they are not living in a shelter for the homeless somewhere or standing in a soup line.

Many of those poor people would be thrilled to have that job, despite its imperfections. They would be more than willing to put up with a not-so-perfect boss in order to have a regular income, live in their own home and cook their own food.

Maybe you do need a better paying job or perhaps you do have a boss who treats you unfairly. That is unfortunate, but the way out is not through complaining.

Don't Fret or Worry — Pray and Give Thanks!

Do not fret or have any anxiety about anything, but in every circumstance and in everything, by prayer and petition (definite requests), with thanksgiving, continue to make your wants known to God.

Philippians 4:6

In this verse the Apostle Paul teaches us how to solve our problems. He instructs us to pray *with thanksgiving* in *every* circumstance.

The Lord taught the same principle to me this way: "Joyce, why should I give you anything else, if you're not thankful for what you already have? Why should I give you something else to complain about?"

If we cannot offer our current prayer requests from a foundation of a life that is currently filled with thanksgiving, we will not get a favorable response. The Word does not say pray with complaining, it says pray with thanksgiving.

Murmuring, grumbling, faultfinding and complaining usually occur when either something or someone has not gone the way we want it to, or when we are having to wait for something longer than we expected. The Word of God teaches us to be patient during these times.

I have discovered that patience is not the ability to wait, but the ability to keep a good attitude while waiting.

It is very important that this matter of complaining and all related types of negative thinking and conversation be taken very seriously. I sincerely believe that God has given me a revelation on how dangerous it is to give our mind and mouth over to them.

God told the Israelites in Deuteronomy 1:6, ... **You have dwelt long enough on this mountain.** Perhaps you have been around the same mountain many times and are now ready to press on. If so, it will be good for you to remember that you will not go forward in any positive way as long as your thoughts and conversation are filled with complaining.

I did not say it would be easy not to complain, but you do have the mind of Christ. Why not make the most of it?

Chapter
20

"Don't make me wait for anything;
I deserve everything immediately."

Wilderness Mentality #5

"Don't make me wait for anything; I deserve everything immediately."

Wilderness Mentality #5

Impatience is the fruit of pride. A proud person cannot seem to wait for anything with the proper attitude. As we discussed in the previous chapter, patience is not the ability to wait, it is the ability to keep a good attitude while waiting.

So be patient, brethren, [as you wait] till the coming of the Lord. See how the farmer waits expectantly for the precious harvest from the land.[See how] he keeps up his patient [vigil] over it until it receives the early and late rains.

JAMES 5:7

This Scripture does not say "be patient if you wait," it says "be patient *as* you wait." Waiting is part of life. Many people don't "wait well," and yet, we actually spend more time in our lives waiting than we do receiving.

What I mean is this: we ask God for something in prayer, believing, and then we wait and wait for the manifestation. When it arrives, we rejoice because we have finally received what we have been waiting for.

However, because we are goal-oriented people who must always have something to press toward — something to look forward to — we go right back into the process of asking and believing God for something else, and waiting and waiting some more until that next breakthrough comes.

Thinking about this situation made me realize that I end up spending much more time in my life waiting than I do receiving. So I decided to learn to enjoy the waiting time, not just the receiving time.

We need to learn to enjoy where we are while we are on our way to where we are going!

Pride Prevents Patient Waiting

For by the grace (unmerited favor of God) given to me I warn everyone among you not to estimate and think of himself more highly than he ought [not to have an exaggerated opinion of his own importance], but to rate his ability with sober judgment, each according to the degree of faith apportioned by God to him.

Romans 12:3

It is impossible to enjoy waiting if you don't know how to wait patiently. Pride prevents patient waiting because the proud person thinks so highly of himself that he believes he should never be inconvenienced in any way.

Although we are not to think badly of ourselves, we are also not to think too highly of ourselves. It is dangerous to lift ourselves up to such an elevated place that it causes us to look down on others. If they are not doing things the way we want, or as quickly as we think they should be done, we behave impatiently.

A humble person will not display an impatient attitude.

Be Realistic!

...In the world you have tribulation and trials and distress and frustration; but be of good cheer [take courage; be confident, certain, undaunted]! For I have overcome the world. [I have deprived it of power to harm you and have conquered it for you.]

John 16:33

Another way that Satan uses our mind to lead us into impatient behavior is through thinking that is idealistic rather than realistic.

If we get the idea in our heads that everything concerning us and our circumstances and relationships should always be perfect — no inconveniences, no hindrances, no unlovely people to deal with — then we are setting ourselves up for a fall. Or, actually, I should say that Satan is setting us up for a fall through wrong thinking.

I am not suggesting that we be negative; I am a firm believer in positive attitudes and thoughts. But I am suggesting that we be realistic enough to realize ahead of time that very few things in real life are ever perfect.

My husband and I travel almost every weekend to a different city to hold seminars. Many times we rent hotel ballrooms and civic or convention centers. In the beginning, I would get impatient and frustrated every time something went wrong in one of these places — things like the air-conditioning not working right (or perhaps not working at all), insufficient lighting in the conference room, chairs that were stained and ripped with the stuffing hanging out, or remains of the cake from the previous night's wedding reception still on the floor.

I felt that we had paid good money for the use of these rooms and that we had rented them in good faith expecting them to be in proper order, so I was irritated when that was not the case. We did everything we could to try to ensure that the places we rented were clean and comfortable, and yet, in about 75 percent of them something did not live up to our expectations.

There were times when we had been promised early check-in for our travel team; yet we would arrive and be told there would be no rooms available for several hours. Hotel employees often gave out wrong information concerning the times of our meetings, even though we had told them repeatedly, and had even sent printed material to them, showing the exact dates and times. Frequently, hotel and banquet employees were rude and lazy. Many times the food we had ordered for seminar luncheons was not what it was supposed to be.

I remember one time in particular when the dessert served to our Christian women (approximately eight hundred of them) was laced with rum. The kitchen got the dishes mixed up with what was being served at a wedding reception. Needless to say, we were a little embarrassed when the women started telling us the dessert tasted like it had liquor in it.

I could go on and on, but the point is simply this: occasionally, but very rarely, we ended up with a perfect place, perfect people and a perfect seminar.

I finally realized that one of the reasons these situations left me impatient and behaving badly was because I was being idealistic and not realistic.

I don't plan for failure, but I do remember that Jesus said that in this world we will have to deal with tribulation and trials and distress and frustration. These things are part of life on this earth — for the believer as well as the unbeliever. But all the mishaps in the world cannot harm us if we will remain in the love of God, displaying the fruit of the Spirit.

PATIENCE: POWER TO ENDURE

Clothe yourselves therefore, as God's own chosen ones (His own picked representatives), [who are] purified and holy and well-beloved [by God Himself, by putting on behavior marked by] tenderhearted pity and mercy, kind feeling, a lowly opinion of yourselves, gentle ways, [and] patience [which is tireless and long-suffering, and has the power to endure whatever comes, with good temper].

Colossians 3:12

I turn to this Scripture often to remind me of what kind of behavior I should be displaying in all situations. I remind myself that patience is not my ability to wait, but my ability to keep a good attitude while I wait.

PATIENCE IS BROUGHT OUT BY TRIALS

Consider it wholly joyful, my brethren, whenever you are enveloped in or encounter trials of any sort or fall into various temptations.

Be assured and understand that the trial and proving of your faith bring out endurance and steadfastness and patience.

But let endurance and steadfastness and patience have full play and do a thorough work, so that you may be [people] perfectly and fully developed [with no defects], lacking in nothing.

James 1:2-4

Patience is a fruit of the Spirit (Galatians 5:22) and is deposited in the spirit of every born-again person. The display or manifestation of patience by His people is very important to the Lord. He wants other people to see His character through His children.

Chapter 1 in the book of James teaches us that when we have become perfect, we will be lacking in nothing. The devil cannot control a patient man.

James 1 also teaches us that we should rejoice when we find ourselves involved in difficult situations, knowing that the method God uses to bring out patience in us is by what the *New King James Version* calls "various trials."

I have found in my own life that "various trials" did eventually bring out patience in me, but first they brought out a lot of other things that were not godly traits: things like pride, anger, rebellion, self-pity, complaining and many others. It seems that these other things must be faced and dealt with before patience can come forth.

Trial or Inconvenience?

And they journeyed from Mount Hor by the way to the Red Sea, to go around the land of Edom, and the people became impatient (depressed, much discouraged), because [of the trials] of the way.

Numbers 21:4

If you remember, an impatient attitude was one of the wilderness mentalities that kept the Israelites wandering in the wilderness for forty years.

How could these people possibly be ready to go into the Promised Land and drive off the current occupants so they could possess the land if they could not even remain patient and steadfast during a little inconvenience?

I really encourage you to work with the Holy Spirit as He develops the fruit of patience in you. The more you resist Him, the longer the process will take. Learn to respond patiently in all kinds of trials, and you will find yourself living a quality of life that is not just endured but enjoyed to the full.

THE IMPORTANCE OF PATIENCE AND ENDURANCE

For you have need of steadfast patience and endurance, so that you may perform and fully accomplish the will of God, and thus receive and carry away [and enjoy to the full] what is promised.
Hebrews 10:36

This Scripture tells us that without patience and endurance we will not receive the promises of God. And Hebrews 6:12 (KJV) tells us that it is only through faith and patience that we inherit the promises.

The proud man runs in the strength of his own flesh and tries to make things happen in his own timing. Pride says, "I'm ready now!"

Humility says, "God knows best, and He will not be late!"

A humble man waits patiently; he actually has a "reverential fear" of moving in the strength of his own flesh. But a proud man tries one thing after another, all to no avail.

A STRAIGHT LINE IS NOT ALWAYS

THE SHORTEST DISTANCE TO A GOAL

There is a way that seems right to a man and appears straight before him, but at the end of it is the way of death.
Proverbs 16:25

We must learn that in the spiritual realm sometimes a straight line is not the shortest distance between us and where we want to be. It may just be the shortest distance to destruction!

We must learn to be patient and wait on the Lord, even if it seems that He is taking us in a roundabout way to get to our desired destination.

There are multitudes of unhappy, unfulfilled Christians in the world simply because they are busy trying to make something happen, instead of waiting patiently for God to bring things to pass in His own time and His own way.

When you are trying to wait on God, the devil will pound your mind continuously demanding that you "do something." He wants to move you in fleshly zeal because he knows that the flesh profits nothing. (John 6:63; Romans 13:14).

As we have seen, impatience is a sign of pride, and the only answer to pride is humility.

HUMBLE YOURSELF AND WAIT ON THE LORD

Therefore humble yourselves [demote, lower yourselves in your own estimation] under the mighty hand of God, that in due time He may exalt you.

1 Peter 5:6

This phrase "lower yourself in your own estimation" does not mean to think badly of yourself. It simply means, "Don't think you can solve all your problems on your own."

Instead of pridefully taking matters into our own hands, we must learn to humble ourselves under God's mighty hand. When He knows that the time is right, He will exalt us and lift us up.

As we wait on God and refuse to move in fleshly zeal, there is a "dying to self" that takes place. We begin to die to our own ways and our own timing and to become alive to God's will and way for us.

We should always be promptly obedient to do whatever God tells us to do, but we should also have a godly fear of fleshly pride. Remember: it is pride that is at the root of impatience. The proud man says, "Please don't make me wait for anything; I deserve everything immediately."

When you are tempted to become frustrated and impatient, I recommend that you begin to say, "Lord, I want Your will in Your timing. I do not want to be ahead of You, nor do I want to be behind You. Help me, Father, to wait patiently on You!"

Chapter
21

*"My behavior may be wrong,
but it's not my fault."*

Wilderness Mentality #6

"My behavior may be wrong, but it's not my fault."

Wilderness Mentality #6

An unwillingness to take responsibility for one's own actions, blaming everything that is wrong or goes wrong on someone else, is a major cause for wilderness living.

We see the problem manifesting from the beginning of time. When confronted with their sin in the Garden of Eden, Adam and Eve blamed each other, God and the devil, thus evading personal responsibility for their actions.

And the man said, The woman whom You gave to be with me – she gave me [fruit] from the tree, and I ate.

...And the woman said, The serpent beguiled (cheated, outwitted, and deceived) me, and I ate.

GENESIS 3:12,13

IT'S ALL YOUR FAULT!

Now Sarai, Abram's wife, had borne him no children. And she had an Egyptian maidservant whose name was Hagar.

So Sarai said to Abram, "See now, the Lord has restrained me from bearing children. Please, go in to my maid; perhaps I shall obtain children by her." And Abram heeded the voice of Sarai.

Then Sarai, Abram's wife, took Hagar her maid, the Egyptian, and gave her to her husband Abram to be his wife, after Abram had dwelt ten years in the land of Canaan.

So he went in to Hagar, and she conceived. And when she saw that she had conceived, her mistress became despised in her eyes.

Then Sarai said to Abram, "My wrong be upon you! I gave my maid into your embrace; and when she saw that she had conceived, I became despised in her eyes. The Lord judge between you and me."

So Abram said to Sarai, "Indeed your maid is in your hand; do to her as you please." And when Sarai dealt harshly with her, she fled from her presence.

Genesis 16:1-6 NKJV

The same scenario played out between Adam and Eve is seen here in the dispute between Abram and Sarai. They were tired of waiting on God to fulfill His promise of a child born to them, so they got in the flesh and "did their own thing." When it turned out badly and started causing trouble, they began to blame each other.

In the past, I observed this same kind of scene countless times in my own home between Dave and me. It seemed that we were continually evading the real issues in life, never wanting to face reality.

I vividly remember praying for Dave to change. I had been reading my Bible and was seeing more and more of his flaws, and how much he needed to be different! As I prayed, the Lord spoke to me and said, "Joyce, Dave is not the problem...you are."

I was devastated. I cried and cried. I wept for three days because God was showing me what it was like to live in the same house with me. He showed me how I tried to control everything that went on, how I nagged and complained, how hard it was to please me, how negative I was — and on and on. It was a shocking blow to my pride, but it was also the beginning of my recovery in the Lord.

Like most people, I blamed everything on someone else or some circumstance beyond my control. I thought I was acting badly because I had been abused, but God told me, "Abuse may be the reason you act this way, but don't let it become an excuse to stay this way!"

Satan works hard on our minds — building strongholds that will prevent us from facing truth. The truth will set us free, and he knows it!

I don't think there is anything more emotionally painful than facing the truth about ourselves and our behavior. Because it is painful, most people run from it. It is fairly easy to face truth about someone else — but when it comes to facing ourselves, we find it much harder to handle.

IF...

And the people spoke against God and against Moses, Why have you brought us out of Egypt to die in the wilderness? For there is no bread, neither is there any water, and we loathe this light (contemptible, unsubstantial) manna.

Numbers 21:5

As you recall, the Israelites complained that all their problems were the fault of God and Moses. They successfully evaded any personal responsibility for why they were staying in the wilderness so long. God showed me this was one of the major wilderness mentalities that kept them there forty years.

It was also one of the main reasons I spent so many years going around and around the same mountains in my life. My list of excuses for why I was behaving badly was endless:

"If I hadn't been abused as a child, I wouldn't have a bad temper."

"If my children would help me more, I would act better."

"If Dave didn't play golf on Saturdays, I wouldn't get so upset with him."

"If Dave would talk to me more, I wouldn't be so lonely."

"If Dave would buy me more presents, I wouldn't be so negative."

"If I didn't have to work, I wouldn't be so tired and cranky." (So I quit work, and then it was...)

"If I could just get out of the house more, I wouldn't be so bored!"

"If we only had more money..."

"If we owned our own home..." (So we bought one and then, it was...)

"If we just didn't have so many bills..."

"If we had better neighbors or different friends..."

If! If! If! If! If! If! If! If! If! If!

BUT...

And the Lord said to Moses,

Send men to explore and scout out [for yourselves] the land of Canaan, which I give to the Israelites. From each tribe of their fathers you shall send a man, every one a leader or head among them.

So Moses by the command of the Lord sent scouts from the Wilderness of Paran, all of them men who were heads of the Israelites....

And they returned from scouting out the land after forty days.

They came to Moses and Aaron and to all the Israelite congregation in the Wilderness of Paran at Kadesh, and brought them word, and showed them the land's fruit.

They told Moses, We came to the land to which you sent us; surely it flows with milk and honey. This is its fruit.

But the people who dwell there are strong, and the cities are fortified and very large; moreover, there we saw the sons of Anak [of great stature and courage].

Numbers 13:1-3,25-28

"If" and "but" are two of the most deceptive words that Satan ever plants in our minds. The twelve spies who were sent into the Promised Land as a scouting party came back with one bunch of grapes so large it had to be carried by two people on a pole, but the report they gave to Moses and the people was negative.

It was the "but" that defeated them! They should have kept their eyes on God and not on the potential problem.

One of the reasons our problems defeat us is because we think they are bigger than God. That may also be the reason why we have such a hard time facing the truth. We are not sure God can change us, so we hide from ourselves rather than facing ourselves as we really are.

It is not as difficult now for me to face a truth about myself when God is dealing with me, because I know that He can change me. I have already seen what He can do, and I trust Him. However, in the beginning of my walk with Him it was difficult. I had spent most of my life hiding from one thing or another. I had lived in darkness for such a long time that coming out into the light was not easy.

TRUTH IN THE INNER BEING

Have mercy upon me, O God, according to Your steadfast love; according to the multitude of Your tender mercy and loving-kindness blot out my transgressions.

Wash me thoroughly [and repeatedly] from my iniquity and guilt and cleanse me and make me wholly pure from my sin!

For I am conscious of my transgressions and I acknowledge them; my sin is ever before me.

Against You, You only, have I sinned and done that which is evil in Your sight, so that You are justified in Your sentence and faultless in Your judgment.

Behold, I was brought forth in [a state of] iniquity; my mother was sinful who conceived me [and I too am sinful].

Behold, You desire truth in the inner being; make me therefore to know wisdom in my inmost heart.

Psalm 51:1-6

In Psalm 51, King David was crying out to God for mercy and forgiveness because the Lord had been dealing with him about his sin with Bathsheba and the murder of her husband.

Believe it or not, David's sin had occurred one full year prior to the writing of this psalm, but he had never really faced it and acknowledged it. He was not facing truth, and as long as he refused to face truth, he could not truly repent. And as long as he could not truly repent, God could not forgive him.

Verse 6 of this passage is a powerful Scripture. It says that God desires truth "in the inner being." That means that if we want to receive God's blessings, we must be honest with Him about ourselves and our sins.

CONFESSION PRECEDES FORGIVENESS

If we say we have no sin [refusing to admit that we are sinners], we delude and lead ourselves astray, and the Truth [which the Gospel presents] is not in us [does not dwell in our hearts].

If we [freely] admit that we have sinned and confess our sins, He is faithful and just (true to His own nature and promises) and will forgive our sins [dismiss our lawlessness] and [continuously] cleanse us from all unrighteousness [everything not in conformity to His will in purpose, thought, and action].

If we say (claim) we have not sinned, we contradict His Word and make Him out to be false and a liar, and His Word is not in us [the divine message of the Gospel is not in our hearts].

1 John 1:8-10

God is quick to forgive us if we truly repent, but we cannot truly repent if we will not face and acknowledge the truth about what we have done.

To admit that we have done something wrong, but then make an excuse for it, is still not God's way of facing truth. Naturally we want to justify ourselves and our actions, but the Bible says that our justification is found only in Jesus Christ. (Romans 3:20-24.) You and I are made right with God after sinning only by the blood of Jesus — not by our excuses.

I remember when a neighbor called me one day and asked me to take her to the bank right away, before it closed, because her car would not start. I was busy doing "my thing" and did not want to stop, so I was rude and impatient with her. As soon as I hung up the phone, I knew how terrible I had acted and that I needed to call her, apologize and take her to the bank. My mind was full of all the excuses I would give her for why I had reacted so badly: "I did not feel good...." "I was busy...." "I was having a rough day myself...."

But deep in my spirit, I could sense the Holy Spirit telling me not to make any excuse!

"Just call her and tell her you were wrong, period! Say no more than 'I was wrong, and there is no excuse for the way I behaved. Please forgive me and allow me to take you to the bank.'"

I can tell you it was hard to do. My flesh was having a fit! I could feel this little thing running around in my soul desperately trying to find a place to hide. But there is no hiding from the truth, because truth is light.

TRUTH IS LIGHT

In the beginning [before all time] was the Word (Christ), and the Word was with God, and the Word was God Himself.

He was present originally with God.

All things were made and came into existence through Him; and without Him was not even one thing made that has come into being.

In Him was Life, and the Life was the Light of men.

And the Light shines on in the darkness, for the darkness has never overpowered it [put it out or absorbed it or appropriated it, and is unreceptive to it].

John 1:1-5

Truth is one of the most powerful weapons against the kingdom of darkness. Truth is light, and the Bible says that the darkness has never overpowered the light, and it never will.

Satan wants to keep things hidden in darkness, but the Holy Spirit wants to bring them into the light and deal with them, so you and I can be truly and genuinely free.

Jesus said it was truth that would set us free. (John 8:32.) That truth is revealed by the Spirit of Truth.

THE SPIRIT OF TRUTH

I have still many things to say to you, but you are not able to bear them or to take them upon you or to grasp them now.

But when He, the Spirit of Truth (the Truth-giving Spirit) comes, He will guide you into all the Truth (the whole, full Truth)....

John 16:12,13

Jesus could have showed His disciples all the truth, but He knew they were not ready for it. He told them that they would have to wait until the Holy Spirit came down from heaven to abide with them and to dwell in them.

After Jesus had ascended into heaven, He sent the Holy Spirit to work with us, preparing us continually for God's glory to be manifested through us in varying degrees.

How can we have the Holy Spirit working in our lives if we will not face truth? He is called "The Spirit of Truth." A major facet of His ministry to you and me is to help us face truth — to bring us to a place of truth, because only the truth will set us free.

Something in your past — a person, event or circumstance that hurt you — may be the source of your wrong attitude and behavior, but don't allow it to become an excuse to stay that way.

Many of my behavior problems were definitely caused from being sexually, verbally and emotionally abused for many years — but I was trapped in the wrong behavior patterns as long as I used the abuse as an excuse for them. That is like defending your enemy by saying, "I hate this thing, but this is why I keep it."

You can definitely experience glorious freedom from every bondage. You don't have to spend forty years wandering in the wilderness. Or if you have already spent forty years or more out there because you didn't know that "wilderness mentalities" were keeping you there, today can be your day of decision.

Ask God to start showing you the truth about yourself. When He does, hang on! It won't be easy, but remember, He has promised, "I will never leave you nor forsake you." (Hebrews 13:5.)

You are on your way out of the wilderness; enjoy the Promised Land!

Chapter
22

"My life is so miserable; I feel sorry for myself because my life is so wretched!"

Wilderness Mentality #7

"My life is so miserable; I feel sorry for myself because my life is so wretched!"

Chapter
22

Wilderness Mentality #7

The Israelites felt exceedingly sorry for themselves. Every inconvenience became a new excuse to engage in self-pity.

I remember when the Lord spoke to me during one of my "pity parties." He said, "Joyce, you can be pitiful or powerful, but you cannot be both."

And all the congregation cried out with a loud voice, and [they] wept that night. All the Israelites grumbled and deplored their situation....

NUMBERS 14:1,2

This is a chapter that I don't want to skim over too quickly. It is *vitally* important to understand that *we cannot entertain demons of self-pity and also walk in the power of God!*

ENCOURAGE AND EDIFY ONE ANOTHER

Therefore encourage (admonish, exhort) one another and edify (strengthen and build up) one another, just as you are doing.
1 Thessalonians 5:11

Pity was hard for me to give up; I had used it for years to comfort myself when I was hurting.

The minute someone hurts us, the moment we experience disappointment, the devil assigns a demon to whisper lies to us about how cruelly and unjustly we have been mistreated.

All you need to do is listen to the thoughts rushing into your mind during such times and you will quickly realize how the enemy uses self-pity to keep us in bondage.

The Bible, however, gives us no liberty to feel sorry for ourselves. Instead, we are to encourage and edify one another in the Lord.

There is a true gift of compassion, which is having godly pity toward others who are hurting, and spending our life relieving their suffering. But self-pity is perverted, because it is taking something that God intended to be given to others and turning it in on ourselves.

Love is the same way. Romans 5:5 (KJV) says that the love of God has been shed abroad in our hearts by the Holy Ghost. He has done this so we might know how much God loves us and that we may be able to love others.

When we take the love God meant to be given away and turn it in toward ourselves, it becomes selfishness and self-centeredness, which actually destroys us. Self-pity is idolatry — turning in on ourselves, concentrating on us and our feelings. It makes us only aware of our own selves and our own needs and concerns — and that is certainly a narrow-minded way to live.

THINK OF OTHERS

Let each of you esteem and look upon and be concerned for not [merely] his own interests, but also each for the interests of others.
Philippians 2:4

Recently one of our speaking engagements was unexpectedly canceled. It was one I had been looking forward to, and initially, I was a bit disappointed. There was a time when an incident like that would have thrown me into a fit of self-pity, criticism, judgment of the other party and all kinds of negative thoughts and actions. I have since learned in that kind of situation just to be quiet; it is better to say nothing than to say the wrong thing.

As I sat quietly, God began to show me the situation from the viewpoint of the other people involved. They had been unable to locate a building in which to hold the meeting, and God showed me how disappointing it was to them. They were counting on the meeting, looking forward to it with great expectation, and now they could not have it.

It is amazing how easy it is to stay out of self-pity if we look at the other person's side and not just at our own. Self-pity is supported by thinking only of us and no one else.

We literally exhaust ourselves sometimes trying to gain sympathy. Yes, self-pity is a major trap and one of Satan's favorite tools to keep us in the wilderness. If we are not careful, we can actually become addicted to it.

An addiction is something done as an automatic response to some stimulus — a learned behavior pattern that has become habitual.

How much time do you spend in self-pity? How do you respond to disappointments?

A Christian has a rare privilege when he experiences disappointment — he can be re-appointed. With God there is always a new beginning available. Self-pity however, keeps us trapped in the past.

LET GO AND LET GOD!

Do not [earnestly] remember the former things; neither consider the things of old.

Behold, I am doing a new thing! Now it springs forth; do you not perceive and know it and will you not give heed to it? I will even make a way in the wilderness and rivers in the desert.

Isaiah 43:18,19

I wasted so many years of my life feeling sorry for myself. I was one of those cases of addiction. My automatic response to any kind of disappointment was self-pity. Satan would immediately fill my mind with wrong thoughts, and not knowing how to "think about what I was thinking about," I simply thought on whatever fell into my head. The more I thought, the more pitiful I felt.

I often tell stories about the early years of our marriage. Every Sunday afternoon during football season, Dave wanted to watch the games on television. If it was not football season, it was some other "ball season." Dave enjoyed it all, and I did not enjoy any of it. He liked anything that involved a bouncing ball and could easily get so caught up in some sports event that he didn't even know I existed.

One time I stood right in front of him and said very clearly, "Dave I don't feel well at all; I feel like I'm going to die."

Without raising his eyes from the television screen, he said, "Uh huh, that's nice, dear."

I spent many Sunday afternoons angry and in self-pity. I always cleaned house when I got mad at Dave. I know now that I was trying to make him feel guilty for enjoying himself while I was being so miserable. I would storm around the house for hours, slamming doors and drawers, marching back and forth through the room where he was, vacuum sweeper in hand, making a loud display of how hard I was working.

I was, of course, trying to get his attention, but he hardly noticed me at all. I would give up, go to the back of the house, sit on the bathroom floor and cry. The more I cried, the more pitiful I felt. God gave me a revelation in later years about why a woman goes to the bathroom to cry. He said it is because there is a big mirror in there, and after she has cried a long time, she can then stand up and take a long look at herself and see how truly pitiful she looks.

I looked so bad sometimes that when I saw my reflection in the mirror I'd start crying all over again. Finally, I would make my sorrowful last stroll through the family room where Dave was, walking slowly, and ever so pitifully. He would occasionally look up long enough to ask me to bring him some iced tea if I was going to the kitchen.

The bottom line is, it didn't work! I exhausted myself emotionally — often ending up feeling physically sick due to all the wrong emotions I had experienced all day.

God will not deliver you by your own hand, but by His. Only God can change people! Nobody but the Almighty could have discouraged Dave from wanting to watch as many sports as he did. As I learned to trust the Lord and to stop wallowing in self-pity when I did not get my way, Dave did come into more balance concerning watching every sporting event.

He still enjoys them, and now it really does not bother me. I just use the time to do things I enjoy. If I really do want or need to do something else, I ask Dave sweetly (not angrily) and most of the time he is willing to alter his plans. There are those times though — and there always will be — when I don't get my way. As soon as I feel my emotions starting to rise, I pray, "Oh God, help me pass this test. I don't want to go around this mountain even one more time!"

Chapter
23

"I don't deserve God's blessings
because I am not worthy."

Wilderness Mentality #8

"I don't deserve God's blessings because I am not worthy."

Chapter

23

Wilderness Mentality #8

After Joshua had led the Israelites across the Jordan River into the Promised Land, there was something God needed to do before they would be ready to conquer and occupy their first town, which was to be Jericho.

> *And the Lord said to Joshua, This day have I rolled away the reproach of Egypt from you. So the name of the place is called Gilgal [rolling] to this day.*
>
> JOSHUA 5:9

The Lord ordered that all the Israelite males be circumcised, since this had not been done during the entire forty years they had wandered in the Wilderness. After this was done, the Lord told Joshua that He had "rolled away" the reproach of Egypt from His people.

A few verses later in Chapter 6, the account begins of how God led the Children of Israel to overcome and capture Jericho. Why did the reproach have to be lifted off of them first? What is a reproach?

REPROACH DEFINED

The word *reproach* means "blame...disgrace: shame."[1] When God said that He would "roll away" the reproach of Egypt from the Israelites, He was making a point. Egypt represents the world. After a few years of being in the world and becoming worldly, we all need the reproach of it rolled away.

Because of the things I had done and what had been done to me, I had a shame-based nature. I blamed myself for what had happened to me (even though much of it had taken place in my childhood, and there was nothing I could have done to stop it).

We have said that grace is the power of God coming to us, as a free gift from Him, to help us do with ease what we cannot do ourselves. God wants to give us grace, and Satan wants to give us disgrace, which is another word for reproach.

Disgrace told me that I was no good — not worthy of God's love or help. Shame had poisoned my inner man. I was not only ashamed of what had been done to me, but I was ashamed of myself. Deep down inside, I did not like myself.

God's rolling away the reproach from us means that each of us must receive for ourselves the forgiveness He is offering for all our past sins.

You must realize that you can never deserve God's blessings — you can never be worthy of them. You can only humbly accept and appreciate them, and be in awe of how good He is and how much He loves you.

Self-hatred, self-rejection, refusal to accept God's forgiveness (by forgiving yourself), not understanding righteousness through the blood of Jesus and all related problems will definitely keep you wandering in the wilderness. Your mind must be renewed concerning right standing with God through Jesus — and not through your own works.

I am convinced, after many years in ministry, that about 85 percent of our problems stem from the way we feel about ourselves. Any person you know who is walking in victory is also walking in righteousness.

I know I don't deserve God's blessings, but I receive them anyway because I am a joint-heir with Christ. (Romans 8:17 KJV.) He earned them, and I get them by placing my faith in Him.

HEIR OR LABORER?

Therefore, you are no longer a slave (bond servant) but a son; and if a son, then [it follows that you are] an heir by the aid of God, through Christ.

Galatians 4:7

Are you a son or a slave — an heir or a bond servant? An heir is one who receives something other than by merit, as when property is passed down from one person to another through a will. A bond servant or laborer, in the biblical sense, is one who is weary from trying to follow the Law. The term denotes burdensome toil and trouble.

I wandered around in the wilderness for years as a laborer, trying to be good enough to deserve what God wanted to give me freely by His grace. I had a wrong mindset.

First, I thought that everything must be earned and deserved: "Nobody does anything for you for nothing." I had been taught that principle for years. Over and over I had heard that statement while growing up. I was told that anyone who acted like he wanted to do something for me was lying and would take advantage of me in the end.

Experience with the world teaches us that we must deserve everything we get. If we want friends, we are told, we must keep them happy all the time or they will reject us. If we want a promotion on our job, everyone says, we must know the right people, treat them a certain way and maybe one day we will get a chance to go forward. By the time we are finished with the world, the reproach of it lies heavy upon us and definitely needs to be rolled away.

How Do You See Yourself?

There we saw the Nephilim [or giants], the sons of Anak, who come from the giants; and we were in our own sight as grasshoppers, and so we were in their sight.

Numbers 13:33

The Israelites had that reproach on them. The fact that they had a negative opinion of themselves is seen in this verse. Ten of the twelve spies who were sent in to scout out the Promised Land before the entire nation crossed over the Jordan came back saying that the land was inhabited by giants who saw them as grasshoppers — and so they were in their own eyes.

This plainly lets us know what these people thought of themselves.

Please be aware that Satan will fill your mind (if he is allowed to) with all types of negative thinking about yourself. He began early building strongholds in your mind, many of them negative things about you and about how other people feel about you. He always arranges for a few situations in which you experience rejection, so he can bring the pain of it back to your remembrance during a time when you are trying to make some progress.

Fear of failure and rejection keep many people in the wilderness. Being slaves in Egypt for so many years and living under severe mistreatment had left a reproach on the Israelites. It is interesting to note that almost none of the generation that originally came out with Moses entered the Promised Land. It was their children who went in. Yet God told them He had to roll away the reproach from them.

Most of them had been born in the wilderness after their parents had left Egypt. How could they have the reproach of Egypt upon them when they did not even live there?

Things that were on your parents can be passed on to you. Attitudes, thoughts and behavior patterns can be inherited. A wrong mindset that your parents had can become your mindset. The way you think about a certain subject can be passed down to you, and you won't even know why you think that way.

A parent who has a poor self-image, an attitude of unworthiness and an "I-don't-deserve-God's-blessings" mindset can definitely pass that mindset on to his children.

Even though I talked about this earlier in the book, because it is such an important area let me mention again that you need to be aware of what goes on in your mind in regard to yourself. God is willing to give you mercy for your failures if you are willing to receive it. He does not reward the perfect who have no flaws and never make mistakes, but those who put their faith and trust in Him.

YOUR FAITH IN GOD PLEASES HIM

But without faith it is impossible to please and be satisfactory to Him. For whoever would come near to God must [necessarily] believe that God exists and that He is the rewarder of those who earnestly and diligently seek Him [out].

Hebrews 11:6

Please notice that without faith you cannot please God; therefore, no matter how many "good works" you offer, it will not please Him if they were done to "earn" His favor.

Whatever we do for God should be because we love Him, not because we are trying to get something from Him.

This powerful Scripture says that God is a rewarder of those who diligently seek Him. I rejoiced when I finally saw this! I know I have made many mistakes in the past, but I also know that I have diligently sought the Lord with all my heart. That means that I qualify for rewards. I decided a long time ago that I would receive any blessing that God wanted to give me.

The Lord wanted to take the Israelites into the Promised Land and bless them beyond their wildest imaginations, but first He had to roll the reproach off of them. They could not have received from Him properly as long as they were burdened down with shame, blame and disgrace.

ABOVE REPROACH

Even as [in His love] He chose us [actually picked us out for Himself as His own] in Christ before the foundation of the world, that we should be holy (consecrated and set apart for Him) and blameless in His sight, even above reproach, before Him in love.

Ephesians 1:4

This is a wonderful Scripture! In it the Lord tells us that we are His and sets forth what He wants for us — that we should know that we are loved, special, valuable and that we should be holy, blameless and above reproach.

Naturally, we should do what we can to live holy lives. But thank God, when we do make mistakes, we can be forgiven and restored to holiness, made once again blameless and above reproach — all "in Him."

WITHOUT REPROACHING OR FAULTFINDING

If any of you is deficient in wisdom, let him ask of the giving God [Who gives] to everyone liberally and ungrudgingly, without reproaching or faultfinding, and it will be given him.

James 1:5

This is another great Scripture that teaches us to receive from God without reproach.

James had been previously speaking to people who were having trials, and now he is telling them that if they need wisdom in their situation, they should ask God. He assures them that He won't reproach or find fault with them — He will just help them.

You will never make it through the wilderness without a great deal of help from God. But, if you have a negative attitude about yourself, even when He does try to help you, you won't receive it.

If you desire to have a victorious, powerful, positive life, you cannot be negative about yourself. Don't look only at how far you have to go, but at how far you have come. Consider your progress and remember Philippians 1:6, ...I am convinced and sure of this very thing, that He Who began a good work in you will continue until the day of Jesus Christ [right up to the time of His return], developing [that good work] and perfecting and bringing it to full completion in you.

Think and speak positively about yourself!

Chapter

24

*"Why shouldn't I be jealous and envious
when everybody else is better off than I am?"*

Wilderness Mentality #9

"Why shouldn't I be jealous and envious when everybody else is better off than I am?"

Wilderness Mentality #9

In John 21 Jesus was conversing with Peter regarding the hardships that he would have to endure in order to serve and glorify Him. As soon as Jesus had said these things to him, Peter turned, saw John and immediately asked Jesus what His will was for him. Peter wanted to make sure that if he were going to have to go through rough times ahead, so would John.

> When Peter saw him (John), he said to Jesus, Lord, what about this man?
>
> Jesus said to him, If I want him to stay (survive, live) till I come, what is that to you? [What concern is it of yours?] You follow Me!
>
> JOHN 21:21,22

In answer, Jesus politely told Peter to mind his own business.

Minding (having our mind set on) other people's business, will keep us in the wilderness. Jealousy, envy and mentally comparing ourselves and our circumstances with others is a wilderness mentality.

BEWARE OF JEALOUSY AND ENVY

A calm and undisturbed mind and heart are the life and health of the body, but envy, jealousy, and wrath are like rottenness of the bones.
Proverbs 14:30

Envy will cause a person to behave in a way that is callous and crude — even animalistic at times. Envy caused Joseph's brothers to sell him into slavery. They hated him because their father loved him so much.

If there is someone in your family who seems to have more favor than you, don't hate that individual. Trust God! Do what He asks you to do — believe Him for favor — and you will end up like Joseph — extremely blessed.

Vine's *An Expository Dictionary of New Testament Words* defines the Greek word translated *envy* as "the feeling of displeasure produced by witnessing or hearing of the advantage or prosperity of others."[1] *Jealousy* is defined by Webster as "feelings of envy, apprehension, or bitterness."[2] I interpret this definition as being fearful of losing what you have to another; resentment of another's success, arising from feelings of envy.

DON'T COMPARE AND COMPETE

Now an eager contention arose among them [as to] which of them was considered and reputed to be the greatest.

But Jesus said to them, The kings of the Gentiles are deified by them and exercise lordship [ruling as emperor-gods] over them; and those in authority over them are called benefactors and well-doers.

But this is not to be so with you; on the contrary, let him who is greatest among you become like the youngest, and him who is the chief and leader like one who serves.

Luke 22:24-26

In my early life, I had an abundance of struggles with jealousy, envy and comparison. This is a common trait of the insecure. If we are not secure concerning our own worth and value as a unique individual, we will naturally find ourselves competing with anyone who appears to be successful and doing well.

Learning that I was an individual (that God has a unique, personal plan for my life) has indeed been one of the most valuable and precious freedoms the Lord has granted me. I am assured that I need not compare myself (or my ministry) with anyone.

I am always encouraged that there is hope for me when I look at Jesus' disciples and realize that they struggled with many of the same things I do. In Luke 22 we find the disciples arguing over which of them was the greatest. Jesus responded to them by saying that the greatest was actually the one who was willing to be considered the least or the one who was willing to be a servant. Our Lord spent a great deal of His time trying to teach His disciples that life in the Kingdom of God is usually the direct opposite of the way of the world or the flesh.

Jesus taught them things like, "Many who are first will be last, and the last will be first," (Mark 10:31), "Rejoice with those who are blessed," (Luke 15:6,9 KJV), "Pray for your enemies, and bless those who mistreat you." (Matthew 5:44.) The world would say that this is foolishness — but Jesus says it is true power.

AVOID WORLDLY COMPETITION

Let us not become vainglorious and self-conceited, competitive and challenging and provoking and irritating to one another, envying and being jealous of one another.

Galatians 5:26

According to the world's system, the best place to be is ahead of everyone else. Popular thinking would say that we should try to get to the top no matter who we have to hurt on the way up. But the Bible teaches us that there is no such thing as real peace until we are delivered from the need to compete with others.

Even in what is supposed to be considered "fun games," we often see competition get so out of balance that people end up arguing and hating one another, rather than simply relaxing and having a good time together. Naturally, human beings don't play games to lose; everyone is going to do his best. But when a person cannot enjoy a game unless he is winning, he definitely has a problem — possibly a deep-rooted one that is causing other problems in many areas of his life.

We should definitely do our best on the job; there is nothing wrong with wanting to do well and advance in our chosen profession. But I encourage you to remember that promotion for the believer comes from God and not from man. You and I don't need to play worldly games to get ahead. God will give us favor with Him and with others if we will do things His way. (Proverbs 3:3,4 KJV.)

Jealousy and envy are torments from hell. I spent many years being jealous and envious of anyone who looked better than I did or had talents I didn't have. I secretly lived in competition with others in ministry. It was very important to me that "my" ministry be bigger in size, better attended, more prosperous, etc. than anyone else's. If another person's ministry surpassed mine in any way, I wanted to be happy for that individual because I knew it was God's will and way, but something in my soul just would not allow it.

I found as I grew in the knowledge of who I was in Christ, and not in my works, that I gained freedom in not having to compare myself or anything I did with anyone else. The more I learned to trust God, the more freedom I enjoyed in these areas. I learned that my heavenly Father loves me and will do for me whatever is best — for *me*.

What God does for you or for me may not be what He does for someone else, but we must remember what Jesus said to Peter, "Don't be concerned about what I choose to do with someone else — you follow Me!"

A friend of mine was once given something as a gift from the Lord that I was believing for and had wanted a long time. Now, I did not consider this friend to be nearly as "spiritual" as I, and so I became very jealous and envious when she excitedly came to my front door sharing with me what God had done for her. Of course, in her presence, I pretended to be happy for her, but in my heart I wasn't.

When she left, attitudes rolled out of me that I never would have thought were in me! I actually resented God's blessing her because I did not think she deserved it. After all, I stayed home, fasted and prayed while she ran around with her friends and had a good time. You see, I was a "Pharisee," a religious snob, and did not even know it.

God arranges events quite often in a way that we would not choose because He knows what we really need. I needed to get rid of my bad attitudes much more than I needed whatever it was that I was believing for. It is important for God to arrange our circumstances in such a way that we have to eventually face ourselves. Otherwise, we never experience freedom.

As long as the enemy can hide in our soul, he will always have a certain amount of control over us. But when God exposes him, we are on our way to freedom, *if* we will put ourselves in God's hands and permit Him to do quickly what He desires to do.

God had, in fact, already purposed for my life that the ministry He would make me steward over was to be quite large and reach millions of people by radio and television, seminars, books and tapes. But He would not bring me into the fullness of it, except to the degree that I "grew up" in Him.

GET A NEW MINDSET!

Beloved, I wish above all things that thou mayest prosper and be in health, even as thy soul prospereth.

                                                3 John 2 KJV

Consider this Scripture carefully. God *desires to bless us even more than we desire to be blessed.* But He also loves us enough not to bless us beyond our capacity to handle the blessings properly and to continue giving Him glory.

Jealousy, envy and comparing oneself with others is childish. It belongs entirely to the flesh and has nothing to do with spiritual things. But it is one of the major causes for wilderness living.

Take account of your thoughts in this area. When you recognize wrong thought patterns beginning to flow into your mind, talk to yourself a little. Say to yourself, "What good will it do me to be jealous of others? It won't get me blessed. God has an individual plan for each of us, and I am going to trust Him to do the best thing for me. It isn't any of my business what He chooses to do for other people." Then deliberately and purposely pray for them to be blessed more.

Don't be afraid to be honest with God about your feelings. He knows how you feel anyway, so you may as well talk to Him about it.

I have said things to the Lord like this: "God, I pray for _____ to be blessed even more. Cause her to prosper; bless her in every way. Lord, I am praying this by faith. In my spirit, I feel jealous of her and inferior to her, but I *choose* to do this Your way whether I feel like it or not."

Recently I heard someone say that no matter how well we can do something, there will always arise someone who can do it better. This statement had an impact on me because I know it to be true. And if this is true, then what is the purpose of struggling all our lives to get ahead of everyone else? As soon as we become number one, someone will be competing with us and, sooner or later, that one person will appear who can do whatever we're doing a little better then we can.

Think of sports; it seems that no matter what record some athlete sets, eventually another athlete comes along and breaks it. What about the entertainment field? The current star is only tops for a certain period of time and then someone new comes along to take his place. What a terrible deception it is to think that we must always struggle to get ahead of everyone else — and then fight to stay there.

God told me a long time ago to remember that "shooting stars" rise quickly and get a lot of attention, but usually they are around for only a short period of time. Most of the time they fall as quickly as they arise. He told me that it is much better to be around for the long haul — hanging in there — and doing what He has asked me to do to the best of my ability. He has assured me that He will take care of my reputation. For my part, I have decided that whatever He wants me to do and be is all right with me. Why? Because He knows what I can handle better than I do.

Perhaps you have had a mental stronghold for a long time in this area. Each time you come across someone who appears to be a little ahead of you, you feel jealousy, envy or a desire to enter into competition with that person. If so, I exhort you to get a new mindset.

Set your mind to be happy for others and trust God with yourself. It will take some time and persistence, but when that old mental stronghold has been torn down and replaced by the Word of God, you will be on your way out of the wilderness and into the Promised Land.

Chapter
25

"I'm going to do it my way,
or not at all."

Wilderness Mentality #10

"I'm going to do it my way, or not at all."

Chapter
25

Wilderness Mentality #10

The Israelites displayed much stubbornness and rebellion during their years in the wilderness. That is precisely what caused them to die out there. They just would not do what God told them to do! They would cry out to God to get them out of trouble when they got into a mess. They would even respond to His instructions with obedience — until circumstances improved. Then, repeatedly, they would go right back into rebellion.

That they might set their hope in God and not forget the works of God, but might keep His commandments

And might not be as their fathers – a stubborn and rebellious generation, a generation that set not their hearts aright nor prepared their hearts to know God, and whose spirits were not steadfast and faithful to God.

PSALM 78:7,8

This same cycle is repeated and recorded so many times in the Old Testament that it is almost unbelievable. And yet, if we are not walking in wisdom, we will spend our lives doing the same thing.

I suppose some of us are just by nature a little more stubborn and rebellious than others. And then, of course, we must consider our roots and how we got started in life, because that affects us also.

I was born with a strong personality and probably would have spent many years trying to "do it my way" no matter what. But the years I spent being abused and controlled — added to an already strong personality — combined together to develop in me the mindset that nobody was going to tell me what to do.

Obviously, God had to deal with this bad attitude before He could use me.

The Lord demands that we learn to give up our own way and be pliable and moldable in His hands. As long as we are stubborn and rebellious, He can't use us.

I describe "stubborn" as obstinate; difficult to handle or work with, and "rebellious" as resisting control; resisting correction, unruly; refusing to follow ordinary guidelines. Both of these definitions describe me, as I was!

The abuse I had suffered in my early life caused a lot of my out-of-balance attitudes toward authority. But as I said earlier in the book, I could not allow my past to become an excuse to stay trapped in rebellion or anything else. Victorious living demands prompt, exact obedience to the Lord. We grow in our ability and willingness to lay aside our will and do His. It is vital that we continue to make progress in this area.

It is not enough to reach a certain plateau and think, "I've gone as far as I'm going to go." We must be obedient in all things — not holding back anything or keeping any doors in our lives closed to the Lord. We all have these "certain" areas that we hang onto as long as possible, but I exhort you to remember that a little leaven leavens the entire lump. (1 Corinthians 5:6 KJV.)

God Wants Obedience, Not Sacrifice

Samuel said (to King Saul), **Has the Lord as great a delight in burnt offerings and sacrifices as in obeying the voice of the Lord? Behold, to obey is better than sacrifice, and to hearken than the fat of rams.**

For rebellion is as the sin of witchcraft, and stubbornness is as idolatry and teraphim (household good luck images). Because you have rejected the word of the Lord, He also has rejected you from being king.

1 Samuel 15:22,23

An examination of Saul's life shows us vividly that he was given an opportunity to be king. He did not maintain the position for long because of stubbornness and rebellion. He had his own idea about things.

One time when Samuel the prophet was correcting Saul for not doing what he had been instructed to do, Saul's reply was, "I thought." He then proceeded to express his idea of how he thought things should have been done. (1 Samuel 10:6-8; 13:8-14.) Samuel's answer to King Saul was that God desires obedience, not sacrifice.

Often, we don't want to do what God asks, and then we attempt to do something to compensate for our disobedience.

How many of God's children fail to "reign as kings in life" (Romans 5:17; Revelation 1:6 KJV) because of their stubbornness and rebellion?

The introduction to the book of Ecclesiastes in *The Amplified Bible* says this, "The purpose of this book is to investigate life as a whole and to teach that in the final analysis life is meaningless without proper respect and reverence for God."

We must understand that without obedience, there is no proper respect and reverence. The rebellion shown by many children today is caused by a lack of proper respect and reverence for their parents. This is usually the fault of the parents because they have not lived in front of their children a life that would evoke respect and reverence.

Most scholars agree that the book of Ecclesiastes was written by King Solomon who was given more wisdom from God than any other man. If Solomon had so much wisdom, how could he have made so many sad mistakes in his life? The answer is simple: it is possible to have something and not use it. We have the mind of Christ, but do we always use it? Jesus has been made unto us wisdom from God, but do we always use wisdom?

Solomon wanted to go his own way and do his own thing. He spent his life trying first one thing and then another. He had anything and everything that money could buy — the best of every worldly pleasure — and yet this is what he said at the conclusion of the book:

All has been heard; the end of the matter is: Fear God [revere and worship Him, knowing that He is] and keep His commandments, for this is the whole of man [the full, original purpose of his creation, the object of God's providence, the root of character, the foundation of all happiness, the adjustment to all inharmonious circumstances and conditions under the sun] and the whole [duty] for every man.

Ecclesiastes 12:13

Let me put into my own words what I receive from this Scripture:

The whole purpose of man's creation is that he reverence and worship God by obeying Him. All godly character must be rooted in obedience — it is the foundation of all happiness. No one can ever be truly happy without being obedient to God. Anything in our lives that is out of order will be brought into adjustment by obedience. Obedience is the whole duty of man.

As far as I am concerned, this is one awesome Scripture, and I encourage you to continue studying it on your own.

OBEDIENCE AND DISOBEDIENCE:

BOTH HAVE CONSEQUENCES

For as by one man's disobedience many were made sinners, so by the obedience of one shall many be made righteous.

Romans 5:19 KJV

Our choice to obey or not to obey not only affects us, but multitudes of others. Just think of it: if the Israelites had promptly obeyed God, how much greater their lives would have been. Many of them and their children died in the wilderness because they would not submit to God's ways. Their children were affected by their decisions, and so are ours.

Recently, my oldest son said, "Mom, I have something to tell you, and I may cry, but hear me out." He then went on to say, "I have been thinking about you and Dad and the years you have put into this ministry, and all the times you chose to obey God and how it has not always been easy for you. I realize, Mom, that you and Dad have gone through things that nobody knows about, and I want you to know that this morning God made me aware that I am benefitting greatly from your obedience, and I appreciate it."

What he said meant a lot to me, and it reminded me of Romans 5:19.

Your decision to obey God affects other people, and when you decide to disobey God, that also affects others. You may disobey God and choose to stay in the wilderness, but please keep in mind that if you now have or ever have children, your decision will keep them in the wilderness with you. They may manage to get themselves out when they are grown, but I can assure you they will pay a price for your disobedience.

Your life might be in better shape now if someone in your past had obeyed God.

Obedience is a far-reaching thing; it closes the gates of hell and opens the windows of heaven.

I could write an entire book on obedience, but for now I simply want to make the point that a life of disobedience is the fruit of wrong thinking.

Bring Every Thought
Into Captivity to Christ

For the weapons of our warfare are not physical [weapons of flesh and blood], but they are mighty before God for the overthrow and destruction of strongholds,

[Inasmuch as we] refute arguments and theories and reasonings and every proud and lofty thing that sets itself up against the [true] knowledge of God; and we lead every thought and purpose away captive into the obedience of Christ (the Messiah, the Anointed One).

2 Corinthians 10:4,5

Our thoughts are what get us into trouble quite often.

In Isaiah 55:8 the Lord says, **For My thoughts are not your thoughts, neither are your ways My ways....** No matter what you or I may think, God has written His thoughts down for us in His book called the Bible. We must choose to examine our thoughts in light of the Word of God, always being willing to submit our thoughts to His thoughts, knowing that His are best.

This is exactly the point made in 2 Corinthians 10:4,5. Examine what is in your mind. If it does not agree with God's thoughts (the Bible), then cast down your own thoughts and think on His.

People living in the vanity of their own mind not only destroy themselves, but far too often, they bring destruction to others around them.

The mind is the battlefield!

It is on this ground of the mind that you will either win or lose the war that Satan has launched. It is my most heartfelt prayer that this book will assist you in casting down imaginations, and every high and lofty thing that exalts itself against the knowledge of God, bringing every thought into captivity, into obedience to Jesus Christ.

Endnotes

Chapter 7

[1] W. E. Vine, *An Expository Dictionary of New Testament Words* (Old Tappan: Fleming H. Revell, 1940), Vol. IV., SET-Z, p. 190.

[2] James Strong, *The New Strong's Exhaustive Concordance of the Bible* (Nashville: Thomas Nelson Publishers, 1984), "Greek Dictionary of the New Testament," p. 24.

[3] *Webster's II, New Riverside University Dictionary* (Boston: Houghton Mifflin Company, 1984), s.v. "meditate."

[4] Vine, Vol. III. LO-SER, p.55.

Chapter 9

[1] *Webster's II*, s.v. "wander."

[2] *Webster's II*, s.v. "wonder."

Chapter 10

[1] *Webster's II*, s.v. "reason."

Chapter 11

[1] Vine, Vol. I: A-DYS, p. 335.

[2] Vine, Vol. IV: SET-Z, p. 165.

Chapter 12

[1] *Webster's II*, s.v. "worry."

[2] *The Random House Unabridged Dictionary*, 2nd ed. (New York: Random House, 1993), s.v. "worry."

Chapter 13

[1] Vine, Vol. II: E-LI, p. 281.

[2] Vine, "Hebrew and Greek Words," Vol. II: E-LI, p. 280.

Chapter 15

[1] *Webster's II*, s.v. "depress."

2 *Webster's II*, s.v. "depressed."

3 Vine, Vol. II: E-Li, p. 60.

4 Vine, Vol. IV: Lo-Ser, p. 55.

5 *Strong's New Exhaustive Concordance,* "Hebrew and Chaldee Dictionary," p. 32.

Chapter 23

1 *Webster's II*, s.v. "reproach."

Chapter 24

1 Vine, Vol. II: E-Li, p. 37.

2 *Webster's II*, s.v. "jealousy."

Bibliography

Random House Unabridged Dictionary, 2nd ed. New York: Random House, 1993.

Strong, James. *The New Strong's Exhaustive Concordance of the Bible.* Nashville: Thomas Nelson Publishers, 1984.

Vine, W. E. *An Expository Dictionary of New Testament Words.* Old Tappan: Fleming H. Revell Company, 1940.

Webster's II New Riverside University Dictionary. Boston: Houghton Mifflin Company, 1984.

About the Author

Joyce Meyer has been teaching the Word of God since 1976 and in full-time ministry since 1980. She is the bestselling author of more than sixty inspirational books, including *In Pursuit of Peace, How to Hear from God, Knowing God Intimately,* and *Battlefield of the Mind*. She has also released thousands of teaching cassettes and a complete video library. Joyce's *Enjoying Everyday Life* radio and television programs are broadcast around the world, and she travels extensively conducting conferences. Joyce and her husband, Dave, are the parents of four grown children and make their home in St. Louis, Missouri.

To contact the author write:

Joyce Meyer Ministries
P. O. Box 655
Fenton, Missouri 63026
or call: (636) 349-0303
Internet Address: www.joycemeyer.org

*Please include your testimony or help received from this book
when you write. Your prayer requests are welcome.*

To contact the author
in Canada, please write:
Joyce Meyer Ministries Canada, Inc.
Lambeth Box 1300
London, ON N6P 1T5
or call: (636) 349-0303

In Australia, please write:
Joyce Meyer Ministries—Australia
Locked Bag 77
Mansfield Delivery Centre
Queensland 4122
or call: 07 3349 1200

In England, please write:
Joyce Meyer Ministries
P. O. Box 1549
Windsor
SL4 1GT
or call: (0) 1753-831102

Books by Joyce Meyer

Battlefield of the Kid's Mind (Spring 2006)
Approval Addiction (Spring 2005)
Ending Your Day Right
In Pursuit of Peace
The Secret Power of Speaking God's Word
Seven Things That Steal Your Joy
Starting Your Day Right
Beauty for Ashes Revised Edition
How to Hear from God
How to Hear from God Study Guide
Knowing God Intimately
The Power of Forgiveness
The Power of Determination
The Power of Being Positive
The Secrets of Spiritual Power
The Battle Belongs to the Lord
Secrets to Exceptional Living
Eight Ways to Keep the Devil Under Your Feet
Teenagers Are People Too!
Filled with the Spirit
Celebration of Simplicity
The Joy of Believing Prayer
Never Lose Heart
Being the Person God Made You to Be
A Leader in the Making
"Good Morning, This Is God!" Gift Book
Jesus—Name Above All Names
"Good Morning, This Is God!" Daily Calendar
Making Marriage Work
(Previously published as *Help Me—I'm Married!*)
Reduce Me to Love
Be Healed in Jesus' Name
How to Succeed at Being Yourself
Eat and Stay Thin
Weary Warriors, Fainting Saints
Life in the Word Journal
Life in the Word Devotional

Joyce Meyer Spanish Titles

By Dave Meyer

Donald Judd

WITHDRAWN

DONALD JUDD

Edited by Nicholas Serota

D.A.P. / Distributed Art Publishers, Inc.

First published in 2004 by order of the Tate Trustees
by Tate Publishing, a division of Tate Enterprises Ltd,
Millbank, London SW1P 4RG
www.tate.org.uk
on the occasion of the exhibition at
Tate Modern, London
5 February – 25 April 2004
K20 Kunstsammlung Nordrhein-Westfalen, Düsseldorf
19 June – 5 September 2004
Kunstmuseum Basel
2 October 2004 – 9 January 2005

Published in North America by D.A.P./
Distributed Art Publishers, Inc.
155 Sixth Avenue, 2nd floor
New York, New York 10013
www.artbook.com

ISBN 1-891024-89-2

Library of Congress Control Number: 2003116492

Designed by Rutger Fuchs, Amsterdam

Printed and bound in Italy by Conti Tipocolor

Measurements of works of art are given in centimetres,
height before width before depth, followed by inches in
brackets.

Works by Judd dating from 1974 or earlier are followed
by a reference number, beginning 'DSS'. This refers to the
numbering system used in Brydon Smith's catalogue
raisonné of paintings, objects and wood-blocks 1960–1974.
See Selected Reading for further details. Later works are
followed by a fabrication number where available.

Cover: *Untitled* 1972 (no.22)
    Tate Photography (Marcus Leith/Andrew Dunkley)
Frontispiece: Donald Judd at The Architecture Studio,
    formerly the Marfa National Bank, with *Untitled* 1961
    (DSS 24), 1994. Copyright © Laura Wilson

Contents

Foreword

One of the most significant American artists of the post-war period, Donald Judd changed the course of modern sculpture. This exhibition is the first full retrospective of his sculpture since 1988 and the first to cover Judd's entire career from the time that he first developed his own language until his death in 1994.

Emerging in the 1960s in New York, Judd became known as a major exponent of 'Minimalism' – a label that he strongly rejected, describing his work as 'the simple expression of complex thought'. Concentrating on a limited number of forms, strikingly rendered in contrasting materials and colours, Judd created an astonishing range of moods and experiences. The austerity of Judd's forms contrasts with the rich sensuousness of the objects that he created.

Judd's engagement with philosophy, architecture, design and politics both informed his own work and influenced the practice of succeeding generations of artists and designers. It is possible to identify Judd's influence on the pared-down forms and the sensuous use of industrial materials that are so frequently a feature of contemporary architecture and design. It seems particularly fitting to show Judd's work in the former industrial spaces of Tate Modern, while recognising that his own installation of his works in these spaces would probably have taken a very different form. The exhibition will also be shown at K20 Kunstsammlung Nordrhein-Westfalen, Düsseldorf, and at the Kunstmuseum Basel.

In developing and preparing the exhibition we are especially indebted to the trustees of the Judd Foundation – Flavin Judd, Maureen Jerome, Louisa Sarofim, Richard Schlagman, Marianne Stockebrand, and particularly to Rainer Judd, in her role as President – for providing such generous support on so many aspects of the project. We have also been very fortunate to have had the support and advice of Marianne Stockebrand, Director of the Chinati Foundation, whose knowledge and understanding of Judd's work have been invaluable.

The exhibition provides an unprecedented opportunity to see some of Judd's most significant works brought together from collections around the world. Despite the often monumental proportions of Judd's work, the surfaces are extremely delicate and we are therefore deeply grateful to all those who have generously lent to the exhibition.

We would also like to convey our thanks to those who have assisted us in the course of preparing and researching the exhibition, including Brooke Alexander, Douglas Baxter, Paula Cooper, Rudi Fuchs, Madeleine Hoffman, Thomas Kellein, Jeffrey Kopie, Thomas Lighton, Craig Rember, Hester van Roijen, Ellen Salpeter, Annemarie Verna and Rob Weiner.

At Tate Modern we would particularly like to thank curator Helen Sainsbury, who has steered the organisation of the exhibition through to completion. Thanks are also due to Emma Dexter, Jacky Klein, Tanya Barson, Zoe Lewis, Paula Feldman and the late Monique Beudert for their contribution to the early stages of the organisation. The complexities of delivering and installing the exhibition have been ably handled by registrars Stephen Dunn and Gillian Smithson, exhibition manager Stephen Mellor, art installation manager Phil Monk, the Art Handling team, and conservators Derek Pullen, Calvin Winner and Tim Green. We are also grateful to all those who have contributed to the wide range of activities that support and interpret the exhibition, including Dennis Ahern, Elisabeth Andersson, Simon Bolitho, Sophie Djian, John Duffett, Sue Glasgow, Will Gompertz, Brian Gray, Adrian Hardwicke, Sioban Ketelaar, Rebecca Lancaster, Brad Macdonald, Jemima Montagu, Bernadette O'Sullivan, Ruth Pelopida, Maeve Polkinhorn, Caroline Priest, Jane Scherbaum, Calum Sutton, Mary Taylor, Nadine Thompson, Sheena Wagstaff and Dominic Willsdon.

The catalogue, elegantly designed by Rutger Fuchs, who worked with Judd in the realisation of several book designs, has benefited from the excellent contributions by David Batchelor, Rudi Fuchs, Jeffrey Kopie, David Raskin, Richard Shiff and Marianne Stockebrand. We would like to thank John Jervis for his skilful management of the catalogue, as well as his colleagues at Tate Publishing, especially Sarah Tucker, Alessandra Serri, Odile Matteoda-Witte, Clare Manchester, James Attlee, Celia Clear, Roger Thorp and Tim Holton. We would like to thank Mr and Mrs James R. Hedges IV for their early and generous commitment to the exhibition by making a donation which has enabled us to publish an extended catalogue.

We are grateful to Tate Members for generously supporting the exhibition in London. Their ongoing commitment to supporting a wide range of activities, acquisitions and projects at Tate is much appreciated. We would also like to thank our American Exhibition Patrons for their support of the exhibition. Each year, this group aims to support an American exhibition at Tate and we are delighted that the Donald Judd exhibition will be the recipient of this year's grant.

Nicholas Serota   Armin Zweite   Bernhard Mendes Bürgi
Director, Tate   *Director, Kunstsammlung Nordrhein-Westfalen*   *Director, Kunstmuseum Basel*

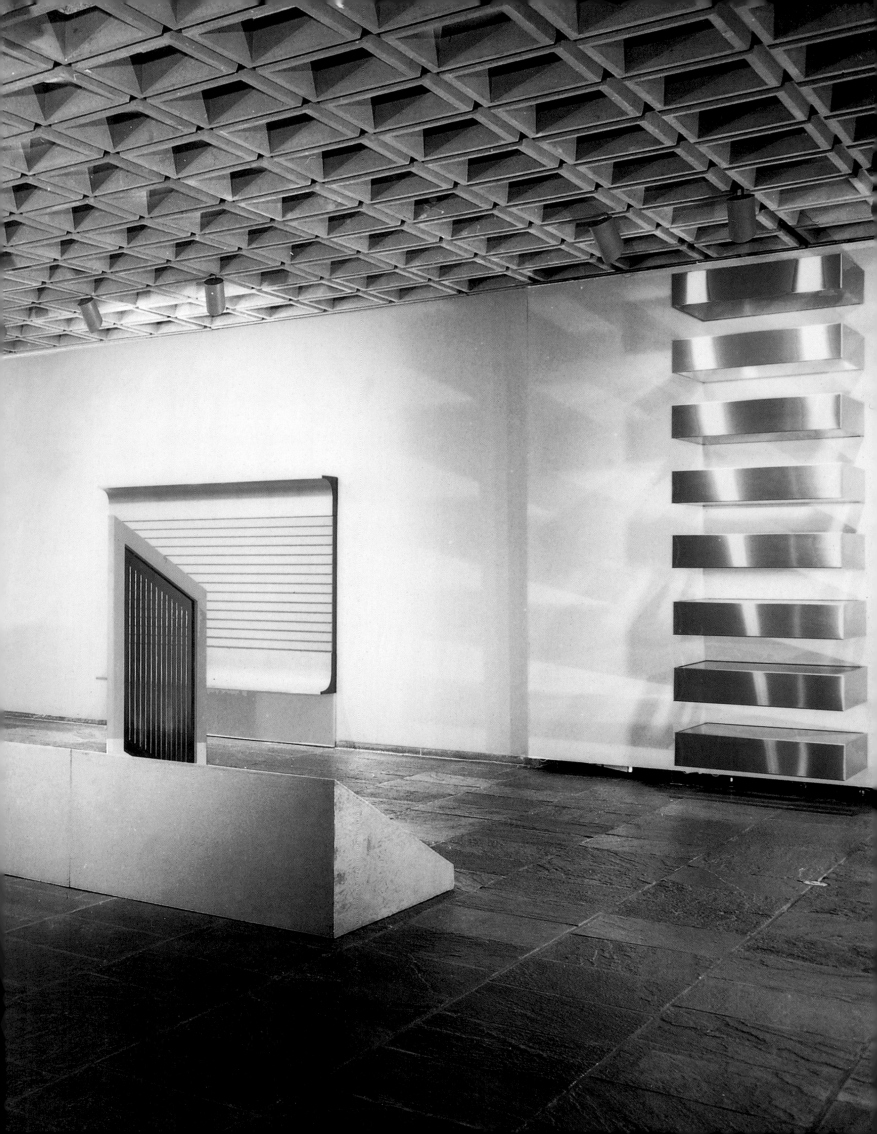

The Chinati Mountains, Presidio County, Texas

Donald Judd (Artist at Work)

RUDI FUCHS

Things are not done
beautifully. The beauty is an
integral part of their being done.

Robert Henri (1865–1929)

In the last years of his life, when he was living in West Texas, Donald Judd began to spend more and more time on the remote ranch at Las Casas down by the Mexican border. Here, in this wide, harsh and rocky valley, he was finally laid to rest in a solitary grave next to the grave of a previous rancher. There were perhaps twenty to thirty of us who brought him there, family and close friends. The ceremony was short and simple and tense. The rectangular coffin was built in unpainted plywood by Peter Ballantine who also built most of Judd's plywood sculpture. It took us two hours, maybe more, to get there from Marfa. Somewhere half way the unpaved road turned into a rough track. There we were, in Robert Halpern's Jeep, slowly bumping over rocks and gullies behind the big black four-wheel-drive hearse. It felt like a comedy Western. Judd had been pleased that there was no proper road to the ranch. When he was down there, on his own most of the time, we would talk over the telephone – at night for me in Holland, but daytime for him, in the dry sharp light and the stillness of that place. 'I have to restore this ranch back to nature', he would say. The previous rancher had been engaged in cutting roads violently, using dynamite. The explosions and the roar of heavy machinery had scared away the birds and other shy animals. 'The landscape has to be healed', he said, 'of its wounds and scars'; and one night he told me that certain birds had returned to the valley. He was as angry about the damage done to the landscape as he was, always, about damage done to artworks. The motive for the Marfa project was that, by installing artworks there in permanence, and when possible under the supervision of the artist, they would be saved from the temporary exhibition business which, he knew by experience, often led to bad and stupid installations and damage. By owning land he could prevent its exploitation; it was that simple. Once he showed me on the sectioned map of Presidio County which sections he had gradually acquired, section by section – and added, grinning, that if one had time and money enough one could buy the entire State of Texas.

No real road to Las Casas also meant, he said, that he would be protected from unwanted company. People could not just swing by for a casual visit. He told me about a trip to Australia and the outback there, years after he had settled in West Texas. So? 'That is where I should have gone', he said. Why? 'Too many people here.' We were standing on a high plateau over his other, smaller ranch closer to Marfa, the Casa Perez. (This ranch is much more idyllic than the remote one where he was buried: the vegetation is more green than grey and there are a few trees.) A western windmill was slowly chirping away. For me, from Europe, we were in the

middle of nowhere: arid stony land, mostly olive-grey in colour, sloping down to the Rio Grande and the purple Mexican mountains beyond. (On my second trip, passing through customs in Houston, the officer called out to his colleague: 'Hey, Pete, these guys are going to Marfa' – and then they laughed.) The people in Marfa, quite rightly, considered Europe far away and did not think much about it. But New Yorkers too thought Marfa was remote. That was why Judd had chosen it; and now I was only here because he lived here. It was his place of work; it was where the studio was. When you want to know more about a living artist you go and see him where he makes his art. There was some production in Marfa, mainly of Cor-ten pieces, because he found someone who could make them. Most of the time, however, when I visited Judd, he was developing a new complex of works begun in the mid-1980s: horizontal wall pieces of brightly coloured rectangular metal panels screwed together. The panels were all equal in height but varied in width. In their syncopated lateral composition, then, they reflected the much earlier progressions but with a different structural logic. What I found in the studio when he reluctantly let me in were mostly preparations for those colour works. I will come back to them; for now I want to remember the concentration and sense of focus present in Judd's large studio (a former supermarket). That is what I had come to Marfa for: the long tables lined up and on the tables, cardboard colour samples laid out in sequences; sheets of paper with studies of sequences of colour proportions. Two or three pieces that had grown out of these studies were installed on a wall. On another table I saw scores of samples of transparent or opaque Plexiglas in all colours. He had always used Plexiglas for its spotless luminosity and for its clear-cut sharpness. He liked industrial materials (aluminium, steel, copper and plywood among others) because they could be cut sharply and used with precision. They were not artistic. Their surface was blank: they carried no history. The studio was orderly, quiet and relaxed. I felt no obsession or hurry.

fig.1   Rudi Fuchs and Donald Judd at the
Stedelijk Museum, Amsterdam, 1993

It was important and instructive to see the studio. Looking with him at work in progress led to conversations about practice that were marvellously concrete. What was being carried out there was plotting, probing, testing, pushing the work on. There was also writing to do and design work for furniture and architecture. The town of Marfa was suffering from bad economic circumstances because profits from the cattle business were failing. For Judd this meant that buildings became available, and that allowed him to organise discrete workspaces for the separate activities of his enterprise all around the railway crossing in the centre of the small town. I think that the separation helped him to concentrate better. Somehow it gave him more time to be patient. Furthermore the luxury of space at prices he could afford made it possible to install some of his own earlier work. That was crucially important. When plotting and designing new work he liked to look at his old work because each of these pieces implied artistic decisions that had led his work on to what it was next. He wanted that history present; and then of course there was always the idea that after his death the work should remain where he himself had installed it, immaculate and precise, a final definitive document. Nothing was more fundamental to Judd's practical understanding of art than the notion that works of art, and in particular sculpture, create space and define the dynamic nature of space. He dwelt on this proposition at length in his last and most profound public lecture (in a sense an elaboration of his famous essay published in 1965, 'Specific Objects'). In November 1993, a few months before his death, he was to accept the Sikkens Award in Amsterdam, for his contribution to the use of colour. He and Marianne Stockebrand had come to Amsterdam and had seen, in the afternoon before the ceremony the next day, a small exhibition of his work that I had installed in the Stedelijk Museum with works from Dutch public collections, some sixteen pieces covering most of his career. I think he liked the installation which, contrary to his habit, had been done in his absence. There was one recent wall piece, blue and yellow, which for some reason the Stedelijk had on loan from him. He might have forgotten. 'That piece', he said, 'should stay with the others.' He donated it. At dinner that evening he felt unwell. 'It will pass', he said. The next morning he phoned. He was very ill, he had to go with Marianne to Cologne to the hospital. 'You deliver the lecture for me', he said. That was the last time I saw him. The lecture was titled 'Some Aspects of Color in General and Red and Black in Particular'. It also dwells, at times erratically as was his style, on problems of space – in particular on how art and architecture, when they are good, make space visible and how space is a precious quality. The lecture is packed with observations that I will not repeat (the text is reprinted here). But when I stood there behind the rostrum and read it, I felt the great urgency in his convictions and also an anger with how, in his view, the quality of space was compromised and squandered everywhere now. In view of this conviction, the careful installations in Marfa were, for him, an exemplary demonstration and now, in a sense, a site of remembrance. Art should not just be jerked around in some gallery or museum. As far as Judd was concerned that is what most exhibitions came down to. Each work of art required an installation that was precise, individual and sensitive. That is, in tune with the physical nature of the piece: whether it was vertical or horizontal, on the wall or on the floor,

brightly coloured or not. All of this counts and is important to allow a piece to project and define its space. In a rough field of dry grass in Marfa, some fifteen, large, man-high concret blocks have been placed in a somewhat irregular row, but they stand there with the unassailable nobility of Egyptian pyramids. Relentless, somebody said. The pieces give the field a enormous dignity and beauty; and that is what they are there for. 'Hopefully', said Judd i one conversation, 'they convince people that quality is possible and that then they won't an longer put up with all the slipshod ugliness and the crap and the lack of attention to simpl detail we have to endure every day.' He had given me a book with the writings of Thoma Jefferson, and we jokingly concluded that a fourth 'unalienable right' should be added to th three in the Declaration of Independence: life, liberty and the pursuit of happiness. The ne right should be the right to beauty and quality for everyone.

When I first saw Judd's work, in 1966 in Holland, my understanding of it was entirely intelle tual and academic. Some young artists of my acquaintance in Holland, such as Ad Dekker were making austere abstract-geometric work. As a young art critic I wrote about it and s became aware of other artists in Europe such as François Morellet or Richard Paul Lohse, wh had taken abstract geometry in art a step further. I knew the work of Frank Stella and Ellswort Kelly. It was easy to conclude that the work made by Judd and other Minimalists was part (a logical development that was evidently bound to happen and for which the moment ha simply arrived. That was the reasoning of traditional art history: that a new and vigorous sty emerges when the previous style begins to lose its dynamism. In our Dutch perception th remarkable new phase of abstraction, terse, precise and profoundly unsentimental, was direct consequence of Mondrian, De Stijl and Bauhaus, and the various ramifications (abstraction that had emerged, stylistically, out of that great moment early in the twentiet century. Mondrian had raised the stakes very high and he himself, in his curious writing had given his art a foundation of idealism and utopia: his paintings propagated a new worl Others in his circle made similar claims. I remember the discussions in the late 1960s whe the new generation was attacked for making this new art that, the general public said, di not even look like art. We argued that these objects were idealistic representations, that i their artistic motivation there was much more than one could actually see, and that they ha a mysterious clarity of insight. After all Mondrian had also been a Symbolist. An utopian aur surrounded these works – and when Minimal art arrived in Holland (and it arrived quite ear because we were prepared) it was seen, of course, in similar utopian and idealistic terms. Th is how I intellectually interpreted Judd's art when I first saw it. Years later, after I had been t West Texas many times, Judd gently corrected me. When we had our annual open-house mee ings in Marfa, *urbi et orbi* as it were, it had become my duty as president of his Chinati Fou dation to make a short speech of welcome before the lavish and festive Mexican dinner cou begin. (Judd liked such proper protocol.) As we were far away from any great centre, I invar ably used the metaphor of a remote monastery where the real faith was kept alive while the was heresy and pestilence in the outside world; we were part of this utopian enterprise.

always worked. But one day Judd was being interviewed in his studio by a German television crew. I was present as I would be next. They asked: 'What is this site here in Marfa exactly?' 'Well', Judd answered, 'Rudi here thinks it is utopia but for me it is just real.' It was this casual remark that made me realise that the place *was* real. It suddenly made the work more exciting. Mondrian too became more exciting now that I could forget my academicism. The pieces were not expressions of emotion or mystic insight. They were moments of realised conviction, arrived at by quiet, patient, emotional reasoning and probing. In the Amsterdam lecture, Judd argued that once an artist had come to a pragmatic conclusion, based on honest practice, to give a piece a definite shape and colour, that definition was not a whim of style. It was a fact that, by its very existence, became as objective as any piece of knowledge that is added to all we know in the world. That is what *real* means. The knowledge exists forever, as a fact. What becomes known cannot just be made unknown.

But now we go back in time: I wanted to make a Judd exhibition at the Van Abbemuseum in Eindhoven to commemorate his first show there in 1970. (That exhibition was also shown in London, in the Whitechapel Art Gallery, in the same year.) I had met Judd in the flesh in Bern, where he had made an exhibition at the Kunsthalle in 1976, with my friend Johannes Gachnang. Instead of bringing work from elsewhere and making the usual show, Judd had specially built plywood works that fitted and spatially articulated each room of the Kunsthalle perfectly. The exhibition was a statement of intent. Present at the opening was the old warrior of geometric abstraction Richard Paul Lohse who, at one point much moved, grabbed Judd by his arms and exclaimed: 'Long live the right angle!'

It was at this time that Judd, for many reasons, some personal, had become very preoccupied with the Marfa project. The type of work that he and some of his friends such as Dan Flavin and John Chamberlain were making was very sensitive to how it was spatially installed. Marfa, conceived as a safe-haven for art, offered the possibility to install work as it should be installed – and permanently, just as a Bernini sculpture in an Italian church. So, when we met in Eindhoven in 1978 to discuss our show there, Judd was quite adamant. Why make an exhibition? He knew the reality of Marfa. 'Works of art have to be saved from the exhibition business', he said. Then he became intrigued, and we finally settled for something similar to Bern, an exhibition of plywood pieces mostly made specifically for the Eindhoven galleries, that would be destroyed afterwards. An exhibition, then, as a demonstration of how art occupies and defines space. It was a wonderful show. To prepare and build it Judd spent a summer in Eindhoven with his two children. During this period our conversations were often about Marfa and the project. Yet it was only in 1987, notwithstanding Judd's entreaties, that I first went to Marfa where I became closer to the work.

Donald Judd was a wilful but also a very shy man. Only now writing this, does it occur to me that the pace of the art life in a hectic competitive centre like New York simply did not suit his temperament. One cannot say that his mind was slow; but his mind was careful. The nervous competitiveness of modern city art life disrupted his concentration. He felt he had to

withdraw his art from the competition because it would inevitably lead to compromise. That is what we talked about that summer in Eindhoven and subsequently. When one considers the phases of development in the work, the pace is remarkably unhurried. In terms of the art market, Judd was not as exciting as, for example, Warhol or Oldenburg. Many said his work was boring, lacking adventure. But, as we certainly now know, his work was as authoritative and important as the work of Mondrian or Malevich. *And Judd knew that.* He knew that he had entered (or discovered) a field of insight and definition that would prove to be of central importance. One could hear this conviction in that last Amsterdam lecture where he listed what his art had achieved – but also explained that it was little understood. There was a certain melancholy in that lecture. The move from New York to Marfa was to protect his independence and to give him the space to work carefully and unhurried at his own pace. For such reasons Tolstoy retired to his country estate: not to be bothered anymore. When in the end the annual Marfa gatherings became popular, when the place became quaintly exotic and fashionable (like Taos, New Mexico, where Georgia O'Keeffe once resided) he retired to his ranch and was seen in town only rarely. Judd had a property in Switzerland, an old country inn near Lucerne that he was fashioning in his own strict idiom. Occasionally I went to see him there. One evening he started to talk about Richard Paul Lohse. 'We took it for granted', he said, 'that we in America would invent everything anew. We were so eager. But then there was Lohse here, and we should have been aware of that.' 'But', he said, 'we did not know.'

Untitled 1989 is a large floor piece that was acquired by the Stedelijk Museum, Amsterdam, in 1993 (fig.2). Since then we have installed it many times in different exhibitions. I thought I knew it well, but when I began to look at it more carefully for this article it turned out that my perception of that sculpture had been shamefully superficial. The seemingly straightforward simplicity of the piece is deceptive. Just looking at it and saying, this is a horizontal construction of elongated rectangular panels in four different colours (red, turquoise, blue, yellow) that alternate in such a way that one colour never appears next to or above itself, is not sufficient even though you might think that you have then seen it. After all, that is what the *organisation* of the sculpture comes down to. Yet, as we will see, such a manner of perception is just too casual. That, however, is how most people stroll at their leisure through a gallery. They think that an artwork can be seen at a glance. Yet the same people are quite content to listen to a Mozart symphony for as long as the composer wanted the music to last. Casual perception seems to be even more a problem with work that emerged under the generic denomination of Minimal art in the late 1960s. Judd often complained about that, as did others with whom it came up in conversation, such as Carl Andre and Sol LeWitt. When, for instance, we look at a small, intimate panel painting such as the bridal portrait of Giovanni Arnolfini and his wife (1434) by Jan van Eyck, we are expected to notice and consider minute details because such is obviously the character of the painting. It is an amazing example of delicate minuteness; that is why it is so enchanting and wonderful. One afternoon in 1991, when Judd had an exhibition in the Vienna Museum of Applied Arts, the director of the Albertina, Konrad Oberhuber, showed us all the Raphael drawings in its collection. It was a great pleasure to

look at these drawings closely and calmly as if one was reading a book; and on that occasion we talked about detail and about the fact that all art is, by its very nature, very detailed. But Minimal art looked different: precisely formulated but not, in the classic sense, detailed. At least since Impressionism, art had looked so much less detailed than before. With Impressionism formal experimentation in art began in a new, nervous way: personal vision and expression got in the way of naturalistic description. From there on, art, whether it was Picasso or Schwitters or Mondrian or Pollock, seemed primarily engaged in the experimental formulation of form. The first noticeable thing about a Picasso nude was that it is, in its curious design, different from a nude by Raphael. The difference is that Picasso took more licence, formally, than Raphael. Picasso's art form is a figure for expression and rhetoric. Think only of his most famous work, *Guernica* 1936. (The problem with Raphael's truthfulness to nature, I must add, is complicated; it was not by accident that Mannerism germinated in his late work and in his studio.) From this general perspective, however, Minimal art was an extreme case by itself. Picasso and Pollock, even Mondrian and Barnett Newman, at least showed traces of the hand and the brush in their paintings; but Minimal art, in that respect, was neutral and blank. Yet Judd's drawings are certainly as precise in the formulation of their artistic objective as any drawing by Raphael. That afternoon Judd looked very intensely at the Raphael drawings, but without reverence. He was an equal colleague, he understood Raphael; he knew what drawing is. But then his anger came back. He hated the term Minimal art, he said. He felt that it did not apply to his work, and never had. The term, of course, refers primarily to the formal aspect of the work; and that is where the problem lies. These were works that employed (certainly compared to Abstract Expressionism) simple forms in straightforward industrial materials – not artistic materials. So the focus became that formal simplicity. It was no longer necessary to look at these so-called 'Minimal' works with careful precision because they were just minimal – nothing more than shapes and outlines. The critical debate about Minimal art became a somewhat philosophical debate: what did this art actually mean? What moved artists to make this kind of object? This discussion took place, and is still going on, without most participants taking the trouble to actually *look* at these objects. There was no reason to look. The work was simple and minimal; we see that, but then what? These were the days during which Judd, if he was not just dismissed, was regarded as that artist who just made cubes. Whereas the reality is that Judd never made a cube in his entire career.

All this came back to me when the Stedelijk Museum acquired *Untitled* 1989. Some time earlier, the museum in Rotterdam had bought a floor piece from the same group of pieces that Judd had been working on, off and on, since the mid-1980s. There are, I think, six of these related works: large pieces that have developed in the context of the multicoloured wall pieces that he began to construct around the same time. I do not remember why the acquisition of one of these large and major pieces by the Stedelijk Museum became an issue in the press. A curator of the Rotterdam museum was quoted saying that he did not understand why the Stedelijk had bought this sculpture as they already had a very similar piece in Rotterdam. I only report this incident because it is so weirdly indicative of the formidable misunderstanding that

Judd's art has had to endure. The Rotterdam curator had said that the piece in Amsterdam was, formally, the same as that in Rotterdam, *only the colours were different.*

Here the misunderstanding is complete. Imagine a gallery acquiring a Frans Hals portrait, and another gallery protesting that it already has such a portrait, actually the same thing, only the position of the hands is somewhat different – for the rest it is as always mainly black. This would be unthinkable; but regrettably with contemporary art, such superficial judgements are all too common. It shows that we still find it generally very difficult to accept that a work by a contemporary artist might be of the same excellence as any great Old Master painting. That is a weakness in our society; and it allows the casual and facile perception of new work to continue as it does, to our detriment.

There is always the first impression of a work of art: that is when you begin to find a work interesting and attractive and beautiful. The first impression decides whether you bother to look again. So I look again at *Untitled* 1989 in Amsterdam. The measurements of the piece are: height 150 cm (59 in), width 750 cm (295 $^1/_4$ in), depth 165 cm (64 $^{15}/_{16}$ in). This overall size is, however, accidental. It is the result of addition; for the proportional unit used by Judd in planning and constructing the piece measures 30 × 150 cm (11 $^{13}/_{16}$ × 59 in): that is the size of the single-colour panels he designed as constituent elements. These panels have a rim of 6.5 cm (2 $^1/_2$ in) in height, so they are like long shallow boxes. The rim is, first, a technical feature: that is where the panels can be screwed together. They also serve, however, to establish a sharp articulation between the panels and thus the colours. Yet I suspect there is also an aesthetic side to this. Judd had always made boxes to which the inside back panel (or in standing boxes the floor panel) was given a colour. The colour, then, appeared as an apparition from inside the shadow of the interior. Even the shallow boxes in *Untitled* 1989 create that slight difference in lighting or subtly illuminating colour. I think Judd liked that effect. When he died he was working on vertical stacks of velvety Cor-ten boxes in which each box had a different sweet Plexiglas colour emanating from the soft shade of the interior.

These last pieces were voluptuous in a way that nobody had ever associated with Judd's intentions. He had been seen as an austere, puritan artist. Then when people finally got used to the tough classic works in plain aluminium, steel or plywood, with their strict architectural articulation of shape, proportion and interior space, he began, in the mid-1980s, to make multicoloured wall pieces with those bright and mellow and sexy colours he had never used before. What was this frivolity? I think that the gradual retirement, first to Marfa and then to the remote ranch, gave him the strength and serenity of mind necessary to embark on something as new and fundamental as the multicoloured pieces. Of all things in art, colour is the most difficult. In a sense, drawing is easy because, whatever one draws (a nude, a tree, a square) there is an object in mind that leads to a definition. Colour, however, is extremely elusive. When an artist, for example Malevich, paints a red square we can, by measurement, very precisely define that square; but the colour red, the kind of red, is indescribable. Picasso is a superb draughtsman but Mondrian is a great colourist; and that is why Mondrian is the greatest

21

former supermarket. Later I also came across drawings and collages in which colour alterna
tions and sequences were mapped out, with precise notations on the proportion of eacl
colour. That patient figuring things out was what was going on there in West Texas.

In each wall piece, two colours per section (30, 60 or 90 cm; 11 $^{13}/_{16}$, 23 $^{5}/_{8}$ or 35 $^{7}/_{16}$ in) rotate il
alternation around the core which is void. If one of the colours turns up again in the adjacen
section, it will never, except at the corners of an element, touch the same colour. That is th
organisational principle. On the front of the piece one sees the choreography of alternatio:
of *all* the colours present in the piece. Before the choreographical permutations begin, th
gamut of colours is presented. For example, from left to right, there are three sections: orang
over red (90 cm; 35 $^{7}/_{16}$ in), blue over yellow (60 cm; 23 $^{5}/_{8}$ in), red over blue (30 cm; 11 $^{13}/_{16}$ in
then, per section, the colours rotate round. This is a simple example: the possibilities to mak
the alternations more complex are almost endless. There are pieces in which the sequence c
colours in the upper band of elements is reversed in the lower band, and the proportions ar
also reversed. There are works consisting of two wall pieces above each other, one the counte
structure of the other. At the same time Judd designed pieces with just two colours in a sim
ple arrangement. *The colours are always just gorgeous.* That is why many people distrusted thes
pieces. They are simply too beautiful, and that kind of beauty was not associated with Min
mal art. There had always been the notion that Minimal art was an objective, frugal and pur
tan art; but now, evidently, one of its leading practitioners had started to follow his instinc
his mood, his subjective sense of beauty. He said: 'I have always worked like that. Whateve
method there is in my work, it is always purely practical, a matter of experience, explorin
how what I know can be made into something else. I am not a doctrinaire artist. I follov
instinct.' It was late evening and we were sitting in the dark on the bench in front of his hous
in Marfa, looking at the stars and sipping a coarse Mexican *aguardiente*. 'I have also', he sa:c
'used colour in a very intense manner, always; not only painted or added [Plexiglas] colou
but also the beautiful colour of materials such as copper or aluminium or plywood. It is s
obvious; but why can people not just accept what they see? If anything that is exactly the g:
of art: that maybe you see something you have never seen before. That is exciting, don't yo
think? Instead when people see something new they get nervous because they prefer to se
what they had hoped to see: that is, more of the same.'

The Amsterdam floor piece, *Untitled* 1989 (fig.2), consists of eighty-five colour panels in tota
each 30 × 150 cm (11 $^{13}/_{16}$ × 59 in). I cannot make out a particular system in the way the fou
colours (again yellow, blue, turquoise, red) wind themselves around the supporting form. Thi
is different from the wall pieces where the programme of alternation is always clear and ca
culated. There is, however, a gradual development in the big floor piece; colours go up or dow
step by step. I have the impression of garlands winding around; and when I look hard I als
see groupings of, each time, two colours emerging – which then change. I see blue over re
and then, suddenly, blue over yellow or turquoise under red and then the reverse of that. I se
unexpected contractions of colour. I see colours shifting position. That is what this work

about. Of the eighty-five panels, twelve touch the floor. They make contact with other, different colours on three sides. The other seventy-three panels make contact on four sides. That means that there are altogether 328 contacts of one colour with a different colour, 328 shifting movements. That is the carnival of colour that goes on in this piece; a narrative is developed of four colours and 328 shifts. That is how we should look at it, at the incredible density; and because, as I believe, something quite new is happening here, precision and patience are needed in one's perception of the piece.

Somehow in Judd's earlier work (and some work he still did simultaneously with the multi-coloured pieces) form and shape were the first components of a piece. First they were subtle phrasings of proportion and interior space. That was their direction or ambition. Certainly, colour was added but mostly in relation to the function of formal and spatial concerns. Colour was used to clarify relationships within the formal construction of a piece. In *Untitled* 1989 in Amsterdam this is quite the other way around: in this work the single colours *make the form* through their quiet movement and alteration. They constitute the form by maintaining their position in the general choreography of colour. They do that quietly. Compared to the marvellous repose of the floor pieces (which sit there solidly like Cézanne's Mont Sainte-Victoire on its horizon) the wall pieces are more nervous and experimental in terms of the behaviour of colour. Their colour is swift and agile. Perhaps the slower floor pieces are themselves moments of repose and of reflection, in the exciting experimental production of the smaller and more staccato wall pieces. They are certainly masterpieces and, I think, strangely philosophical in character. And, given their different schemes of colour, I wonder whether they can be compared to the ancient traditional cycle in painting of the Seasons – in which the Amsterdam piece, with its lush ripe colours, would represent the height of Summer. The piece in the Tate Gallery, in galvanised iron, represents Winter. The very colourful works with eight colours in St Gallen, or with eight colours and galvanised iron in Düsseldorf, are phases of Spring, with flowers in bloom. The very mellow colours in the Herbert piece should represent Autumn and the harvest of grapes for wine. The piece in Rotterdam, then, would be late Summer or early Autumn. Donald Judd, who so much liked the land and the colour changes in the land, might just have agreed with these descriptions. But then he might not have; he distrusted romantic notions. An artist makes work according to his ideas and beliefs. After that each individual fantasy, like mine or yours, is equally real because that is how a work lives on in time: by being seen and remembered.

Leo Castelli Gallery and Warehouse, New York,
11 April – 9 May 1970

fig.3 JASPER JOHNS

Thermometer 1959

Oil on canvas and thermometer
131.5 × 97.8 (51³/₄ × 38¹/₂)
Seattle Art Museum. Partial and promised gift
of Bagley and Virginia Wright

Donald Judd, Safe from Birds

RICHARD SHIFF

'YOU DON'T HAVE TO MIMIC CHANCE'

ACKNOWLEDGEMENTS
For essential aid in
research, I thank Mette
Gieskes, Eileen Costello,
James Lawrence and
Sherry Smith in Austin;
Marianne Stockebrand,
Rob Weiner, Craig Rem-
ber and the Donald Judd
Estate (now Judd Founda-
tion) in Marfa; Alexander
Dumbadze, Douglas Bax-
ter, Peter Ballantine and
Nan Rosenthal in New
York; David Raskin in
Chicago; and James Cuno
in London. This essay
extends my 'Donald Judd:
Fast Thinking',
published in *Donald Judd:
Late Work*, exh. cat., Pace-
Wildenstein, New York
2000.

In 1970, informed that Barnett Newman had died, Donald Judd felt a deep loss.[1] He and New-man had been cordial friends, sharing political as well as aesthetic views. A generational dis-tance of twenty-three years hardly affected their sympathetic affinities.[2] Acting on his strict principles, Newman combined humour with abrasiveness; famously, he chose an audience of aestheticians to announce that aesthetic science held as much interest for artists as 'ornithol-ogy ... for the birds'.[3] Judd, too, had little use for theoretical generalisation. Although income was a factor, he may have become a writer on art because, like Newman, he was so dissatis-fied with what was available to read.[4] He had extraordinary critical insights and was adept at verbalising his own artistic strategies and credo. Yet even now (again like Newman) his preci-sion may seem overreaching or just as often pass undetected and unappreciated, along with his wry humour. Judd's spare verbal style and insistent scepticism shock prolix academic minds.

When a statement is so pointed as to shock, it sometimes registers without memorable effect. Often I have been taken aback by instances of Judd's concision – little verbal time bombs that explode at random, previously unnoticed in pages I have already read – as here, from 1960, close to the start of his career as an art critic: '*Thermometer* has one.'[5] The 'one' in this sentence refers to the functioning thermometer Jasper Johns attached to one of his works (fig.3). By syntactical reflexiveness, Judd indicated the redundant, non-allusive character of Johns's title: *Thermometer* 1959, contains a thermometer; on the canvas to the instrument's left and right, numbers stencilled in paint calibrate it. The title merely names a material object already there to be seen, not something to be imagined or reconstructed.[6] Judd recognised Johns's *False Start*

1   'I was with [Judd] when he got the call that Barney Newman had died. He was devastated.' Larry Bell, statement in *Artforum*, vol.32, no.10, Summer 1994, p.73.

2   According to Robert Murray, who assisted Newman with sculptural projects, 'Don patterned himself on Barney more than on any other artist.' Statement to author, 11 September 2002. On Newman's links to Judd's generation, see Richard Shiff, 'Whiteout: The Not-Influence Newman Effect', Ann Temkin (ed.), *Barnett Newman*, exh. cat., Philadelphia Museum of Art 2002, pp.77–111.

3   Barnett Newman, 'Remarks at the Fourth Annual Woodstock Art Conference' (1952), *Barnett Newman: Selected Writings and Interviews*, ed. John P. O'Neill, New York 1990, p.247.

4   'An artist paints so that he will have something to look at; at times he must write so that he will also have something to read.' Newman, 'From "The Ideas of Art: The Attitudes of Ten Artists on Their Art and Contemporaneousness"' (1947), Newman 1990, p.160.

5   Donald Judd, 'In the Galleries: Jasper Johns' (1960), *Donald Judd Complete Writings, 1959–1975, Gallery Reviews, Book Reviews, Articles, Letters to the Editor, Reports, Statements, Complaints*, Halifax and New York 1975, p.14.

6   With titles, Judd did Johns one better, designating his own works 'Untitled', the sole exceptions being dedications to named individuals.

1959 as similar. It manifested 'stenciled names of the various colors, seldom in their own' –
their own colours, that is (fig.4). Again, syntactical reflexiveness makes the point; but it may
take a second reading to catch it.

Judd thought the issue worth expanding: 'A curious polarity and alliance of the materiality of
objects and [the] qualities of paint and color are implicit in each of Johns's paintings.' We do
well to paraphrase Judd's perception, because what he was saying back in 1960 remains hard
to appreciate. Material objects and sensory qualities are different entities, he suggests; and
between them there can be both a polarity (a separation) and an alliance (a union). Viewing
False Start, which lacked the blatantly physical materiality of an attached object (such as a
thermometer), Judd determined that here the factor of 'materiality' – he also called it 'actuality' – was the stencilling itself. It was identical to lettering that might appear 'on a box', a
real-life feature that might be 'attached' to any surface. Johns's 'amorphous' brushwork, to
the contrary, introduced as a purely sensory quality the visible texture and colour of paint.[7]

In Judd's view, paint as Newman used it was also a matter of pure sensory quality, nothing more.
Typically, it would bleed under Newman's strips of masking tape as he constructed his bands
of colour. Sometimes the narrowest bands were created by brushing over tape to leave a reserve
of white or raw canvas surrounded by feathery strokes, as in *Shining Forth (To George)* 1961 (fig.5).
Judd refused to view such markings as a calculated aesthetic refinement, a reference to tradition. He explained in 1964 that Newman's effects resulted from the straightforward 'way
the paint was applied'.[8] Later he commented that Newman's 'brushiness' was 'used as the
nature of the edge, the process of making the edge. That has to do with brushwork as con-
trasted with making [illusionistic] space.'[9] Here, by Judd's reckoning, paint is allowed to be
paint; its appearance is not of illusion, expression or gesture, but merely traces the artist's
process of manufacture. And so with Jackson Pollock: 'The dripped paint ... is dripped paint
... It's not something else that alludes to dripped paint.'[10] Neither Newman's nor Pollock's self-
evident technique ought to have encouraged critics to search for a more general aesthetic category or rationale.

Judd had a wonderful way of making his argument: 'You don't have to mimic chance ...
Pollock and those people [the Abstract Expressionists] represent actual chance.'[11] The New
York School did not need European Surrealist methods; chance, contingency, uniqueness
would be present in any event, in the actuality of every brushstroke. Things happen, Judd
believed, and chance is the way things are (with Newman or Pollock, the 'way the paint was
applied'). When artists imitate what convention dictates to be the *look* of chance, say, with
self-conscious gestures, they distance themselves from the specific reality of the mark and
its colour. Instead, Judd advises, 'use a simple form that doesn't look like either order or
disorder', one that looks like what it is. Referring to his own work of 1964 (fig.6), he stated
that 'the piece with the brass [horizontal bar] and the five [blue-lacquered] verticals is above
all *that shape*'. It presents no definitive ordering of parts, nor is it formless. Because of the
size, colour, surface quality and relatively deep spatial projection of the opposing elements –
as well as the position of the entire work, its top set near eye level – the verticals appear

7   Judd, 'In the
Galleries: Jasper Johns'
(1960), Judd 1975, p.14.
8   Judd, 'Barnett
Newman' (written 1964,
published 1970), Judd
1975, p.202.
9   Judd in Jeanne
Siegel (ed.), 'Around Barnett Newman', *Artnews*,
vol.70, no.6, October
1971, p.60.
10   Judd, 'Jackson
Pollock' (1967), Judd 1975
p.195.
11   Judd, 'Questions
to Stella and Judd', interview by Bruce Glaser, ed.
Lucy Lippard, *Artnews*,
vol.65, no.5, September
1966, p.58, order of phrases reversed. Glaser's initial interview occurred in
February 1964 and includ-
ed Dan Flavin; this seg-
ment of Judd's commen-
tary was added by Judd
and Glaser in December
1965.

fig.4 JASPER JOHNS
False Start 1959

Oil on canvas
170.8 × 137.2 (67 ¼ × 54)
Private collection

fig.5 BARNETT NEWMAN
Shining Forth (To George) 1961

Oil on canvas
289.6 × 441.9 (114 × 174)
Musée National d'Art Moderne, Centre Georges
Pompidou, Paris. Gift of the Scaler Foundation, 1978

fig.6 DONALD JUDD
Untitled 1964

Brass and blue lacquer on galvanised iron
103 × 213.4 × 17.2 (40¹/₂ × 84 × 6³/₄)
DSS 55
National Gallery of Canada, Ottawa.
Purchased 1974

neither to support nor to be hung from the bar directly above them. They are simply 'there', without a generalising relationship (of support and dependency) that would transform them into some kind of anthropomorphic anecdote, the projection of feelings not derived directly from the object.[12] At about the same time, Judd argued similarly that Newman's work was 'concomitant with chance and one person's knowledge [based on experience] ... It doesn't claim more than anyone can know ... The color, areas, and stripes are not obscured or diluted by a hierarchy of composition and a range of associations.' According to Judd, Newman's painting never became an organised 'picture'.[13]

A certain history supports this view of Newman's and Pollock's significance, and Johns's too, none of whom was making a 'picture'. At stake for Judd was a problem that had been increasingly acknowledged by critics and theorists throughout the nineteenth and twentieth centuries: to the extent that the material features of a painting were sufficiently prominent to draw attention to themselves, they interfered with illusionistic representation (the 'picture'). Accentuated materiality nevertheless had its advantages: it stimulated sensation (not only the viewer's but also the artist's) and asserted the act or presence of the individual maker. Yet the extreme specificity of an artist's accentuated mark threatened to terminate the process of cultural association, disabling interpretive commentary. Modern works – such as Paul Cézanne's, with their aggressive, repetitive marks and unruly figuration – were characterised as much by material interference as by anything else. They divided appreciative critics between those who would attend to 'painting for itself' (medium and form) and those who would struggle to decipher the eccentric depiction (image and content).[14]

One thing was recognised by all participants to the debate: the intellectual abstractions associated with artistic 'content' or subject matter were cultural constructions linked to massive ideological generalisations. Judd said of Newman that his art 'didn't claim more than anyone [any one person] can know'. It represented personal experience, not a collective intellectual abstraction. To assert individual liberty, an artist could stress working from experience, as Newman presumably did; the results would be inherently opposed to cultural ideologies and their fixed conventions. Within a nineteenth-century context, early modernist artists who wished to resist the given institutional culture shifted from its approved thematic subject matter to concentrate on immediate, sensory aspects of nature, a realm of experience they

12   Judd in Glaser 1966, p.58. Analogously, Judd later recalled that 'in a work placed on the floor, made in 1963, a trough cut in the upward surface is very carefully placed on no particular division at all, which is not so easy'. Judd, 'Symmetry' (1985), *Donald Judd Complete Writings 1975–1986*, Eindhoven 1987, p.94. The earliest

examples of this type are *Untitled* 1963 (no.9), and *Untitled* 1963 (DSS 41, light cadmium red oil on wood). Judd's avoidance of both order and disorder parallels his desire to escape reference to cultural values attached to either traditional craft or modern industrialism ('I wasn't really so interested in being anti anything ...

I wanted to do something of my own'); see Judd in David Batchelor, 'A Small Kind of Order', *Artscribe International*, no.78, November/December 1989, pp.63–4.
13   Judd, 'Barnett Newman' (1964), Judd 1975, p.202.
14   Emile Bernard's early responses to Cézanne outline the

issue: 'He opened to art this amazing door: painting for itself ... The more he works, the more his work removes itself from the external view [and] the more he abstracts the picture'. 'Paul Cézanne', *Les hommes d'aujourd'hui*, vol.8, no.387, February–March 1891, n.p.; 'Paul Cézanne', *L'Occident*, vol.6, July 1904, p.21.

felt able to appropriate as their own. Ultimately, they would concentrate on the studio materials used to render naturalistic effects. Turning inwards in a physical rather than intellectual sense – to focus on paper, canvas, wood, metal, graphite or paint – artists evaded the most obvious ideological clichés. They found individual expression by engaging with ordinary physical matter, yielding themselves to it, abandoning the 'self' formed by cultural templates. The consequent discovery might be something very small, but presumably one's own, real and reliable.[15]

Expressed in works of art, the desired experience of inwardness, individuality and actuality assumed outward, interpretable signs. Attention to the mundane, an awkward or jarring style, rudimentary design, suggestions of naiveté and spontaneity – these were indications during the nineteenth century that the refinements of the traditional culture were being rejected. A new cultural code supplanted the old, at least in certain circles. Once established, this new code came under suspicion as a set of Romantic affectations, moves as calculated and formulaic as any acquired academic mannerism. In 1841, the educator Ludovic Vitet was already warning artists to be wary of 'intentional and systematic naiveté'.[16] It was a misstep analogous to what Judd, in his late twentieth-century context, called mimicking chance. Judd rejected what had become his generation's signs of cultural rejection. Most critics continued to discern features of this sort in Newman's art, for example, an expressive 'tremor of the hand'.[17] Judd challenged the expressionist interpretation with a suitably brute account of the irregularities that seemed to violate Newman's otherwise affectless manner: 'Everything is specifically where it is ... Infrequently [his colour] is thin enough to show brush marks and becomes a little illusionistic [but] that is the way the paint was applied.'[18]

In at least one respect, Judd represents the extreme end of a long modernist tradition. As much as his nineteenth-century predecessors were concerned with individual expression, they also worried that its material means, taken too far, would destroy the intelligible order of representation and the social system it supported. Many believed that they had to choose between one kind of meaning and the other – emotional expression of individual values through form or intellectual expression of social values by way of thematics. Under pressure, even Newman sometimes separated the two realms of experience, using his polished verbal argument to insist that visual art was about immediate feeling: 'I work only out of high passion', he replied

15 'One does not learn naiveté. Naiveté comes from the heart, not the brain.' Champfleury (Jules Fleury), *Histoire de l'imagerie populaire* (1869), Paris 1886, p.xlvi. For details of this line of argument, see Richard Shiff, 'Natural, Personal, Pictorial: Corot and the Painter's Mark', Andreas

Burmester, Christoph Heilmann and Michael F. Zimmermann (eds.), *Barbizon: Malerei der Natur – Natur der Malerei*, Munich 1999, pp.120–38; 'From Primitivist Phylogeny to Formalist Ontogeny: Roger Fry and Children's Drawings', Jonathan Fineberg (ed.), *Discovering Child Art: Essays on Childhood, Primitivism, and Mod-*

ernism, Princeton 1998, pp.59–80; 'Mark, Motif, Materiality: The Cézanne Effect in the Twentieth Century', Felix Bauman, Evelyn Benesch, Walter Feilchenfeldt and Klaus Albrecht Schröder (eds.), *Cézanne: Finished – Unfinished*, Ostfildern-Ruit 2000, pp.99–123.

16 Ludovic Vitet, 'Eustache Lesueur', *Revue*

des deux mondes, sér.27, 1 July 1841, p.58. The Romantic-modernist issue of artificial naiveté had been articulated by Immanuel Kant, *The Critique of Judgment* (1790), trans. James Creed Meredith, Oxford 1952, p.166–7; and Friedrich Schiller, *On the Naive and Sentimental in Literature* (1795–6), trans. Helen

Watanabe-O'Kelley, Manchester 1981.

17 Lawrence Alloway, 'Field Notes: An Interview, interview by Michael Auping, 26 September 1986, Michael Auping (ed.), *Abstract Expressionism: The Critical Developments*, New York 1987, p.135.

18 Judd, 'Barnett Newman' (1964), Judd 1975, p.202.

to the suggestion that his painting was 'excessively logical [and] intellectual'.[19] Like Newman, but much more radically, Judd inverted the usual concerns. He worried that residual elements of representational illusionism, thematic allusion and even (contra Newman) the intent to express emotion, would interfere with the chance sensuous reality, the only reliable reality, of art.[20]

FAST THINKING

Judd regarded Newman, as well as Pollock, Mark Rothko and Clyfford Still, as immediate precedents for his practice.[21] These Americans had struggled to liberate painting from its 'European' compositional hierarchies and illusionism. They succeeded in producing material objects that held specific 'interest' (a central concept for Judd), as opposed to creating 'pictures' that evoked generalised notions drawn from aesthetics and politics.[22] Like them, Judd preferred to leave the surfaces of his materials without superfluous layers of beautification or the enhancements of metaphoric association. 'Sheet aluminum is sheet aluminum', he said, just as in Newman 'the few parts [are] all equally primary'.[23] Judd preferred materials that retained a very specific appearance in their customary use, such as industrial metals, Plexiglas and plywood. The common culture thought differently, as Judd noted caustically, late in his career: 'An imitation wooden surface of plastic is the symbol of the century. All classes love it.'[24]

19   Newman, '"Frontiers of Space", Interview with Dorothy Gees Seckler' (1962), Newman 1990, p.248. Similarly, Newman explained that his allusive titles were intended to evoke the 'emotional content ... the meaning that the painting had when I was painting it'. 'Interview with Emile de Antonio' (1970), Newman 1990, p.305.

20   Judd, 'Jackson Pollock' (1967), Judd 1975, p.195. See my final section, 'Safe from birds'.

21   Judd in Batchelor 1989, p.63.

22   On the constellation of Pollock, Still, Rothko and Newman (especially the latter three), compare Clement Greenberg, '"American-Type" Painting' (1955) and 'After Abstract Expressionism' (1962), Clement Greenberg: The Collected Essays and

Criticism, ed. John O'Brian, I–IV, Chicago 1986–93, III, pp.217–36, IV, pp.121–34. In art reviews from the 1940s on, Greenberg commented on how the modern public's materialistic, positivistic and scientist values corresponded to the increasing desire among artists to found their expression in a self-contained, specific materiality; this would be opposed to an art consciously directed at the representation of generalised cultural themes, social relations, and ideological values. Links between Greenberg's critical analysis and the practices of Judd and other members of the Minimalist generation have been studied from a number of historical and critical perspectives. For my own views and citations to other relevant sources, see Shiff, 'Breath of

Modernism (Metonymic Drift)', Terry Smith (ed.), In Visible Touch: Modernism and Masculinity, Chicago 1997, pp.184–213; 'Autonomy, Actuality, Mangold', Shiff, Robert Storr, Arthur Danto, Nancy Princenthal and Sylvia Plimack Mangold, Robert Mangold, London 2000, pp.7–57. See also Thierry de Duve, 'The Monochrome and the Blank Canvas', Serge Guilbaut (ed.), Reconstructing Modernism: Art in New York, Paris, and Montreal 1945–1964, Cambridge, Massachusetts, 1990, pp.244–310; Thierry de Duve, Clement Greenberg Between the Lines, trans. Brian Holmes, Paris 1996; Yve-Alain Bois, 'The Limit of Almost', William Rubin (ed.), Ad Reinhardt, New York 1991, pp.14–17; Yve-Alain Bois, 'Greenberg's Amend-

ments', Kunst & Museumjournaal, vol.5, no.1, 1993, pp.1–9. In 1991, Judd stated, 'I thought we [he and Greenberg] wanted the same thing.' Interview by James Meyer, quoted in Meyer, Minimalism: Art and Polemics in the Sixties, New Haven 2001, p.140.

'Interest' and 'interesting', as Judd used these terms, imply an intense combination of thought and feeling, the recognition of a value that confirms one's established interest: 'The thing as a whole, its quality as a whole, is what is interesting.' Judd, 'Specific Objects' (1965; written 1964), Judd 1975, p.187. Such a statement is double-edged because the work's qualities and their 'wholeness' both solicit and retain the viewer's interest (a complex of intellectual and

emotional predispositions), while also enhancing that interest in the way that sensation is intensified when stimulated. Ralph Barton Perry, an important philosophical source for Judd, wrote of this commutability factor in interest: 'the object [of aesthetic interest and enjoyment] is so commingled with the feeling [of enjoyment] that the feeling appears as a "tertiary" quality of the object: the delight taken in the object becomes the object's "delightfulness".' Ralph Barton Perry, Realms of Value: A Critique of Human Civilization, Cambridge, Massachusetts, 1954, p.332, emphasis eliminated. Michael Fried's misconstrual or belittling of Judd's sense of 'interest' (commentary appearing first in Fried, 'Shape As Form:

Of Newman and his New York School cohorts, Judd said: 'The first two necessities … were to create a new reality and a new wholeness. The only thing they could claim to be whole was themselves. A person thinking, feeling and perceiving, which occurs all at once, is whole.'[25] A 'wholeness … which occurs all at once': here psychological integration seems to acquire a temporal dimension, an immediacy, that is hard to imagine.[26] As for Newman, if he as a person was whole, then by his own estimation he transferred that wholeness to his art: 'My painting … are not a construction … the wholeness has no parts.'[27] The psychological and temporal whole becomes a material and spatial whole. Both exist. Judd often evoked the same relationship between the quality of his experience (his existence) and the quality of his three dimensional objects. Although constructed, the objects had no 'parts', at least not in the sense of parts of a similar nature being arranged to form a whole.[28] If there were parts, they remained separate and *dissimilar*, despite the sensation of combined wholeness. Just as an individual person is a complex of qualities, such material elements do not become 'parts' in the usual sense because none is subordinate to whatever the whole is. Dissimilarity of the elements preserves the identity of their distinct qualities within a wholeness.

With Judd it seems that dissimilarity became a visual quality in itself: 'The box with the Plexiglas inside is an attempt to make a definite second surface', he stated in 1971; 'the inside is radically different from the outside. While the outside is definite and rigorous, the inside is indefinite.'[29] Judd achieved this type of effect in many formats, including an aluminium floor box, open at the ends, with an interior of violet Plexiglas (*Untitled* 1969; no.17) as well a

Frank Stella's New Paintings', *Artforum*, vol.5, no.3, November 1966, p.27, n.8) led Judd to focus on the concept of interest in interviews (unpublished interview by Margot Willett, 1968, Judd Foundation, Marfa, Texas) and writings ('Complaints: Part I' [1969], Judd 1975, p.198). When Frances Colpitt in 1980, and later James Meyer in 1991, questioned Judd on this issue in connection with their dissertations on Minimalism, the artist referred them to Perry's philosophical discussion of interest: see Ralph Barton Perry, *General Theory of Value: Its Meaning and Basic Principles Construed in Terms of Interest*, London 1926; Perry 1954; Frances Colpitt, *Minimal Art: The Critical Perspective*, Ann Arbor 1990, pp.120–8; Meyer 2001,

pp.140–1. By linking the judgement of moral and psychological 'value' to 'interest', Perry believed he was merely extending established philosophical convention: 'It is held at the present day with something approaching unanimity that value in the generic sense has to do with a certain constant that we may call *bias* or *interest*.' Ralph Barton Perry, 'The Definition of Value', *The Journal of Philosophy, Psychology and Scientific Methods*, vol.11, 12 March 1914, p.149, original emphasis. On Judd's philosophical formation, see also Thomas Kellein, 'The Whole Space', *Donald Judd: Early Work 1955–1968*, exh. cat., Kunsthalle Bielefeld 2002, pp.14–17; Rainer Crone, 'Symmetry and Order: Formal Logic in the

Sculptures of Donald Judd', Rudi Fuchs (ed.), *Donald Judd*, exh. cat., Stedelijk Van Abbemuseum, Eindhoven 1987, pp.61–75. The most comprehensive account of Judd's educational background and its relevance to his later philosophical and political positions has been developed in David Raskin, 'Donald Judd's Skepticism', unpublished dissertation, The University of Texas at Austin 1999. See also Raskin, 'Specific Opposition: Judd's art and politics', *Art History*, vol.24, no.5, November 2001, pp.682–706. On 'interest', see Raskin, 'Judd's Moral Art', in this catalogue.

23 Judd in Batchelor 1989, p.64; 'Barnett Newman' (1964), Judd 1975, p.202. See also Judd, 'Statement' (1968), Judd 1975,

p.196: 'A shape, a volume, a color, a surface is something itself. It shouldn't be concealed as part of a fairly different whole.' For Judd's related views on the colours of materials, see Jochen Poetter (ed.), 'Back to Clarity: Interview with Donald Judd', *Donald Judd*, exh. cat., Staatliche Kunsthalle Baden-Baden 1989, pp.94–5; Angeli Janhsen (ed.), 'Discussion with Donald Judd', *Donald Judd*, exh. cat., Kunstverein St Gallen 1990, p.54.

24 Judd, 'Art and Internationalism: Prolegomena' (1992), *Donald Judd*, exh. cat., Gallery Yamaguchi, Osaka 1992, p.8.

25 Judd, 'Abstract Expressionism' (1983), Judd 1987, pp.41–2.

26 Judd argued that time and space are abstractions or generalities made real only through person's specific actions 'Time and space don't exist; they are made by events and positions.' 'On Russian art and its relation to my work' (1981), Judd 1987, p.17.

27 Newman, supplemental statement (1965) to 'Interview with David Sylvester' (1965–72). Newman 1990, p.254.

28 Judd defined conventional painting in terms of 'the quality of the parts [being] like the quality of the whole'. Judd, 'Jackson Pollock' (1967), Judd 1975, p.195.

29 Judd in John Coplans, 'An Interview with Don Judd', *Artforum*, vol.9, no.10, June 1971, p.50.

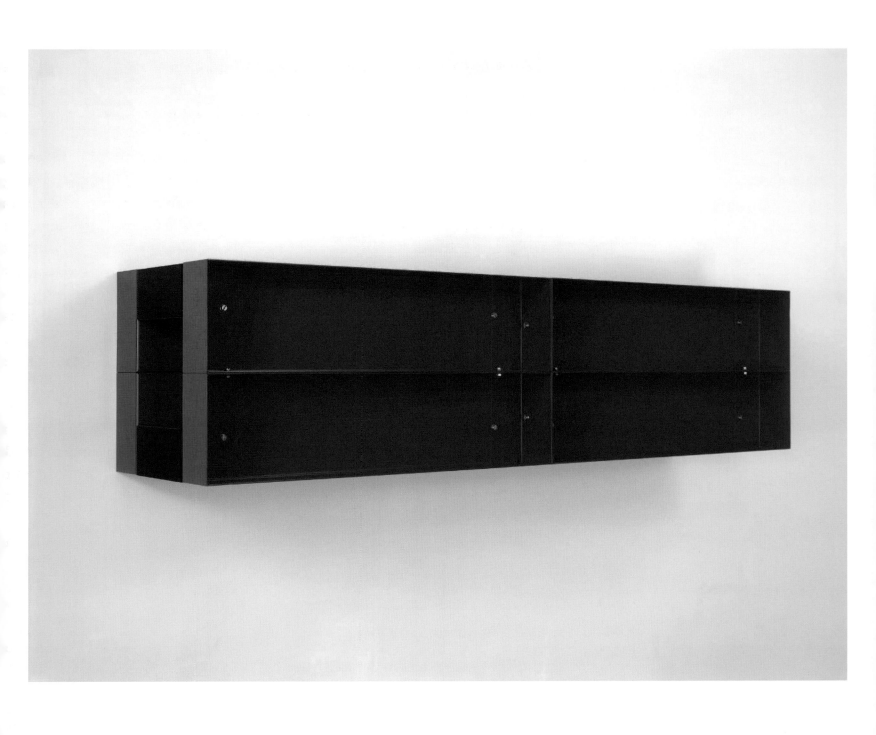

fig.7 DONALD JUDD

Untitled 1989

Red and black enamelled aluminium
30 × 120 × 30 (11 $^{13}/_{16}$ × 47 $^{1}/_{4}$ × 11 $^{13}/_{16}$)
89-48
Courtesy PaceWildenstein, New York

a copper floor box, open at the top, with an aluminium bottom enamelled in red (*Untitled* 1972; no.22). His concern to combine definite and indefinite features or 'qualities' recalls what he had written about Johns's *False Start*, appreciating it for its 'curious polarity' of 'formal' stencilled lettering and 'amorphous' brushstrokes of pure colour. There was 'polarity', Judd wrote, but also 'alliance'.

In a statement prepared not long before his death in 1994, Judd referred to his juxtaposition of red and black panels as a familiar 'two-color monochrome' (see *Untitled* 1989; fig.7). Apparently, the contradiction in terms did not trouble him. 'If there were an identifiable feeling to red or to red and black together they would not be usable to me', he wrote. 'Color is like material. It is one way or another, but it obdurately exists. Its existence as it is is the main fact and not what it might mean, which may be nothing.' The exception, which Judd would avoid, occurred when an 'association is cultural ... light blue and white [as] the colors of peace, of the cops and the United Nations'. For multicoloured works such as *Untitled* 1989–90 (no.37), Judd extended his principle in a way that recalls his recommendation to 'use a simple form that doesn't look like either order or disorder': 'I especially didn't want the combinations to be harmonious ... or to be inharmonious in reaction ... I wanted a multiplicity all at once that I had not known before.'[30] Perhaps we should view Judd's multicoloured floor and wall pieces as if they were multicoloured monochromes. We know at least the negatives: he sought neither formal arrangement, nor anti-formal arrangement, nor any allusion to cultural themes.

Judd's idea of sensory wholeness – polarity in alliance, the two-colour monochrome – parallels a notion he developed with great consistency, particularly in his later writings: the need to integrate thought with feeling. We have already seen the evidence in the way Judd articulated his appreciation of the personal origin of Newman's art ('a person thinking, feeling and perceiving ... all at once'). Judd understood experience as thought and feeling together, linked perhaps by everything that might be called sensation:

> I've always considered the distinction between thought and feeling as, at the least, exaggerated ... Emotion or feeling is simply a quick summation of experience, some of which is thought, necessarily quick so that we can act quickly ... Otherwise we could never get from A to Z, barely to C, since B would have to be always rechecked. It's a short life and a little speed is necessary.[31]

We have to 'act quickly', Judd says. He means relatively quickly, of course, given the number of considerations that must somehow be taken into account with efficiency. To reach a goal, we take chances with our reasoning; we guess, letting thought be guided by feeling. If we do not take chances, we get no further than 'B', which is hardly anywhere. What we cannot prove to be correct, we can *feel* to be correct; and feeling, Judd implies, should be considered a valid cause of action. In fact, feeling is thinking of a certain sort – thinking that passes too fast to be 'thought' or analysis. 'Insight' and 'intuition' are other words for fast thinking: an immediate apprehension of an object or a situation by either the mind or the senses. With such

30   Judd, 'Some Aspects of Color in General and Red and Black in Particular' (1993), *Artforum*, vol.32, no.10, Summer 1994, p.113. Reprinted on pp.144–59 of this catalogue. On the monochromatic effect of dissimilar colours ('not harmonic [but] monochromatic when grouped'), see also Judd, 'Malevich: Independent Form, Color, Surface' (1974), Judd 1975, p.214. Possibly, a 'two-color monochrome' of contrasting hues would depend on an equivalence of saturation value. Judd explains the effect in Malevich as applying hues that are 'full color, simple, primary'. Later he expanded his categories: 'Every easily known color paired with either black or white forms [a two-color] monochrome: orange, yellow, blue, green ... The contrasting pairs are just as well known: red and blue, red and green [and so forth]. All colors of the same value ... make pairs. All values of the same color make pairs. Full [saturated] colors pair.' Furthermore, a 'sharp and acid color' can pair with 'one white and full'. And the listing continues. Judd 1994, p.113.

31   Judd, 'Art and Architecture' (1983), Judd 1987, p.30.

immediacy, the distinction between mind and sense, thought and feeling breaks down. Judd merely asks us to accept this fact and profit from what it allows – 'a little speed'.

Is quickness consistent with the fundamentals of Judd's practice? We might not think so, given the delay between the designing, sketching, looking, thinking, pondering ... and the eventual execution of a work by fabricators. (After 1964, Judd no longer crafted works himself but employed artisans and manufacturers with highly specialised skills and knowledge.) A piece was not complete until Judd had seen it, experienced it, thought-felt it in its material specificity after fabrication: 'Even if you can plan the thing completely ahead of time, you still don't know what it looks like until it's right there ... One thing I want is to be able to see what I've done ... Art is something you look at.'[32] Judd's waiting to see might have been slow, but quickness can be a psychological phenomenon, a certain feeling that accompanies a certain thought, perhaps occurring both before and after the relatively slow fabrication of a work.

Charles Sanders Peirce, the great American pragmatist – as such, one of the heads of Judd's intellectual lineage – stressed the factor of speed in thinking.[33] If a scientist were to use a system to test all possible hypotheses concerning a single problem, Peirce argued, he would be unlikely to reach a solution during 'the whole time that has elapsed since the earth was solidified'.[34] The choice of a hypothesis that actually proves true, winning the bet with chance, faces infinitely unfavourable odds. Yet, to a statistician's amazement, our choices, our guesses, are sometimes correct – 'wrong oftener than right, yet the relative frequency with which [we are] right is on the whole the most wonderful thing in our constitution'.[35] If we can guess or intuit the correct hypothesis rather than working through the entire system, we radically increase our speed of intellectual production.

'Everything which happens is infinitely improbable.'[36] This is one of Peirce's characteristically odd statements and rather Judd-like. Its validity lies in the realisation that 'everything which happens' has an infinite number of opportunities to happen otherwise – in principle, not to happen at all. Perhaps this is why a species of bird that one has not previously encountered is interesting. Even though it may share features with other species, we wonder why it looks and acts *this* way and not some other way. Something of the sort may be what Judd was thinking when he wrote, 'Things that exist exist, and everything is on their side ... Everything is equal, just existing, and the values and interests they have are only adventitious.'[37] By existing, the things that exist, like brushstrokes by Pollock, Newman or Johns, have already beaten the odds. The pictorial references of traditional art add potentially distracting, general values to a specific object brought into existence by an artist. Existence in its specificity is sufficient to develop a personal interest on the part of the viewer, especially when the qualities of the object escape familiar categories, making *this* existence informative and 'interesting'.

Works of art enter the world as hypotheses, attempts at meaningful integrations of thought and feeling. Thought without feeling would not have the force of hypothesis, which is a premature or guessed conclusion. In many of his writings, Peirce called hypothetical guesswork by a technical term, 'abduction', which, like an aesthetic judgement, feels correct but cannot

32   Judd in Glaser 1966, pp.60–1.

33   On the details of Judd's education and the origins of his empiricism and pragmatism, see Raskin 1999; Kellein 2002. Judd quoted a passage from Peirce at the conclusion of his 'A long discussion not about masterpieces but why there are so few of them, Part II' (1984), Judd 1987, pp.85–6.

34   Charles Sanders Peirce, 'Lectures on Pragmatism' (1903), *Collected Papers of Charles Sanders Peirce*, ed. Charles Hartshorne and Paul Weiss, I–VI, Cambridge, Massachusetts, 1960, V, p.106.

35   Peirce 1960, 'Lectures on Pragmatism' (1903), V, pp.106–7.

36   Peirce, 'Illustrations of the Logic of Science: Deduction, Induction, and Hypothesis', *Popular Science Monthly*, vol.13, May–October 1878, p.481.

37   Judd, 'Black, White, and Gray' (1964), Judd 1975, p.117.

be proven: 'No reason whatsoever can be given for it, and it needs no reason, since it merely offers suggestions.'[38] As both critic and artist, Judd operated within this realm of suggestiveness that also entailed a certainty: 'It's not possible to prove a proposition about the world [as opposed to a proposition concerning logic]. One can only assert, point and list characteristics. The proof of a high level of [artistic] resolution, of high quality, falls into this familiar quandary.'[39]

A work by Judd is an hypothesis materialised, an aesthetic proposition. Peirce described the act of hypothetical inference not only as thought but as emotion – 'a single feeling of greater intensity ... belonging to the act of thinking the hypothetic conclusion ... Hypothesis produces the *sensuous* element of thought.'[40] Concerning the feeling of a thought, its bare sensation, another passage from Peirce is illuminating, his definition of the category of experience he called both 'Firstness' and 'Originality': 'something which is what it is without reference to anything else within it or without it, regardless of all force and of all reason'.[41]

For Judd, then, looking could be a form of feeling, a sensory and emotional experience, neither preliminary to nor dependent on thinking, but itself a fast or accelerated thinking. When asked in 1990 whether his viewer should 'understand something' or 'just look', Judd replied:

> That's the division between thought and feeling. You have to do it [think and feel] all at once. You have to look and understand, both. In looking you understand; it's more than you can describe. You look and think, and look and think, until it makes sense, becomes interesting.[42]

ILLUSION

When Judd said, 'Things that exist exist and everything is on their side', he was taking the side of sensory specifics as opposed to conceptual generalities. He was looking at things, feeling something, thinking ('in looking you understand'). Critics, however, often think first, before feeling. They think in order to understand how to look. Thinking by way of their medium of written language, they drift into disembodied reference: words suggest other words; allusive metaphors and metonymies are tempting; ideas expand; the concrete specifics become conceptual abstractions and cultural clichés. Consider what has happened to the issue of illusion and illusionism in relation to Judd's art.

Judd's interpreters have often argued that the complex optical qualities of his three-dimensional works contradict his indictment of illusionism in painting. Rosalind Krauss initiated this line of commentary in 1966 when she noted, astutely, how deceptive the experience of an object by Judd was likely to be. Frontal and perspectival views of one and the same work did not readily predict each other and were difficult to relate logically. (Think, for example, of Judd's progressions [no.16, fig.26] and later, his works in bent aluminium [nos.27–9, 31] where what appears to be a solid bar-like construction proves to be a hollow tube.) Krauss concluded that Judd's art was 'play[ing] off the illusory quality of the thing itself as it presents

38   Peirce 1960, 'Lectures on Pragmatism' (1903), V, p.106. In summation Peirce wrote: 'Deduction proves that something *must* be; Induction shows that something *actually is* operative; Abduction merely suggests that something *may be*', original emphasis.

39   Judd, 'Abstract Expressionism' (1983), Judd 1987, pp.39–40. Compare Judd, 'Statement which appeared in "ABC Art" by Barbara Rose' (1965), Judd 1975, p.181: 'It is silly to have opinions about many things that you're supposed to have opinions on. About others, where it [having an opinion] seems necessary, that necessity and the opinion are mostly guess.' Also Greenberg, 'The Bennington College Seminars' (1971), *Homemade Esthetics: Observations on Art and Taste*, New York 1999, p.99: 'You "intuit" quality. But you can't analyze it.'

40   Peirce 1878, pp.481–2 (original emphasis).

41   Peirce 1960, 'Partial Synopsis of a Proposed Work in Logic: Originality, Obsistence, and Transuasion' (1902–3), II, p.46.

42   Judd in Janhsen 1990, p.54.

itself to vision alone.'[43] As a kind of deception, this effect of 'illusion' might be linked to everything from the craft of *trompe-l'oeil* to the fundamental 'illusionism' of the Western painting tradition, threatened by modernist materiality. Illusionism is the effect of a certain cultural conditioning, determining that we see any rectangular surface through the space and perspective of a window view, and any two juxtaposed colours as situated on different representational planes.[44] Such ubiquitous 'illusionism', associated with representational depiction and orderly composition, became problematic for Judd and others of his generation: 'Two colors on the same surface almost always lie on different depths ... Except for a complete and unvaried field of color or marks, anything spaced in a rectangle or on a plane suggests something in its surround, which suggests an object or figure in its space, in which these are clearer instances of a similar world – that's the main purpose of painting.'[45] In the context of his discussion of Newman, Judd offered a variant formulation: 'Ordinary abstract painting and expressionistic painting ... [have] a residual naturalism ... They are still pictures.'[46] And 'pictures' are illusionistic.

Over the years, as Judd's constructions evolved and viewers became conscious of an increasing complexity of perspectival and colouristic effects, critics noted an apparent split between Judd the artist and Judd the critic-theorist-polemicist. The terms 'illusion' and 'illusionism' were used loosely in this discussion, sometimes with the acknowledgement, but often not, that they invoke two distinct categories of phenomena: illusion as a natural condition of vision, a physiological fact; illusionism as a constructed effect for the pictorially indoctrinated.[47] Because the words overlap, suggesting similarity where it may not exist, it becomes difficult to keep the referential fields apart.[48] The problem was initially present in Yve-Alain Bois's commentary of 1991, but he quickly corrected it: 'I detected a contradiction between Judd's anti-compositional position ... and the voluptuous luxuriance of his materials ... I saw it as a lapse into the very illusionism that Judd, to his credit, had always strongly opposed.' The correction – or rather adjustment, for Bois was merely recounting a series of his impressions – came in a note to the text: 'From the 1970s on, in his many interviews, Judd was at pains to distinguish between the spatial illusionism proper to painting ... and all other forms of illusion.'[49]

Judd did take pains, going so far as to point out that, among all the subjective psychological experiences people have, optical illusions (such as chromatic afterimages) are 'absolutely

43   Rosalind Krauss, 'Allusion and Illusion in Donald Judd', *Artforum*, vol.4, no.9, May 1966, p.26.

44   With conventional sculpture, a similar illusionism results from the fact that any three-dimensional object set on a base evokes a figure in space.

45   Judd, 'Specific Objects' (1965), Judd 1975, p.182.

46   Judd, 'Barnett Newman' (1964), Judd 1975, p.202.

47   Judd himself does not appear to confuse these two terms; see his repeated references to illusionism in 'Specific Objects' (1965), Judd 1975, pp.181–9.

48   Note Judd's response to comparing a Newman painting to a Byzantine Madonna set

against a solid gold field: 'A lot of things look alike, but they're not necessarily very much alike.' Glaser 1966, p.61.

49   Yve-Alain Bois, 'The Inflection', *Donald Judd: New Sculpture*, exh. cat., The Pace Gallery, New York, and Galerie Lelong, Paris 1991, n.p. For other references to the contradiction of Judd's 'illusionism', see Prudence

Carlson, 'Donald Judd's Equivocal Objects', *Art in America*, vol.72, no.1, January 1984, p.117; William C. Agee, 'Donald Judd and the Endless Possibilities of Color', Dietmar Elger (ed.), *Donald Judd: Colorist*, exh. cat., Sprengel Museum, Hanover 2000, p.44; Martin Engler, 'Specific Objects – The Illusion of Factuality', Elger 2000,

pp.58, 73. William Agee's observation that Judd 'seemed uncharacteristically quiet or even perplexed' by the problem of lighting conditions and reflections is especially provocative; see Agee, 'Donald Judd in Retrospect: An Appreciation', *Donald Judd: Sculpture*, exh. cat., PaceWildenstein, New York 1994, pp.13–14.

objective'.[50] Everyone sees optical illusions in the same situations, under the same conditions. Such illusions are not only objective but real – real illusions.[51] They have little to do with illusionism. What Judd said of the modern artist's emphasis on colour – that it produced 'an immediate sensation, a phenomenon', that it 'destroyed the earlier representational painting' – applied also to optical illusion. The 'illusions' of illusionism, to the contrary, were effects neither physiologically nor phenomenologically inherent in the direct apprehension of an object. Illusion is the way things are. Illusionism is the way things are not.

Judd's critical reviews indicate that he regarded optical illusion as one of a number of features proper to painting, as much a perceived quality of the medium as colour and shape. Illusion factored into his appreciation of the early Frank Stella, whose work he considered the only true rival of Pollock's 'drip' paintings with respect to escaping pictorial reference and illusionism; even Newman did not quite make the cut.[52] Here is Judd's concise yet detailed description of Stella's U-shaped canvas *Lake City* 1960–1 (see the version of 1963–4; fig.8), which I supplement for emphasis:

> The geometric field initially appears rigid, objective and somewhat oppressive. The successive angles at the two turns align into diagonals. That, the greater distance between the lines [along the diagonal, as they turn] and the paint reflecting differently [from one side of the right-angle turn to the other] cause the surface surrounding the angles to borrow the diagonal direction. The sensation is optical and definite. [This is what we would call, in another context, an optical illusion.] The [illusory] diagonals are free and electric in a static field. The [painting is] both objective, like geometric work, and truculently subjective, unlike that.[53]

'Optical' (that is, illusory) and 'definite'; 'electric' (that is, moving) and 'static'; 'subjective' and 'objective': these improbable pairings depend largely on the play of light against the grain of Stella's paint. At the angles, light produces a difference in perceived colour while the physical layer of pigment remains uninflected; the viewer perceives a diagonal where Stella never drew one. These illusory but real and inescapable effects join other material qualities to secure for Stella's art 'the absence of illusionistic space'.[54] There is so much to see precisely as it is that nothing drifts off into illusionism. Interviewed along with Judd in 1964, Stella said that

---

50 Judd 1994, p.77.

51 In 1975, Agee, responding to 'a striking illusion of receding shapes' in Judd's large floor pieces, made the correct distinction: 'the illusionism is real – a physical consequence of the structure of the work, not depicted or suggested as in painting'. Agee, 'Unit, Series, Site: A Judd Lexicon', *Art in America*, vol.63,

no.3, May–June 1975, p.46. Another example of 'real' illusion would be the dramatic and somewhat confusing effects of shadow cast at various times of the day on Judd's outdoor concrete works at Marfa. William James and other philosophers with whom Judd was familiar distinguished clearly between 'physiological' illusion and 'psychological'

effects dependent on acquired experience, which would include illusionism. See William James, *The Principles of Psychology*, Cambridge, Massachusetts, 1981, p.876. Newman, too, knew the difference: '[An edge] might have been an illusion, but [Cézanne] insisted on painting this illusion [as] the reality of sensation.' Newman,

'Review of *Abstract Painting: Background and American Phase* by Thomas B. Hess' (1951), Newman 1990, p.122.

52 Judd, 'Jackson Pollock' (1967), Judd 1975, p.195.

53 Judd, 'In the Galleries: Frank Stella' (1962), Judd 1975, p.58, paragraphing suppressed.

54 Ibid. p.57.

fig.8   FRANK STELLA

Lake City (second version) 1963–4

Copper paint on canvas
210 × 280 (82 ⁵/₈ × 110 ¹/₄)
Museum Kunst Palast, Düsseldorf
Lake City (first version) 1960–1 was destroyed
in the early 1960s

his painting was 'based on the fact that only what can be seen there *is* there ... What you se
is what you see.'[55] For Judd, illusion was an accepted feature of 'what you see'.[56]

When Judd prepared sketches and instructions for fabricators, he was careful to specify whethe
an application of paint should be glossy or matt; from the 1960s on, he used both kinds o
paint finish just as he used both shiny and matt metals.[57] Reflectiveness, along with all th
illusions and complex chromatic effects it might generate, was a fundamental consideratio
and could be either featured or suppressed. A work might revel in it, such as certain types o
floor boxes Judd created during the 1970s and 1980s (for example, *Untitled* 1989, no.33). Fror
within the polished brass or aluminium sides of these open boxes, an atmosphere of blue, rec
orange or amber light emanates. The colour itself belongs to the surface of an interior base
a transversal panel, or both, which may be of either Plexiglas or painted metal. The immate
rial, vaporous effect results from a complicated play of reflection. This is an optical effect c
the same general type that Judd appreciated in Stella – an illusion, which, because it make
no apparent reference to things outside itself, is not illusionistic.[58]

Judd's floor and wall boxes (in both vertical and horizontal arrangements) exploit many othe
optical effects we might be tempted to call illusions: forms seen in various kinds of perspe
tive, partly obscured, multiple in their wholeness, presenting visual contradictions. Consic
er the six wall-box units of *Untitled* 1991 (fig.9), spaced in two tiers. Eye level, always a prim
consideration for Judd, lies between them, with the upper edge of the lower units set a
approximately 150 cm (59 in) above the floor. This forces us to view the group looking into th
lower boxes from above and into the upper boxes from below.[59] Further differentiation with
in the whole results from Judd's having varied the internal panels: some elements are wide
some narrow, some vertical and some horizontal, causing each square box to look as if it wer
skewed towards a uniquely proportioned rectangular form. Such intriguing, but disconcer
ing instances of visual illusion are so conspicuously at the centre of our experience of Judd'
work that we are induced to judge them 'real'. Or at least to regard them, as he did, as th
real alternative to the illusionism of the Western tradition.

Judd intended his boxes to appear as neither low nor high relief in relation to the wall o
floor as their ground plane. Even high relief, he believed, amounted to a kind of flattened pi
torialism – the three-dimensional object behaved like a picture, its real dimensions lost to a

55 Stella in Glaser 1966, pp.58–9, original emphasis.

56 Accordingly, Judd tended to treat Op artists of the 1960s favourably, describing illusory features such as afterimages; see 'In the Galleries: Tadasky' (1965), Judd 1975, pp.162–3.

57 See Judd's notations to his 1965 drawings, illustrated in Walter Hopps (ed.), *United States of America: VIII Sao Paulo Biennial*, exh. cat., Pasadena Art Museum 1965, p.31.

58 Of course, like 'interest', references can be *brought* to a work by its audience. Although illusory effects of light and colour were for Judd non-referential, the suggestion of weight was a different matter: 'I wanted to avoid any sensation of weight. This goes back to the business of representation. I think that most of the European tradition of art represented weight,' Judd in Batchelor 1989, p.64.

59 Because many of Judd's works have so much more width than height (see *Untitled* 1985; no.29) – or, as with the stacks, so much more height than width (see *Untitled* 1968; no.15) – they appear panoramic relative to normal viewing distance, when one stands close enough to perceive surface quality and details of construction. I assume that Judd intended his works to be perceived from near enough not to cancel out such an effect; he commented favourab on the Abstract Expressionists' similar concern '[They] wanted their pair ings to be seen at the usual distance, not fifty feet [15 m] back reducing them to pictures.' 'Abstract Expressionism (1983), Judd 1987, p.47. Compare Newman's sta ment of 1951 in Newman 1990, p.178.

44

fig.9 DONALD JUDD

Untitled 1991

Douglas Fir plywood with red and blue Plexiglas
6 units, each 100 × 100 × 50 (39 ³/₈ × 39 ³/₈ × 19 ¹¹/₁₆)
91-1
Collection Dia Art Foundation, New York

illusionistic effect.[60] The space of Judd's boxes is their own, not some pictorial space that appears more extensive or deeper, yet also flatter, than the actual space of the art. We see Judd's boxes at their true size, neither larger nor smaller than they are, regardless of the viewing position, even though the size of the installation room may affect the number of units displayed. The actual spacing of the units is a factor of their dimensions; for example, the spaces between units in *Untitled* 1991, measure 50 cm (19 $^{11}/_{16}$ in), equal to the depth of each of the units and half their height and width.

'Don thought of scale as fundamentally inherent in an object', the sculptor David Rabinowitch recalled, '[but] I saw it as a function of conditions of observation.'[61] Most people would agree with Rabinowitch. 'Inherent scale' is one of those strange Juddisms, one of his counter-intuitive intuitions. Sometimes it benefits us to suspend what seems like the sophisticated notion – 'a function of conditions of observation' – in order to test out, hypothetically, what seems like the naive one – 'inherent scale', or things as they are. Judd provided a retrospective explanation of his insight in his final essay, albeit cryptically. With regard to the degree of projection from the wall, he stated that this dimension should be 'at least as much as [the object's] height and width'. The principle Judd actually applied in practice was looser: the object's projection should be at least as much as its height *or* its width (not both, although he did create some cubic units). Eventually Judd realised that even this requirement could be

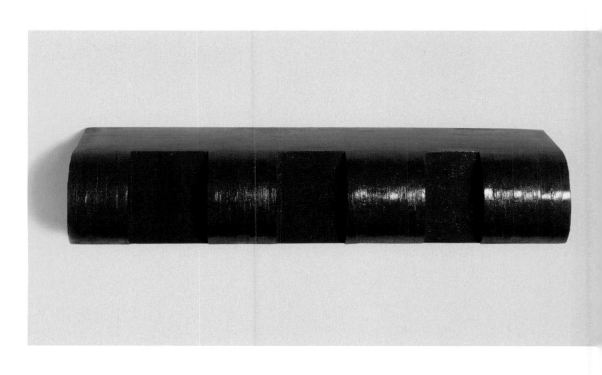

fig.10 DONALD JUDD

     Untitled 1964

Red lacquer on wood
12.2 × 64.8 × 21.3
(4 $^{13}/_{16}$ × 25 $^{1}/_{2}$ × 8 $^{3}/_{8}$)
DSS 45
Courtesy PaceWildenstein,
New York

60   In connection with work in relief, Judd mentions three artists whom he had praised repeatedly as exceptions during his years as an art critic – Claes Oldenburg, Lee Bontecou and John Chamberlain; Judd 1994, p.75. Bontecou recently recalled a telling incident: 'A client wanted to buy [a wall relief], but he wanted it flat against the wall, so Leo [Castelli] suggested I take the [projecting] box part off ... and I realized, They don't get it – they think it's a decoration.' Lee Bontecou, quoted in Calvin Tomkins, 'Missing in Action', *The New Yorker*, 4 August 2003, p.40.

61   David Rabinowitch, statement in *Artforum*, vol.32, no.10, Summer 1994, p.117.

reduced. As long as an object's cantilever from the wall (or rise from the floor) appeared abrupt, with no transition or other concession to the architectural support, space and scale would be the object's own; 'the work [would] not be flattened, low or high, to the wall, whether it be small or large'. The first work to materialise this insight was *Untitled* 1964 (fig.10), which should probably also be regarded as the first of Judd's progressions. It was 'made of left-over plywood semi-circles, and it projected further than its height'. Judd took pride in his scheme for securing or stabilising 'inherent scale' and believed it continued to escape his superficial imitators: 'This invention [of 1964] is still not understood [thirty years later], or rather it is completely lost. Derivations are everywhere, but are always low or high relief, new in appearance only.'[62]

Given Judd's hypothetical conclusion concerning the degree of projection from the wall, I think at least two other factors contribute to the distinctive 'look' of his work. First, as I have already indicated, is the viewing angle dictated by his instructions for hanging. Judd set the height of most of his horizontally oriented wall pieces so that the top edge would be approximately 150 to 160 cm (59 to 63 in) above the floor (also the height of many large floor boxes).[63] This means that the typical viewer looks slightly over the top and perceives the depth both frontally (glimpsing the top) and laterally (glimpsing the sides), with the result that the formal structure seems to regulate and reveal itself, even though elements (sometimes unexpected ones) remain wholly or partly hidden from any particular position. Viewing the work entails moments of surprise (pragmatic, empirical experience) but no mystery (allusion to experience outside real time and space). In certain other works, such as the late series of plywood wall boxes containing cylindrical plywood tubes, the hanging height is set at 174.6 cm (68 $^3/_4$ in) (see *Untitled* 1993; fig.11). This positioning results in the most natural view being directed entirely within the box, all *interior* planes being revealed, including the inside top. Again, the effect is to render the appearance of the form intensely specific, as if its orthogonals could belong to no grid but its own, terminating at the back panel. Judd often layered that panel with transparent, coloured Plexiglas, introducing another specific quality, which is related to the wood only by the chance circumstance of its situation, its mere existence (see *Untitled* 1993, no.41, as a straightforward example of this effect).

The second of the two additional factors in manifesting 'inherent scale' is internal proportions. Note Judd's wording as he addresses this issue:

> My idea of proportion is simpler than [something like the Golden Section], although it's rather complicated to explain. My first work was developed by looking. Then I figured out that many things [that I constructed] were very close to even proportions [such as 1:2]. And slowly I made the proportions even. I think what you see [in the ordinary experience of looking] are just the simple ones, 1:2 and 2:3 and 3:4.[64]

What Judd has described is the process of hypothetical inference, or thinking-feeling, that is, fast thinking. After a period of 'looking', he realises he has been approaching a hypothetical rule, the use of a 1:2 ratio. He decides to use that ratio without ever having proven systemat-

62   Judd 1994, pp.75–6. Despite the existence of certain cubic units (such as the six that constitute the wall piece *Untitled* 1968, DSS 130, Milwaukee Art Center), Judd stated that he 'never made this minimum [degree of projection from the wall], which would be a cube'. He may have meant that he never made a single-unit cubic work. For a more extensive account of Judd's conception of space in three-dimensional work and why his 'invention' was 'new', see Richard Shiff, 'A Space of One to One', *Donald Judd: 50 x 100 x 50, 100 x 100 x 50*, exh. cat., PaceWildenstein, New York 2002, pp.5–23. On the importance of projection, see also Lynne Cooke, 'Donald Judd: Re-ordering Order', *Donald Judd*, exh. cat., Waddington Galleries, London 1989, p.10, n.28.

63   In 1971, Judd stated that 'the viewer is meant to see a little of the tops of the boxes, but the ceiling height doesn't matter. They should be hung at either 62 or 63 inches [158 or 160 cm]. The choice of the height is meant to avoid flattening the boxes when they are on the wall.' Coplans 1971, p.49.

64   Judd in Katharina Winnekes, 'Interview mit Donald Judd', *Kunst und Kirche*, April 1993, p.135. On the ratio 1:2, see also Judd, 'Art and Architecture' (1983), 'Abstract Expressionism' (1983), Judd 1987, pp.33–4, 47.

ically that it generates the best results. 'No reason whatsoever can be given for it', as Peirc[e] said of hypothesis; it simply looks right.[65] '1 to 2 is ... as much its own quality', Judd wrote i[n] 1983, 'as red, or red and black', a two-colour monochrome.[66] Judd's simple ratios, such as 1:[2] and 1:2:4, dominate his late works. A quality of proportion, not a supporting wall, stabilise[s] complex objects such as *Untitled* 1986 (no.30), with its thirty units, each 100 cm (39 $^3/_8$ in) squar[e] and 50 cm (19 $^{11}/_{16}$ in) deep. Was Judd fetishising machine-tooled accuracy with his 'even' me[t]ric numbers? Not at all.[67] Precision of measurement was merely a pragmatic convenience fo[r] the fabrication process. Like a Peircean law (a specific hypothesis generalised), Judd's regu[larity was not strict but flexible: 'Try to verify any law of nature and you will find that th[e] more precise your observations, the more certain they will be to show irregular departur[es] from the law.'[68] Yet the flexibility, like the order, had its limits. Judd needed to avoid any trul[y] complicated or nuanced set of proportions that would approach the compositional rhythm[s,] hierarchies and subordination of parts he associated with 'European' art. 'One or four boxe[s] in a row' – or six, as in *Untitled* 1992 (no.40), which uses the 1:2 ratio – 'is local order, just a[n] arrangement, barely order at all'.[69] Why this order and not that? The reason, if we can call [it] such, was not law, but chance. 'We cannot in any way reach perfect certitude nor exactitud[e] [on matters of fact]', Peirce wrote, 'nor can we with any probability ascertain the exact valu[e] of any measure or general ratio.'[70] Judd made the determinations he could, nothing mor[e.] 'An artist works only step by step into the unknown while ... the particulars of the world ar[e] infinite.'[71]

'POWER LIES IN A POLARIZATION'

If many of Judd's pronouncements challenge common understanding, so do Peirce's. I have bee[n] quoting Peirce here and there because he reminds me of Judd: a pithy, penetrating thinke[r] who often referred to intuition and the way that situations, things and even thoughts fee[l;] who also, somewhat paradoxically, inclined towards exhaustive observational detail. A fin[al] reference to Peirce's discussion of hypothesis and abduction (guesswork that tends to prov[e] correct) enforces Judd's notion of polarisation, which guided his thoughts about Johns ('pola[r]ity and alliance') and perhaps almost everything else. Peirce wrote that 'hypothesis infers fro[m]

65 Peirce 1960, 'Lectures on Pragmatism', v, p.106.

66 Judd, 'Art and Architecture' (1983), Judd 1987, p.34.

67 Compare Judd in Batchelor 1989, p.64.

68 Peirce 1960, 'The Doctrine of Necessity Examined' (1892), vi, pp.36–7. The actual dimensions or placement of an element of a work by Judd might be

slightly at variance with what the official dimensions imply. For example, in order to create a space for a bracket in box units intended to be hung on a wall, Judd typically projected the back plane of the rectilinear prism forward. This enables an unusually snug fit to the wall, but also entails that the interior dimensions of the box fail to match the

exterior dimensions, and that the positioning of modular units set within the box may lack absolute symmetry. This type of irregularity seems to escape ordinary visual inspection, yet an idealist (not Judd) would be concerned that the variation could be measured, even if otherwise undetectable. For Judd, only what a viewer was likely to

notice mattered. Accordingly, with his vertical stacks he took advantage of a hidden economy of incompletion: in cases where the back planes of the units were not exposed to sight, he simply eliminated them (for example, in stacks made entirely of opaque materials, lacking any transparent Plexiglas). Judd

designed his structures as to look a certain way from the positions from which they could be seen not for the sake of some inviolable geometric completeness.

69 Judd, 'Statement' (1968), Judd 1975, p.196.

70 Peirce 1960, 'Fallibilism, Continuity, and Evolution' (c.1897), I, p.6[?]

71 Judd 1994, p.76.

fig.11 DONALD JUDD

Untitled 1993

Douglas Fir plywood with transparent yellow Plexiglas
100 × 100 × 50 (39 $^3/_8$ × 39 $^3/_8$ × 19 $^{11}/_{16}$)
93-4
Courtesy PaceWildenstein, New York

49

facts of one kind to facts of another'; he defined hypothesis as the logic of chance that links dissimilarities rather than deriving 'similar facts' from given ones.[72] Hypothesis operates outside established orders of association.

For his part, Judd argued that the pictorial illusionism he sought to escape had been engineered to extend familiar domains of similarity.[73] His claim to inventiveness rested on his having created paradigms for works that would define space and time in a new way, without becoming part of a synthetic environment of metaphor and anthropomorphism: 'I developed space as a main aspect of art.'[74] He said 'a main aspect', not 'the main aspect'. Instead of becoming a field encompassing all things, rendering each thing like all others in occupying a position within the space, Judd's space was a distinct quality to be sensed along with shape, colour, light and simple proportions such as 1:2. His space was a primary among equals. It became an active element rather than a passive container, no longer the homogenising background of a 'picture'.[75]

In March 1960, within the same set of reviews that included his reference to Johns's 'polarity and alliance', Judd presented his central intuition in relation to Pollock:

> Marks and bare canvas are equally positive, almost in competition for frontality ... Pollock achieves generality by establishing an extreme polarity between the simple, immediate perception of paint and canvas, a reduction to unexpandable sensation [like Johns's 'amorphous' brushwork], and the complexity and overtones of his imagery and articulated structure [like Johns's stencilling]. Such diverse elements combined under tension produce a totality much greater and unlike any of the parts.[76]

In 1967, Judd made analogous observations in an essay devoted to Pollock exclusively: 'The elements and aspects of Pollock's paintings are polarized rather than amalgamated ... Everything is fairly independent and specific.'[77] He restated the idea in two essays of 1983, and yet again at a symposium in 1992.[78] So 'polarisation' was a value of long standing, announced as early as 1960 and repeated thereafter. Judd clearly identified with Pollock's art as much as with Newman's; as I have already noted, he ranked Pollock's achievement somewhat higher, at least in his assessment of 1967, an opinion he 'hate[d] to admit'.[79]

72   Peirce 1878, p.481.

73   Judd, 'Specific Objects' (1965), Judd 1975, p.182.

74   Judd 1994, p.72.

75   This is one of many points at which Judd's thinking converges upon Greenberg's: 'Space is there to be shaped, divided, enclosed, but not to be filled ... [A work] is not so much sculptured as constructed, built, assembled, arranged.' Greenberg, 'The New Sculpture' (revised version, 1958), Art and Culture, Boston 1961, p.142. Compare above, note 22.

76   Judd, 'In the Galleries: Helen Frankenthaler' (1960), Judd 1975, p.13. Judd's 1960 statement on Pollock formed part of his response to the structure of Frankenthaler's painting, which suffered from 'a certain progression into disappearance' (ibid., p.14), that is, a compositional hierarchy. Roberta Smith ('Donald Judd', in Brydon Smith [ed.], Donald Judd, exh. cat., National Gallery of Canada, Ottawa 1975, p.13) recognised the significance of this early review by Judd; it was independently brought to my attention by Alexander Dumbadze.

77   Judd, 'Jackson Pollock' (1967), Judd 1975, p.195.

78   Judd, 'Art and Architecture' (1983), 'Abstract Expressionism' (1983), Judd 1987, pp.34–5, 45; contribution to Barnett Newman symposium, Harvard University, 14 May 1992, audiotape, Harvard University Art Museums, Cambridge, Massachusetts. See also Judd, 'Chamberlain: Another View' (1963), Judd 1975 p.108.

79   Judd, 'Jackson Pollock' (1967), Judd 1975, p.195.

fig.12 JACKSON POLLOCK
Echo: Number 25 1951

Enamel on unprimed canvas
233.4 × 218.4 (91⁷/₈ × 86)
The Museum of Modern Art, New York.
Acquired through the Lillie P. Bequest and
the Mr and Mrs David Rockefeller Fund

Linked together, Judd's various references to polarity in Pollock, from 1960 to 1992, clarify what the term might have meant to him. He spoke of two primary factors: the sensation of 'dripped paint' (Pollock's materiality) and the sensation of the whole composition. In Pollock, these features were 'further apart in quality than is usual'.[80] (Here, as most often with Judd, 'quality' refers to character, not value or level of attainment; but the one can entail the other.) This internal difference led Judd to realise that the whole of a Pollock could never be inferred from a fragment – an interesting notion in the light of Peirce, who defined 'hypothesis' in just this manner, because its elements were dissimilar and its conclusion might appear to have arrived from nowhere. Hypothetical reasoning never moves from like to like. Indeed, Judd countered the common opinion that any one part of Pollock's 'all-over' surface would predict the general character of any other part ('a fragment [has little] of the quality of the whole').[81] To the contrary, each of Pollock's marks retained its distinctness while the artist developed an 'extension of extremes'. 'Most paintings by other artists', Judd argued, 'seem harmonious in comparison', having a 'moderated a priori generality', a lot of like things gathered together. Hence his conclusion: 'The level of quality of a work can usually be established by the extent of the polarity between its generality [the whole composition] and its particularity [in Pollock's case, the material marks].' Reaching still further, Judd stated: 'The greater the polarity of the elements in a work, the greater the work's comprehension of space, time and existence.'[82] With an art of polarity, not only the space but the very 'existence' of the work would become large, commodious, powerful.

Judd's primary examples from Pollock were *Echo: Number 25* 1951 (fig.12), and *Autumn Rhythm: Number 30* 1950 (fig.13). In the case of *Echo*, 'positive and negative areas ... seldom overlap or are

80 Judd's observation parallels the one I stressed at the beginning of this essay: in 1964, he remarked on Newman's having let paint look 'the way [it] was applied'.

81 Judd, 'Jackson Pollock' (1967), Judd 1975, p.195. 'Fragmentation' was a pejorative term in Judd's lexicon; see Judd, '*Jackson Pollock* by Bryan Robertson' (1961), Judd 1975, p.31; 'Abstract Expressionism' (1983), Judd 1987, pp.38–9.

fig.13 JACKSON POLLOCK

Autumn Rhythm: Number 30 1950

Oil on canvas
266.7 × 525.8 (105 × 207)
The Metropolitan Museum of Art,
George A. Hearn Fund, 1957 (57.92)

ambiguous'. I assume Judd was referring to the clustering of marks ('positive') that leave relatively open spaces ('negative') between them. Here the negatives constitute more than just a reserve for the positives; rather than generating a spatial field for an illusionistic 'picture', they become something in themselves, things that exist. In turn, *Echo* becomes a painting of 'extremes', with its elements equivalent, not subordinate.[83] In the case of *Autumn Rhythm*, Judd stressed its near 1:2 proportion, as if Pollock intuited the ratio as a way of ensuring his work's specificity.[84] Proportion, Judd cleverly perceived, represents 'both extremes at once' – extreme generality in the mathematical ratio, extreme particularity in *this* sensory instance of it.[85]

Judd's logic of Peircean abduction, his intuitive guesswork that beats the odds against existence, generates its proper share of surprise. Before reading his collected writings in sequence, I had no inkling that he would apply his notion of Pollock's polarisation to the sculpture of Lee Bontecou. In Peircean terms, this is an instance of inference from 'facts of one kind to facts of another': the works of the two artists are dissimilar, if only because of the difference in medium – two qualitatively different sets of facts (although Bontecou was inspired by Abstract Expressionism). Judd began his line of reasoning with Pollock, but it was with Bontecou that the polarity thesis developed, at least according to the chronological record of the published criticism.

Judd first reviewed Bontecou's works at the end of 1960. He noticed that she was constructing her wall pieces with an unusual degree of projection outwards; *Untitled* 1960 (fig.14), extends forwards from the support wall by 40.5 cm (16 in), nearly half the height of the sculpture. Judd resorted to metaphor to meet this critical challenge: 'Bontecou's constructions stand out from the wall like contoured volcanoes. Their craters are voids but exceedingly aggressive ones ... threateningly concrete holes to be among.'[86] 'Concrete', another term for 'definite' or 'self-defining', is the prescient figure in this context, despite Judd's strongly connoted allusions to aggression, threat and a sexualised topography. Two years later, in early 1963, he made one of his most searching statements:

> The quality of Bontecou's reliefs is exceptionally single. *Often power lies in a polarization of elements and qualities or at least a combination of dissimilar ones.* The four obvious aspects of the reliefs – the broad scale, the total shape, the structure, and the image – combine exponentially into an explicit quality and are the aspects of a single form [Judd would later call this 'wholeness']. The new scale excludes every-

82   Quotations from 'Jackson Pollock' (1967), Judd 1975, p.195; 'Art and Architecture' (1983), 'Abstract Expressionism' (1983), Judd 1987, p.34, 45. Compare Judd, 'Specific Objects' (1965), Judd 1975, p.187: 'In the new work [of the type Judd approves] ...

there aren't any neutral or moderate areas or parts, any connections or transitional areas.'

83   Judd, 'Abstract Expressionism' (1983), Judd 1987, p.45; compare 'In the Galleries: Helen Frankenthaler' (1960), Judd 1975, p.13.

84   Judd, 'Abstract Expressionism' (1983), Judd 1975, pp.45–6.

85   Judd, 'Art and Architecture' (1983), Judd 1987, p.34.

86   Judd, 'In the Galleries: Lee Bontecou' (1960), Judd 1975, p.27.

thing but the positive elements: there is no field in which the structure or the image occurs; there is no supporting context [hence, no illusionistic 'space']. The entire shape, the structure and the image are coextensive.[87]

Judd repeated these same observations when he authored a feature article on Bontecou in 1965, adding: 'The black hole does not allude to a black hole; it is one.'[88] Yet, as always in her case, he admitted a certain allusiveness in the work, which suggested at least two channels of interpretation, one regarding the 'image' and the other the politics of art. Judd set politics at the end of his account, but we can consider it first; it casts his objection to 'European' composition in the socio-historical light in which Newman, too, had seen it:

> The explicit power which displaces generalizations is a new and stronger form of individuality. Bontecou's work has an individuality equaled in the work of only a few artists. These are mostly Americans. The various American hierarchies [social and political] are bad enough, but apparently those elsewhere are worse.[89]

More evident than Bontecou's implicit 'American' politics was the 'image' in her work. In his writings on the artist, Judd used several metaphors, not just the 'volcano' of 1960. The problem he had to negotiate was this: although Bontecou's 'black hole' was decidedly a black hole, it also became a complex of cultural and psychological allusions extending 'from something as social as war to something as private as sex – from bellicosity – to invitation'.[90] In other words, the thing that merely was what it was, a certain concrete particularity, also encompassed a set of metaphorically linked generalities. In the language Judd applied to Pollock, we would say that Bontecou had developed an 'extension of extremes'.

Although Judd let little if anything of 'image' into his own art, he was such a flexible critic that he could appreciate imagistic features in others, so long as the 'image' remained a quality with its own impact. This explains not only why he could accept simultaneous sensations

---

87   Judd, 'In the Galleries: Lee Bontecou' (1963), Judd 1975, p.65, emphasis added. At the end of the same year, in an essay on Chamberlain, Judd linked Pollock to his developing thoughts on polarity: 'The polarity of [Pollock's] work, greater than that of Chamberlain's, is based on corresponding extremes of form. A point of sensation, the immediacy of the dripped paint, is opposed to a volume of structural and imagistic forms.' 'Chamberlain: Another View' (1963), Judd 1975, p.108.

The material factor in Chamberlain's art, like that in Pollock's and Bontecou's, achieved 'an independent power' because it was never subordinated to illusionistic likeness or compositional hierarchy. Judd 1975, p.110; see also Raskin 1999, pp.56–9. As in the case of 'illusion', Judd's sense of 'power' has been misconstrued because of the generalised preconceptions of many of his readers. For example, when relating Judd's views to issues of power, Anna Chave ignores his state-

ments on Bontecou and confuses his interest in the 'power' of a work's separate qualities with the more traditional concern for a 'singular, coherent totality'. 'Minimalism and the Rhetoric of Power', *Arts Magazine*, vol.64, no.5, January 1990, p.56. Judd insisted that the 'qualities' retain their power independent of the power of wholeness.

88   Judd, 'Lee Bontecou' (1965), Judd 1975, p.178.

89   Ibid., pp.179–80. On the related perspective

of Newman, see Shiff, 'Introduction', Newman 1990, pp.xiii–xxviii.

90   Judd, 'Lee Bontecou' (1965), Judd 1975, p.179. Whatever else he said of Bontecou, Judd avoided describing her work as mysterious, as others did (see, for example, Gerald Nordland, 'West Coast in Review', *Arts Magazine*, vol.36, no.3, December 1961, p.64). Like Judd, the majority of critics appear to have called Bontecou's work 'powerful' and 'strong'.

fig.14 LEE BONTECOU
Untitled 1960

Welded metal and canvas assemblage
88.9 × 139.7 × 40.6 (35 × 55 × 16)
Collection of Halley K. Harrisburg and Michael
Rosenfeld; Courtesy of Michael Rosenfeld Gallery

of sex and war in Bontecou's work, but also why he remained a lifelong admirer of Claes Oldenburg, another creator of forms that were 'sexual' (Judd's term) and therefore seemingly referential.[91] Judd's 1962 review of Wayne Thiebaud hints at what will come: 'Oldenburg [unlike Thiebaud] makes his cakes and pies and other foods and articles actual objects, which is different epistemologically from illustration.'[92] An Oldenburg pie is like a Bontecou black hole (or like paint by Pollock, Newman, Johns or Stella): it is what it is. According to Judd, Oldenburg's materials *looked* like what they were: his vinyl was slick; his canvas was matt; both were flaccid. The materials need not match the sensory qualities of the things to which the image might be alluding; they were distinct, self-referential, 'objective'.[93] 'Objective', as we know, was the term Judd would later apply to optical illusions, another category of sensory quality that remained true to itself, referring materially nowhere else.

If a work by Oldenburg calls up a range of emotion while conveying its own material look, this too is independent of its imagistic references. Judd's point is easy to miss, unless we join him in fast thinking:

> Oldenburg's pieces have nothing to do with the objects they're like ... The pieces have only the emotion read into [such] objects ... They're exaggerated, as [subjective] interest is ... The grossness of the scale, simplicity and surface make it obvious that it's the interest in the object that is the main thing, not the object itself ... [Oldenburg has] made the emotive form, with him basic and biopsychological, the same as the shape of [a new] object, and by blatancy subverted the idea of the natural presence of human qualities in all things.[94]

By 1966, this was Judd's way of saying that the emotional content belonged specifically to what could be seen and felt in Oldenburg's art; it did not derive from thinking through a chain of metaphoric associations, leading back to either culture or nature. Oldenburg took

91   Judd, 'Claes Oldenburg' (1966), Judd 1975, pp.192–3. However forthright Judd was in his judgements, he also behaved generously toward friends such as Oldenburg, perhaps putting extra effort into analysing their art. In 1968 he told an interviewer: 'I only feel competitive when people whose work I don't like very much receive undue attention. I'm very much in favor of people I like.' Unpublished interview by Margot Willett, Judd Foundation, Marfa, Texas, quotation courtesy of the Judd Foundation and David Raskin.

92   Judd, 'In the Galleries: Wayne Thiebaud' (1962), Judd 1975, p.60.

93   Judd, 'Specific Objects' (1965), Judd 1975, p.187.

94   Judd, 'Specific Objects' (1965), 'Claes Oldenburg' (1966), Judd 1975, pp.189, 191–2. On Judd's notion of 'interest' (as in this passage), see above, note 22.

the emotion that cultural associations might attach to an everyday object and literalised o
actualised that feeling in an object of his own creation, to which he gave an appropr_at
form, in some respect an exaggeration or distillation of an ordinary quality ('[he] has mad
something that didn't exist before').[95] The new object became specific to the feeling, and th
feeling to the object. Oldenburg's art converted fictive 'anthropomorphism' into 'biopsychc
logical' fact – a movement that would parallel the conversion of illusionism or illusionisti
effects into 'real' (optical) illusions.[96] To the typical, literal-minded critic, Oldenbur;
appeared intent on evoking consumer objects in the everyday world. Judd, with his greate
concentration on sensation, saw that Oldenburg was creating a parallel world from his chc
sen materials, where outside references were unnecessary and even irrelevant to undei
standing. To limit an Oldenburg pie to a reference to pies and the society of consumption
was to miss the experience that the newly created object offered through its qualities o
image and form (fig.15).

fig.15 CLAES OLDENBURG
Small Yellow Pie 1961

Muslin soaked in plaster over wire frame,
painted with enamel
45.7 × 41.9 × 19.1 (18 × 16$^1/_2$ × 7$^1/_2$)
Collection Claes Oldenburg and Coosje van Bruggen

95   Judd, 'Claes Olden-
burg' (1966), Judd 1975,
p.191.

96   Judd linked anthro-
pomorphism to illusion-
ism and a generalised
rationalism in essays such
as 'Specific Objects' (1965),
Judd 1975, p.189, and
'Claes Oldenburg' (1966),

Judd 1975, p.191, as well
as elsewhere in his writ-
ings. He did not insist
that Oldenburg had elim-
inated anthropomor-
phism, but instead was
transforming it; compare
his remarks in 'In the Galleries: Claes Oldenburg'
(1964), Judd 1975, p.133.

fig.16 CLAES OLDENBURG
Soft Switches (Version 2) 1963–9

Vinyl filled with dacron and canvas
105 × 105 × 27.9 (41 $^5/_{16}$ × 41 $^5/_{16}$ × 11)
Collection of William Hokin

If I read Judd on Oldenburg correctly, taking his commentary on Bontecou as a precedent, it seems that Oldenburg represented a case of the convergence of thought and feeling.[97] With extreme concision (which I supplement) Judd wrote:

> The sense of objects occurs with forms that are near some simple, basic, profound forms you feel [each of which is a 'particularity']. These disappear when you try to make them into imaginable visual or tactile forms [by applying the generalities of illusionism]. The reference to objects gives them [that is, the basic emotive forms] a way to occur. The reference [a kind of thinking] and the basic form [which is sensed or felt] as one thing [a wholeness] is Oldenburg's main idea.[98]

In Oldenburg's art, referential thought and emotive form constitute a polarity, yet a wholeness. As an example, Judd proposes one of Oldenburg's soft switches of stuffed vermilion vinyl, which he relates to nipples – but not to real nipples, rather, to the 'feeling' or emotion of nipples (compare *Soft Switches (Version 2)* 1963–9; fig.16):

> The whole switch is big and soft and the nipples [the toggle elements of the switch] are enormous – the main things ... The two switches aren't separate from the rectangle; the three physically separable parts [two switches, one rectangle] don't, visually, add up to the whole. They're made as a whole. They're the same material and it bulges and sags the same throughout.

One feeling, one thought, perhaps even one physicality that 'bulges and sags the same throughout' – but a polarity of references to nipples and switches. It does not 'add up' visually, and certainly is not integrated by any anatomical metaphor, because 'there aren't two breasts, just two nipples'.[99] Yet ... there it is.

'SAFE FROM BIRDS'

Judd mentioned the colour of Oldenburg's *Soft Switches* only in naming it, responding without analysis. Surely, however, this blatant, monochromatic vermilion was as primary to the work as its shape, its softness and its image. The colour was a quality of the material and hence of the work; but it neither identified its substance as vinyl nor categorised it otherwise, any more than the giant size of the switches – or of certain Judd boxes – would establish their place in an industrial, social or cultural order. Colour, size and the other qualities of *Soft Switches* were specific, 'just existing'.

Oldenburg's vermilion epitomised one of the hyper-material aspects of modern art that distinguished it from earlier art, interfering with the long tradition of illusionism. 'Even in the work of [Edvard] Munch, whose work is not considered abstract', Judd wrote, 'color is amplified beyond anything seen for centuries ... Color is an immediate sensation, a phenomenon, and in that [respect] leads to the work of [Dan] Flavin, [Larry] Bell, and [Robert] Irwin.'[100] As his terminal examples, Judd chose three artists who, strictly speaking, were neither painters nor

97   The Bontecou-Oldenburg connection is especially apparent whe Judd writes that 'Oldenburg's objects involve an analogy between psychological, erotic and other wise profound forms on the one hand, and pieces of food and clothing on the other. The two kinds of form are co-existensiv [sic], but with different references.' 'Local History' (1964), Judd 1975, p.153. Oldenburg's commingling of eroticism and consumerism parallels Bontecou's sex and war.

98   Judd, 'Claes Oldenburg' (1966), Judd 97 p.192.

99   Ibid., p.193.

100   Judd 1994, p.77, order of phrases adjuste for clarity.

sculptors; in their mature work, they used light as their source of colour, a real illusion with 'none of painting's scheme of something framed ... [its] illusionistic space [and] modulated surfaces'.[101] In 1964, Flavin himself described his work in accord with Judd's fast thinking: 'Each [fluorescent] tube exists of itself, you know, as an equal entity in the whole ... They are independent of each other, though they can appear to be related. For instance, I can use all white tubes, and yet there are different whites.'[102] (fig.17) As if in response, Judd observed that Flavin's cool-white tubes caused his daylight-white tubes to appear blue. It was more important to notice this than explain it; Flavin's arrangement was 'simple, unstressed, unconcluded'.[103] Judd later complained that viewers refused to see his own work as 'something itself ... so they look for something [else] to put into it'.[104]

At the time that Judd referred to red and black as a two-colour monochrome and, beyond that, to desiring 'a multiplicity [of colours] all at once', he was working with brilliantly enamelled bent-aluminium constructions (see fig.7 and nos.27–9, 31, 37).[105] I am tempted to regard Flavin's arrangements of fluorescent tubes analogously, even in cases where the colour contrast remained subtle. His two whites together were separate, furthering neither composition nor hierarchy. Judd provided a gloss on the situation by taking the history of art back to its origins:

> The necessities of representation inhibited the use of color [in traditional European art] ... The simulation of appearance, the depiction of objects in their space, upon a flat surface, a simulation of reality that must be ... believed by the viewer, is not compatible with a developed interest in color. The painting by Zeuxis that the birds pecked at could not have been like the painting on Attic vases, flat areas of red and black ... Romanesque painting, which has clear and strong and well organized areas of color, has always been safe from birds.[106]

The birds developed interest in grapes not colour, and Zeuxis appealed to them with his studied illusionism. He simulated and the birds 'believed', as if guided by a visual logic they could never have perceived in 'flat areas of red and black', an unmodulated two-colour monochrome. With his witty remark, Judd showed no more respect for the soul of birds than Zeuxis had. He leaves us to infer that birds are victims of their own expectations – in Newman's terms, more like aestheticians than like artists. Newman, however, had allowed avians a certain dignity, not so much in his famous 'for the birds' statement, but through another aspect of the analogy. He observed that birds possess an aesthetic sense that lifts them above their ordinary affairs and appetites: 'The loon gliding lonesome over the lake, with whom is he communicating?'[107] Newman implied that the loon took as much 'interest' (to use Judd's word) in the air and the height as in indications of food that might at times distract it from the 'wholeness' of the view and the experience of space itself.

Judd wanted an art 'safe from birds'. Living in his late-modern era, he suspected that it might take more than clear, strong colour, Romanesque or modern, to accomplish this. Taking leave of Newman, he imagined 'the birds' as people who confuse emotion with sensation, projecting

101 This is Judd's early response to Flavin's work; Judd, 'In the Galleries: Dan Flavin' (1964), Judd 1975, p.124.
102 Flavin in 'New Nihilism or New Art: Dan Flavin, Don Judd, and Frank Stella Discuss Contemporary Art' (February 1964), moderated by Bruce Glaser, audiotape, Pacifica Radio Archive, North Hollywood, California.
103 Judd, 'In the Galleries: Dan Flavin' (1964), Judd 1975, p.124. Judd was reviewing Flavin's Kaymar Gallery show of March 1964.
104 Judd in Batchelor 1989, p.63.
105 Judd 1994, p.113.
106 Ibid., pp.72–3.
107 Newman, 'The First Man Was an Artist' (1947), Newman 1990, p.159.

fig.17 DAN FLAVIN

Untitled 1963–6

Fluorescent light fixtures with cool-white
and warm-white lamps
Overall height 305 (120)
Solomon R. Guggenheim Museum,
New York. Panza Collection, 1991

general meaning into their felt experience of chance appearances. To birds, colour was not colour but a sign for fruit, the satisfaction of pre-existing desire. The problem with the emotionally 'expressive' kind of art, so common in the modern era, was that it transferred the experience of an external object or situation to the feeling of an artwork. When the sensation of an artwork served only to refer back to an emotional experience, the emotion became the generalised meaning. What resulted was not so different from the hybrid 'imitation wooden surface of plastic' that Judd abhorred ('all classes love it'), or the experience of birds who mistake modulations of red and black for grapes.[108] In both instances, the living wholeness of colour, form, substance and space is lost.

Art could portray an emotion, or it could present a sensation. It was most important, Judd thought, to realise that 'what you feel and what things are aren't the same'.[109] Emotion and sensation were both valid artistic interests, so long as there was no confusion. Oldenburg took one direction: '[His] work involves feelings about objects; his objects are objects as they're felt, not as they are.'[110] Pollock took the other: '[His] painting is dripped paint. It's that sensation, completely immediate and specific ... [His] paintings don't involve the immediate emotions of traditional art.' Between these artists – and within each of them as well – there was polarity and wholeness.

Judd was more Pollock than he was Oldenburg, but still more he was himself. We do not yet have comfortable terms for what he accomplished. Nor did he. Asked if he was a sculptor, he replied: 'No, it means carving to me ... I never had a word; I don't know.'[111] I continue to wonder why his art of 1:2 proportions and two-colour monochromes is so emotionally and even intellectually satisfying. It was not derived from nature and offered nothing for the birds: 'Time and space can be made and don't have to be found like stars in the sky or rocks on a hillside' (or grapes on a vine).[112] The space of art, Judd proclaimed, 'is made by thought'.[113] What Judd invented – by thinking, feeling, fast-thinking – is so fundamentally human that we sense its quality, both character and value, 'just existing'.

108 Judd 1992, p.8.
109 Judd, 'Jackson Pollock' (1967), Judd 1975, p.195.
110 Judd, 'Claes Oldenburg' (1966), Judd 1975, p.192.
111 Judd in Winnekes 1993, p.136.
112 Judd, 'On Russian art and its relation to my work' (1981), Judd 1987, p.17.
113 Judd 1994, p.70.

Whitechapel Art Gallery, London,
29 September – 1 November 1970

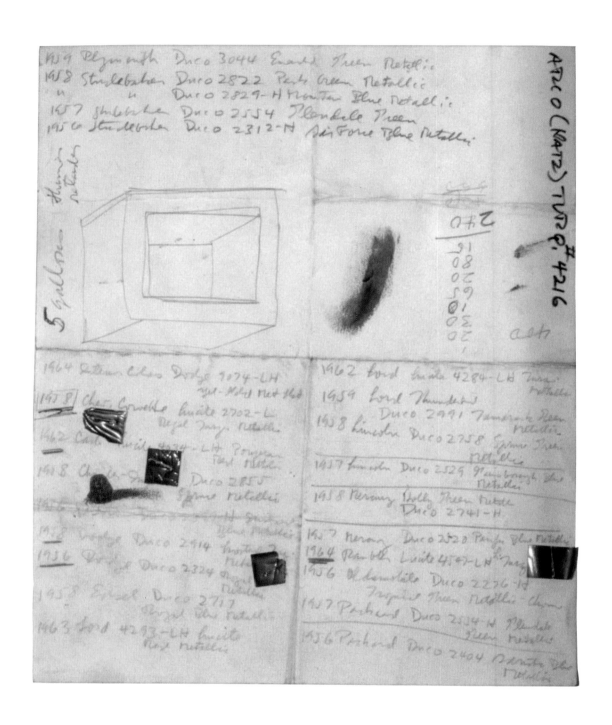

fig.18 DONALD JUDD

Untitled c.1964

Pencil and colour samples on paper
35 × 29 (13 3/4 × 11 3/8)
Collection of Judd Foundation

Everything as Colour

DAVID BATCHELOR

I am looking at a reproduction of an undated drawing by Donald Judd. Perhaps 'drawing' isn't the right word here, as the small sheet of paper, evidently once folded into four quarters, is mostly covered in hand-written notes in pencil, together with a diagram of what appears to be a mid-1960s floor-based box-like structure (fig.18). The yellowing paper also has six postage-stamp-sized patches of colour either attached to or smeared on the surface. Artists' notes of this kind are always fascinating – if often also frustrating – in the way they hint at an over-the-shoulder insight into the working procedures of the artist. Here is the private and unself-conscious studio activity of thinking, observing, testing and recording made available to the outside world. At the same time, this sheet of paper is only a minute fragment in what was already by then becoming an enormous body of work by the artist, and fragments such as these can often make for unreliable documents. Nevertheless, this particular fragment is both unusual and revealing, and highly suggestive, and what follows is simply an occasion to follow up some of those suggestions.

The notes by Judd are not thoughts or reflections, but a list of nearly thirty different commercially available colours. All the listed colours were produced by the American automotive industry between 1956 and 1964, and all are metallic. The list begins with '1959 Plymouth Duco 3044 Emerald Green Metallic' and continues in the same form to detail colours produced by Studebaker, Lincoln, Ford, Oldsmobile, Packard, Dodge, Chrysler, Mercury and Chevrolet. Clearly, for Judd at this time – 1964 or shortly afterwards – it was the colours and surfaces of cars, rather than the traditional colours and surfaces of painting, that had come to inform and shape elements of his work. And yet we are rarely invited, either by Judd himself or by subsequent critics and historians, to imagine his work in relation to these emblems of modernity and the city.

For me, the broader questions prompted by this piece of paper are: Where is the car in the art of the industrial world? Why is it so hard to find any plausible representation of a motor vehicle in the history of modern art? Why – given so many artists' and critics' century-and-a-half-long preoccupation with modernity, the everyday, and the painting of modern life – have these objects and other kinds of machinery remained almost invisible and, when made visible, made visibly unconvincing? What is it about this defining bit of modernity that has proved so resistant to being depicted? The problem with this kind of question is that it turns you into an art-historical trainspotter, quite literally at first because you have to go back to

Impressionism and the several artists who, with the words of Baudelaire ringing in their ears, began to confront the early products of industrialisation, mostly, if not exclusively, in the form of the steam train. But why is it that for the most part the results were either located in the distant upper left corner of an otherwise pleasantly rolling landscape or, when close up, a great deal more steam than they were train? And why, some years later, when the Futurists returned to the subject with Marinetti's talk of a great art of mechanical production ringing in their ears, were the painters' and sculptors' allegories of dynamism realised mostly in divisionist horses, dashing nudes or cinematographic daschunds? It appears that for both the Impressionists and the Futurists it was possible to accommodate the mechanical into their art only by dissolving or otherwise converting it into a kind of nature: into an enveloping natural atmosphere or into a symbolic natural force. It is as if the summoning up of the spirit of industrialisation also appeared simultaneously to necessitate its suppression: it could be evoked, suggested, hinted at, but not addressed directly. But at least in these works there is a tension between the forces of nature and the forces of the city, even if it is finally resolved emphatically in terms of the former. By the time Matisse had got around to painting a car – in 1917, when industrialisation was settling into its long and passionate relationship with barbarism – it is as if he already knew there was absolutely no energy left in the subject for the painter. *The Windshield, On the Road to Villacoublay* 1917 (fig.19) is a curiously lacklustre painting. Without any particular tension – between interior and exterior or between form and colour or between nature and culture – it therefore also lacks any particular harmonic resolution of tension of the kind that animates almost all of Matisse's work.

A couple of years before Matisse approached and then quickly abandoned the automobile, Francis Picabia had begun to tackle the subject from another, radically divergent angle. In the

fig.19 HENRI MATISSE

*The Windshield, On the Road to
Villacoublay* 1917

Oil on canvas
38.2 × 55.2 (15 × 21³/₄)
The Cleveland Museum of Art, 2002.
Bequest of Lucia McCurdy McBride in
memory of John Harris McBride II, 1972.225

process he also turned the relationship between nature and culture in art on its head. *Portrait of a Young American Girl in a State of Nudity* 1915 (fig.20) is neither a portrait nor a painting. A diagrammatic ink drawing of a spark plug with an entirely nominal (but infinitely suggestive) reference to a figure, this and other mechanomorphic images by Picabia and Duchamp are perhaps some of the very few emphatically *artificial* works of the first half of the twentieth century. Several other Dadaists and many of the Soviet Constructivists also set out to produce works which were similarly or otherwise *against* or somehow *beyond* nature. Of them Malevich perhaps tried hardest also to remain a painter, and this led to some rather odd couplings, such as a black square compared, figuratively, to the front end of a locomotive or a black square tied, literally, to the front end of a truck (fig.21).

There is something almost comical, deliberately or otherwise, in the artistic flirtation with the automobile in the first half of the twentieth century. But this should not disguise the seriousness of the problem that confronted these artists. The work of Picabia and Duchamp, of Malevich, Tatlin and others suggests that, in order to confront technological modernity in art, in order to deal directly or indirectly with its characteristic forms, shapes, surfaces and effects, some alternative had to be found to the illusionistic space of painting and to its characteristic surface effects. For Picabia and others this sometimes took the form of the diagram, a type of drawing functionally tied to mechanical engineering and, by extension, to the world made in its image. For others, arguably, what has become conventionalised in art as the ready-made and the monochrome might initially have served a similar purpose. And then of course there was the photograph. What these different avant-garde forms share is both a series of negative attributes – they are not autographic, not expressive, not painterly – and at the same time the positive attribute that they are all themselves mechanical, or at least can be made to appear so more convincingly than conventional pictures or sculptures.

fig.20 FRANCIS PICABIA
Portrait of a Young American Girl in a State of Nudity
1915

Ink on paper
Private collection

fig.21 The arrival of the funeral procession of Kasimir Malevich at the Moscow station, Leningrad, 15 May 1935

fig.22 ANDY WARHOL

White Disaster 1 1963

Silkscreen ink and acrylic paint on canvas
269.2 × 208 (106 × 81 ⁷/₈)
Staatsgalerie Stuttgart

68

It is as if, in order to approach the mechanical world in art, the work of art itself had to become, in some broad sense, machine-like, to become like or to be made like the world it sought to represent. This would be one possible description of Leo Steinberg's argument in his (until recently largely underrated) essay 'Other Criteria', published in 1972 and based largely on a reading of Robert Rauschenberg's early work.[1] Steinberg argued that here the residual window-onto-the-world naturalism of painting (including most abstract painting) had been finally superseded in the 'flatbed picture plane'. This reorientation whereby 'pictures no longer simulate vertical fields, but opaque flatbed horizontals' was for Steinberg a technical analogue of 'the shift from nature to culture'; above all it was 'a pictorial surface that let the world in again', or, more particularly, it was a 'picture plane ... for the consciousness immersed in the brain of the city'. In some senses Steinberg's argument is not entirely at odds with Michael Fried's more or less contemporary suggestion that painting had been faced with a 'gradual withdrawal ... from the task of representing reality – or of reality from the power of painting to represent it'.[2] The second half of the proposal now seems more interesting than the first: the idea that something has happened to the world so that it has in some way become beyond the power of painting to represent it. As far as I am aware, Fried never states exactly what that something was, but painting nevertheless would have to continue despite it. For Steinberg the world had to be let back in again and the means for achieving this was a radical reorientation and literalisation of pictorial space, a reorientation that would 'contaminate all purified categories', including the assumed categorical distinctions between painting and sculpture, and between art and non-art.

The point about the car perhaps is that it already *is* a painting (and a sculpture, and an object of aesthetic interest). And it is a very particular kind of painting: a bright, colourful, shiny, industrial paint job. This kind of painting-in-the-world, and many of the colours and surfaces of other industrial commodities, have shown themselves to be all but beyond painting-as-art or, more specifically, painting-as-representation. And this is, I think, largely because artists' colours – oils and watercolours in particular – and their brushes and palettes were developed to mimic the language of nature, in all its modulated glory, and as such have not been able to adapt easily to the phenomenological or psychological experience of the modern city. When artists have adopted the colour and paint technology of industry – Rauschenberg in the early 1950s, Stella in the late 1950s, Oiticica, Pistoletto and Richter amongst others in the 1960s – they have produced paint-job paintings, truly flat abstractions, unmodulated monochromes of everyday life.

It wasn't until the 1960s that the car began to find a credible place in painting, and it did so mainly through the work of Andy Warhol and Ed Ruscha. But in Warhol's remarkable *Disaster* series the car gets into the space of painting only when the car has in one sense ceased to be a car and only when the space of painting has been pretty much cleared of paint (fig.22). Warhol's 'paintings' are, after all, mostly screenprints of photographs. They are also in important ways both partial ready-mades and partial monochromes, and the pictorial image survives in the work because, as Jeff Wall has suggested, it is preceded by these conditions and subject to their terms.[3]

1   Leo Steinberg, 'Other Criteria' (1972), *Other Criteria*, Oxford 1972, pp.55–91.

2   Michael Fried, 'Art and Objecthood' (1967), *Minimal Art: A Critical Anthology*, ed. Gregory Battcock, New York 1968, pp.116–47.

3   Jeff Wall, 'Monochrome and Photojournalism in On Kawara's *Today* Paintings' (1993), *Robert Lehman Lectures on Contemporary Art*, 1, ed. Lynne Cooke and Karen Kelley, New York 1996, pp.135–56.

There is one important exception, an occasion where artists attempted to represent rather than reproduce the colours and surfaces of industrial technology: the episode of Photorealism in the 1970s. These are works that fascinate, largely in the sense that they seem to want to bewitch the viewer (fig.23). They are obviously highly accomplished, but at the same time are often also without intensity. Their precisionist virtual space leaves little room in which to move around, there are no gaps or holes; and there are thus few spaces for the viewer. For the most part they are detached, clinical, miniaturist and, above all, *static*. They ask you to stand still. With a Rauschenberg you occupy the *same* space as the painting; it asks you to move around and it rewards you for this. A Richard Estes painting may show reflections; a Rauschenberg black painting makes reflections. In doing so it also isolates, embodies and conveys something of the specificity of urban experience. The work is like the world but more in the manner of a sample than a picture: it refers, but not pictorially.

It should be clear that my question about the car was not entirely about cars. Rather the car stands here as an instance of something more general to our experience of modernity: the question of modern materials and colours. It is, for example, an obvious but often unremarked fact that our experience of colour has been transformed over the last hundred or so years. This revolution in colour, a small but highly visible part of the larger revolutions in industry, electrification and electronics, has meant that the colours of the modern city are almost entirely new and completely unnatural. Most of the colours we now see are chemical or electrical;

fig.23 RICHARD ESTES
Untitled 1973–4

Screenprint on paper
85.1 × 119.1 (33 $^{1}/_{2}$ × 46 $^{7}/_{8}$)
Tate

they are plastic or metallic; they are flat, shiny, glowing or flashing (or they are broken, switched off and as if they were never there). These colours are intense but also ephemeral; they are vivid but also contingent. And they are ubiquitous: always everywhere allied to commerce and the street. As such they are always also impure, and largely indifferent to the protocols of traditional colour theory.

This is where Judd comes in. His own development as an artist could be seen in terms of a considered response to the colours and materials of modernity. Flanked by John Chamberlain on one side and Dan Flavin on the other, Judd first abandoned pictorial space, then painting, then painter's paints – but without ever fully abandoning the problems which painting had carried with it for over a century. On the contrary, it was perhaps precisely in order to address the problems of painting that Judd found he had to abandon the traditional materials and tools of the painter.

By the early 1960s Judd had begun to combine oil paints with increasingly unconventional supports and structures, as a few examples of the materials for specific works indicate: 'light cadmium red oil and wax on liquitex and sand on masonite and wood with aluminium and black oil on wood' (1962); 'oil on wood with galvanised iron and aluminium' (1963); 'oil on plywood, aluminium tube' (1963). By 1964 the oil had gone from Judd's repertoire and his materials had become both more industrial and more exotic sounding, including for example: 'orange pebbled Plexiglas and hot-rolled steel' (1964); 'galvanised iron and red enamel' (1965); 'black anodised aluminium and bronze Plexiglas' (1965/90); 'red fluorescent Plexiglas and steel' (1965); 'stainless steel and amber Plexiglas' (1966); 'turquoise enamel on aluminium' (1966); 'cold-rolled steel and turquoise enamel' (1969).

It is a fairly extraordinary list of materials by any standards, but it is also one strikingly, bizarrely, even deliriously at odds with the category 'Minimalism' and its standard predicates – 'reduction', 'austerity', 'rationality' and so forth. As I have argued elsewhere, Judd's colours have remained largely invisible for nearly four decades.[4] The chromophobia that has enveloped the discourse on Minimalism is part of a much larger resistance to colour in the West, and the more intense the colour the more invisible it has tended to remain. You would not know, for example, from reading Anna Chave's account of Minimalism and masculinity, that most works by Judd and Flavin are not only stunningly colourful – a quality which is habitually associated with the feminine, the irrational or the infantile rather than the masculine or the authoritarian – but that they are often weird and weightless too.[5] Even more sympathetic commentators, such as Hal Foster, have remained entirely silent on this critical dimension of the art of the 1960s.[6] It has been left mainly to Judd himself and to his artist contemporaries, such as Flavin and Robert Smithson, to stress the significance of colour in his work, and to the occasional critic, such as Rosalind Krauss and William C. Agee.[7] During the 1960s all these commentators noted this aspect of Judd's work; only very recently has his colour begun to get the attention it deserves again.[8]

The list of materials says a lot about Judd's work. There is the importance of Plexiglas, an American trade name for cast or extruded acrylic sheet. In the 1950s plastics of various kinds were

4   See David Batchelor, *Chromophobia*, London 2000.

5   Anna Chave, 'Minimalism and the Rhetoric of Power', *Arts Magazine*, vol.64, no.5, January 1990, pp.44–63.

6   Hal Foster, 'The Crux of Minimalism', *The Return of the Real*, Cambridge, Massachusetts, 1996, pp.34–69.

7   See Robert Smithson, 'Donald Judd', 'The Crystal Land' and 'Entropy and the New Monuments', *Robert Smithson: Collected Writings*, ed. Jack Flam, Berkeley 1996, pp.4–23; Rosalind Krauss, 'Allusion and Illusion in Donald Judd', *Artforum*, vol.4, no.9, May 1966, pp.24–6; William C. Agee, 'Don Judd', *Don Judd*, exh. cat., The Whitney Museum of American Art, New York 1968.

8   Two recent exhibitions of Judd's work have focused directly on his work as a colourist: *Dan Flavin/Donald Judd: Aspects of Color*, The Menil Collection, Houston, 1998, and *Donald Judd: Colorist*, Sprengel Museum, Hanover, 2000.

still novel enough for intellectuals and cultural critics to speculate about their effects, almost as if they were drugs. It is hard now to recover exactly how for Roland Barthes plastic was 'the stuff of alchemy' which could induce 'wonder', 'amazement', 'reverie' and 'euphoria', while at the same time being a 'disgraced', 'artificial', 'imitation material'.[9] For Aldous Huxley, writing at the same time as Barthes, the promised ubiquity of plastics was experienced entirely as a threat, a degradation of the rare colour of jewels and stained glass.[10] For both, the colours of plastic were seductive but false, and finally its 'undoing'. Describing it as 'hollow and flat' like its sound, Barthes saw plastic as capable of retaining only the most 'chemical-looking' hues: 'Of yellow, red and green, it keeps only the aggressive quality, and uses them as mere names, being able to display only concepts of colours.' *Mythologies*, the volume that contains Barthes's short essay 'Plastic', was published in 1957; within a few years plastics such as Plexiglas had become commercially available in a wide range of colours, including fluorescents, as well as in different degrees of transparency, opacity and surface finish. For Judd the 'chemical' hues of Plexiglas were clearly a part of its attraction: here finally was a material that had an intrinsic colour that was also a brilliant colour. Previously Judd had had to apply layers of light cadmium red oil paint to plywood surfaces in order to generate vivid planes of colour, and that almost inevitably left some visible brushwork. After 1963 and for the next thirty years Judd's palette became in effect a variety of commercial colour samples and swatch books, ready-made industrial monochromes that could be ordered up from a range of suppliers (figs.24–5).

9   Roland Barthes, 'Plastic', *Mythologies*, trans. Annette Lavers, London 1972, pp.97–9.

10   Aldous Huxley, *Heaven and Hell*, London 1956.

fig.24   Colour samples at Donald Judd's studio at Marfa, Texas, 1995

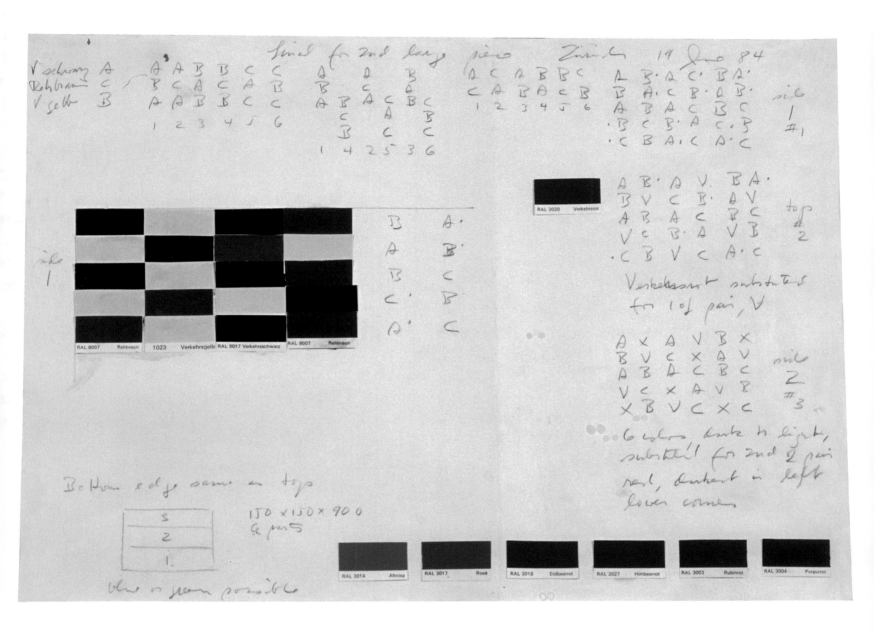

fig.25 DONALD JUDD

Untitled (Final for 2nd large piece Zurich 19 June 1984) 1984

Pencil and colour samples on paper
34 × 48 (13 ³/₈ × 18 ³/₄)
Collection of Judd Foundation

73

It is clear from Judd's vocabulary of materials that he was drawn to vivid, bright and above all *impure* colours. Turquoise, amber and bronze allude to the colours of precious stones and metals; they are not spectrum colours or hues codified in the traditional hierarchy of primaries and secondaries. William Agee is the only commentator I am aware of who has made an explicit connection between Judd's work of the 1960s and car colours, including the glorious 'Harley-Davidson Hi-Fi Red' and '1958 Chevrolet Regal Turquoise'.[11] These colours and colour names would have been seen by many, and probably are still seen by many, as gaudy, vulgar and almost pathetically *aspirational*. Or, to put it another way, these colour names are so not-high-culture in their artifice, in their apparent longing for status and their craving for respect. If they belong to art at all it is to Pop, the art which is too often assumed to be somehow in opposition to Minimalism in its embrace of mass culture. But then Judd always had great respect for Warhol's colour, and, like many artists, complete disrespect for terms such as 'minimalism' and 'pop'. It is interesting that, in an essay more concerned with the work of Warhol and Ruscha than Judd, Dave Hickey begins with a discussion of the aesthetics of 1950s and 1960s custom cars. Before describing how this prepared him for the aesthetics of Warhol and Ruscha – and a car is always somehow just around the corner from a Ruscha painting – he lists the colours of his own vehicles of the time: 'a coral-and-cream 1955 Ford, a turquoise-and-white Chevrolet Bel Air, a bronze-lacquered 1937 Chevrolet pick-up ... '[12]

Looking at a sample of Judd's materials also shows very clearly how he nearly always used them in combination, sometimes in quite dramatic pairings. Further, these combinations nearly always consist of one or more highly reflective as well as coloured surfaces. The effects are both complex and richly sensuous. Judd's earlier three-dimensional works would often combine the applied colour of paint and the intrinsic colour of, say, a section of metal. This is continued in later works when the applied colour would typically be industrially coated – anodised or enamelled, for example – and the intrinsic colour would be one of a wide range of metals – from Cor-ten steel to brass – which themselves could be either dull or highly polished, or somewhere inbetween. Plexiglas again offered a quality of colour and surface which was intrinsic yet intense, and Judd's many 'stacks' look like experiments in combinations of different metals with Plexiglas of different colours and degrees of transparency or opacity. The resulting works can become almost fluid or almost crystalline as they shine or glow. Colours reflect off each other and bleed onto the supporting wall; highlights glint at the right-angle edges and corners; surfaces dissolve and then reassert themselves as the viewer moves around; planes become mirrors reflecting other planes in the work or beyond it. The colours both hold the work together and begin to break it apart. The excess of colour and reflection is often at least partially held in by the repeated geometry of the work, but sometimes it is also emphasised by the same geometry as each mirror-like surface is itself mirrored. Even the uncolourful colours of materials such as plywood and galvanised steel – materials that serve to stabilise and soak up the liquidity of other colours – nevertheless participate in the complex play of polymonochromatic plane and space. As Judd once noted: 'It's best to consider everything as color.'[13]

11   See Agee, 'Donald Judd and the Endless Possibilities of Color', Dietmar Elger (ed.), *Donald Judd: Colorist*, exh. cat., Sprengel Museum, Hanover 2000, pp.33–5:.

12   Dave Hickey, 'The Birth of the Big, Beautiful Art Market', *Air Guitar: Essays on Art & Democracy*, Los Angeles 1997, pp.61–72.

13   Jochen Poetter (ed.), 'Back to Clarity: Interview with Donald Judd', *Donald Judd*, exh. cat., Staatliche Kunsthalle Baden-Baden 1989 p.94.

There is of course nothing in Judd's writing to suggest he ever intended his work to be viewed as a contribution to the painting of modern life. Rather the opposite: he was emphatically, almost pathologically, averse to the idea of art as representation in any form. And yet, when considered from the perspective of his colour and surfaces, it would seem perverse to deny there was anything less than a profound and deeply felt relationship between his work and the spaces and surfaces of the modern city. In particular, the relationship between colour and reflection, while not unique to Judd's work, exists at a more highly developed level than just about anything that was being made at the time or since. The point, however, is not that these works do not *refer*, but that they are not *pictures* and they don't represent pictorially. They are, as Steinberg had said about Rauschenberg, not windows onto a world but objects in the world. They are, as Richard Shiff has noted, not concerned with traditional illusionism but with making *real* illusions.[14] They refer not by picturing but by presenting, not by evoking but by embodying the colours and surfaces of the city. In doing so they locate, isolate and begin to bring into view one of the most vivid and elusive, one of the most visually complex and overlooked aspects of our social environment.

14   See Richard Shiff, 'Donald Judd, Fast Thinking', *Donald Judd: Late Work*, exh. cat., PaceWildenstein, New York 2000, pp.4–23.

Lisson Gallery, London,
22 January – 23 February 1974

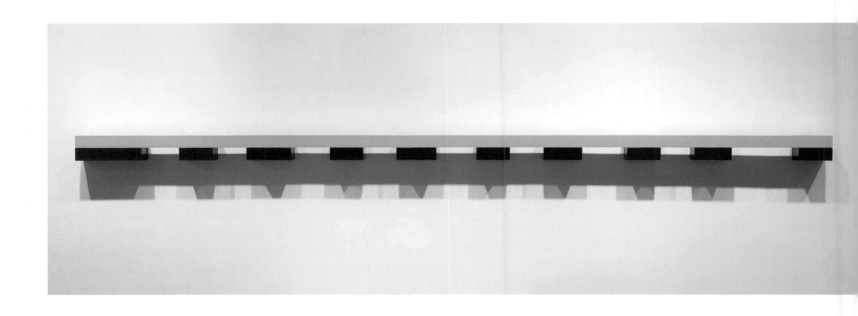

fig.26 DONALD JUDD

Untitled 1966

Aluminium and purple lacquer on aluminium
$21 \times 642.6 \times 21$ ($8\,^{1}/_{4} \times 253 \times 8\,^{1}/_{4}$)
DSS 84
Whitney Museum of American Art, New York. Gift of
The Howard and Jean Lipman Foundation, New York

Judd's Moral Art

DAVID RASKIN

I would like to acknowl-
edge the helpful com-
ments on drafts of this
essay from Clifford Allen,
Jodi Cressman, Irmgard
Emmelhainz, David
Getsy, Raja Halwani,
Clare Manchester,
Margaret Olin, George
Roeder, Mike Schreyach
and Richard Shiff.

For JRC.

1. SEEING OURSELVES

Despite Donald Judd's desire to eliminate every last trace of allusion and illusionism from his art, Rosalind Krauss saw both in spades.[1] This was in 1966 – nearly forty years ago! – and her bold critique has held sway ever since.

For Krauss, one of Judd's untitled progressions from 1966 suggested that something was amiss (fig.26). From the front, this twenty-one-foot-wide (642.6-cm) work looked to her as if Judd had made it by hanging ten purple bars of various widths from a single length of brushed alumini-um. But when she moved to the side, she realised that the purple elements did not really hang since they turned out to be both L-shaped and to cradle the upper bar. Instead of clarifying the nature of Judd's object, this side view created a new problem. From this perspective, she could not deduce the mathematical formula he had used to determine the widths of the purple forms and the intervening gaps. It was precisely this disparity between her visual observations and the work's physical existence that bothered her; her discrete impressions failed to disclose the piece's actuality. She found that she was only able to resolve this problem by walking around the object, that is, by accumulating a series of perspective views (which in turn seemingly alluded to 'the colonnaded nave of Brunelleschi's "San Lorenzo"' [fig.27][2]). This reciprocal interaction of critic and art – her moving, it revealing – proved that something called 'lived illusion' was the principal feature of Judd's art, a realisation that she celebrated with a didactic claim about life. Krauss thought that the experience of lived illusion rightly demonstrated that it is the very interplay between a person and the world that gives meaning to both, that makes each exist.[3]

But in 1971 Krauss rebelled against her own claims, against what she thought Judd's art taught about life. The lived perspective that had once made such sense now seemed circular and deeply flawed. She had come to believe that private 'lived' experience was unverifiable, since it provided no objective means to distinguish between knowing and believing, and conse-quently no sure foundation for truth. If the self and the world induce each other, where, she objected, are 'the grounds for certainty'?[4] Or to put her question another way, when physi-cally objective material (purple aluminium, for instance) capitulates to point of view (one per-spective after another), what stands against the circular egoism of Descartes's *cogito ergo sum*, against the wrongheaded belief that apperception alone provides a firm basis for conviction? Judd's great failure, she now scolded, was in forwarding a dishonest metaphysics by traffick-ing (so she argued) in exactly the egoistic experience she now rejected but had earlier praised. But just two years later Krauss changed her position again and in the process made her most

1   Rosalind E. Krauss,
'Allusion and Illusion in
Donald Judd', *Artforum*,
vol.4, no.9, May 1966,
p.24.
2   Ibid., p.25.
3   Ibid., p.26.
4   Krauss, 'Problems
of Criticism, X: Pictorial
Space and the Question of
Documentary', *Artforum*,
vol.10, no.3, November
1971, p.70.

fig.27 The interior of San Lorenzo, Florence, by Filippo Brunelleschi c.1423

5   Krauss, 'Sense and Sensibility: Reflections on Post '60s Sculpture', *Artforum*, vol.12, no.3, November 1973, p.47, emphasis in the original. Although a general claim, she was actually speaking about Frank Stella's deductive paintings, postulating a shared foundation for Minimal, Post-Minimal, and Conceptual art. She continued, 'The significance of the art which emerged in this country in the early 1960s is that it staked everything on the truth of that model. Ibid., p.48.

6   Ibid., p.50.

7   Ibid., p.49.

8   Ibid.

9   Krauss, 'Reception of the Sixties', roundtable discussion, *October*, no.69 Summer 1994, p.9. Her first explicit externalisation thesis appeared in Krauss, 'A View of Modernism', *Artforum*, vol.11, no.1, September 1972, pp.48–51.

10   Judd admired the Lee Bontecou's work 'excludes grand interpretations. The explicit power ... displaces generalizations.' Donald Judd, 'Lee Bontecou' (1965), *Donald Judd Complete Writings 1959–1975, Gallery Reviews, Book Reviews, Articles, Letters to the Editor, Reports, Statements, Complaints*, Halifax and New York 1975, pp.179–80.

11   Judd, 'Art and Architecture' (1983), *Donald Judd Complete Writings 1975–1986*, Eindhoven 1987, p.32.

important judgement in terms of her own intellectual development. She claimed that art like Judd's successfully exposed the drawback of trusting sensations to provide understanding, since it proved that there could never be direct sensory access to reality, which instead waited to be discovered by other analytical means. It now communicated that '*meaning* ... is unintelligible apart from ... the semiological conventions of a public space'.[5] Accordingly, she no longer believed that Judd was promoting the wholesale egoism that she had previously denounced.[6] Instead she held that his project pushed the conventional nature of the relationship between a person and his world to its logical and extreme end, to the 'complete externalization of the Self'.[7] It was exactly this discovery that Judd's (and certain other) art now offered, a revelation that 'leads away from any notion of consciousness as unified within itself. For the self is understood as completed only after it has surfaced into the world'.[8] This view leaves no *cogito* whatsoever; rather, the self is simply the world's symptom.

And with this final step Krauss accomplished her own critical goal, the repudiation of modernism's stubborn individualism, its values of 'authenticity, originality, expressiveness'.[9] Judd's art showed her that human agency was subordinate to a world that mechanically composed the scope of our existence, an existence that can be known and analysed.

However, Judd himself objected to these sorts of 'grand interpretations' of art; good art, he believed, 'displaces generalizations'.[10] Art's address is instead ineffable, and to claim otherwise 'risk[ed] placing it among metaphysics and religion, both destructive illusions'.[11] In a morality that directly clashed with Krauss's, he held that it was precisely the artist's partiality that constituted the value of art.

Judd 'leapt into the world an empiricist', as he put it on one of a number of occasions.[12] But his avowals have confused matters for decades, since his empiricism was a knotty species now long out of fashion. It was behaviourist.

Behaviourism was extremely popular from the 1920s through the 1950s; one of its major exponents was Ralph Barton Perry (1876–1957). Now largely forgotten, Perry was editor of American philosopher William James's (1842–1910) works, author of some two-dozen books, President of the American Philosophical Association and a professor at Harvard University for nearly the entire first half of the twentieth century. Forwarding the sceptical mandate of seventeenth- and eighteenth-century British philosophers such as John Locke, George Berkeley and David Hume, this empiricist way of thinking tests the validity of ideas against experiences, rejects all innate beliefs and anchors knowledge only in concrete facts and observable phenomena. Judd was well educated in this Anglo-American tradition, earning a Bachelor of Science in philosophy from Columbia University in New York City in 1953 after a thorough grounding of fifteen classes in the discipline. In interviews and his own essays, he argued that this training informed his artistic practice. He specifically insisted on his debt to Perry's ideas.[13]

Behaviourism encompasses philosophy, experimental psychology and the natural sciences as its advocates aimed to create a unified theory of human existence. In this thinking, inner psychological states are extensions of external behaviour, but it is solely the latter that can be objectively observed and investigated. As Perry wrote, 'The so-called "states" of mind, or "contents of consciousness" … are identified with the environment of behavior, being mental only in so far as behavior selects and combines them.'[14] Such behaviourist externalisation seemingly resolves the classic puzzle of the relationship between mind and body since it substitutes an holistic motor-affective account that unites the two.[15] Feelings, desires and emotions are actions in the world, not affairs of the mind.[16] It is thus a view devised to overcome the seeming inability of introspection to provide verifiable accounts of experience.

This behaviourist externalisation initially sounds similar to Krauss's deferral to what she called 'public space', since both views are broadly empirical in that tangible data alone account for the immaterial psyche. And the resemblance makes sense because both the artist and the critic

12   Judd, 'On Russian art and its relation to my work' (1981), Judd 1987, p.15.

13   See Judd, 'Complaints: Part I' (1969), Judd 1975, p.198; Judd, 'Interview with Margot Willett', tape recording, 1968, Archives of American Art, Smithsonian Institution, Washington, DC; Frances Colpitt, Mini-

mal Art: The Critical Perspective (1980), Seattle 1997, p.123; James Meyer, Minimalism: Art and Polemics in the Sixties, New Haven and London 2001, p.140.

14   Ralph Barton Perry, General Theory of Value: Its Meaning and Basic Principles Construed in Terms of Interest (1926), Cambridge, Massachusetts, 1954, section 58.

Parts of Perry's argument were previously published in an article entitled 'A Behavioristic View of Purpose', Journal of Philosophy, 1921.

15   Perry wrote, 'Behaviorism, in the general sense, is simply a return to the original Aristotelian view that mind and body are related as activity and organ.

The activities of mind, so construed, are observable and describable function of the physical organism.' Perry 1926, section 58.

16   Perry believed that a behaviourist 'does not abandon consciousness, but the introspective theory of consciousness'. Ibid., emphasis in the original.

shared the view that looking at art was a 'way of finding out what the world's like'.[17] The ke
difference is that Judd's specific behaviourist theory insisted on the quantifiable, yet accor
modated the indefinite: 'All experience is knowledge', he offered, 'subjective experience
knowledge; objective experience, which is science, is obviously knowledge.'[18] In this remai
from 1993, he used the term 'knowledge' differently from how he had meant it in the pas
here switching from a philosophically narrow definition such as justified true belief to
broader, more colloquial use. In 1968, for example, he had told one interviewer, 'It's impo
tant that the extent of knowledge is made clear so that it doesn't get muddled. They know s
much about geology. They know so much about physics ... And since that constitutes knov
edge and is reasonably factual ... that's what should be taken seriously or believed.'[19] But son
twenty-five years later, tired I think of the misperception such statements had created – th
his art barred passion – he extended 'knowledge' to include more than just the hard fact
He wanted to make it perfectly clear that he had always believed, 'art isn't a factual matte
really, anyway'.[20]

According to Perry, all behaviour stems from *interest*, a broad concept that Judd repeatedly insis
ed he made central to his own aesthetics. As Perry wrote, 'The really important claim made i
behalf of interest is the claim that things happen *because* of interest.'[21] He used interest in
counter-intuitive way, defining it as a kind of moral agency. Interest combines action wit
expectation, which creates a class of valuing actions such as liking or disliking, loving or ha
ing, desiring or avoiding, and so forth.[22] It is a synonym for 'the motor-affective life' in its entir
ty.[23] As an example of what he had in mind, he explained that a cat values cream whether sh
can imagine 'cream' or not. The cat's valuing – her interest – isn't a mental event but is instead
unification of desire with action; the cat laps the cream.[24] Any lack of interest is indifference, .
is the case with dogs. The dog laps cream, beer, mud, everything, not being either for or again
anything.[25] Whether cats, dogs or people, it is behaviour alone that shines light on values.

A particular category of interest, aesthetic interest, concerns this discussion most. 'The aesthet
interest', Perry wrote, 'is an interested *activity* – a mode of dealing of which its object provid
the appropriate occasion.'[26] Those objects, Judd once contended, could even be concrete bloc

17   The phrase is Judd's, which Krauss quotes in three places. Judd in Bruce Glaser, 'Questions to Stella and Judd' (1964 broadcast, 1966 publication), Gregory Battcock (ed.), *Minimal Art: A Critical Anthology*, New York 1968, p.151. Krauss, *Passages in Modern Sculpture* (1977), Cambridge, Massachusetts, and London 1981, pp.245 and 266; and Krauss, 'The Mind/Body Problem: Robert Morris in Series', *Robert Morris: The*

Mind/Body Problem, exh. cat., The Solomon R. Guggenheim Foundation, New York 1994, p.11.

18   Judd, 'Some Aspects of Color in General and Red and Black in Particular' (1993 speech), *Artforum*, vol.32, no.10, Summer 1994, p.77. Reprinted on pp.144–59 of this catalogue.

19   Judd, 'Interview by Lucy R. Lippard', New York, 10 April 1968, Lucy R. Lippard Papers, Archives of

American Art, Smithsonian Institution, Washington, DC, p.54.

20   Ibid. The relationship between art and knowledge is the focus of my currently unpublished essay, 'Illusionism in Krauss and Judd', December 2002 (under editorial review).

21   Perry 1926, section 58, emphasis in the original.

22   Perry, *Realms of Value: A Critique of Human Civilization* (1954), New York 1968, p.7. (Colpitt quoted from

this page, see Colpitt 1980, p.123.) Previously Perry had explained, 'It is characteristic of the living mind to be *for* some things and *against* others.' Perry 1926, section 49, emphasis in the original. Perry considered the 1954 volume a sequel to the work of 1926.

23   Perry names *interest* an 'all-pervasive characteristic of the motor-affective life, this *state, act, attitude or disposition of favor or disfavor*', Perry 1926, section 49,

emphasis in the origina (Colpitt quoted this sam statement as it appeare in an ethics reader, see Colpitt 1980, p.123.)

24   Perry 1926, section 49. Perry took the cat example from D.W. Prall. See also Perry 195 p.15.

25   Perry 1954, p.7. (Colpitt quoted from th page, see Colpitt 198c, pp.122–3.)

26   Perry 1954, p.32 emphasis in the origina

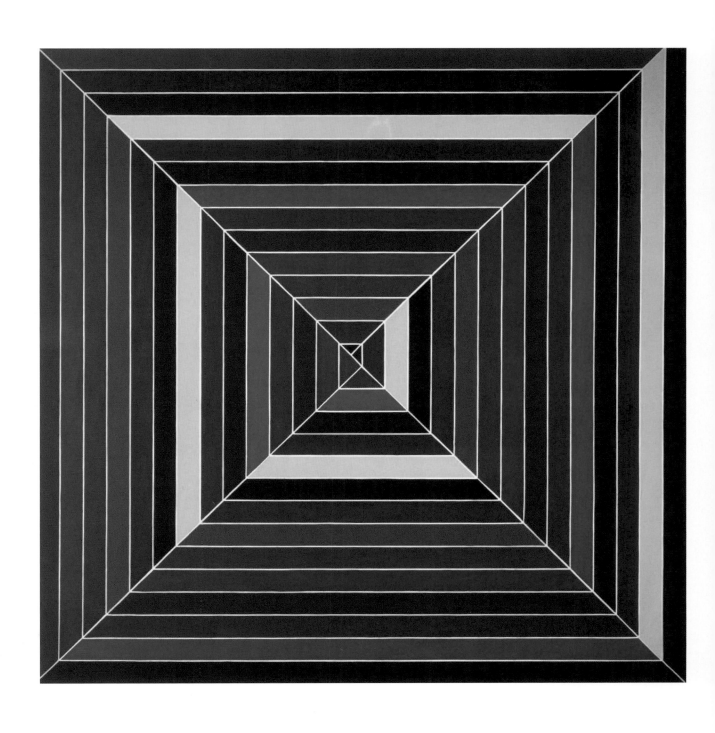

fig.28 FRANK STELLA

Hyena Stomp 1962

Oil on canvas
195.6 × 195.6 (77 × 77)
Tate

by the side of the street; aesthetic interest could transform all material things into works of art.[27] And though blocks could function as art, Judd actually thought the inverse transformation was best: he claimed that art should be 'experienced as an object'.[28] Object status – the palpable combination of material and image – was the source of art's 'power', of its 'amplified intensity', two descriptions he used when applauding Lee Bontecou, John Chamberlain, Frank Stella, Claes Oldenburg, Lucas Samaras and others (fig.28).[29] It is my contention that Judd made Perry's interest his main principle, for it reconciled verifiable physical characteristics and private responses, acknowledging that art is both an objective experience and a valuing one.[30]

Judd declared this behaviourist position throughout his essay 'Specific Objects' of 1965, which is often considered Minimalism's manifesto (but was never thought so by Judd himself).[31] In the well-known first sentence, he observed that some artists were creating a new kind of art

fig.29 Installation view of *Primary Structures: Younger American and British Sculptors*, The Jewish Museum, New York, 27 April – 12 June 1966, showing DSS 85 and DSS 86

27   Judd, 'Interview with Margot Willett', 1968.

28   Judd, 'Lee Bontecou' (1963), Judd 1975, p.65.

29   Judd, 'Local History' (1964), Judd 1975, pp.152–3.

30   A copy of Perry's *Present Philosophical Tendencies* (1912) is in Judd's personal library in Marfa, Texas; Part V is on interest. It is an unusual book for anyone but a specialist to own,

given that the tendencies discussed date to the turn of the twentieth century. Chris Cook kindly located this volume by Perry in Judd's library, summer 2002. Although Judd's behaviourist principles and practice are frequently mistaken for some sort of phenomenological commitment, especially one influenced by French

philosopher Maurice Merleau-Ponty (1908–1961), it should now be clear that these two stands diverge most strongly; the behaviourist holds that the real world exists in a meaningful manner outside of our engagement with it, but as Merleau-Ponty himself wrote, 'The perceived world is the always presupposed foundation

of all rationality, all value and all existence.' Maurice Merleau-Ponty, 'The Primacy of Perception and Its Philosophical Consequences' (1946 address, 1947 publication), *The Primacy of Perception*, ed. and intro. James M. Edie, Evanston, Illinois 1964, p.13.

31   Judd repeatedly asserted that this article

was not a manifesto. For one such instance, see Judd in David Batchelor, 'A Small Kind of Order', *Artscribe International*, no.78, November/ December 1989, p.62. Judd also used the behaviourist concept of interest in his earlier reviews. See, for example, Judd 1975, pp.67, 72, 95.

that was 'neither painting nor sculpture', a type called 'specific objects'.[32] This practice indicated a widespread *disinterest* in traditional media, which had run their course. 'The disinterest in painting and sculpture', Judd proclaimed, 'is a disinterest in doing it again.'[33] The issue was more than a wish for novelty, since Judd, in a slight variation from Perry's terminology, held that disinterest was not mere indifference (the dog's demeanour), but was instead a negative valuing action (the cat rejecting spoiled cream).[34] The abandonment of painting and sculpture was valuing action, since Judd believed those forms of art presented a view of existence that cried out for repudiation. As he contended elsewhere, 'All that art is based on systems built beforehand, a priori systems; they express a certain type of thinking and logic that is pretty much discredited now.'[35] This a priori system was none other than Thomist Christianity (and the ensuing rational philosophy of Descartes), which Judd believed arrested life with absolutes.[36] And it was precisely because painting and sculpture were grounded in such peremptory values that he (and certain other artists, he thought) found them immoral. 'A person', he later wrote, 'lives with a little solid knowledge, a great deal of fragmentary knowledge, a lot of assumptions and many provisional solutions and reactions made from day to day.'[37] Accordingly, Judd held that art itself was not simply good or bad, but was right or wrong in moral terms. Morally wrong art is disinteresting art. And he made this claim over and over again. Once, when asked, 'Aren't you saying then that the reading of the painting is where the correction should take place [to restore its credibility]', he replied, 'No, it's decidedly *in* the painting.'[38] Again he followed Perry's lead, for as the latter explained, 'in theory of value it is this *object*, and not the acts of judgment themselves, which is primarily in question'.[39] Judd's moral injunction was understood quite clearly in the 1960s, even if not everyone agreed. George Segal, for one, accused Judd of making 'value judgments', while Robert Rauschenberg, for another, objected, 'But you're talking about a kind of morality.'[40]

Judd's call was for 'a new thing itself' – moral art – and not for a hybrid combination of painting and sculpture, which would have been a form rotten to its core.[41] In 1966, perhaps trying

32   Judd, 'Specific Objects' (1965), Judd 1975, p.181.

33   Ibid.

34   It is on this particular point of terminology that Judd's use of 'interest' differed from Perry's in a technical manner. For Perry, interest is an act of valuing either positively or negatively; no valuing accompanies indifference, which is the condition of no interest. In Judd's less precise use, which I will follow, interest mainly implies a positive act of valuing, while disinterest is its negative condition. I would like to emphasise that Perry's and Judd's Anglo-American empirical understanding of the aesthetic act as an active, valuing action is extremely different from Kant's transcendental aesthetics. Despite a similarity in vocabulary, Kant, unlike Perry or Judd, held that the aesthetic experience is disinterested, meaning that it is both impartial and lacking in selfish ambition. In distinguishing Perry from Kant, I am disagreeing with Colpitt's Kantian interpretation of 'interest', and, in insisting the issue is one of values and not merely value, with Meyer's understanding of 'interest' as a neutral sounding term for the active judgement of quality. Nevertheless, their research into this issue is extremely valuable, and I have gratefully built upon it; Colpitt was the first scholar to take Judd's ideas about interest seriously, and they are two of the three interviewers who pressed Judd himself on this important concept. See Colpitt 1980, pp.120–5; Meyer 2001, pp.140–1, 294 n.104.

35   Judd in Glaser (1964), Battcock 1968, p.151.

36   Judd, 'Statement' (1968), Judd 1975, p.196.

37   Judd, 'Art and Architecture' (1983), Judd 1987, p.29.

38   Rose and Judd, quoted in 'Is Easel Painting Dead?', November 1966, symposium transcript, Barbara Rose Papers, Archives of American Art, Smithsonian Institution, Washington, DC, p.31, emphasis added.

39   Perry 1926, section 54, italics in the original.

40   George Segal quoted in 'Tape-Recording of Waldorf Panel II On Sculpture, Tape #1', 17 March 1965, symposium transcript, Archives of American Art, Smithsonian Institution, Washington, DC, p.62; Robert Rauschenberg, quoted in 'Is Easel Painting Dead?', 1966, p.31.

41   Judd in Batchelor 1989, p.63.

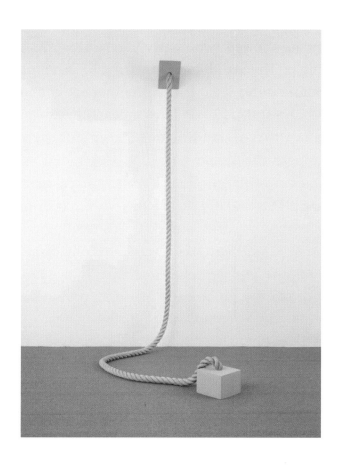

fig.32 ROBERT MORRIS
Rope Piece 1964

Rope and wood, painted
556.2 × 25.5 × 25.5 (219 × 10 × 10)
The Museum of Modern Art, New York.
Gift of Philip Johnson

fig.33 ROBERT RAUSCHENBERG
Bed 1955

Combined painting: oil and pencil on
pillow, quilt and sheet on wood supports
191.1 × 80 × 20.3 (75 $^3/_4$ × 31 $^1/_2$ × 8)
The Museum of Modern Art, New York.
Gift of Leo Castelli in honour of
Alfred H. Barr, Jr.

tional forms: 'Because the nature of three dimensions isn't set, given beforehand, something credible can be made, almost anything', a principle aligned with his rejection of metaphysical givens.[46]

Mathematical sequences and geometric shapes are themselves, it might be argued, devices aimed towards the viewer's intellect. But in art, as Perry explained, maths and geometry are 'viewed through a sensory medium' and are consequently only 'approximately logical, mathematical, or conceptual'.[47] With their abstraction instead made phenomenal, they function as a kind of material itself, and so do not rely on recognition for discernment (but this does not prevent them from being deciphered or analysed like any other material). And Judd believed Perry's ideas; he told one interviewer that maths was 'just ... like finding a material', and another that he used geometry to make it 'evident that the scheme was given, not composed – that I didn't adjust all these little parts'.[48] Nor was Judd's conception an uncommon one for his era, though again the issue was much disputed. In 1966 Robert Smithson, in agreement with Judd, characterised maths and geometry in art like Judd's as 'synthetic', that is, as 'separated from [their] original meaning'.[49]

46   Judd, 'Specific Objects' (1965), Judd 1975, p.184.

47   Perry 1954, p.332, emphasis removed from the original. Perry's comment is similar to Judd's remarks that '[y]ou don't walk up to it and understand how it is working. but I think you do understand that there is a scheme there'. Judd in John Coplans, 'An Interview with Don Judd', *Artforum*, vol.9, no.10, June 1971, p.49.

48   Judd, 'Interview by Friedrich Teja Bach', 5 May 1975, Archives of the Judd Foundation, Marfa, Texas; Judd, 'Interview by Daniel De Wilde', 1979, p.3.

49   Robert Smithson, 'Entropy and the New Monuments' (1966), *Robert Smithson: The Collected Writings*, ed. Jack Flam, Berkeley, Los Angeles and London 1996, p.23.

As Judd recognised, aesthetic interest does not readily surrender the sensuous to the analytic.[50] It takes its art 'all at once', an idea that Perry demonstrated with a charming simile: 'neither the warp nor the woof, but the warp and the woof together with the nap and the dye – in short, the carpet'.[51] Perry's example received vanguardist life with Judd's more famous formulation in 'Specific Objects': 'It isn't necessary for a work to have a lot of things to look at, to compare, to analyze one by one, to contemplate. The thing as a whole, its quality as a whole, is what is *interesting*.'[52] In this sense, art's success or failure depends on its ability to stave off contemplation, to generate and hold a single prolonged sensation, since, as Judd believed, 'all first-rate art has been based on an immediate phenomenon'.[53] He offered Lee Bontecou's work as an example (fig.34). Although she made her art by combining fabric scraps, saw blades, metal cylinders and electric lights on jutting metal armatures, he beheld only the sensual unity of these components, which generated a singleness he thought had once exceeded that of his own art: 'Each ... is an image ... primarily a single emotive one ... essentially new and surprising; an image has never before been the whole work, been so explicit and aggressive.'[54] Her art was interesting and, accordingly, satisfying. In trying to make art like hers, Judd wanted his objects, in their heterodoxy, to present strong sensations that escaped habit and custom, that were seemingly autonomous (fig.35).[55] And although

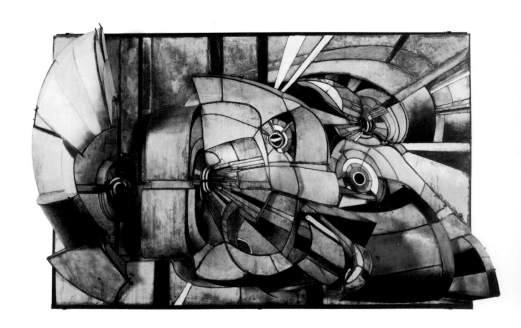

fig.34 LEE BONTECOU

Untitled 1966

Welded steel, wire and canvas
199.4 × 302.3 × 78.7 (78 1/2 × 119 × 31)
Museum of Contemporary Art, Chicago.
Gift of Robert B. Mayer Family
Collection 1991.85

50 Perry 1954, p.328.
51 Ibid., p.348. Perry more directly explained that 'aesthetic interest ... contemplates not bare relations, arrangements, organizations, variables – but terms in relation, subject matter arranged and organized, values or variables. The objects so contemplated escape both the schematic thinness of con-

cepts, and the chaotic plethora of sense-perception.' Ibid., p.347.
52 Judd, 'Specific Objects' (1965), Judd 1975, p.187, emphasis added.
53 Judd, 'Art and Architecture' (1983), Judd 1987, p.35.
54 Judd, 'Specific Objects' (1965), Judd 1975, p.188. Richard Shiff made the important observation that Judd was amenable to 'metaphorically

linked generalities' in art other than his own, and thus was willing to embrace sexual and violent content in Bontecou's art. Shiff's explanation of this aspect of Judd's beliefs – his polarity – is a signal contribution. Richard Shiff, 'Donald Judd: Fast Thinking', *Donald Judd: Late Work*, exh. cat., PaceWildenstein, New York 2000, p.15.

55 Judd said, 'I never took sculpture as a model, although I was impressed, not influenced exactly, but pushed somewhat by quite a few people, for example, by Bontecou and Chamberlain, who at one time I thought did stronger work than I could possibly do.' Judd quoted in, 'The New Sculpture: A Symposium on Primary Structures',

2 May 1966, transcript, Archives of the Jewish Museum, New York, p.9. Though I am singling out Bontecou for special attention, arguments could be made for the importance to Judd of art by John Chamberlain, Claes Oldenburg, Jackson Pollock and, to a slightly lesser extent, Barnett Newman and Frank Stella.

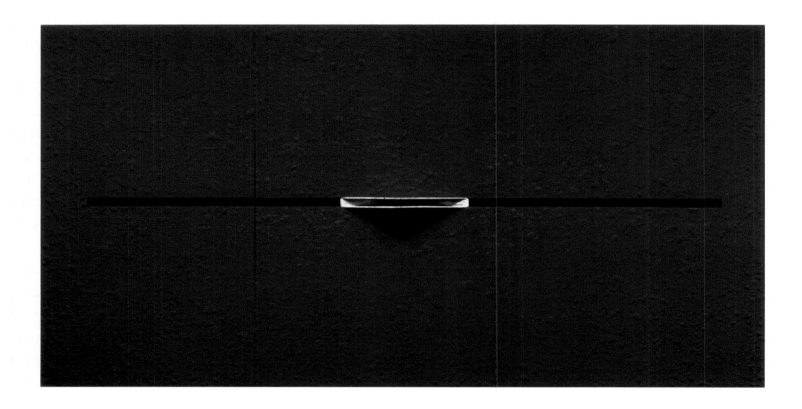

fig.35 DONALD JUDD

Untitled 1962

Light cadmium red oil and wax on liquitex and sand
on masonite and wood, with aluminium and black
oil on wood
122 × 243.8 × 19 (48 × 96 × 7 ¹/₂)
DSS 28
Collection of Judd Foundation

viewers have long tried to find the comfort of the familiar in them, those like Krauss who look hard enough discover only frustration, a fault not of Judd's art but of society itself. 'The Don Quixote of our time', Judd conjectured, 'would be against all stories and words. We're brought up on stories: Children's stories, literature, movies, trite expectations, if this then that.'[56] For far from providing any allegorical meaning, the specific object breathes at a motor-affective level; it is not art as idea, but art as idea and feeling and value all at once.[57] In short, interesting. 'A work', Judd notoriously asserted, 'needs only to be interesting', a demand that sets the bar awfully high.[58]

Judd's insistence that right art was sensually single also explains why he believed that materials should safeguard their character. 'There is an objectivity to the obdurate identity of a material', he contended, unlike in, say, a Willem de Kooning painting where the impasto partly serves representational ends.[59] He consistently repeated this belief, later telling one interviewer, 'I am very interested in the materials as materials, for themselves, for the quality they have, and retaining that quality, not losing it.'[60] This position was not reductive formalism, but was instead the commitment to a sure foundation for truth, one that does not 'go against what is known scientifically'.[61] This kind of integrity is vital to a specific object's credibility, since, as Perry explained, 'the work of art may be criticized on the ground of the purity or impurity of the creative motive'.[62] And Judd tested his own art in Perry's terms: 'I'm making it for a quality that *I* think is interesting and more or less true.'[63] Spared the imprecision of reference, material – scientific – fidelity provides the objective ground and, correspondingly, the phenomenal clarity that conveys art's subjective dimension. The physical object becomes an 'emotive form', a work of art that Judd asserted in 'Specific Objects' transmits 'biopsychological' energy from the artist to the viewer.[64] This energy is specifically, Judd elsewhere explained, the artist's 'assertion of herself, of what she feels and knows'.[65] Interest is powerful; it is 'primitive, oppressive and unmitigated ... '.[66] Raw.

56   Judd, unpublished note, 15 November 1988, Archives of the Judd Foundation, Marfa, Texas.

57   That modernist art 'breathes' is Richard Shiff's contention in his important study, 'Breath of Modernism (Metonymic Drift)', *In Visible Touch: Modernism and Masculinity*, ed. Terry Smith, Chicago 1997, pp.185–213.

58   This is one of Judd's two most debated claims, the one that has led scholars to investigate what exactly he meant by the concept 'interesting'. Judd, 'Specific Objects' (1965), Judd 1975, p.184. Compare Michael Fried, 'Art and Objecthood', Battcock 1968, p.142, and Judd, 'Complaints: Part I' (1969), Judd 1975, p.198.

59   Judd, 'Specific Objects' (1965), Judd 1975, p.187.

60   Judd, 'Interview by Paul Cabon, France' (after 1989), Archives of the Judd Foundation, Marfa, Texas, p.10.

61   Judd, quoted in video interview, Marfa, Texas, June 1992, Archives of the Judd Foundation, Marfa, Texas.

62   Perry 1954, p.340. Judd similarly claimed, 'Nothing made is completely objective, purely practical or merely present.' Judd, 'Specific Objects' (1965), Judd 1975, p.189.

63   Judd in Glaser (1964), Battcock 1968, p.151, emphasis in the original.

64   The quoted words are Judd's; biopsychological is a behaviourist concept, a synonym for motor-affective. Judd, 'Specific Objects' (1965), Judd 1975, p.189. On art as 'the transmission of some kind of energy', see George Kubler, *The Shape of Time: Remarks on the History of Things*, New Haven and London 1962, p.9.

65   Judd, 'Lee Bontecou' (1965), Judd 1975, p.179. Judd repeated this contention in 'Art and Architecture' (1983), Judd 1987, p.33.

It is no surprise that viewers have long had visceral reactions to Judd's art, weighing it (him) against what they feel and know. James Mellow had an 'almost chilling' experience.[67] Richard Serra found the works 'unnerving'.[68] Robert Pincus-Witten felt them to be 'particularly coercive'.[69] Karl Beveridge and Ian Burn discovered themselves 'forced ... to deal with [our] own presence'.[70] Michael Fried complained that the art 'refuse[d] to stop confronting him, distancing him, isolating him'.[71] These are motor-affective responses to biopsychological energy. They are behaviourist displays of apprehension and unease, of heeding the call for valuing action. 'The motive to change', Judd seconded, 'is always some uneasiness: nothing setting us upon the change of state, or upon any new action, but some uneasiness.'[72] And herein lies art's great civic promise: 'You have to change the behavior of the whole country', Judd repeated, 'People have to change their lives.'[73] Judd's art indicts.

fig.36 Advertisement for 'Citizens for Local Democracy' in *Public Life*, vol.2, nos.16–18, October–November 1970

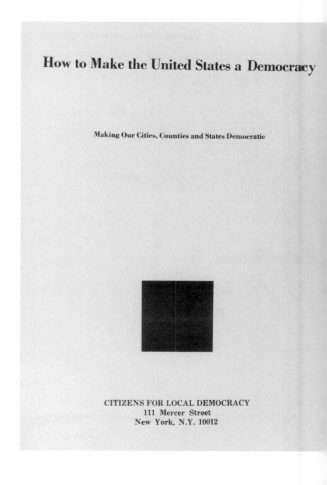

66   This is how Judd described Bontecou's interesting art. Judd, 'Lee Bontecou' (1965), Judd 1975, p.179.

67   James Mellow, '"Everything Sculpture Has, My Work Doesn't"', *New York Times*, 10 March 1968, p.26 (D).

68   Richard Serra, 'Reminiscence', included as a sidebar in Judd 1994, p.114.

69   Robert Pincus-Witten, 'Fining It Down: Don Judd at Castelli', *Artforum*, vcl.8, no.10, June 1970, p.48.

70   Karl Beveridge and Ian Burn, 'Don Judd', *The Fox*, no.2, 1975, p.132.

71   Fried, 'Art and Objecthood', Battcock 1968, p.140. Fried was writing in the third person.

72   Judd, 'Specific Objects' (1965), Judd 1975, p.181. These sentences are actually John Locke's statement, which Judd quoted without identifying its author, although it did appear inside quotation marks. See John Locke, *An Essay Concerning Human Understanding* (1690), New York 1959, bk.II, ch.21, sectio 29. For Perry's discussion of biopsychological motvation, see Perry 1926, section 58.

73   These are President Bill Clinton's words, which Judd quoted. Judd 1994, pp.78 110.

In turning value over to conviction, interest provides the intuition of morality but not a specific code of morals. It does not presume to tell people how they should live their lives because it does not provide a specific set of rules or a standard against which to judge behaviour. Accordingly, in exactly the same way that Judd would soon decide to broaden his definition of knowledge, he finally made a point of ensuring that his charge was not construed as a dogmatic one, saying in 1989, '[Art]'s not a medium for something else, so it's not teaching. It's not a moral thing, it's not an ethical thing, it's not a scientific thing; it's art.'[74] For with interest as value, morality's address is solely to intuition – exactly as art's should be – in that its compass is satisfaction or unease, the feelings that compel us to act and which verify our course every step of the way. Beliefs are constantly tested for their ability to help us live better lives. 'He who knows values, and takes account of them', Perry wrote, 'profits from that knowledge through his better adaptation to the environment in which he lives; and he who ignores them, does so at his peril.'[75] In this evolutionary maxim, the world is understood not as an abstraction but as behaviour, real events and local affairs only; it is incapable of being modelled, represented or even known in any comprehensive manner.[76] Instead, our ever-changing world takes shape through the process of attempting to achieve consensus, which guides and reforms the four major social institutions, which Perry identified as 'conscience, polity, law, and economy'.[77] This conception makes democracy an instrument of morality and morality a means for democracy.[78] To pursue one's own satisfaction in consensus with others is to act morally. Morality and democracy become one and the same agent, each penetrating all the features of public life, synonyms for social compassion and liberal progress. And the principle that behaviour, democracy and morality are united guided Judd's lifelong commitment to political activism (fig.36).

I have elsewhere said a good deal about Judd's actions, which flowered in the late 1960s and early 1970s and again in the early 1990s, but I would like to touch on some of the highlights here as well, since for Judd, both aesthetically and personally, conviction alone is not action – deeds matter.[79] In 1969, he assisted his wife Julie in the formation of Artists Against the Expressway, part of a coalition that opposed the construction of a proposed thoroughfare that would have cut through the heart of Soho where they lived. Judd helped AAX assemble a prominent steering committee and wrote and signed letters on its behalf, including one to the mayor and another (a mass mailing written by Julie) that called for a rally at the Whitney Museum.[80]

74 Jochen Poetter (ed.), 'Back to Clarity: Interview with Donald Judd', *Donald Judd*, exh. cat., Staatliche Kunsthalle Baden-Baden 1989, p.96. Sandra Delacourt questioned me about this statement.

75 Perry 1926, section 57.
76 Compare to Mark Bauerlein, *The Pragmatic Mind: Explorations in the Psychology of Belief*, Durham and London 1997, pp.106–7.
77 Perry 1954, p.342.

78 Perry made the fearless claim for the 'identity between democracy and morality'. Perry 1954, p.274.
79 Raskin, 'Specific Opposition: Judd's art and politics', *Art History*, vol.24, no.5,

November 2001, pp.682–706.
80 Judd to Mayor John V. Lindsay, 9 January 1969, Archives of Julie Finch, New York. The mass mailing letter was dated 7 June 1969. Copies of it are in the Lucy R. Lippard

Papers, Archives of American Art, Smithsonian Institution, Washington, DC, and the Robert Smithson and Nancy Holt Papers, Archives of American Art, Smithsonian Institution, Washington, DC.

The *New York Times* (and other newspapers) reported the group's protest, noting that more tha
6,000 artists lived in the threatened district then mostly known for its nineteenth-century
cast-iron buildings, which would be destroyed.[81] Julie, the group's chairwoman, reached ou
for the support of the Citizens for Local Democracy, asking for its help; she also enlisted th
aid of the War Resisters League in which she and Judd were already active.[82] In the face of th
mounting opposition, the city cancelled its plans; the WRL even sent a telegram to the Judd
congratulating them 'on victory in xway affair'.[83]

After collaborating with the Citizens for Local Democracy, Judd became increasingly active i
the organisation, writing for its newspapers and serving on its advisory committee.[84] The CLD
main goal was to fracture the central government of New York City and replace it with som
fifty small townships, a plan that would restrict the reach of government by limiting powe
to neighbourhoods alone.[85] The current situation, as CLD described it, was intolerable: 'In th
absence of local democracy within the city, New York ... is virtually an elective monarchy wit
8,000,000 subjects.'[86] Judd agreed with them, believing that townships would check the con-
solidation of political rule since each resident would have an immediate and equal share o
power. It was in this respect that he told one of CLD's reporters, 'the only defense and the onl
way to regain the rights everyone is supposed to have is to form a permanent organization o
citizens'.[87] With politics confined to location and with the locale of restricted size, peopl
would be obligated to cooperate for their mutual well being. In this 'plan without a maste
(as CLD's slogan ran), not only would neighbours count, they would exercise their democra
ic and moral responsibilities.[88]

The CLD naturally embraced the Civil Rights movement, explaining that 'local self-governmer
would put an end to the racism that now flourishes in our cities'.[89] For after the Reverend D
Martin Luther King, Jr spoke out against the Vietnam War in April of 1967, individual righ
and the peace movement became tied hand in glove, uniting the two major protest causes tha
characterised the era in the United States. And Judd fully agreed with the necessity of th
alliance: 'All those who seek to destroy the liberties of a democratic nation', Judd wrote quo
ing Alexis de Tocqueville, 'ought to know that war is the surest and the shortest means t

81   Grace Glueck, 'Artists Assail Downtown Expressway', *New York Times*, 20 June 1969.

82   On 3 March 1969, Julie Judd wrote to the editors of the *Public Life*, which was the newspaper of the Citizens for Local Democracy, asking if they were 'interested in hearing more or working with us'. One subsequent AAX press release was signed by Marvin Gelfand, a member of Citizens for

Local Democracy. Archives of Julie Finch New York.

83   Ralph DiGia, War Resisters League, telegram to Donald and Julie Judd, 21 July 1969, Archives of Julie Finch, New York.

84   See 'Ad Hoc Committee to Save Corona' [advertisement], *Newspaper of Lower Manhattan Township*, vol.1, no.1, 1971, n.p.

85   *Public Life*, vol.2, nos.16–18, October–November 1970, n.p.

86   Ibid.

87   Judd quoted in ibid.

88   Ibid.

89   *Public Life*, vol.1, no.19, 7 November 1969, pp.3–4.

90   See Judd's so-called 'yellow poster' of 1971. Its contents are reproduced as 'Quotes for the War Resisters League' in Judd 1975, pp.205–7. I once wrongly claimed that this poster was slightly misdated – it is

not. I had mistaken the Westbeth Peace Festival 1970 for one held the following year, 1971, where the poster was sold to raise funds for the New York Peace Action Coalition a Student Mobilization Committee to End the War i Vietnam. Letters in the Lucy R. Lippard Papers, Archives of American A Smithsonian Institutio Washington, DC, confir that 1971 is the correct date.

accomplish it'.[90] War prevents liberty, a pacifist thinks, by coercing minority groups and individuals into obedience to the state or silence.[91]

Judd, who continued his association with WRL, later characterised this broad activist climate as a reaction to Cold War oppression, which consisted of '40 years of aggression, which keeps everyone poor and scared'.[92] But his political commitments have often been dismissed, and at the end of his life he asked, 'Why is it idealistic ... to want to do something new and beneficial, practical also, [resulting] in a new civilization?'[93] Judd's greatest accomplishment was in keeping people sovereign, whether in politics or in art.

But Krauss, Judd's most important critic, saw things differently. Instead of trusting people to make their own decisions, she subordinated agency to the prevailing conditions, which perpetually construct the borders of our lives. What Judd found interesting, then, was precisely the value that Krauss found objectionable. The individual, above all else.

91   Compare to Randolph Bourne, 'War is the Health of the State' [from Bourne, *The State*, 1919], in *The Anarchist Reader*, ed. George Woodcock, Atlantic Highlands, New York, 1977, pp.98–103.

92   Judd, 'A long discussion not about masterpieces but why there are so few of them, Part II' (1984), Judd 1987, p.84.

93   Judd 1994, p.78.

Galerie Heiner Friedrich, Cologne,
1 June – 10 July 1974

fig.37 DAN FLAVIN

Untitled (Marfa Project) 1996

Detail from Building Three
Permanent collection the Chinati Foundation,
Marfa, Texas

Donald Judd: A Sense of Place

NICHOLAS SEROTA

> *The painting should give man a sense*
> *of place, that he knows he's there,*
> *so he's aware of himself.*[1]
>
> Barnett Newman (1905–1970)

PRACTICE AND PLACEMENT

Donald Judd's *Last Will and Testament*, completed three years before his death, not only divides his assets but also gives instructions and sets out his beliefs as guidance for his executors. The Will is characteristic of Judd in its moral as well as practical purpose, and is a succinct statement of his views about the relationship between man, art and nature. High on his list of priorities is the proper display of his own work and the preservation of the installations that he had realised in New York and Texas. 'Too often I believe, the meaning of a work of art is lost as a result of thoughtless or unsuitable placement of the work for display. The installation of my own work, for instance, as well as that of others, is contemporary with its creation, and the space surrounding the work is crucial to it. Frequently as much thought has gone into the placement of a piece as into the piece itself.'[2]

The attention and discipline that Judd brought to the installation of his own work began early in his career.[3] The practice developed through a sequence of domestic spaces and culminated in the series of buildings and structures that he created and populated with work in and around Marfa, Texas, between his first arrival in the town in November 1971 and his death in 1994. It was Judd's habit to install his own work and that of friends within his living space, so that he could learn from its immediate availability and presence. In 1968 he acquired a cast-iron-frame building which filled a 22.9 by 7.6 m (75 ft by 25 ft) lot on a corner of Spring Street in Soho, New York.[4] His conversion and occupation of this space set the model for most of his later projects. The former garment factory and showroom was gutted, removing accretions and opening up the floors to reveal the plain structure and allow abundant natural light to fill the spaces. Each floor was given a single designated purpose: eating, living, sleeping and the making of art; and in each a sofa, chairs or a bed were placed to create a space for relaxation and for contemplation of the art that had been carefully installed in every space. Over the years, paintings and sculptures by contemporaries such as Frank Stella, Claes Oldenburg and Dan Flavin, as well as objects by Judd himself, gradually moved into appointed locations.

When Judd established himself in Marfa during the 1970s, converting industrial buildings in the town as quarters for living and working, similar principles prevailed. Over a twenty-year period Marfa slowly declined in prosperity and Judd acquired a range of redundant buildings across the town – several houses, a former bank, a hotel, a supermarket, aeroplane hangars and warehouses and an army barracks. Each was dedicated to a single purpose, so that even-

1. Barnett Newman, 1967, cited by Judd in 'Abstract Expressionism' (1983), *Donald Judd Complete Writings 1975–1986*, Eindhoven 1987, p.41.

2. *Last Will and Testament of Donald C. Judd*, 10 December 1991.

3. Judd mentions the practice in connection with an apartment in which he lived on 19th Street, New York, during the late 1950s.

4. For Judd's description of the space see '101 Spring Street', *Donald Judd, Architektur*, exh. cat., Westfälischer Kunstverein, Münster 1989, pp.18–19.

tually he could boast separate buildings to house studios for sculpture, printmaking, drawing and architecture, as well as other buildings in which he had installed specific groups of works.[5]

Judd gradually settled himself and his young children into the complex of buildings in Marfa now known as the Mansana de Chinati. There he followed the example of Spring Street in making installations, primarily of his own existing works. In the East Building, a former World War I aircraft hangar, he spent some years installing a group of early painted works. In the West Building he placed a group of later wall and floor sculptures constructed out of a range of metals and differing types and hues of Plexiglas.

With the support of the Dia Foundation, he later took over the decayed and spoiled land of the former army headquarters at Fort Russell, situated at the southeast edge of Marfa. There he achieved a closer synthesis between his own objects and the buildings or the landscape. In two former artillery sheds, an installation of one hundred milled-aluminium sculptures and the modification of the sheds themselves were developed as a single project. His description is revealing of his care for detail: 'the buildings, and the works of art that they contain, were planned together as much as possible. The size and nature of the buildings were given. This determined the size and scale of the works. This then determined that there be continuous windows and the size of their divisions. The windows replaced derelict garage doors closing the long sides. A sub-division of nine parts, for example, would have been too complicated in itself.'[6] Similarly, fifteen groups of three large concrete sculptures were placed out in the field beyond the artillery buildings: a project on the scale of Stonehenge and equally responsive to changing conditions of light and the seasons.[7]

Unusually, Judd's commitment to installations of art extended to the work of other artists. In Marfa he had given over a former wool and mohair factory and warehouse to the presentation

5. Of the houses Judd acquired, several were eventually dedicated to the display of specific groups of work, e.g. the Cobb House, in which his early paintings were presented on bare pink plaster walls, and the Whyte House, devoted to the presentation of painting from the period 1960–1 with furniture by Rudolf Schindler.

6. Judd, 'Artillery Sheds', *Donald Judd, Architektur* 1989, pp.72–3.

7. The arrangement of the groups is typical of Judd in that all the possible presentations are not exhaustively followed; rather only those which register as having most resonance and difference are selected.

fig.38 JOHN CHAMBERLAIN

23 works in painted and chromium
steel 1972–83
Architectural adaptation by Donald Judd
Permanent collection the Chinati
Foundation, Marfa, Texas

of a group of sculptures by John Chamberlain, an artist for whom Judd had longstanding admiration (fig.38).[8] At Fort Russell, the expanse of the landscape, the number of buildings and the scale of the opportunity encouraged him to invite close friends to propose projects. These included Ilya Kabakov, whose *School No.6* 1993 now occupies one of the former barrack buildings, and Flavin, who proposed a series of light sculptures to fill six of the U-shaped barrack quarters. Flavin's extravagant and glamorous project was planned in great detail, but following a disagreement with Judd, was eventually realised only in 2000 after the deaths of both artists (fig.37).[9]

Each of these projects was developed through a sequence of drawings. Judd made use of these sketches to clarify proportions, sub-divisions of space and relationships between objects. Increasingly, and especially in the large-scale installations such as the artillery sheds or Flavin's barracks, Judd's aim was to create an installation that would endure. The commitment to permanence had its origins in his observation that 'the art and architecture of the past that we know is that which remains. The best is that which remains where it was painted, placed or built. Most of the art of the past that could be removed was taken by conquerors. Almost all recent art is conquered as soon as it is made since it's first shown for sale and once sold is exhibited in alien museums. The public has no idea of art other than that it is something portable, that it can be bought … this situation is primitive in relation to a few earlier and better times.'[10] He continued, 'most art is fragile and some should be placed and never moved again … somewhere a portion of contemporary art has to exist as an example of what the art and its context were meant to be. Somewhere, just as the platinum iridium meter guarantees the tape measure, a strict measure must exist for the art of this time and space.'[11]

Judd's desire for permanence was born out of a frustration with collectors, dealers and even more particularly museums. From the 1970s onwards he had 'complained' loudly that museums frequently treated art badly and artists even worse.[12] 'The gallery is fairly controllable, if limited, the public space slightly, the collector's glasshouse ranch not at all. Most owners of art install it badly; little can be expected. The museum should be serious and competent and much is expected, but it's a disappointment and a failure.'[13] Judd came to believe that the only museum installations of value were those in which groups of works were placed on permanent display. There were some powerful precedents for this view. Clyfford Still, for instance, was praised by Judd for having given a body of work to the Albright Knox Museum in Buffalo

8. Judd's admiration for Chamberlain preceded his own move into three dimensions. He wrote about Chamberlain's first exhibition in 1960: 'Colored sculpture has been discussed and hesitantly attempted for some time, but not with such implications. The color here is insufficient, but the possibilities exciting and Chamberlain has a long time and the start to find them.' Judd, 'John Chamberlain' (1960), republished in *Donald Judd Complete Writings, 1959–1975: Gallery Reviews, Book Reviews, Articles, Letters to the Editor, Reports, Statements, Complaints*, Halifax and New York 1975, p.10.

9. The Flavin project was realised by the Chinati Foundation 1996–2000, following detailed specifications by the artist.

10. Judd, 'Statement for the Chinati Foundation' (1986), Judd 1987, p.111.

11. Ibid.

12. See Judd 'Complaints: Part I' (1969), Judd 1975, pp.197–9; and 'Complaints: Part II' (1973), Judd 1975, pp.207–11.

13. Judd, 'On Installation' (1982), Judd 1987, p.20.

fig.39 DONALD JUDD

Untitled 1964

Blue lacquer on galvanised iron
152 × 68.6 × 61 (6 × 27 × 24)
DSS 69
Private collection
Illustrated example fabricated 1969

and another to the San Francisco Museum of Modern Art on the condition that these groups were installed permanently.[14] Brancusi had set an example, leaving his studio to the French nation on condition that his studio and its contents be kept intact, as had Beuys with his installation of a group of his works at Darmstadt in 1969. In the 1970s others were working with a similar purpose, notably the de Menil family in Houston, and Heiner Friedrich through his Dia Art Foundation, for a period a partner of Judd in Marfa.[15] Nevertheless, Judd was more dogged and more ambitious than most. The installations of his own work and that of others, notably Chamberlain and Flavin, both at Spring Street and in Marfa, although not yet fully realised, are more complete and more authoritative than almost any other permanent installation. As such they have been enormously influential on a generation of curators and museums, and have encouraged a general move towards long-term installations, such as those achieved for Cy Twombly at The Menil Collection in Houston in 1995, and more recently the installation of the Dia collection itself in Beacon, New York.

SPECIFIC LOCATIONS

The root of Judd's concern with the placement of his own work, and that of the artists whom he admired, lay deeper than the simple fact that the appearance or meaning of a work could be 'harmed' or 'helped', as he put it, by where it was placed. As he wrote in 1993, 'There is no neutral space since space is made, indifferently or intentionally, and since meaning is made ignorantly or knowledgeably.'[16] For Judd, space, as well as material and colour, were the principal constituents of the visual. He regarded the concept of 'space' in art as being poorly understood and barely explored in past practice, and he believed that this was an area to which he had made a very significant contribution. 'The smallest simplest work [of mine] creates space around it, since there is so much space within ... This is new in art, not in architecture, of course.'[17] In Judd's view, sculpture from the Greeks to the mid-twentieth century had been totemic in character and therefore deriving from the human figure. He admired the sculpture of David Smith, but described Smith as 'the last of the stone in the field'.[18]

Judd himself, although we now regard him as a 'sculptor', practised as a painter for the first third of his career. These paintings, later valued by Judd and installed in the Cobb House in Marfa, were abstract, expressive, and grew out of consideration of interiors and landscapes. They also reflected an admiration for the work of Stuart Davis. Judd created his first free-standing object only at the relatively advanced age of thirty-four, but in preparing the catalogue raisonné of his work in 1975, he deliberately expunged from the record all the paintings covering the period 1948–59.[19] It is therefore easy to overlook the fact that Judd brought the sensibility of the painter to the interrogation of the third dimension. Like Degas, Picasso, Matisse, Newman and Twombly, Judd is a painter whose contribution to sculpture decisively changed our understanding of the medium.[20]

In the early 1960s Judd struggled to free his painting from the 'European' attributes that he regarded as inimical to the successful work of contemporary art: composition and illusionism

14. Judd complained about both buildings and collections: 'A museum is the collection of an institution and it's an anthology. A few anthologies are all right, but some hundred in the United States alone is ridiculous. It's freshman English forever and never no more literature.' Judd, 'On Installation' (1982), Judd 1987, p.21.

15. The Dia Art Foundation, established by Heiner Friedrich and Philippa de Menil, was also responsible for the realisation of Walter de Maria's *Lightning Field* in New Mexico and his *New York Earth Room* (both 1977).

16. Donald Judd, '21 February 1993', *Donald Judd: Large Scale Works*, exh. cat., The Pace Gallery, New York 1993, p.9.

17. Ibid.

18. Ibid.

19. The exemplary catalogue raisonné of his work up until 1974, published on the occasion of his retrospective exhibition in Ottawa, begins in 1960. Brydon Smith (ed.), *Donald Judd Catalogue Raisonné of Paintings, Objects, and Wood-Blocks, 1960–1974*, exh. cat., National Gallery of Canada, Ottawa 1975.

20. For an extended examination of the contribution of painters to the development of twentieth-century sculpture see Lynne Cooke, *In Tandem: the Painter-Sculptor in the Twentieth Century*, exh. cat., Whitechapel Art Gallery, London 1986.

in painting and anthropomorphism in sculpture. His regard for Pollock, as well as for Still and later Newman, was founded on these painters' ability to circumnavigate the twin traps of composition and illusionism. In his own painting, Judd steadily suppressed gesture and sought to bring the space of the picture close to the surface of the picture plane, as he had observed Stella doing in his black and metallic paintings of 1960. Gradually compositional elements in Judd's paintings were removed, with symmetry replacing balance as the guiding principle. Judd praised Pollock above all, but also Newman, Still and Rothko, for making 'their work a reality not a picture of it'.[21] By 1962 Judd had incorporated found objects in his paintings: in one a baking pan (no.3), in another the letter 'O' from a Plexiglas sign (no.4). These were formal devices included not for their anecdotal or metaphorical associations, but because they allowed depth without creating illusion. In a series of rapid but carefully considered moves, Judd steadily developed the projection of his works off the wall, cantilevering the paintings beyond the point at which they could properly be described as 'reliefs'. To Judd's surprise, one of these objects found itself on the floor and became a free-standing object without need of support from the wall. In less than two years, and in a mere handful of works, Judd formulated his essential vocabulary and set out a series of propositions that he was to explore over the next thirty years: volume, interval and space, and the relationship of a work of art to the wall, the floor and the room.

The astonishing speed with which Judd's language developed was governed by a desire to explore aspects of sculpture that had remained unexamined. The increasing depth of his paintings was the symptom of an ambition to explore volume. A similar ambition determined his choice of the box as the principal form for his sculpture and his use of materials such as machined sheet metal and Plexiglas that would ensure precision and disclose the volume of the interior.

The exploration of vertical and horizontal intervals in the stacks and progressions established a direct connection between the sculpture, the viewer and the space in which both stand. The viewer reads the sculpture by scanning the relationship between the parts of the sculpture and the dimensions of the room. Thus, the interval and size of the original vertical stack of 1965 was determined in part by the distance between the floor and the ceiling (fig.42). The size and characteristic number of units (ten) became fixed by 1966, although stacks continued to be made in two sizes: 15.2 × 68.6 × 61 cm (6 × 27 × 24 in) – a private, domestic scale – and 22.9 × 101.6 × 78.7 cm (9 × 40 × 31 in) – a public, institutional scale. Judd similarly adopted three sizes in the horizontal progressions, deploying different combinations of materials.

Each of Judd's works, although comprising several units or components, is distinguished by the fact that the rules of composition, taste and balance are absent. Of course, Judd's eye is present, for example in the subtle adjustment of the size of the units in the prototype stack, from 22.9 × 101.6 × 76.2 cm (9 × 40 × 30 in) to the dimensions of 22.9 × 101.6 × 78.7 cm (9 × 40 × 31 in) which became his convention. However, the form of the work is determined by simple rules of proportion and arithmetic, while its placement shapes the viewer's perception, both of the sculpture itself and of the space that it inhabits.

21. Judd, 'Abstract Expressionism' (1983), Judd 1987, p.41.

By the mid-1960s Judd was also occasionally making works in which the interval between a number of units of a given size was adjusted in order to fill the available wall space, rather than being fixed and related to the size of the four or six boxes placed on the wall. At the end of the decade he went a step further in conceiving works which deliberately occupy and dominate space: a wall of steel 'boxes' stacked three-high in the Castelli Gallery in 1969 and 1970 (see pp.26–7). now installed in the West Building at the Mansana de Chinati,[22] and the 'wall' of plates, set at 20.3 cm (8 in) from the perimeter of the gallery in 1970.[23] However, in contrast to work like *8 Cuts* 1967, by Carl Andre (fig.40), Judd's sculptures do not activate the space, but remain discrete objects set within it.[24] In the early 1970s Judd began to use plywood as a material for larger scale works. The wood was cheap, conformed to his requirement for a material to be light, plain and consistent, and was easily assembled on site. By 1975 he was using it to construct works that had a more direct relationship to the architectural space of the room. Characteristic of these was the sculpture designed to occupy snugly the space between the symmetrical projecting pilasters of the Lisson Gallery in London (see pp.76–7). The following year he made a series of five large plywood sculptures for the Kunsthalle in Bern, in which the size of each work was influenced by the condition that they should extend to a fixed distance 152.4 cm (60 in) from the walls of the room (see pp.142–3).[25] Even here, however, Judd resisted any temptation to allow his sculpture to follow slavishly the plan of the rooms with their eccentric cut-off corners. Each sculpture retained its rectilinear autonomy, related to but not determined by the space. Each sculpture was placed in a room, but was neither at one with the room

22. *Untitled* 1969 (DSS 160), galvanised iron, 57 units.

23. *Untitled* 1970 (DSS 221), hot-dipped galvanised iron, 18 units.

24. *8 Cuts* 1967 was one of a number of works in which Andre made sculptures that cut into space, e.g. *Lever* 1966 and *Equivalents I–VIII* 1966, which can be seen as positive counterparts to *8 Cuts*.

25. See *Donald Judd: Skulpturen*, exh. cat., Kunsthalle Bern 1976.

fig.40 CARL ANDRE

8 Cuts 1967

1472 concrete block capstones
5.1 × 934.9 × 1300 (2 × 368 × 512)
Original installation:
The Dwan Gallery, Los Angeles
Courtesy of Virginia Dwan

nor functioned as a catalyst to activate the space. The impact was not on the space, but on th
viewer whose experience was defined by their perambulation of the room and by the effect of
large object, the top surface of which was deliberately set at 1.2 m (4 ft), or chest height. In th
same way, another plywood sculpture, *Untitled* 1981, filled the whole wall of the Castelli Galler
on Greene Street, but is also a sculpture of great complexity and subtlety that obliges the viewe
to attend to its concerns rather than those of the space that it occupies (see pp.160–1).[26]

This focus on the relationship between the viewer and the sculpture itself is one of the centra
preoccupations of Judd's work. He was uninterested in geometry, mathematics and system
but he did use simple arithmetic and proportion to establish a relationship between the phy
ical presence of the sculpture and the viewer. He may have abhorred anthropomorphism in
work of art, but his sculpture is fundamentally connected to the human body and to the ph
nomenological experience of standing in a space and confronting the work. Most of his wa
works carry an instruction that the top edge should be located at 157.5 or 160 cm (62 or 6
in), eye level for someone of Judd's stature, and the height at which it is possible to perceiv
that the works have depth and volume rather than simply surface.

Judd had a profound belief in the value of prolonged 'looking'. The incorporation of a simpl
wooden bench, chairs or frequently a bed in many of his installations at Spring Street and i
Marfa was a practical device to encourage extended contemplation of the work. Judd disco
ered through personal experience that long scrutiny of a work in the right conditions wou
yield understanding, and oblige him to make continual refinements to the installations i
New York, Texas and elsewhere. His attitude towards installation was therefore empiric
and pragmatic, seeking the best position for each piece by a process of trial and error. H
wanted to give each work its own space, but also a proper relationship with its neighbour c
counterpart elsewhere in the room. This intuitive process characterised Judd's who
approach to making art. When asked whether he wanted an observer to understand som
thing, or simply look at the work, he replied, 'that's the division between thought and fee
ing. You have to do it all at once. You have to look and understand, both. In looking yc
understand; it's more than you can describe. You look and think, and look and think, until
makes sense, becomes interesting.'[27]

ARCHITECTURE AND ENCLOSURE

Judd's activity of transforming buildings and his desire to be present at the installations of h
work, pacing the space, seated on a chair or reclining on a bed covered by a Navaho blanke
reflected an abiding interest in architecture. In 1946–7 while serving in Korea, where one
his more satisfying tasks had been to erect simple prefabricated buildings, he had considere
becoming an architect. However, he had ultimately decided against the idea on the groun
that it might involve too much compromise and negotiation with others. Twenty years late
he began to explore space and volume within buildings using the straightforward pragmat
principles that had governed his approach to making sculptural objects.

26. The sculpture was specifically designed to fill the full length of the wall at Castelli and was subsequently installed at the Saatchi Gallery, London, on a wall adapted to the same dimensions.

27. Angeli Janhsen (ed.), 'Discussion with Donald Judd', *Donald Judd*, exh. cat., Kunstverein St Gallen 1990, p.54.

fig.41 Exterior front view of north artillery shed facing south. The Chinati Foundation, Marfa, Texas

In architecture Judd's touchstones were consistent: the early twentieth-century pioneers of modernism Frank Lloyd Wright, Le Corbusier and Mies van de Rohe, as well as the classical simplicity of Louis Kahn. In his modifications of existing buildings and occasional opportunities to create new structures (more were planned but not realised for want of funds) Judd developed simple rules. These involved establishing and reinforcing symmetry through the axial alignment of doors and windows, and dividing the space by means of simple rhythms and ratios.[28] He considered proportion, achieving balance through the harmony of structure, scale and material, an essential of architecture. His interest in building, like his parallel interest in furniture, was triggered by his own requirements for a kind of space in which he and later his children could live, work, eat, sleep, entertain and contemplate the art he was making. His architecture grew naturally from this wish to inhabit space, to take over raw volume – most often in the form of simple industrial structures – and to turn them into plain but comfortable rooms. Austerity was not Judd's taste, but all his interiors are characterised by spareness. This was a means of ensuring that nothing should interfere with the prime focus of attention, works of art installed in the rooms themselves. Where replacement or sub-division of space demanded invention and design, Judd adopted the most direct of solutions, looking for models in the vernacular buildings around him. The new windows and doors of the

28. 'I long ago reached an agreement with what I consider the primary condition: art, for myself, and architecture, for everyone, should always be symmetrical except for good reason.' Judd, 'Symmetry' (1985), Judd 1987, p.92.

old equestrian arena at Fort Russell, the warehouse housing Chamberlain's installation and the artillery sheds, for instance, are all based on a simple quartering device. Similarly, the design of the roofs of the artillery buildings (fig.41), required to shed water from the original flat and leaking surface, derive from tunnel-like agricultural buildings seen 48 km (30 miles) away. The proportions, however, are Judd's. By choosing simply to double the height of the building Judd avoided an architectural solution based on aesthetic principles, such as the application of a 'golden' section.

In Spring Street, Judd's search for simplicity and a lucid relationship between parts was achieved by stripping away accretions to expose the inherent logic of the building. In Texas he was obliged to establish his own order, especially in situations where he was working with two or three buildings on a plot. In the early 1970s he found himself living with his family in four almost identical 3.4 m by 3.4 m (11 ft by 11 ft) rooms, two for sleeping and one each for living and eating. The experience of such close proximity caused him to reflect on the improvements that could follow from moving these functions slightly apart, opening the space between the rooms by introducing aisles or courtyards.[29] The courtyard, which he had observed as a very satisfactory building form in early societies and other contemporary cultures, became his favoured solution for creating generous living space that also gave personal privacy. The volume of a courtyard can be read as 'unseen' space, an equivalent to the volume that could be discovered in the interior of his sculpture. The Mansana de Chinati, for instance, was created by building a 2.8-m (9-ft) high adobe wall around the perimeter of his property in order to enclose the original single dwelling and two aeroplane hangars. The wall defines the extent, creates seclusion and above all gives protection to a compound that provides for daily tasks to be undertaken in appropriate locations. The Mansana de Chinati is a personal settlement within the city, rather like a Roman encampment with its separate structures and buildings for bathing outdoors and indoors, working, eating, reading and sleeping. Within the courtyard, order is created by the alignment of structures and by simple sub-divisions of the open ground.

Judd's creation of a compound at the Mansana de Chinati was an act of recuperation: he took a plot of apparently waste ground and a handful of semi-derelict buildings, and with a few deft moves transformed the plot into a 'place' with identity and purpose. In Judd's view the relationship between buildings and terrain had to be one of harmony not abrasion. He strongly believed that most modern development was wasteful of resources and insensitive to the natural environment. In developing his plans at Marfa, he therefore made every effort to reuse old structures and to restrict his new building to land that had already been 'damaged'. For instance, his plans for a group of buildings in concrete designed to house two groups of wall and floor pieces were conceived for an overgrown but spoiled site overlooking the abandoned buildings at Fort Russell.[30] In several of his essays on architecture Judd criticised the waste involved in conventional twentieth-century town planning, in which ribbon development along expressways to the suburbs resulted in the successive neglect of the city centre and later regeneration based on the creation of shopping malls.[31]

29. Judd conceived and drew many variant arrangements of buildings around courtyards, but was only rarely able to develop these ideas in reality, as for instance through his creation of the compound containing the buildings at Mansana de Chinati. See however, 'Casa Luan', *Donald Judd, Architektur* 1989, pp.29–30; and 'Horti Co clusi', ibid., pp.40–1.

30. Judd, 'Concrete Buildings', *Donald Judd, Architektur* 1989, pp.88–

31. Judd, 'On Architecture' (1984), Judd 198 p.88.

fig.42 DONALD JUDD

Untitled 1965

Galvanised iron
7 units, each 23 × 101.6 × 76.2 (9^1/$_{16}$ × 40 × 30)
DSS 65
Moderna Museet, Stockholm

Throughout his practice as a maker of buildings Judd therefore sought to make whole tha
which had been destroyed, abandoned or left derelict. A similar instinct governed h
approach to his rare commissions for outdoor sculpture. In these projects he consistent
sought to complement rather than dominate the landscape, producing works that subt
exploit the fall of the terrain, just as he had done with the adobe wall at the Mansana d
Chinati.[32] In the few instances in which he took over new ground, as on his ranch Ayala d
Chinati to the south of Marfa, he confined his new building to temporary structures in woo
in order to preserve a balance between man and the natural environment. He became extrem
ly critical of others who had built on unspoiled wilderness and devoted ever greater parts (
his income to the acquisition and preservation of land. In his Will almost as much attentio
is devoted to his ranch property as to his art, with instructions that the ranch, which 'has si,
nificant ecological and botanical value', should be given to a 'qualified entity or governmer
tal unit which will best be able to preserve this property in its natural state for the benefit (
the scientific community and the general public'.[33]

Judd's work as an artist, an architect, a designer of furniture and rancher is all of a piece. Ther
is a striking consistency of purpose and method. At its centre lies a concern for space ard fo
the phenomenological relationship between objects and the viewer.[34] Judd explicitly denie
that his ambition was the creation of a spiritual experience or spiritual space. For Judd spac
was palpable, to be observed and felt. In contrast to the sacred contemplative space that w
have come to associate with Rothko through his chapel in Houston, or the mystical kabbali
tic space to which Newman alludes in his architectural project for a synagogue, Judd's spac
lies much closer to the empirical observations of nature by Henry David Thoreau. In this Jud
distances himself from the previous generation of painters whose work develops from Eur
pean antecedents, and shows himself to be an American original.

32. *Last Will and Testament of Donald C. Judd*, 10 December 1991.

33. 'My first and largest interest is in my relation to the natural world, all of it, all the way out. This interest includes my existence, a keen interest, the existence of everything and the space and time that is created by existing things. Art emulates this creation or definition by also creating, on a small scale, space and time.' Judd, 'Art and Architecture' (1983), Judd 1987, pp.32–3.

National Gallery of Canada, Ottawa,
24 May – 6 July 1975

101 Spring Street, New York

PHOTOGRAPHS BY TODD EBERLE

101 Spring Street, New York. Exterior.

Area of the Chinati Foundation near Marfa
with barracks and artillery sheds.

Chinati Foundation. Arena, interior
with furniture and doors by Donald Judd

Chinati Foundation. North artillery shed, side view, roof and windows by Donald Judd.

Judd Foundation. La Mansana de Chinati.
West Building, permanent installation of works
by Donald Judd.

Judd Foundation. La Mansana de Chinati. East Building,
permanent installation of works by Donald Judd.

Judd Foundation. La Mansana de Chinati. West Building,
permanent installation of works by Donald Judd.

Judd Foundation. Interior of former
Marfa National Bank, paintings by
Donald Judd.

Judd Foundation. Whyte Building. Interior
with paintings by Donald Judd and furniture
by Rudolf Schindler.

141

Kunsthalle Bern,
14 April – 30 May 1976

Leo Castelli Gallery, New York,
10 September – 31 October 1981

4   *Untitled* 1962

Light cadmium red oil on liquitex and sand
on masonite with yellow Plexiglas
122 × 243.8 × 7 (48 × 96 × 2 ³/₄)
DSS 30
San Francisco Museum of Modern Art.
Bequest of Phyllis Wattis

As one of the most colourful works from this period,
this painting benefits from the experience of the previous one, and also uses an alien object to add actual depth
to the flat picture surface. In this case a yellow Plexiglas
letter, turned on its side, is inset into the picture plane
so that the letter appears to be gouged out of the picture
surface. As in the black composition with a baking pan
(no.3), here the form and the size of the flat letter 'O'
affect the form and size of the overall work. In fact the
rectangle is proportioned 1:2, as are a number of Judd's
paintings from 1961–2. During this period, Judd increasingly used the colour light cadmium red (here for the
second time, and over a considerable surface). This was
the dominant colour in his work until the end of 1964;
it still occurs in the work after this date but to a lesser
extent. Judd favoured this colour because every detail
of a painting was so extremely important to him,
and light cadmium red showed up edges, lines and
textures, unlike black, for instance, which tended to
obscure them.

     For some time Judd had been struggling with the
fact that the canvas was a rectangle that had to be filled
somehow. In these last works (nos.3, 4) he had found a
way to define the rectangle from within, and to calculate
its size and dimensions in direct proportion to the object
in the centre. 'Representation' and format became one,
and the fact that the central focus was a real object that
existed in its own right reinforced Judd's determination
to create works of art that referred solely to themselves.
The advances he made in these paintings paved the way
for his first forays into three-dimensionality, on which he
embarked straight after finishing this piece. This was his
last work to hang flat on a wall and the conclusion to the
chapter called painting.

5   *Untitled* 1962
     exhibited example fabricated 1988

Light cadmium red oil on wood with iron pipe
122 × 84 × 54.6 (48 $^1/_{16}$ × 33 $^1/_{16}$ × 21 $^1/_{2}$)
DSS 33
Collection of Judd Foundation
Illustrated example fabricated 1979

This right angle, constructed from two wooden panels painted red and straddled by a bent, black metal pipe, is the second free-standing work Judd made, and the first that can be considered to be independent of painting. Made in 1962, it follows a series of paintings with rough surfaces and inserted objects; it was made concurrently with a small number of wall reliefs, and marks the beginning of Judd's oeuvre in three dimensions.

The pipe was found in a hardware store on Canal Street, as were many other objects that were integrated into paintings during 1961–2; these objects provided real depth to the otherwise flat paintings and were used as devices to help define the paintings' size and shape.

Determined to move away from traditional composition as an order relating to something external, Judd explored other ways to give structure to his work. Just as the baking pan dictated the proportions of the black rectangle in which it was embedded (no.3), the lengths of the two arms of the metal pipe fulfil the same purpose in the free-standing red angle. The ends of the pipe were centred in the two wooden panels, thus determining the width of the panels.

Remembering these beginnings in an interview with John Coplans in 1971, Judd admitted that he had been puzzled by his first two pieces standing in the middle of the room. 'I didn't quite know what to make of it', he explained, 'they suddenly seemed to have an enormous number of possibilities. It looked at that point and from then on that I could do anything. Anyway, I certainly didn't think I was making sculpture.'[1]

The possibilities lay in the qualities of the angle produced between the two panels, which created space without enclosing it. 'There is scarcely an inside and an outside, only the space within the angle and the space beyond the angle. The only enclosed space is inside the pipe. This slight linear space determines the dimensions of the broad planes. The shell of this narrow space passes through the breadth of the inner angle, a definite space through a general space.'[2]

This red angle is no longer placed on a pedestal, but rather directly on the floor. Although it is vertical, it is neither reminiscent of a figure, nor of anything else. Judd had already tried to remove representation from his paintings in order to achieve something 'in its own right'. It was his attempt to make art that did not try to represent or comment on something that existed in some other form but one that has its own rules and qualities, and is something in itself.

1   'Don Judd: An Interview with John Coplans', *Don Judd*, exh. cat., Pasadena Art Museum 1971, p.30.
2   Donald Judd, *Some Aspects of Color in General and Red and Black in Particular*, Sassenheim 1993, p.11. Reprinted on pp.144–59 of this catalogue.

172

6   *Untitled* 1962

Light cadmium red oil on striated plywood, black oil
on wood with galvanised iron and aluminium
193 × 244.5 × 30 (76 × 96 ¹/₄ × 12)
DSS 34
Öffentliche Kunstsammlung Basel, Kunstmuseum

The two-dimensional plane dominated Judd's work for
more than a decade. Although this was still true in 1961
and 1962, his work also began to move modestly beyond
the flatness of the canvas. Objects, such as a baking pan
or an oval-shaped letter, were inserted into the surface of
the paintings, which were often made with masonite.
Routed lines and a rough, sandy texture were additional
techniques used to open up the two-dimensionality of the
picture plane and create a surface that was more palpable
and defined. In the course of these articulations Judd created a new type of work that occupies a position between
painting and free-standing sculpture. These reliefs, of
which only five were made between 1961 and 1963, are
hung flat against the wall, but seem to want to roll away
from it. The curved metal bands at the top and bottom jut
forward out of the picture plane and enter three-dimensional space. The rectangular middle area is made from
striated wood painted light cadmium red, the colour Judd
used predominantly from 1961 – which saw the onset of
his interest in real space – until 1964, when his first works
were fabricated from metal. The reliefs are his earliest
works to use galvanised iron, which was to become a
favourite material in the following years.

Curving the top and bottom bands results in an
odd and yet intriguingly original shape. It was by this
means that Judd made the transition from the flat surface to the shallow wall box, using a quarter-circle curve
to elegantly lead from one dimension into the next. The
reliefs confidently suggest that painting is past and something else lies ahead. References to the earlier two-dimensional works are largely absent, including compositional
devices and centrality. Handmade elements are reduced,
giving way to a more technical appearance and a new
sense of rigidity and directness. Interestingly, the middle
field has the same dimensions of 121.9 by 244.5 cm (48 by
96 ¹/₄ in) that are characteristic of several earlier paintings
(nos. 2 and 4), and the 121.9-cm (48-in) length is repeatedly
used in three-dimensional works (nos.5, 7 and 8).

8   *Untitled* 1963

Light cadmium red oil on wood with purple Plexiglas
49.5 × 123.2 × 123.2 (19 ¹/₂ × 48 ¹/₂ × 48 ¹/₂)
DSS 38
Estate of Dan Flavin
Illustrated example fabricated 1969

Judd reached a point where his interest in three-dimensional work was fully established fifteen years after he began studying art at the Art Students League in 1948. He now felt that many possibilities were inherent in his approach to volumetric shapes. Looking back some years later he observed that, 'The first work that an artist feels is theirs is not a solution limiting the possibilities but is work that opens to limitless possibilities', and, as he stated, 'The problem for any artist is to find the concatenation that will grow.'[1]

This first fully enclosed volume is a square, divided diagonally to a depth half its height, with one side of the top removed so that the shape appears as both a square and as two triangles. The piece is made from wood, painted red, except for the diagonal cut which stands out in purple Plexiglas, making the side from which it is visible the 'show side'. Although there is no real front or back, the view in which both the upper and lower sections are visible with the purple diagonal running across the square is more interesting than the view from the opposite side where only the solid red section is visible.

Judd was interested in shapes with defined edges and perceivable volumes. Drawings from the same year show that he contemplated cutting into a cube diagonally and lengthways, with narrower and wider angles (fig.47), to various depths. The step-like configuration created a less static and more dynamic shape that presents itself differently from different angles. The classical front-back standpoint no longer applies and all four sides have equal value.

Judd had predominantly used light cadmium red in his paintings since 1960, and subsequently also used it for his three-dimensional works. Red was accompanied by black, metal or purple, this last a new colour that first appeared in his palette in 1963. Red and purple, a compelling combination, were combined in several pieces built in the coming years. In the early years purple was applied as lacquer on metal surfaces; later it also became available as anodised aluminium.

This floor piece is the first to incorporate Plexiglas, a new material that would subsequently be used in many works. Judd's interest in Plexiglas derived from its colour, which is inherent to it and not merely applied. He was also intrigued by its transparency, which made it possible to delineate a volume without closing it off. Purple is bold and unusual in art. Judd thought long and hard about colour, and dedicated his last essay to this subject.[2] Certain colours are identified with certain artists, he explained, and each must find their own colours. Judd admired Roger van der Weyden (1399/1400–1464), but when he tried to employ van der Weyden's blue and red in a small painting as a student, he realised that they were not his colours, and painted them over. Light cadmium red was already Judd's colour by 1963; red and purple became – next to red and black – a typical Juddian combination.

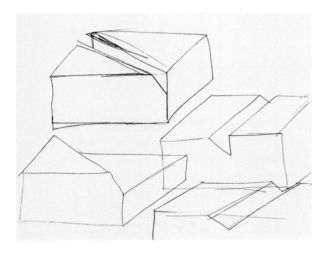

fig.47 *Studies for a sculpture* 1963

Pencil on paper
27.8 × 35.7 (11 × 14)
Collection of Judd Foundation

1   Donald Judd, 'Abstract Expressionism' (1983), *Donald Judd Complete Writings 1975–1986*, Eindhoven 1987, p.42.
2   Donald Judd, *Some Aspects of Color in General and Red and Black in Particular*, Sassenheim 1993.

10   *Untitled* 1964

Chartreuse oil on wood and yellow enamel on iron
49.5 × 122 × 86.4 (19 ¹/₂ × 48 ¹/₁₆ × 34)
DSS 46
The Helman Collection

This piece has almost identical dimensions to the previous work (no.9), and is painted in chartreuse green. In this case there is a semicircular pipe on the top side that finishes flush with the short sides of the rectangle into which it is set; the pipe is enamelled yellow. This work marks the appearance of a new colourfulness in Judd's work. A vibrant yellow had already appeared in his painting (no.4) along with light cadmium red, which predominated by 1961 at the latest. This red is generally combined with black and, more rarely, with purple or metal or its equivalent, grey. Despite Judd's fondness for chartreuse, he seldom used it, and it only reappears years later in a positively fluorescent version as factory-made anodised

aluminium. Chartreuse had the same quality that he valued so much in light cadmium red, that is to say, every nuance of the form showed up with complete clarity. Years later he specifically commented on the 'somewhat sharp and acid color opposed to one white and full'.[1]

Above all, this piece once again demonstrates Judd's extremely distinctive sense of colour; after the palpable colour in numerous red works, this chartreuse box confirms that shapes and contours are defined by colour. The sharp green seems almost iridescent, an impression that is reinforced by the yellow, which creates the effect of a light strip and so calls to mind Barnett Newman's work.

1   Donald Judd, *Some Aspects of Color in General and Red and Black in Particular*, Sassenheim 1993, p.28.

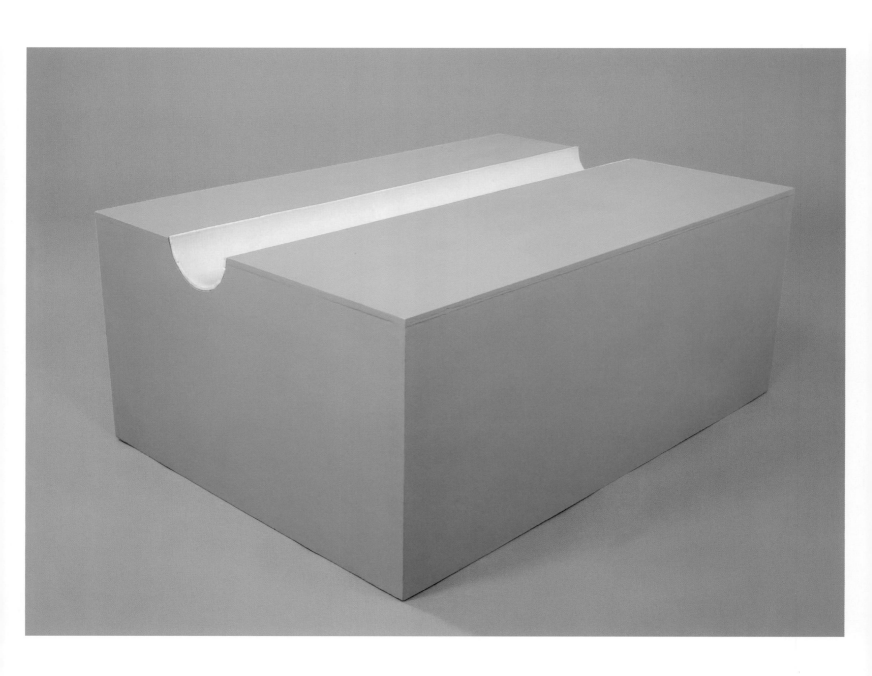

11   *To Susan Buckwalter* 1964
exhibited example fabricated 1965

Galvanised iron and blue lacquer on aluminium
76.2 × 358.2 × 76.2 (30 × 141 × 30)
DSS 56
Addison Gallery of American Art, Phillips Academy,
Andover, Massachusetts (Gift of Frank Stella [PA 1954])
Illustrated example fabricated 1964

In 1964 Judd began to have his works constructed by
fabricators. Handmade items were still made concurrently with fabricated works during the first part of the year,
but by the summer he was commissioning all his pieces.
Judd worked with a number of fabricators who specialised in different materials and techniques throughout his life. In general he would deliver a sketch which
would be rendered into a construction plan by the fabricator; the piece would then be built upon approval from
the artist.

    To Susan Buckwalter consists of four cubes of gal-
vanised iron connected by a square pipe running along
the top front edges. This pipe is made of blue-lacquered
aluminium. Open at both ends, it is inset into the top
edge of the cubes, flush with fronts and tops. All the
surfaces have a slight shine and softly reflect the light.
In the early years, galvanised iron was Judd's preferred
metal because it was the most affordable and had no historical baggage like, for instance, bronze. At the same
time, it is the only metal that has a surface pattern, with
occasional flecks of colour – bluish or reddish – that give
it a painterly quality, although the material itself is tough
and durable.

    The four cubes are aligned at intervals of approxi-
mately one quarter their length, creating compressed
spaces between them like ravines. These spaces clarify
the work's depth and emphasise a pull from front to back
as well as the alternation of enclosed and open volumes.
This is the first work in which the distances between the
single parts create distinctly defined spaces. This idea
will soon be employed in more works, most powerfully
in the stacks.

    The experience gained from the preceding works
which were to be viewed from any number of angles led to
Judd's interest in creating more complex spatial intercon-
nections than he had hitherto done. The alternation of
open and closed volumetric shapes now formed the basis
of many works; this alternation is established by means of
repetition, with the result that from now on sequences of
identical components become a recognisable constant in
Judd's oeuvre. The shortest sequences consist of four
units; other sequences frequently run to six, eight or even
ten identical elements. In the Buckwalter piece space is
oriented in two directions at once, from front to back and
from left to right, with the lengthways direction linking
the separate elements. By late 1964 Judd's work looked

simpler and sharper, even tougher and more technical, and involved more complex spatial relationships than before.

Three examples of this piece were made; the first in December 1964, which remained in the artist's collection, and two at the end of the following year, 1965. While Judd generally had one example of every work made, he occasionally decided on more. These may have been fabricated at the same time, or at different times; each is always considered an original, not an edition. Judd dedicated this work to Susan Buckwalter, a collector of contemporary art from Kansas City, Missouri, who died in January 1965.

12   *Untitled* 1965

      exhibited example fabricated 1968

Red lacquer on galvanised iron
12.7 × 175.3 × 21.6 (5 × 69 × 8 $^1/_2$)
DSS 70
Froehlich Collection, Stuttgart

See no.14

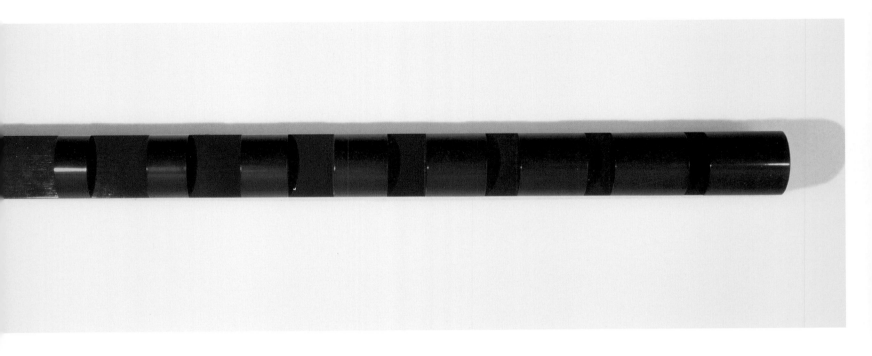

13   *Untitled* 1966

Amber Plexiglas and stainless steel
50.8 × 122 × 86.4 (20 × 48 × 34)
DSS 82
Froehlich Collection, Stuttgart
The form of this work was used first
in DSS 58 (1965)

It took Judd an astonishingly short time to familiarise
himself with the technical potential of industrial production processes and to learn how to make best use of these
for his own purposes. In this new incarnation, the already
familiar floor box becomes stunningly sophisticated: two
side panels of stainless steel plus three Plexiglas panels
make up the box. There is no base panel. The result is a
volumetric shape with utterly clear dimensions that is
transparent and coloured and entirely free of allusions
to anthropomorphic forms or other narrative elements.
Judd no longer needed to make incisions in order to
reveal the interior or the construction of the piece.
Here the facts are plain for all to see: steel wires running
between the two steel panels maintain the tension
between them; the steel panels in turn stabilise the
lighter, more flexible Plexiglas panels.

14 *Untitled* 1966

Stainless steel
36.8 × 194.3 × 64.8 (14$^1/_2$ × 76$^1/_2$ × 25$^1/_2$)
DSS 117
Museum Ludwig (Donation Ludwig 1976)
The form of this work was used first
in DSS 77 (1965)

Close connections sometimes exist even between very different-looking works. The origins of an elongated horizontal wall piece, with a mathematical sequence of rounded shapes protruding forwards, can be found in an iron pipe that Judd had set into a red box two years earlier (no.9). In his efforts to open up the volume, he cut half-sections out of the pipe and ultimately removed it altogether, dividing the volume under it into segments by means of these semicircular excisions (figs.48–9). The same principle is visible here in 'negative' form. The first instance of the principle being applied in 'positive' form occurred when Judd took the leftover semicircular sections of wood and fixed them to a flat wooden block in a simple progression of 6 to 7 to 8 to 9 (fig.10).[1] A year later this prototype was recreated in metal, and in a second version: a long, very narrow form which allows the progression to be stretched, increasing the difference between full and empty forms running in the opposite direction to each other (no.12).

For his first progressions with rounded forms, Judd's preferred metal was galvanised iron painted with clear red varnish so that its characteristic pattern of 'ice flowers' could shimmer through. Later he also used blue varnish, or left the metal in its natural state. Over time Judd also worked with brass, copper and stainless steel. Besides the very elongated version (no.12), there is also a second more compact one, albeit on a larger scale (no.14). The four convex sections and the negative spaces between them are also based on a simple progression, which is less dramatic as it contains fewer elements. These wall pieces no longer treat the wall as a projection surface; in addition they have little to do with reliefs, as they are approximately twice as deep as they are high. Initially a painter, Judd began to feel constrained by the fact that painting is so closely connected with walls. Gradually he moved away from the wall and out into three-dimensionality. Although he continued to create works with a wall in mind, these by definition go beyond traditional genres. As he stated, 'Low and high relief are basically painting, possessing the same problems, as well as some of their own.' He went on to explain his changed understanding of the function of the wall: 'After I made the first works placed on the floor, knowing the new relationship to a surface, through at least 1963 I didn't think anything could be made which could be placed on the wall. Then I realised that the relationship to the wall could be the same as that to the floor. The work on the floor was not lying flat upon it, therefore it was not low relief on the floor, nor heaped upon it, therefore it was not high relief on the floor ... It was necessary for the work to project sufficiently, at least as much as its height and width.'[2] The extreme horizontality of the elongated piece (no.12) soon established itself as part of Judd's thinking, both in this form and in another type of progression, and he returned to this horizontality in the 1980s in his multicoloured modular wall pieces.

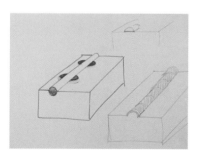

fig.48 *Studies for painted wood sculptures* 1963

Pencil on paper
27.8 × 35.7 (11 × 14)
Kröller-Müller Museum, Otterlo

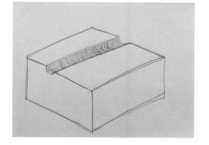

fig.49 *Study for a sculpture* 1963

Pencil on paper
27.8 × 35.7 (11 × 14)
Collection of Judd Foundation

1   DSS 45, Brydon Smith (ed.), *Donald Judd, Catalogue Raisonné of Paintings, Objects, and Wood-Blocks 1960–1974*, exh. cat., National Gallery of Canada, Ottawa 1975, p.117.
2   Donald Judd, *Some Aspects of Color in General and Red and Black in Particular*, Sassenheim 1993, p.12.

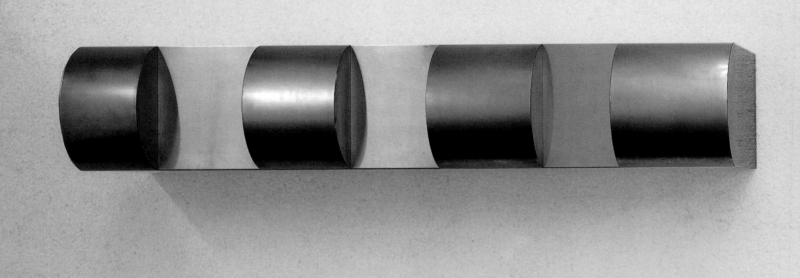

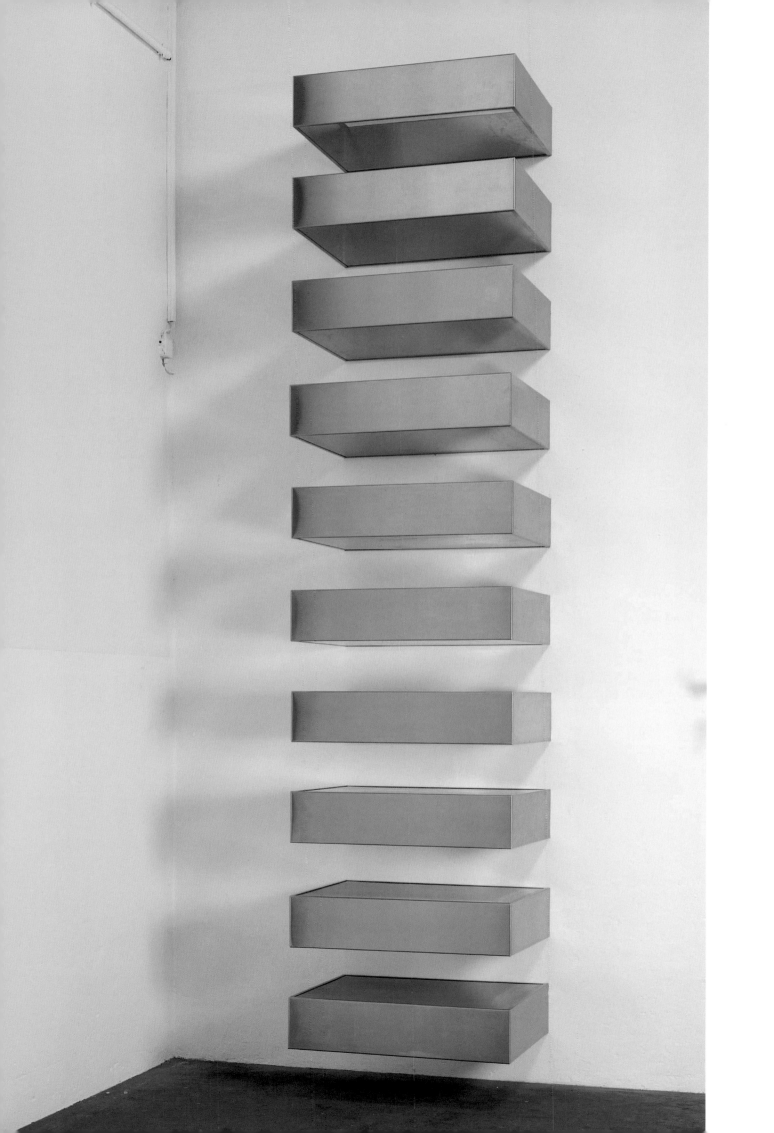

15   *Untitled* 1968

Stainless steel and yellow Plexiglas
10 units, each 23 × 101.6 × 78.7 (9 $^1/_{16}$ × 40 × 31)
DSS 123
Froehlich Collection, Stuttgart
The form and arrangement of this work
were used first in DSS 118 (1968)

Judd's work took an astonishing turn with the invention of vertical pieces, the so-called 'stacks'. These consist of single units (with identical dimensions) hung one above the other on the wall. The intervening spaces have the same dimensions as the units; thus enclosed and open volumes of the same size alternate. Generally ten such units form a work. The distance between the floor and the lowest unit equals the height of one unit. When the ceiling height will not allow for all ten units, fewer are installed. Ideally, they extend from floor to ceiling. Judd made the first stack in galvanised iron in the summer of 1965; it consisted only of seven units (fig.42). The second was made a year later, also from galvanised iron, and it already consisted of ten units which project an inch further out from the wall, as do all subsequent stacks.[1]

The forward-projecting box grew from the notion that a flat volume can also have depth and can stand a good deal further out from the wall than Judd had hitherto imagined. This thought, which combined the idea of elongated four-sided pipes and progressions with rounded fronts, led to the first single stack element which, surprisingly, was attached to the wall by its smallest surface. With this decision, Judd distanced himself from high relief as a genre and entered a realm that we can only describe in terms of such neutral concepts as space and three-dimensionality. In response to the question of how he had decided on the size of the projection, instead of citing some mathematical formula, Judd characteristically came up with an explanation of the relationships involved: 'The [units] couldn't come out too far in relationship to the width, and I didn't want any kind of engineering problem. The projection was a very precise relationship to the width of the piece. The first stack was a 30 in [76.2 cm] projection as against 40 in [101.6 cm] wide. I changed the next one to 31 in [78.7 cm] by 40 in [101.6 cm]. I don't like any dramatic quality or incident or anything archaic. The boxes just hung on the wall in a practical manner.'[2] After Judd had experimented with several single boxes of this kind and had studied the effects of different colours, he crucially decided to present them in a vertical line. Identical in size, these boxes link the floor to the ceiling and are the first indication of his interest in integrating art and architecture, and in reflecting the spatiality of the art in its relationship to the spatiality

of the architecture. In all of this, transparency continues to be important, both in connection to the forms the works take and to the legibility of the spatial parameters. The stacks measure out the space vertically, cut through it with their horizontal elements, but leave the wall intact as a necessary foil. The alternation of closed and open volumes makes it possible to achieve the desired degree of transparency, and it becomes evident that the stacks consist of separate elements that are not physically connected because they conform to an order that has no need for a physical link. The distances between the units become part of the work; far from being formless, they function as open volumes. Giving this 'nothingness' a spatial identity was one of Judd's major achievements, and it was in the vertical stacks that he first put it into practice with virtuosic skill.

The mid-1960s mark the beginning of industrial production in Judd's oeuvre, and much of his output at that time was fabricated from galvanised iron, sometimes finished with coloured paint. From 1967 onwards the work grew decidedly more colourful, and as the amount of colour increased so, too, did the level of transparency. The vertical panels continued to be made from metal – which included stainless steel, copper, brass and aluminium – whereas the top and bottom of each unit were made from coloured, transparent Plexiglas. The effect is astonishing: colour glows in the interstices and, seen as a whole, the vertical stacks look like gently gleaming columns; yet the actual structures appear so light that the metal bands seem to do no more than contain the colour radiating outwards. A third variant first appeared in 1970; in this case the top and the bottom of each box are made from metal, while the sides are finished with coloured, opaque Plexiglas.[3] In these works the colour cuts more sharply into the space, and the undersides of the shallow boxes reflect the upper side of the box below, intensifying the light between them with the result that they appear to partially dissolve. Judd made all three variants in numerous metals and combinations with Plexiglas, later adding anodised aluminium in various colours; each outcome has its own sensuality, be it a 'hard' combination like galvanised iron and sharp green Plexiglas or a 'soft' one like copper and fluorescent red Plexiglas.

1   DSS 78, Brydon Smith (ed.), *Donald Judd, Catalogue Raisonné of Paintings, Objects, and Wood-Blocks 1960–1974*, exh. cat., National Gallery of Canada, Ottawa 1975, p.135. In general there are two kinds of stacks, the larger of which measure 22.9 × 101.6 × 78.7 cm (9 × 40 × 31 in) (height × width × depth) and the smaller of which measure 15.2 × 68.6 × 61 cm (6 × 27 × 24 in).

2   'Don Judd: An Interview with John Coplans', *Don Judd*, exh. cat., Pasadena Art Museum 1971, p.39.

3   DSS 208, Smith 1975, p.209.

16   *Untitled* 1969

Clear anodised aluminium and brushed aluminium
21 × 642.6 × 20.3 (8 ¹/₄ × 253 × 8)
DSS 175
Van Abbemuseum, Eindhoven

At the same time as he was working on the progressions
with rounded sections, Judd was also developing another
kind of progression that combines aspects of *To Susan Buck-walter* (no.11) with the extremely elongated progression. The
squared pipe is retained, again placed at the front and flush
with the front edge of the work. Fixed to the pipe, under-
neath and behind it, is a series of boxes that are deeper than
the pipe, thus keeping the pipe away from the wall. The
boxes precisely double the height and the depth of the work.

In his determination to liberate himself from traditional forms of composition and to work with given orders
instead, progressions based on different number sequences
became a key motif in Judd's work. Following the simple
additive progressions in the previous works, the Fibonacci
sequence and inverse natural numbers also started to feature as design elements. The Fibonacci sequence is associated with natural processes; except for the first two, each
number is the sum of the preceding two, thus producing
the sequence 1, 1, 2, 3, 5, 8, 13, 21 and so on. Translated into
volumetric forms, the result of this sequence is that shapes
which start small very rapidly increase in size – almost
disproportionately. The interstices follow the same pattern
but run in the opposite direction so that the longest shapes
are separated by the shortest openings. *Untitled* 1969 (no.16)
embodies the Fibonacci sequence with its unequal, acceler-
ating steps.

Judd's progressions based on inverse natural numbers appear much more uniform by comparison. This
sequence is built on alternating addition and subtraction:
$1, -^1/_2, +^1/_3, -^1/_4, +^1/_5, -^1/_6$, and so on; thus the values increasingly converge. Translated into three dimensions, the
shapes are arranged from left to right according to the
numerical sequence, and are interrupted by spaces whose
dimensions follow the same pattern, but progress in the
opposite direction (no.20).

A third type of progression, not illustrated here, is
based on values that continually double – 1, 2, 4, 8, 16 –
and was used mainly for shorter pieces. The shortest progressions measure 190.5 cm (75 in), the longest measure
642.6 cm (253 in) and, as such, are his most extreme horizontal works. The first was made in 1965 using the characteristic pairing of light cadmium red and purple; this is
followed by combinations such as brass and red, purple and
clear aluminium, blue and galvanised iron, or more delicate
pairs such as smoothly matt aluminium and gleaming
brushed aluminium.

18 *Untitled* 1969

exhibited example fabricated 1970

Cold-rolled steel
6 units, each 100 × 100 × 100 (39 ³/₈ × 39 ³/₈ × 39 ³/₈),
with 25 (9 ³/₄) intervals
DSS 186
Öffentliche Kunstsammlung Basel, Kunstmuseum
The form and arrangement of this work were used first
in DSS 88 (1966)

Six closed cubes stand in a row, separated by a distance
a quarter of their own length. The cold-rolled steel from
which they are made has a dark grey colour and a muted
gleam. Although the joints are precise and all but seamless,
it is still just possible to see the thickness of the sheet metal.
    In his lengthy last essay, 'Some Aspects of Color in
General and Red and Black in Particular', Judd opens with
the words: 'Material, space and color are the main aspects of
visual art.'[1] He bemoans the fact that our knowledge of
space is so scanty, and freely admits that his own efforts to
discover more about space and its qualities are still at an
early stage. His questions focus on the shape of a volume –
which he illuminates by drawing an analogy with rocks –
the quality of its surface, the inclination of the ground
beneath it and the number of volumes: 'How far apart are
the two rocks? Is one larger than the other? Two rocks of
equal size and the space between them is a situation which
is very different from that of a small rock and a large rock
with the same space between. Do the rocks have the same
shape or is one pointed and the other round? If they are on a
slope, which is higher, which joins the plane as an entity?'[2]
Although these lines, written at the end of his life, are a
reflection on his oeuvre as a whole, they still nevertheless
echo his thoughts from three decades earlier. His entire output is an attempt to find answers to these questions, with
each individual work providing a partial answer to a specific aspect. Six closed volumes of the same size alternate in a
recurring rhythm with open volumes that are a quarter of
the size of the cubes; all are completely free-standing and
make no reference to the wall. The configuration is similar
to that of the four-part work *To Susan Buckwalter* 1964 (no.11),
although the 1964 work is oriented towards the wall and
the parts are connected with a narrow square pipe. In this
1969 work (no.18), Judd eliminates the connecting element,
confident that the chosen distance between the pieces, as a
defined space, would hold the volume together. As he says
in his essay on colour: 'If two objects are close together they
define the space in between ... These definitions are infinite
until the two objects are so far apart that the distance in
between is no longer space.'[3]

1 Donald Judd, *Some
Aspects of Color in General
and Red and Black in Particular*, Sassenheim 1993, p.5.

2 Ibid., p.6.
3 Ibid.

19   *Untitled* 1969

Copper
10 units, each 23 × 101.6 × 78.7 (9 $^1/_{16}$ × 40 × 31)
DSS 204
Solomon R. Guggenheim Museum, New York.
Panza Collection, 1991
The form and arrangement of this work
were used first in DSS 78 (1966)

See no.15

20   *Untitled* 1970

Clear anodised and purple anodised aluminium
20.5 × 644 × 21 (8 $^1/_{16}$ × 253 $^9/_{16}$ × 8 $^1/_4$)
DSS 224
Moderna Museet, Stockholm. New York Collection 1973
The form of this work was used first in DSS 84 (1966)

See no.16

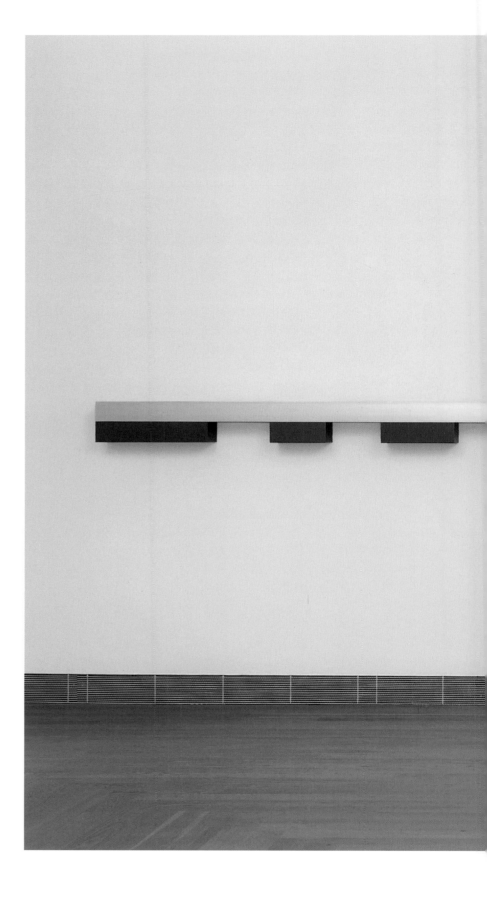

21   *Untitled* 1970

Clear anodised aluminium
10 units, each 23 × 101.5 × 79 (9 $^1/_{16}$ × 39 $^{15}/_{16}$ × 31 $^1/_8$)
DSS 239
Öffentliche Kunstsammlung Basel, Kunstmuseum
The form and arrangement of this work
were used first in DSS 78 (1966)
Illustration shows installation of 8 units

See no.15

22   *Untitled* 1972

Copper and light cadmium red enamel on aluminium
91.6 × 155.5 × 178.2 (36 × 61 $^1/_4$ × 70 $^3/_{16}$)
DSS 271
Tate. Presented by the American Fund
for the Tate Gallery 1992

This copper box is a fascinating example of the way that
Judd was able to combine material, colour and light.
The piece is high enough to reveal its interior when seen
from afar, and low enough to discover from nearby that
the interior base is made of another material. The base
has a smooth surface in light cadmium red that reflects
off the copper walls, turning the interior into a red glow,
a volume of red. The edges of the work appear blurred
and the distinction between copper and red is dimin-
ished. This illusion has a physical cause. The choice of
red in combination with copper is an example of Judd's
liking for similarities – similar values, similar hues, similar kinds of colours – although he also liked differences

and contrasts and, accordingly, made another copper
box with an ultramarine base.[1]

    The knowledge gained of the qualities of metal
and the impact of light, combined with the knowledge
gained from structuring a contained space, eventually
led to Judd's largest creation, one hundred pieces in
mill aluminium (created for the Chinati Foundation
between 1982 and 1986 – see pp.130–1) that manipu-
late light in astonishing ways. The bluntness of a container and the efflorescence of colour come together
in the copper box where two aspects, material and
colour, affect a third, space, in an unforeseen and
slightly enigmatic fashion.

1   DSS 321, Brydon
Smith (ed), *Donald Judd,
Catalogue Raisonné of Pain-
ings, Objects, and Wood-
Blocks 1960–1974*, exh.
cat., National Gallery of
Canada, Ottawa 1975,
p.270.

205

206

23   *Untitled* 1973

Plywood
7 units, each 195.6 × 195.6 × 195.6 (77 × 77 × 77),
with 10.2 (4) intervals
DSS 279
Museum Wiesbaden
Illustration opposite shows installation of 5 units

Judd's first three-dimensional works were constructed
from wood and painted in various colours. In the mid-
1960s he started to use metal instead, and only returned
to wood in 1972, albeit plywood (preferably Douglas Fir).
Sheets of plywood have the advantage that they do not
bend or buckle, which means that even large formats can
be constructed very precisely. Judd seized on this quality
and immediately began a series of multi-part works that
turned out to be comparatively large. The seven-part work
illustrated here is the second to be made in plywood and
one of the largest of its kind. The open cubes relate to
both the wall and the floor; coming after the stacks, this
was a new aspect in Judd's work and one that allowed him
to overcome the constraints of the 'relief' genre, and to
add another dimension to the definition 'free-standing'.

fig.50 *Untitled* 1973 installed with all seven
units during the *Don Judd* exhibition at the
Leo Castelli Gallery, New York, 1973

207

24 *Untitled* 1973

Brass and red fluorescent Plexiglas
6 units, each 86.4 × 86.4 × 86.4 (34 × 34 × 34),
with 20.3 (8) intervals
DSS 282
Solomon R. Guggenheim Museum, New York.
Panza Collection, 1991
The form and arrangement of this work
were used first in DSS 80 (1966)

This is one of Judd's most opulent works, in which he used brass and fluorescent Plexiglas – industrial equivalents for yellow and red – which seem to shower sparks of fire around them. A static photograph cannot begin to convey the spectrum of red tones that is produced by the transparent Plexiglas – ranging from orange to raspberry to purple – as the light changes, and which continues to change with every movement the viewer makes. A whole range of colour tones can appear at once in a single sheet of Plexiglas, allowing the series of cubes to apparently have multicoloured side panels. The red tones radiate into the gaps between the cubes, thereby bridging the intervals between them. The series illustrated here can be read as a horizontal equivalent of the vertical stacks; the first version of the horizontal works was made in 1966, about a year before the first vertical stacks with Plexiglas were fabricated. While this earliest version only consisted of four cubes, all the later ones were comprised of six. In contrast to the stacks, which were to become Judd's trademark, only a handful of the horizontal works were realised. When John Coplans observed that, 'the horizontal wall boxes don't seem to be explored in their variations as much as the stacks', Judd responded by pointing out the practicalities of his situation: 'It had a lot to do with money. There has been quite a demand for the stacks and next to none for the four or six boxes in a row. Along with that, the six boxes in a row are bigger and consequently cost more than the stacks to make.'[1] Initially the horizontal works were constructed using stainless steel and amber or yellow Plexiglas, a combination that is also typical of the vertical stacks from around the same time. The alliance of brass and red fluorescent Plexiglas first appeared in a vertical stack in 1969, four years before it reappeared in this six-part wall piece.

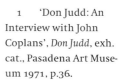

1   'Don Judd: An Interview with John Coplans', *Don Judd*, exh. cat., Pasadena Art Museum 1971, p.36.

25   *Untitled* 1978

Plywood
16 units, each 50 × 100 × 50 (19 $^{11}/_{16}$ × 39 $^3/_8$ × 19 $^{11}/_{16}$)
The Chinati Foundation
Illustrations show 4 units

Each of these sixteen wall pieces has the same exterior
dimensions, while each interior is divided differently.
One has a front panel that is recessed to the centre,
another is divided in half crossways; the front panel of
the next is semi closed, while yet another is divided in
the centre by an angle. A continuous measurement of
10.2 cm (4 in) was used for many of the remaining divisions: an internal open box leaves a space of 10.2 cm
(4 in) between it and the exterior box, as does another
interior box that is closed. A front panel floats 10.2
cm (4 in) in front of the box, or is inset 10.2 cm (4 in)
from the front. A diagonally sloping panel runs from
the back towards the front where it leaves a gap of
10.2 cm (4 in); a rim of that width frames the otherwise
open front.

Judd had been interested in diagonals and sloping panels
since the early 1960s, although they only became a consistent part of his spatial considerations from 1971. He also
began to incorporate tilted panels with a different angle
in each of the four corners of the structure. Straight and
angled dividers, and their combinations, become the subject of several very large works, notably the wall works
shown at the Castelli Gallery in 1981 (see pp.160–1) and
the thirty-part wall piece from 1986 (no.30), both made
from plywood, and the one hundred floor pieces in mill
aluminium made between 1982 and 1986 (see pp.130–1).
It was the experience gained from earlier, smaller works,
the effect of narrow versus wide, open versus enclosed,
single or double angles and the impact of light, that
enabled Judd to embark on such large groups.

26   *Untitled* 1982

Aluminium and purple Plexiglas
3 units, each 100 × 100 × 37 (39³/₈ × 39³/₈ × 14⁹/₁₆),
with 32 (12 ⁵/₈) intervals
82-12
Annemarie and Gianfranco Verna

Following the exhibition at the Castelli Gallery, New York, in autumn 1981 – where Judd showed a wall piece, over 20 m (65 ¹/₂ ft) long and reaching almost to the ceiling, with units subdivided by diagonal plates set at angles ranging from relatively blunt to extremely acute (see pp.160–1) – volumes with internal diagonal dividers increasingly preoccupied the artist. Diagonal dividers can be traced back to the early 1960s (for example no.7), and they reappeared with renewed vigour in the early 1970s, but in the earlier pieces they only occurred in isolation. It was not until 1980 that they established themselves in Judd's vocabulary and subsequently underwent numerous variations.

The wall piece illustrated here consists of three boxes, each with external measurements of 100 × 100 × 32 cm (39³/₈ × 39³/₈ × 14⁹/₁₆ in); the thickness of the metal plates reduces the size of the interior to 96 × 96 cm (38 × 38 in) (height and width) by 32 cm (12⁵/₈ in) (depth). The diagonal plates are set into the piece at an angle of 45°, so that each occupies a third of the overall volume.

The three wall elements demonstrate three possible ways of dividing the boxes: the left-hand box has a diagonal in the centre which precisely – albeit diagonally – halves the volume in such a way that the purple back wall appears as two equal strips. In the middle box, this central diagonal is joined by a second diagonal below it, so that the front is divided into three equal horizontal fields, with the plates clearly acting as reflectors for their own volumes; a gradation of tones is produced, ranging from pale silver to mid-purple to a clear dark purple. In the right-hand box the lower diagonal remains where it is, while the central diagonal is lifted upwards so that the volume opens up noticeably, although only the central strip of the back wall is visible. Here, again, the reflections of the purple Plexiglas and of the silvery aluminium are discernable on the diagonals, turning the whole and its parts into a diverse and complex 'painterly' configuration. With the diagonal, Judd introduces a comparatively dynamic element into his art, which is otherwise predominantly defined by the more static right angle. In contrast to right-angled divisions, the diagonal makes it possible to structure a volume with one area open to the front and another hidden behind it although not closed off from it; consequently the front side and the back wall are subdivided differently. This asymmetry leads to very different areas of light and shadow which – as in this three-part wall piece – create highly differentiated colour effects. Judd used both horizontal and vertical diagonals in his work, ultimately combining diagonals and right angles, as may be seen in the thirty-part wall piece of 1986 (no.30).

work in panels limited the use of ratio, the extent of one color to another, but this is perhaps just as well.'[2] In the major floor pieces (six in total) which he began in 1984 – five multicoloured, one monotone – four, six or eight colours were used and variously organised. An early solution is the spiral; that is the colours are arranged in such a way that they progress diagonally from panel to panel, running across all the long sides including the top, so that all the sides together form a coherent whole. This can be varied by making the pairs 'jump', which helps to prevent the colour distribution becoming too regular and obvious. As a rule Judd chose to make colour pairs that are occasionally connected with other single colours.

The large floor piece, *Untitled* 1989–90 (no.37), uses neighbouring shades of red, blue and yellow: strawberry red and blood orange, sky blue and turquoise blue, sulphur yellow and saffron yellow, plus the contrasting pair of white and black, and galvanised iron as the only single element (fig.52). Of all the metals that Judd used in his artistic work, galvanised iron is the most painterly. Its ice-flower pattern catches the light and reflects touches of colour. It is a metal that combines a 'flowery' pattern with an innate rigour, and it was these qualities that inspired Judd that same year to create a large floor piece using this metal exclusively (no.36). The gentle sheen of its surface adds sharpness to the edges and allows light and shadow to reflect more freely than is the case in the coloured versions. In the context of the coloured surfaces in the Düsseldorf piece, the galvanised iron seems, with its grey tones, to mediate between the richly contrasting colour pairs.

28   *Untitled* 1984

Enamelled aluminium
30 × 180 × 30 (11 $^{13}/_{16}$ × 70 $^{7}/_{8}$ × 11 $^{13}/_{16}$)
84-46
Private Collection

See no.27

fig.51 *Colour study for enamelled work on the wall* 1986

Pencil and colour samples on paper
approximately 22 × 27.9 (8 $^{1}/_{2}$ × 11)
Location unknown

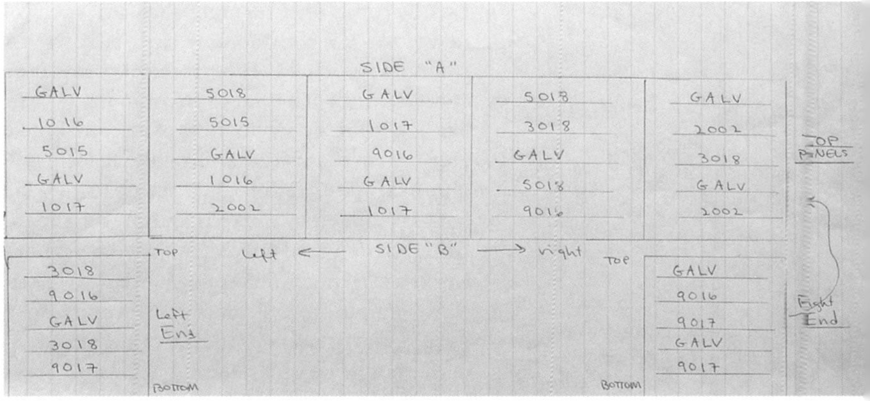

fig.52 Plan made for Judd in 1989 of RAL colour codes for *Untitled* 1989–90 (no.37)
Ink on paper
21.6 × 33.8 (8 $^{1}/_{4}$ × 13 $^{1}/_{4}$)
Collection of Judd Foundation

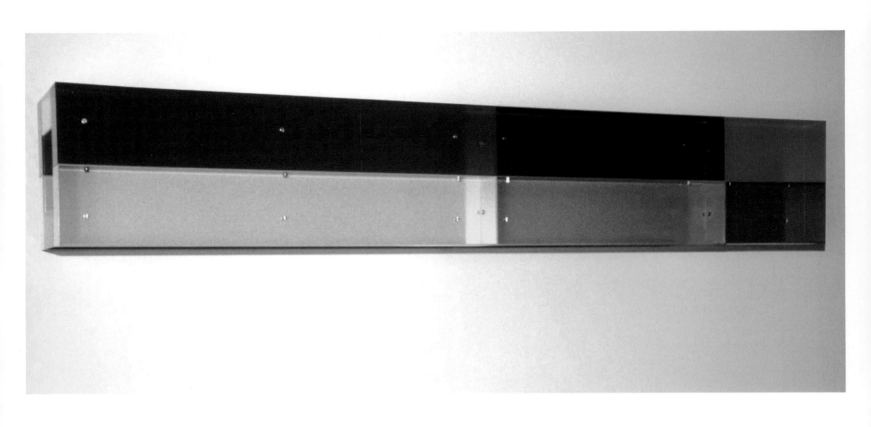

217

29 *Untitled* 1985

Enamelled aluminium
30 × 300 × 30 (11 $^{13}/_{16}$ × 118 $^{1}/_{8}$ × 11 $^{13}/_{16}$)
85-51
Tate. Presented by Janet Wolfson de Botton 1996

See no.27

30 *Untitled* 1986

Douglas Fir plywood and orange, amber, alizarin,
brown, purple and yellow over black Plexiglas
30 units, each 100 × 100 × 50 (39 $^{3}/_{8}$ × 39 $^{3}/_{8}$ × 19 $^{11}/_{16}$)
86-25
Collection of Judd Foundation

In 1986 Judd started to plan one of his most extensive and complicated wall pieces. Of the originally planned sixty-six units, thirty were realised. These were shown in the retrospective of Judd's work at the Whitney Museum of American Art, New York, in late 1988. The remaining thirty-six units were never made. The existing thirty units are hung in three rows at equal intervals from each other. Open-fronted, they are divided internally by vertical panels which reveal more or less of the coloured rear walls. The divisions are clearly rhythmical, although the pattern underpinning the rhythm is not obvious. The dividers can predominate in the left, centre or right half of the shapes, as if a motif were leaping backwards and forwards over a screen until it comes to the finale in a great crescendo. This results in a sense of movement and it is as though the boxes will not allow viewers to remain rooted to the spot but compel them to walk along beside them, gazing forwards and backwards to compare the view that changes every moment.

All thirty units measure 100 cm (39 $^{3}/_{8}$ in) high by 100 cm (39 $^{3}/_{8}$ in) wide by 50 cm (19 $^{11}/_{16}$ in) deep. Internally each one is divided differently. The divisions are made by both straight dividers (perpendicular to the back wall) and angled dividers. Starting with an open undivided box, Judd ran through all the possibilities of angled divisions with the dividers starting in the extreme left corner and moving across in quarter steps until they meet the other side wall. Next he followed the same path with pairs of angled dividers, then with three and lastly with four. He then explored the same possibilities for straight dividers, which in fact produce fewer variants (figs.53–4).

The next stage involved combining these results according to the following pattern:

Single angled divider with single, double and triple straight dividers;

Double angled dividers with single, double and triple straight dividers;

Triple angled dividers with single, double and triple straight dividers;

Quadruple angled dividers with single, double and triple straight dividers.

These twelve combinations produce sixty variants, of which Judd chose forty-eight. Together with the eighteen earlier variants, this gives a total of sixty-six. But at this point complications ensue for the viewer. As in other multi-part works, Judd avoided any apparent sense of

 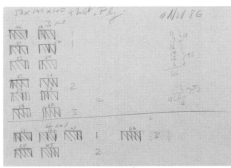

fig.53 *Study for 30-part plywood piece* 1986

Pencil on paper
21 × 29 (8 $^{1}/_{4}$ × 11 $^{3}/_{4}$)
Collection of Judd Foundation

fig.54 *Study for 30-part plywood piece* 1986

Pencil on paper
21 × 29 (8 $^{1}/_{4}$ × 11 $^{3}/_{4}$)
Collection of Judd Foundation

order that would be open to didactic explanation. Instead he confused matters, although there is method behind the apparent confusion. The numbers of variants one to sixty-six are written out in three rows (fig.55) such that in each row the numbers progress in threes, with the top row starting with the number 1, the middle row with the number 2 and the bottom row with 3. This block of numbers is divided into three sections; the first two have seven numbers per row and the last has eight. In order to redress this imbalance, Judd abandoned the last vertical set of three numbers, which reduced the total units to sixty-three.

The complexity does not diminish. The second section of the top row (1, 4, 7 to 61) is now placed below the first section, and the third section below the second. The same process is repeated with the numbers in the second and third rows:

1   4   7   10 13 16 19 2   5   8   11 14 17 20 3   6   9   12 15 18 21
22 25 28 31 34 37 40 23 26 29 32 35 38 41 24 27 30 33 36 39 42
43 46 49 52 55 58 61 44 47 50 53 56 59 62 45 48 51 54 57 60 63

The result is that the first twenty-one variants (the simpler configurations) are all in the top row, the next twenty-one make up the middle row and the most complicated ones are all in the bottom row. Consequently the number of internal dividers increases from top to bottom or, to put it another way, the lower the box, the fuller it is.

The final component in this work is colour. In keeping with the original notion of sections, colours are distributed in groups of seven. The top row of the first section is orange, the second row is amber and the third alizarin; the second section, from top to bottom, is brown, purple and yellow over black (i.e. sheets of Plexiglas laid on top of each other to create a new tone). Unfortunately we have no record of the colours intended for the last section; all we have is Judd's note 'another amber'.

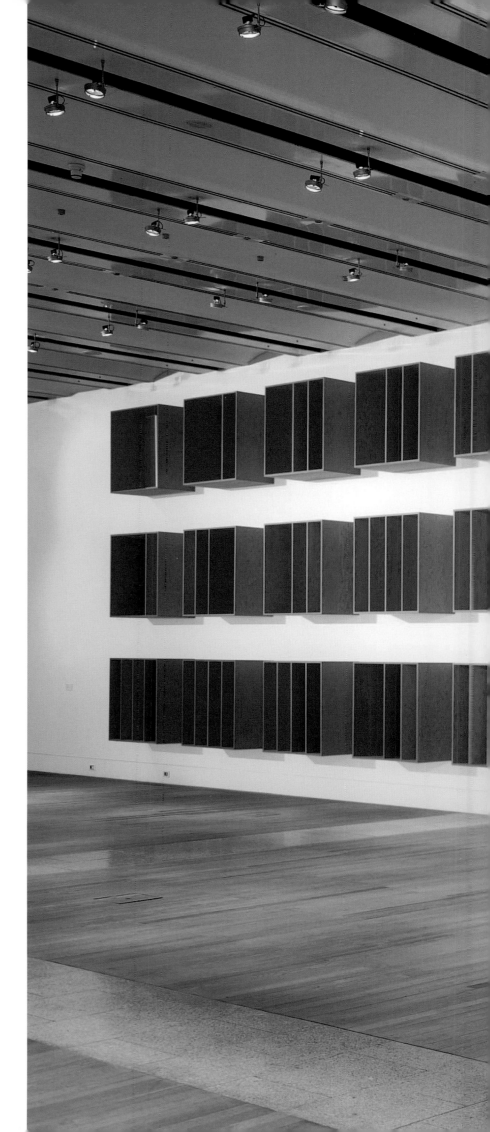

fig.55 *Number sequence for 30-part plywood piece* 1986

Pencil on paper
22.8 × 30.4 (9 × 12)
Collection of Judd Foundation

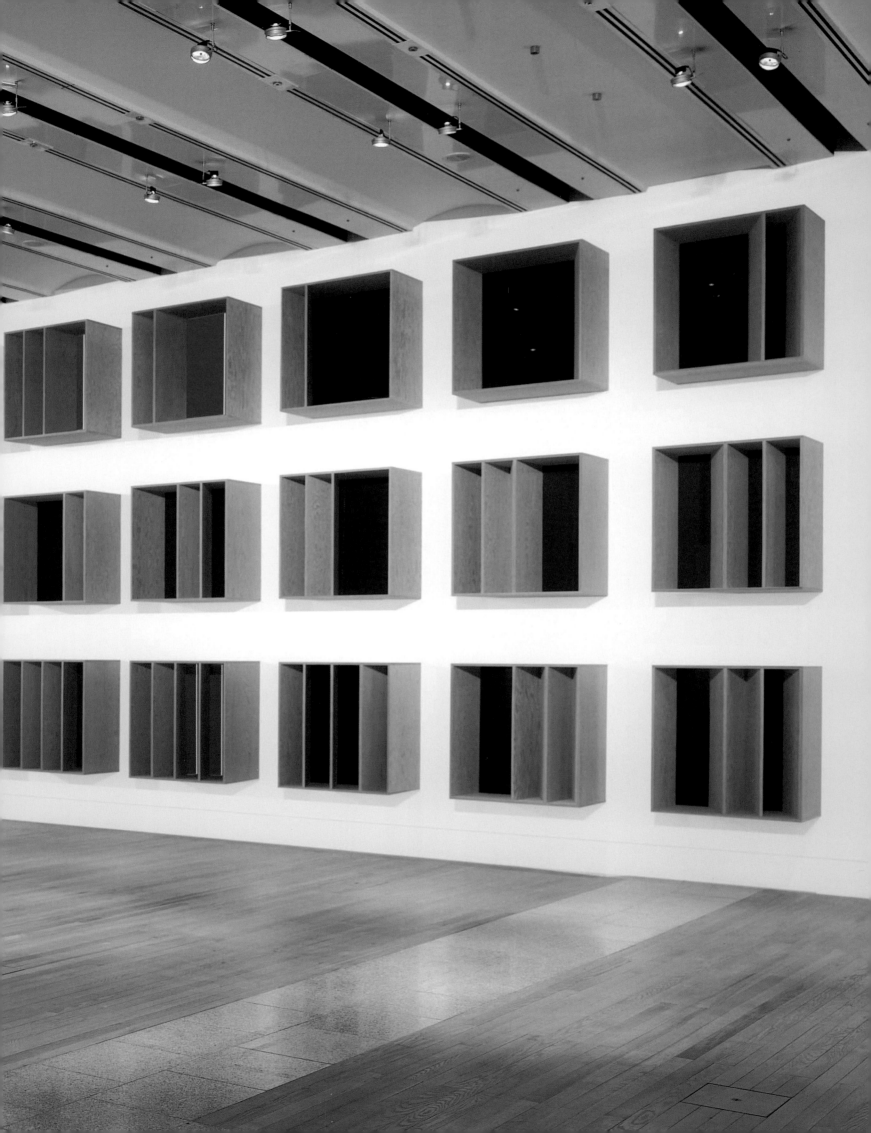

31 *Untitled* 1987

Enamelled aluminium
2 units, each 30 × 360 × 30 (11 $^{13}/_{16}$ × 141 $^{3}/_{4}$ × 11 $^{13}/_{16}$)
87-30
Jamileh Weber Gallery, Zurich

See no.27

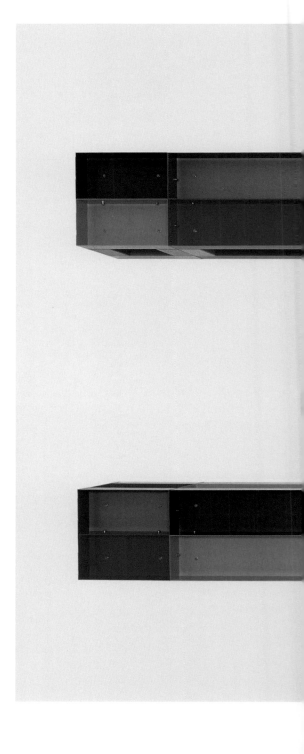

223

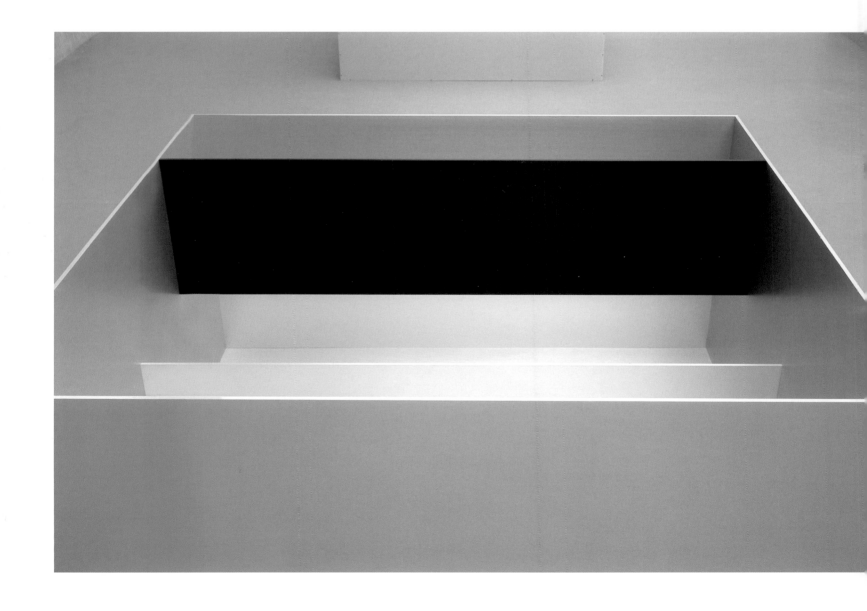

32   *Untitled* 1989

Clear anodised aluminium and black
anodised aluminium
100 × 200 × 200 (39 $^3/_8$ × 78 $^3/_4$ × 78 $^3/_4$)
89-1
Musée d'Art Moderne, Saint-Etienne Métropole

1 Jochen Poetter (ed.),
Donald Judd, exh. cat.,
Staatliche Kunsthalle
Baden-Baden 1989, p.87.

Starting in the late 1980s, Judd had his anodised aluminium works made in a factory in Switzerland. These included twelve floor pieces that were shown in the summer of 1989 at the Staatliche Kunsthalle Baden-Baden, Germany. Four of the twelve have been included here, installed again together in one room. All twelve are open boxes, measuring 100 cm (39 $^3/_8$ in) in height, and 200 cm (78 $^3/_4$ in) in width and depth. They are not a series, but twelve individual works that represent twelve out of a much larger number of possibilities. As Judd explained in an interview published in the exhibition catalogue, the decision to make twelve was determined by the space available in the Kunsthalle and he had 'not tried to think of the total system' nor 'started with all the possibilities and picked twelve'.[1] Although the open-box form is familiar from earlier works, this group posits a new rhythmical division of space. Moreover, this was the first time that Judd used anodised aluminium for such large-scale pieces.

The components for structuring the interiors are mid-point dividers at half or full height, and half-height dividers rising from the base or raised flush with the upper rim, dividing one half of the work into two quarters. Some dividers have a double thickness of 20 mm ($^{13}/_{16}$ in). A second component, colour, was introduced in the Plexiglas sheets laid out on the bases in black, blue and amber,

or in anodised elements in black and blue. Varying combinations of these dividers, colours and materials determine the individual pieces of this group (fig.56).

Aluminium is a metal that is stable yet relatively light; when it is anodised the slightly roughened surface has a completely even, matt sheen. In a secondary process colour can be applied to the anodised panels, which still retain their elegant, brushed-looking surface texture. In contrast to untreated aluminium or other metals, anodised aluminium will neither oxidise nor lose its smooth silvery sheen. The effect of light falling on these surfaces can be magical. The boxes appear to glow from within, although there is no obvious light source – a Rembrandt effect transposed into modernity. The reflections are extremely soft; there are no harsh shadows, only gentle transitions from lighter to darker zones. The outwardly rigorous, hermetic box shapes reveal an inner existence that seems weightless and almost unreal. The interiors appear to embody light, particularly in pieces constructed entirely from clear ('colourless') aluminium. Where coloured elements are introduced, these form fixed points of reference in a context in which actual coordinates seem to dissolve under the gaze.

In these floor pieces, the subtly shimmering colours produced by anodisation are restricted to the dividers.

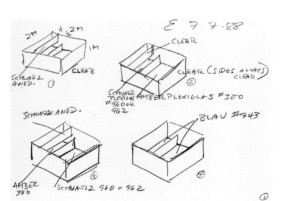 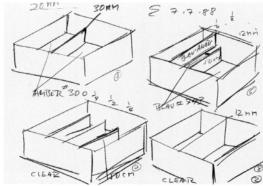 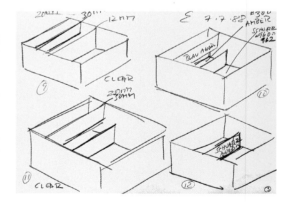

fig.56   *Studies for the Twelve Works exhibited in the Staatliche Kunsthalle Baden-Baden* 1988

Pencil on paper
Each 21 × 29.8 (8 $^1/_4$ × 11 $^3/_4$)
Collection of Judd Foundation

36   *Untitled* 1989

Galvanised iron
150 × 750 × 165 (59 × 295 $^1/_4$ × 64 $^{15}/_{16}$)
89-40
Tate. Presented by the American Fund
for the Tate Gallery 2000
The form of this work was used first in 1984

See no.27

37 *Untitled* 1989–90

Enamelled aluminium and galvanised iron
150 × 750 × 165 (59 × 295 $^{1}/_{4}$ × 64 $^{15}/_{16}$)
Kunstsammlung Nordrhein-Westfalen, Düsseldorf
The form of this work was used first in 1984

See no.27

235

38 *Untitled* 1990

Blue anodised aluminium and clear Plexiglas
10 units, each 23 × 101.6 × 78.7 (9 $^1/_{16}$ × 40 × 31)
90-3
Tate. Presented by the American Fund
for the Tate Gallery 2002
The form and arrangement of this work
were used first in DSS 118 (1968)

See no.15

39 *Untitled* 1992

Cor-ten steel
3 units, each 150 × 150 × 150 (59 $^{1}/_{16}$ × 59 $^{1}/_{16}$ × 59 $^{1}/_{16}$),
with 50 (19 $^{11}/_{16}$) intervals
92-3
Museo Nacional Centro de Arte Reina Sofía, Madrid

Judd first used Cor-ten steel in the 1980s, and then only
for a small number of large-format outdoor pieces. When
the possibility arose of creating a workshop in Marfa
and training a team of assistants, he set up El Taller
Chihuahuanese in an empty factory. From 1989, single
and multi-part works in Cor-ten steel were produced here,
including this three-part floor piece.

    The three cubes are positioned side by side at a
distance of 50 cm (19 $^{11}/_{16}$ in) from each other, which is the
same measurement that determines the short front and
back panels as well as the distance between those panels.
All the cubes are configured in the same way: the two side
panels are recessed by 50 cm (19 $^{11}/_{16}$ in), thus creating two
niches, and between them a tunnel of exactly the same
volume. Where two cubes stand next to each other they
flank a new space equal in size to the central space; at the
same time they enclose a volume equal to that of a whole
cube. Thus the front and back views consist of planes that
are alternately closed and open, with those 'closed'
planes in turn closed and open, either forming enclosed
or open volumes. Because the space between the cubes is
clearly defined, it becomes part of the overall organisation, similar to the volumes between two units in a stack.

40 *Untitled* 1992

Cor-ten steel with green, yellow, purple, ivory,
orange and black Plexiglas
6 units, each 50 × 100 × 50 (19 ^{11}/$_{16}$ × 39 ^{3}/$_{8}$ × 19 ^{11}/$_{16}$),
with 50 (19 ^{11}/$_{16}$) intervals
92-5
Collection of Judd Foundation
Illustration shows installation of 5 units

Cor-ten steel introduced a brown colour with a velvety
surface into Judd's palette, which inspired him to explore
new territory and to create works that, in contrast to the
metals used hitherto, absorb rather than radiate light.
Cor-ten has an evenly matt, slightly grainy surface in a
warm mid-brown. Judd perceived it more as a colour than
as a material – unlike galvanised iron or aluminium, for
instance – and it was this quality that stimulated his
sense of colour and led him to produce single and multi-
part works that revolve around the colour of Cor-ten. He
combined Cor-ten with smoothly reflective Plexiglas in
dark tones (with tonal values equal to that of the brown
steel) or in light contrasting colours.

The vertical arrangement of same-sized boxes at
regular intervals is a continuation of Judd's classical
stacks, which are invariably constituted of same-sized
components. In this later form, which was developed in
the mid-1980s and generally consists of six units rather
than the ten found in the earlier stacks, the individual
units also have a different shape. The internal spaces of
the units can be differently organised and play out ways
of dividing the volume in several versions; alternatively
the divisions can be effected through colour. However, in
Judd's designs using Cor-ten, there is a clear preference
for open, undivided boxes, which thus become a sounding board for different colour tones. The glowing colours
of the six-part wall piece *Untitled* 1992 (no.40) make a particular impact. Each box has a differently coloured back
wall, which appears all the more striking due to the
brown frame around it. All the colours are deep and satu-
rated. The two dark tones, green and black, mark the top
and the bottom of the series. The brighter colours, along
with the purple, are used inbetween these two, although
they are arranged in such a way that each step presents
the greatest possible contrast. Unlike comparable pieces
made from metal, where the interior walls of the box
reflect the colour of Plexiglas, thereby creating an immaterial colour volume, in the Cor-ten works the back walls
– not radiating colour – remain decidedly planar.

In *Untitled* 1993 (no.41), a work made at the same
time with units of exactly the same size in exactly the
same configuration, Cor-ten is replaced with plywood and

opaque Plexiglas is replaced with transparent Plexiglas.
Apart from the physical and optical lightness of plywood
compared to Cor-ten, the main difference between the
two works is the endeavour to fuse colour and its support
into a single entity. Transparent Plexiglas subtly colours
the rear walls of the plywood boxes and allows the grain
of the wood, accentuated by the colour filter, to show
through. This process is similar to that used in earlier
works made from galvanised iron, where Judd prevented
the grey tone from becoming too monotonous by coating
it in clear-coloured varnish, which allowed the pattern
of the metal to remain visible (no.12). Judd was interested
in colour and its carrier becoming one, as exemplified by
both coloured Plexiglas and anodised aluminium; when
that was not possible, as in the case of plywood – where
colour is *on* not *in* the carrier – the two elements were
united as closely as possible, bringing out the character
of the wood rather than hiding it.

Seen together, these two stacks demonstrate
Judd's empathetic handling of colours and materials
and his ability to respond to them with great sensitivity.
Both works alert us again to Judd the colourist. Dan
Flavin had seen him in this light right from the outset
and accordingly dedicated several of his works to 'Don
Judd, colorist'. The rectangular volume becomes a colour
container for a palette that is wide-ranging yet still very
distinctly Judd's own. During the last ten years of his
artistic career he specifically devoted himself to the study
of colour, which he put on a par with space and materials,
as one of the three elements that constitute the distinguishing features of art.[1] Judd believed that we are only
in the earliest stages of the study of colour, and did what
he could to open up the field as far as possible. Having
started his artistic career as a painter, dispersing colour
across a picture plane, Judd then projected colour into
space with his three-dimensional works. This interest
defined his output for the best part of three decades.
But, as William Agee once observed, Judd's thinking was
always connected with painting: 'For Judd, the challenge
was to maintain the integrity of a flat surface on a flat
wall, but to do it in a form other than of a two-dimensional painting.'[2]

1   Donald Judd, *Some
Aspects of Color in General
and Red and Black in Particular*, Sassenheim 1993,
p.5.
2   William C. Agee,
'Donald Judd and the
Endless Possibilities of
Color', Dietmar Elger
(ed.), *Donald Judd: Colorist*,
exh. cat., Sprengel Muse-
um, Hanover 2000, p.46.

41   *Untitled* 1993

Douglas Fir plywood with grey, yellow, brown,
blue, orange and green transparent Plexiglas
6 units, each 50 × 100 × 50 (19 $^{11}/_{16}$ × 39 $^{3}/_{8}$ × 19 $^{11}/_{16}$),
with 50 (19 $^{11}/_{16}$) intervals
93-1
Collection of Judd Foundation
Illustration shows installation of 5 units

See no.40

Staatliche Kunsthalle Baden-Baden,
27 August – 15 October 1989

Chronology

JEFFREY KOPIE

3 June 1928

Donald Clarence Judd is born to Roy and Effie (née Cowsert) Judd in his grandparents' farmhouse in Excelsior Springs, Missouri. His father is employed by the Western Union Telegraph Company, and the family moves to several cities in the Midwestern United States during Judd's childhood. Between 1932 and 1941 the Judds live in Omaha, Nebraska; Kansas City, Missouri; Des Moines, Iowa; and Dallas, Texas. Judd ascribes his lifelong shyness to these moves; the only constancy is summers spent at his grandparents' farm in Missouri. Judd's first private art instruction classes are taken at age ten in Omaha with the support of his parents. At the age of twelve in Dallas, Judd designs a World War II bond poster for a class assignment, but refuses to add text to the work, arguing with his teacher that the addition would ruin the design.

1944

The Judd family moves to Westwood, New Jersey. Judd graduates from Westwood High School in June 1946.

28 June 1946

Enlists in the United States Army.

17 December 1946

En route to his station in Korea, Judd travels by bus with four other soldiers from boot camp in Fort McClellan, Alabama, to Los Angeles, California. He passes through far West Texas and the American Southwest for the first time. He sends a telegram to his mother: 'DEAR MOM VAN HORN TEXAS. 1260 POPULATION. NICE TOWN BEAUTIFUL COUNTRY MOUNTAINS LOVE DON.' In the early 1970s, Judd will return to the area and settle in Marfa, 120 km (74 miles) southeast of Van Horn.

December 1946 – November 1947

Serves as a construction foreman in the army's Corp of Engineers in Korea, surveying an airport landing strip and supervising the erection of prefabricated buildings. He begins to develop an interest in building and architecture.

20 November 1947

His required military service complete, Judd is honourably discharged from the army.

February 1948

Enrols in classes at New York's Art Students League.

September 1948 – June 1949

Attends the College of William and Mary in Williamsburg, Virginia, studying drawing and watercolour, but leaves after two semesters. He is now intent on becoming either an artist or an architect.

June 1949

Returns to the Art Students League and studies painting with Louis Bouché, Reginald Marsh and Luis Bosa, drawing with Bernard Klonis and anatomy with Robert Hale.

This chronology has been compiled with the assistance of the Judd Foundation, which will publish an authorised chronology following further research.

Telegram from Donald Judd to Effie Judd, 17 December 1946

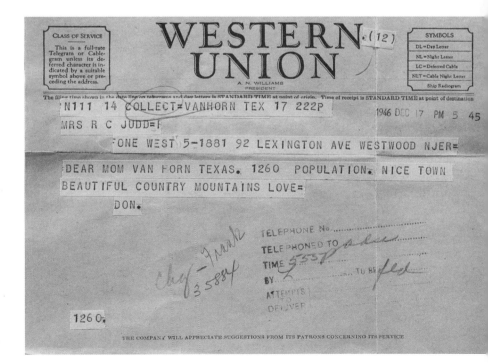

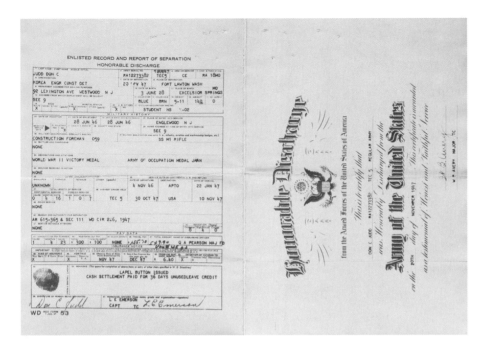

June 1949 – October 1953

Enrols in night classes in the general studies programme at Columbia University, New York City. Graduates with a Bachelor of Science in Philosophy, *cum laude*. The future art critic Barbara Rose is a classmate. Judd studies logical/positivist and pragmatist thought including the philosophies of John Dewey, George Santayana and Henri Bergson with Robert Cummings, and the history of science with Jacob Epstein. An instructor comments that Judd's highly critical piece on Plato's theories of art is a 'good paper – though a little harsh'. Other courses include studies in Metaphysics, the Philosophies of Civilization and History, René Descartes, Baruch Spinoza and the British Empiricists.

September 1952

Awarded first prize by the jury in the Washington Square Outdoor exhibition in New York for his etching *The League Stairwell*.

2–30 November 1952

Participates in the 22nd Annual New Jersey State Exhibition at the Montclair Art Museum. His print *Gramercy Square* is awarded first prize by the jury.

1953

Moves from his parents' home in Westwood to a basement apartment at 304 East 27th Street in Manhattan. Works part-time at Christadora House, a settlement facility in the East Village that provides schooling and recreational opportunities to immigrant children. He also teaches art to underprivileged children at the Police Athletic League, where he meets John J. Jerome, a boxing instructor, who will remain a lifelong friend and will eventually become his lawyer.

June 1954

Participates in the Brooklyn Museum's Eighth National Print Annual.

November 1954

Participates in a group show at City Center in New York. Judd shows an untitled river landscape, which receives positive mention in both *Arts Digest* and the *New York Times*.

10–22 October 1955

First small group exhibition in New York with three other artists at the Panoras Gallery. Judd shows abstract, landscape-based paintings. In a review in the *New York Herald Tribune*, he is singled out for praise: 'A shining star compared to the rest ... sure instinct whose heart and mind work together – composition and originality indicate the makings of a first-rate painter.'

Autumn 1956

Studies contemporary art at New York University for one semester and shows at the Panoras Gallery with Nathan Reisen. Small reviews appear in the *New York Times*, *Arts* and *Art News*.

Honorable Discharge
from the Armed Forces,
20 November 1947

Donald Judd
The League Stairwell 1952
Collection of Judd
Foundation

24 June – 6 July 1957

First solo exhibition, at the Panoras Gallery. Judd shows abstract paintings derived from landscapes. The Staten Island Institute of Arts and Sciences purchases a painting. The exhibition receives small, generally favourable notices in *Art News*, *Arts* and the *New York Herald Tribune*. Judd later refers to the exhibition as 'stupid'.

1958–60

Returns to Columbia University for a master's degree in art history. All prerequisites for the degree are completed except language requirements. His studies include Baroque Painting and Sculpture and Renaissance Architecture with Rudolf Wittkower, Venetian Renaissance Painting, Pre-Columbian Art, Far Eastern Art, Aesthetics, Impressionism, Modern Painting since 1900 and, with Meyer Schapiro, American Painting 1940–50.

Summer 1959

Begins writing for *Art News* – his first reviews appear in the September 1959 issue. He praises seventeenth-century Chinese artist Tao Chi and writes lukewarm notices on portraits by Joseph Stella and a group show at the Tanager Gallery. A positive review of Yayoi Kusama's work follows shortly thereafter. From the outset Judd's criticism is direct, unsentimental and deceptively simple in form and language, yet he exhibits a thorough understanding of art history and great sensitivity as to how individual artists develop. His writing avoids the categorical pigeonholing of artists, focusing instead on each artist's work individually. He leaves *Art News* in November 1959, primarily because of the magazine's tendency to edit his reviews. Writing in July 1974, Judd states, 'I wrote criticism as a mercenary and would never have written it otherwise.'

1 August 1959

Moves to a loft space at 53 East 19th Street – rent is $100 per month.

December 1959

Hired by Hilton Kramer, editor of *Arts* (later *Arts Magazine*), to review exhibitions. Despite their vast philosophical, political and aesthetic differences, Judd will write in 1974 that, 'It may be hard to believe but Hilton Kramer was easy to work for.'

1960

Teaches shop class (basic carpentry) and history at the Allen Stevenson School, a private institution on the Upper East Side of Manhattan.

February 1960

Writes enthusiastically for the first time about the work of John Chamberlain in *Arts*: 'colored sculpture has been discussed and hesitantly attempted for some time, but not with such implications'.

March 1960

Writes in *Arts* that Jasper Johns is 'precise, inventive, authentic, and important'.

December 1960

Praises an exhibition of reliefs by Lee Bontecou, and excoriates shows by Adolph Gottlieb and Michael Goldberg, both of whom he defines as 'second-generation Abstract Expressionists', who he believes are debasing the great paintings of Barnett Newman, Mark Rothko and Jackson Pollock.

Judd's paintings at this time depart considerably from the earlier, landscape-based abstractions: they are larger in both size and scale, and display an increased tendency towards both flatness and geometry.

1961

Judd begins to paint on masonite rather than canvas, often using liquitex mixed with sand or wax. He begins to make these works thicker and adds depth to his paintings through the incorporation of objects – the first is an aluminium baking pan inserted at the centre of a masonite panel. His first work to project out from the wall follows shortly thereafter: a rectangular relief made of a wooden panel painted light cadmium red whose top and bottom edges curve outwards and are covered with galvanised iron.

Summer 1961

Due to a change of ownership and a new policy of fewer reviews, Judd is fired by *Arts*, but is rehired by editor James Mellow in January 1962.

January 1962

Judd essentially abandons painting, turning instead to what he will later term 'a new form of high relief': a wall box with its interior back painted light cadmium red mixed with sand, the exterior sides painted black. A vertical black asphalt pipe is centred at the front and projects beyond the sides.

Autumn 1962

A mutual friend introduces Judd to painter John Wesley. Wesley and Judd remain close lifelong friends.

Autumn 1962 – Spring 1964

Teaches art at the Brooklyn Institute of Art and Science, where he exhibits his first three-dimensional work placed directly on the floor in a faculty show in November 1962.

The work consists of three horizontal wooden boards backed by a curved masonite panel painted with black enamel. An asphalt pipe projects from the back of the masonite through the middle board, flush with its front surface. This is Judd's first work that creates both internal and external space; the work supplies the artist with the beginnings of his working vocabulary.

Winter 1962

Meets Dan Flavin at a planning session for a cooperative art gallery in Brooklyn. They remain close friends and champions of each other's work for the next three decades.

8 January 1963

Exhibits three pieces in *New Work: Part I* at Richard Bellamy's Green Gallery, New York. Other artists exhibiting include Darby Bannard, Flavin, Kusama, Ellsworth Kelly, Robert Morris, Lucas Samaras and George Segal. Judd becomes friends with several of the gallery artists, most lastingly with Samaras and Claes Oldenburg.

May 1963

Exhibits another floor work in a group show at the Green Gallery.

August 1963

Travels by bus from New York to Tucson, Arizona, to visit his younger sister Marcia Lamb. As he later remarked: 'I loved the land around Tucson, chiefly because you could see it.'

17 December 1963 – 11 January 1964

After declining numerous invitations to mount a one-man exhibition, Judd has his first solo show at the Green Gallery. He shows four reliefs and five floor boxes, including two with semicircular channels in their tops. The exhibition also marks Judd's first use of Plexiglas, in a low, square, floor volume, bisected diagonally into triangular halves, one of which is double the height of the other. The interior plane of the higher triangle is faced with purple Plexiglas.

Reviews are mixed. Irving Sandler in the *New York Post* describes the exhibition as 'this world of dead things ... a depressing show'. In the *New York Times*, Brian O'Doherty states, '[the work] tries to achieve meaning by a pretentious lack of meaning' and '[the show] obligingly expires before one's eyes, in a form of suicide'. Hilton Kramer, writing in *Art in America*, bemoans the lack of 'expressive import' in the work. Michael Fried, however, writing in *Art International*, calls the Green Gallery show an 'assured, intelligent show ... one of the best on view in New York this month'.

New Work: Part I,
Green Gallery, New York,
8 January – 2 February
1963

pieces fabricated by Bernstein Brothers. Hilton Kramer, in the *New York Times*, laments the 'extreme of depersonalization' in the work.

27 April 1966

Primary Structures: Younger American and British Sculptors, curated by Kynaston McShine, opens at The Jewish Museum, New York. It is the first show of such work to receive intense attention from the mainstream media. A large number of artists are presented, including Carl Andre, Ronald Bladen, Anthony Caro, Flavin, Robert Grosvenor, Lewitt, John McCracken, Morris, Tony Smith and Robert Smithson. Two Judd works are shown in a room with works by Bladen, Grosvenor and Morris; both consist of four galvanised iron cubes, connected at the top front by a hollow, square, horizontal aluminium tube. One work, with the tube painted blue, is installed on the wall; the other, with a plain aluminium tube, sits directly on the floor.

In the catalogue of the exhibition, Judd writes his first refutation of categorical terms such as Minimalism, ABC Art, anti-art, anti-art art, etc. Stating that labelling is reductive, he writes: 'If someone says his work is art, it's art ... The most reductive can mean is that new work doesn't have what the old work had ... New work is just as complex and developed as old work.'

During a *Primary Structures* panel, sculptor Mark Di Suvero asserts that Judd is not an artist, 'because he doesn't do the work ... a man has to make a thing in order to be an artist'. Judd dismisses the criticism: 'Whether one makes it oneself or doesn't; it's all a case of technique that makes the thing visible, so that I don't see in the long run why one technique is any more essentially art than another technique.'

Summer 1966

Serves as the visiting artist at Dartmouth College, Hanover, New Hampshire.

July 1966

Writes an appreciation of Oldenburg for that artist's exhibition at the Moderna Museet in Stockholm. Oldenburg chooses not to include the essay in the exhibition catalogue, and it remains unpublished until 1975.

Autumn 1966

Judd is invited to teach art at Southern Illinois University but he refuses to take a loyalty oath to the United States; the offer is rescinded.

Primary Structures,
The Jewish Museum,
New York, 27 April –
12 June 1966

December 1966

The US artists from the São Paolo Bienal are presented at
the National Collection of Fine Arts in Washington, DC.
Hilton Kramer, in the *New York Times*, admits to 'gloomy
thoughts about where art is heading'. Another critic calls
the show 'a symptom of brainless passion for novelty ...
their physical existence gives promise of attic clutter for
generations yet unborn'.

January 1967

Makes his first stack that incorporates Plexiglas:
a ten-unit work comprised of stainless steel frames
with translucent green Plexiglas inserted at the top
and bottom of each unit.

Contributes to *Collage of Indignation*, a statement
against the war in Vietnam, organised by Max Kozloff
and Barbara Rose and exhibited at New York University.
Other participating artists include Di Suvero, Nancy
Graves, Roy Lichtenstein, James Rosenquist and Richard
Serra.

April 1967

Judd writes an appreciation of Pollock in *Arts Magazine*.
He regrets that no satisfactory, complete examination of
Pollock's achievement has been produced.

October – December 1967

Conducts a sculpture seminar at Yale University, New
Haven, Connecticut.

December 1967

In *Arts Yearbook 9*, in response to the question, 'Do you
want your work in a museum?', Judd replies, 'Yes, anywhere.' He goes on to explain his ideal museum conditions: 'smooth, square walls ... an unpatterned floor.
Good architecture.'

23 January 1968

Birth of his son, Flavin Starbuck Judd. The first name is
from the artist, the middle name from an ancestor of
Julie Finch Judd.

February 1968

Purchases 101 Spring Street for $68,000, a five-storey, 1870
cast-iron building designed by Nicholas Whyte, with two
basement levels. The building – originally a garment factory – fills a 22.9 × 7.6 m (75 × 25 ft) lot at the corner of
Mercer Street, in the then quiet neighbourhood of Soho.
After removing extensive debris and added partitions
throughout, and assigning specific functions to each
floor, Judd slowly begins to renovate. Both this renovation
and the installation of his works and those of his contemporaries contribute to his developing ideas on large-scale
work, installation and architecture. When complete in
the mid-1980s, the ground floor is used for looking at new
work and showing the work of other artists; the second
floor for cooking and eating; the third floor as a studio.
The fourth floor has wide, pine planks installed as both
floor and ceiling, and serves as a formal dining room; the
fifth floor is a bedroom. The second floor has a mural by
David Novros on one wall, while the fifth floor is dominated by a barrier piece of almost 21.5 m (70 ft) with red

and blue fluorescent lights by Flavin. Judd's work is also displayed, along with pieces by Chamberlain, Oldenburg, Reinhardt, Samaras, Stella and H.C. Westermann. Eighteenth- and nineteenth-century furniture is mixed with twentieth-century modernist pieces by Alvar Aalto and Gerrit Rietveld, along with furniture designed by Judd himself.

27 February – 24 March 1968

A retrospective of Judd's work from 1961 to 1968, organised by William C. Agee assisted by Dudley Del Balso, is held at the Whitney Museum of American Art in New York.

April 1968

Judd hires Dudley Del Balso as his office manager. She establishes a running record of Judd's production and a system of purchase orders to Bernstein Brothers. These become the basis of the artist's catalogue raisonné, which she begins in 1969. Del Balso remains involved in Judd's work almost continuously until early 1984.

Summer 1968

Drives with his wife and son through Colorado, Arizona and New Mexico, searching for a place outside New York where he can develop large-scale work.

Serves as artist-in-residence at the Aspen Center for Contemporary Art. While in Aspen, Judd and his wife publish an advertisement in the *Aspen Times* both against the Vietnam War and in favour of the civil rights movement.

August 1968

Conducts the Emma Lake Artists' Workshop at Lac La Ronge in North Saskatchewan. The workshop consists of numerous seminar discussions.

October 1968

Participates in a benefit exhibition at the Paula Cooper Gallery for Veterans Against the War in Vietnam with Jo Baer, Andre, Flavin, Robert Mangold and Robert Ryman. Around this time, Judd becomes involved with the War Resisters League, an organisation founded by his wife's great aunt, Jessie Wallace Hughan, in 1923. The Judds later host several exhibitions at 101 Spring Street to benefit the League.

Roberta Smith, a senior from Grinnel College in Iowa, begins a study of Judd's transition from two to three dimensions while participating in the Whitney Museum's Independent Study Program. She later spends two years (1972–4) assisting Del Balso on the catalogue raisonné.

January 1969

For his second exhibition at Leo Castelli, Judd creates one of his first works to incorporate the architecture of a space, filling most of Castelli's front room with fifty-seven open-ended folded galvanised iron units (each 304 cm [120 in] deep) arranged in three rows of nineteen. Judd attributes his development of architectural works to the ongoing renovation of 101 Spring Street. The piece is unsold and will eventually be installed at Judd's studio in Marfa, Texas.

March 1969

Meets Harvey Shapiro, editor of the *Public Life* newspaper and founder of Citizens for Local Democracy (CLD), a group devoted to developing greater autonomy and power at the community level. Shapiro's advocacy of smaller, truly representative, community-based government probably influenced Judd's own thinking. Contributing to a symposium titled 'The Artist and Politics' in the September 1970 *Artforum*, Judd acknowledges that the newspaper's politics are more sophisticated than his own. He joins the CLD, becoming a member of its advisory committee along with Hannah Arendt, Noam Chomsky and New York newspaper columnist Murray Kempton. Julie Finch Judd becomes the director of a CLD subcommittee, the Lower Manhattan Citizens for Local Democracy.

April 1969

Publishes 'Complaints: Part I', his most combative essay to date, in *Studio International*. Continuing his argument against the categorisation of new art, Judd accuses the critical establishment of 'attempt[ing] to close the fairly open situation of contemporary art'. He denounces Clement Greenberg's current thinking as 'ignorant and hysterical', and declares Michael Fried's summer 1967 *Artforum* essay 'Art and Objecthood' 'stupid'. Judd writes that the attempt to impose groupings on artists with divergent aims is detrimental to the work being made. In addition, he finds Greenberg's (and his followers') desire to protect the continuation of Abstract Expressionism produces exactly the opposite: 'it destroys the work they try to protect'.

Judd aids his wife in the formation of Artists Against the Expressway, a committee formed to fight New York City's plan to eradicate a large portion of the cast-iron section in southern Soho and build a major highway thoroughfare to connect the East River bridges with the West Side's Holland Tunnel. Julie Finch Judd serves as chair of the organisation. Others on the committee are Agee, Castelli, Richard Feigen, Arnold Glimcher, Lichtenstein, Lucy Lippard, Louise Nevelson, Newman, Kenneth Noland, Yvonne Rainer, Rauschenberg and Stella. In July 1969 New York City abandons its plans for the expressway.

Summer 1969

Drives down to Baja California, Mexico, which he considers 'excessively perfect in its lack of vegetation'. Judd stays a month in the town of El Rosario.

October 1969

For the National Gallery of Canada's Flavin retrospective Judd writes 'Aspects of Flavin's Work', citing Flavin's previous exhibitions at the Kornblee Gallery and at the Museum of Contemporary Art in Chicago as 'among the best things I've seen'.

Winter 1969

Moves with his wife and son to 101 Spring Street.

January 1970

Large solo exhibition curated by Jean Leering opens at the Van Abbemuseum, Eindhoven. The exhibition travels to the Folkwang Museum, Essen, the Kunstverein Hannover and the Whitechapel Art Gallery, London. Positive reviews appear in *The Times*, the *Observer* and the *City Press*.

February – March 1970

Lectures on art at Cranbrook Academy of Art in Michigan and at Columbia University in New York.

April 1970

For his third show at Leo Castelli he shows a second work that engages the architecture of the front gallery: eighteen hot-dipped galvanised iron units are placed 20.3 cm (8 in) from three walls of the gallery and set directly on the floor. During the exhibition Judd meets Italian collector Giuseppe Panza, who begins to collect Judd's works, often only in the form of drawings for pieces to be fabricated in the future.

Designs a platform bed for the fifth floor of Spring Street, fabricated by Peter Ballantine.

Summer 1970

Travels again through the US Southwest, but he finds southern Arizona's population to be growing too quickly, and the climates of northern New Mexico and Arizona too cold. Judd eventually spends two months with his family on the Baja Peninsula, both in El Rosario and at a campsite inland at Rancho El Metate. Begins thinking about work created in specific response to a given landscape.

11 August 1970

Birth of his daughter Rainer Yingling Judd, named after choreographer and filmmaker Yvonne Rainer and a Swedish ancestor from Judd's family.

September 1970

In his contribution to *Artforum*'s 'The Artist and Politics' symposium, Judd states that art should not be used for political activism, excepting extreme cases where 'nothing else can be done'. He expresses his scepticism for the Art Workers Coalition, an artist/activist group started in January 1969, about which he complains that it is 'filled with lawyers and the politics of interest groups'. Peripherally involved with the Art Workers Coalition at its inception, Judd quickly disassociates himself from it, the experience confirming his belief that art cannot effectively serve the causes of political activism.

January 1971

Writes his first overtly political statement for the *Newspaper of Lower Manhattan Township*. 'Individuals and the communities they form should have political power.' Judd argues against the individual's ceding of power to larger political institutions, and stresses that political decisions should be made within the community, thereby guaranteeing genuine democracy. He insists that great caution should be exercised in delegating authority to larger governmental institutions at city, state and national levels.

Don Judd,
Whitechapel Art Gallery,
London, 29 September –
1 November 1970

February 1971

His first outdoor piece, for the collection of Joseph Pulitzer, is completed. Resting on a slope, the work consists of two concentric rectangles made of stainless steel; the top edge of the outer rectangle is level, while the inner one is parallel to the slope. The same principle also appears in two circular works during 1971: two hot-rolled steel circles are installed on the ramp of the Guggenheim Museum in New York, and a thick concrete circle is constructed on the grounds of Philip Johnson's Glass House in New Canaan, Connecticut.

May 1971

Writes 'Greater Westbeth' for the *Newspaper of Lower Manhattan Township*, in which he complains that Soho is becoming too expensive and commercial, thus threatening the existence of a 'live situation' for art.

May – July 1971

Mid-career retrospective organised by John Coplans opens at the Pasadena Art Museum, California. Hilton Kramer in the *New York Times* chooses the adjectives 'remorseless', 'simplified', 'vehement', 'blunt', 'stark' and 'doctrinaire' to describe the exhibition. Robert Hughes, writing more charitably in *Time* in May 1971, remarks that Judd's 'output ... is a kind of critical meditation on what is and what is not intrinsic to sculpture. The lucidity of his argument is what makes his work so influential.'

Summer 1971

Creates a poster with numerous quotes about democracy and war, dating from de Tocqueville to the Nixon Administration, culled from the pages of Shapiro's *Public Life*. Among those quoted are Thomas Jefferson, Walt Whitman, Frederick Douglass, Ralph Waldo Emerson, Henry David Thoreau and Franklin D. Roosevelt. Signed posters are sold to benefit the Peace Action Coalition and the Student Mobilization Committee to End the War in Vietnam.

Judd travels again to Baja California, sketching out ideas for a housing compound to be located in Arroyo Grande, near the town of El Metate, but abandons the idea and intensifies his search for land in the US Southwest.

November 1971

Expanding his search for an area in which to settle, Judd flies to El Paso, Texas, and drives to the area surrounding the Big Bend National Park. He chooses Marfa because 'it was the best-looking and most practical'. Marfa is located in the Chihuahuan Desert, an area of the US once controlled by Mexico, known to the Spanish as *desplobado* and to the Aztecs as *Chichimeca*. He rents a small house in town and also one of two large former

army buildings situated between Marfa's main highway to the south and a cattle feed mill and the Southern Pacific railway tracks to the north. This is the first structure of what will become the Mansana de Chinati (also known as The Block).

January 1972

Returns to Marfa with friend and assistant Jamie Dearing and a truck loaded with his art.

May 1972

In a two-man show with Serra at Leo Castelli, Judd exhibits a large row of open-ended boxes, his first work in plywood since 1964. The piece is made by Peter Ballantine, who becomes the primary fabricator of Judd's plywood work.

November 1972

Shows his first open-front stack, with the frontal planes of each unit recessed to one-half the depth of the units, the Greenberg Gallery, St Louis.

March 1973

Writes 'Complaints: Part II' for *Arts Magazine*. Aimed squarely at museums, Judd complains that a small group of artists supports an enormous number of personnel for the presentation of contemporary art, and that an exorbitant amount of money is spent building new museums, leaving little to nothing left for the purchase of art. He also disparages institutions for their poor handling of works, resulting in damage and/or ruination, and complains that installations are often crowded and careless, thereby doing a disservice to the work.

Summer 1973

Purchases both large former army buildings in Marfa for the price of $48,000.

Autumn 1973

Travels for the first time to Italy to participate in the group exhibition *Contemporanea* in Rome. The experience contributes to his growing disillusionment with large contemporary exhibitions: he designs a site-specific work in plywood, which is then poorly fabricated and incorrectly installed by the exhibition's staff. Leaving Rome, he travels to Arezzo and Florence, then on to Giuseppe Panza's home in Varese, where he attempts to come to an agreement with Panza for the realisation of works purchased from Leo Castelli that exist only on paper.

*Donald Judd Complete
Writings, 1959–1975,
Gallery Reviews, Book
Reviews, Articles, Letters
to the Editor, Reports,
Statements, Complaints,*
Halifax and New York
1975

Donald Judd,
National Gallery of
Canada, Ottawa,
24 May – 6 July 1975

December 1973

Judd's first exhibition at Galerie Annemarie Verna, Zurich,
with whom he shows regularly for the rest of his life.

1974

Buys the remaining portion of what will become the
Mansana de Chinati, including a rectangular two-storey
building, the former offices of the army's Quarter Master
Corps. Judd continues working on the installation of
his early works in the large east building. He later states,
'the main purpose of the place in Marfa is the serious and
permanent installation of art'.

January 1974

Shows large-scale, site-specific plywood structures at the
Lisson Gallery in London. Fabrication of the works is done
locally; Judd is dissatisfied with the construction and
installation of the works.

In its final stages, the catalogue raisonné is given
to Brydon Smith, Curator of Contemporary Art at the
National Gallery of Canada, Ottawa, for completion and
fact-checking.

1975

Karl Beveridge and Ian Burn publish 'Don Judd' in *The Fox*
magazine. The authors question the verity of Judd's political positions, attributing a large measure of his success to
American cultural imperialism. The essay is the most
extensive Marxist critique of Judd's work to date; similar
arguments will appear in *Arts Magazine* in January 1990
and in the summer 1994 issue of *October*. Although he
does not make reference to the authors, Judd writes
'Imperialism, Nationalism and Regionalism' shortly after
the publication of *The Fox* piece. In his essay, Judd asserts
that the attitudes prevalent in nationalism are identical
to those of religion, which he terms 'fully discredited'.
The essay is a vigorous statement against the description
of his art as 'American', insisting that his work is international and not defined by the United States' growing
political and cultural hegemony in the world. In marked
contrast to Marxist critiques of his work, Judd stresses
that no relationship exists between political equality and
artistic excellence.

Spring 1975

*Donald Judd Complete Writings, 1959–1975, Gallery Reviews,
Book Reviews, Articles, Letters to the Editor, Reports, Statements,
Complaints* is published by the Press of the Nova Scotia
College of Art and Design, Halifax, and New York
University Press.

24 May – 6 July 1975

Retrospective exhibition at the National Gallery of Canada, Ottawa, organised by Brydon Smith. The exhibition
publication includes the catalogue raisonné of Judd's
work from 1960 through 1974 (in which the 'DSS' number
assigned to each work reflects the last names of the three
authors – Del Balso, Smith and Smith) as well as a revised
version of Roberta Smith's senior thesis.

February 1976

At the invitation of Ellen Johnson, Judd serves as Baldwin professor at Oberlin College in Ohio, including two public lectures and twenty-four hours of studio instruction.

April 1976

Retrospective of drawings, curated by Dieter Koepplin, opens at the Kunstmuseum Basel. In an effort to defend his work against claims of austerity and impersonality, Judd writes in a catalogue note: 'The popular dichotomy of thought and feeling provides no information and causes a lot of trouble. There isn't such a division. Feelings are intelligent because they have developed through thought and thought is felt because it has been simplified and remembered and believed through feeling.'

Judd travels again to Varese to meet with Panza, where he discovers a poorly fabricated remake of the 1969 galvanised iron wall work previously shown at Leo Castelli. The work has been incorrectly installed in a converted horse stable. Judd protests that fabrication and placement cannot be done without his authorisation.

May 1976

Purchases the Walker House near the centre of town in Marfa.

By the end of 1976, a bedroom and kitchen are completed in the east building at the Mansana. The installation of works in the building's north room is also finalised, consisting of three large vertical stacks and three aluminium floor boxes.

1977

Disgusted with the increasing commercialisation of Soho and committed to the permanent placement of his works in Marfa, Judd declares full-time residency in Texas, where work at the Mansana continues to occupy the majority of his time. For purposes of privacy and noise reduction, he encloses his building in a 2.8 m (9 ft) wall made with adobe bricks from two demolished hotels in Marfa. Responding to his daughter's request for a yard, an alley of grass and plum trees is planted between the wall and the east building.

Judd begins to design furniture for his children. The first piece is a double bed bisected by a vertical plane, allowing them each some privacy in a shared room. Designs of tables, desks and a series of chairs follow shortly after. Some of the work is fabricated by Judd himself, other pieces are made by Marfa native Celodonio Mediano, Judd's construction foreman.

March 1977

Shows fifteen plywood floor works at the Heiner Friedrich Gallery on Wooster Street, Soho, New York. These works will eventually enter the Dia Art Foundation's collection, and be installed at Dia:Beacon, New York, in the spring of 2003.

May 1977

In a catalogue interview with Kasper König for his exhibition at the Moderne Galerie Bottrop, Judd states, 'my thought comes from painting, even if I don't paint'.

June 1977

Installs his first outdoor aluminium work on the campus of Northern Kentucky University, concurrent with an exhibition at the Cincinnati Contemporary Art Center of the fifteen plywood works shown previously at Heiner Friedrich.

Two concentric, concrete rings are constructed adjacent to the Aasee in Münster, Germany, as part of the *Skulptur* exhibition curated by Kasper König and Klaus Bussmann. At the inauguration of the work, Judd writes about public art: 'The categories of public and private mean nothing to me. The quality of a work cannot be changed by the conditions of its exhibition or by the number of people seeing it.'

December 1977

Writes 'In Defense of My Work', although it remains unpublished until 1985. In his most comprehensive statement to date about the importance of installation, Judd laments that the great paintings produced in New York in the 1940s and 1950s have been dispersed around the world, thereby preventing an accurate assessment of the period. He is intent on keeping his work intact: 'to preserve my work and that of others and to preserve this work in spaces I consider appropriate ... [is] a concern second only to the invention of my work ... the two concerns have joined and both tend toward architecture ...

space surrounding my work is crucial to it: as much thought has gone into the installation as into a piece itself'.

1978

Oldenburg moves to a studio above Kusama's in New York. During Judd's frequent visits to Kusama he becomes better acquainted with Oldenburg. In an exchange of work between the artists in 1981, Judd acquires Oldenburg's *Soft La Coupole Light Fixture* 1964, which will eventually be permanently installed on the fifth floor at 101 Spring Street.

June 1978

Judd and the founders of the Dia Art Foundation, Heiner Friedrich and his wife Philippa de Menil, discuss a large-scale project in Marfa. Dia is primarily financed by Philippa de Menil's interest in her family's Houston-based oil drilling manufacturing corporation, Schlumberger. The project is initially named the Art Museum of the Pecos, then changed to the Transpecos Museum.

November 1978

Donald Judd petitions for divorce from his wife in Presidio County, Texas Court. The divorce is finalised in February 1979.

January 1979

Signs a contract with Dia for the fabrication of thirteen 6 m (20 ft) horizontal progressions, three vertical ten-unit wall stacks, two stainless steel floor works, five 4.5 m- (15 ft-) wide channelled steel rectangular floor works, twenty-five large mill aluminium floor boxes, and a group of outdoor sculptures. Although Judd initially wants to construct new buildings, it is decided that the work will be installed in existing structures at Fort Russell, a former US Army cavalry post and subsequent World War II prisoner-of-war camp on the southeast edge of Marfa.

May 1979

Talks continue with the Dia Art Foundation about permanent installations of large-scale works. The scope of the project has increased, with plans for permanent installations by Judd, Flavin and Chamberlain. Judd later envisions individual outdoor works by Andre, Richard Long, Oldenburg and Serra, as well as the re-creation of a two-room installation by Larry Bell, which had previously been shown in 1969 at The Museum of Modern Art, New York. A new contract is signed in which Dia pledges Judd complete financial support for the fabrication, installation and permanent maintenance of his work along with that of Flavin and Chamberlain.

July 1979

Dia purchases the bulk of Fort Russell, as well as the Wool and Mohair Building, a large warehouse in the centre of Marfa, the latter structure for the installation of Chamberlain's work.

March 1980

Dia agrees to the production of an additional seventy-five mill aluminium floor works, to be installed in two artillery sheds at Fort Russell.

Donald Judd, Stedelijk van Abbemuseum, Eindhoven, April 1979

May 1980

Intent on settling his affairs with Giuseppe Panza, Judd travels again to Varese, where he proposes the creation of a permanent installation. No agreement is reached.

Summer 1980

Dia buys the remainder of Fort Russell, including eleven U-shaped barrack buildings, an equestrian arena and an additional 138 hectares (340 acres) adjacent to the fort.

By the end of 1980, two of the fifteen outdoor concrete works have been constructed. When complete, the works will be installed on a north-south axis 1 km ($^2/_3$ mile) long, in a field between the fort's artillery sheds and the fort's eastern edge, which borders Highway 67. Each work will consist of $5 \times 5 \times 2.5$ m ($16\,^1/_2 \times 16\,^1/_2 \times 8$ ft) forms in varying arrangements and numbers of units.

Responding to questions by an Internal Revenue Service auditor about tax deductions taken for travel and property expenses, Judd writes: 'You can't think about pieces without being on the land. That's the circumstances of the piece's invention. The IRS is full of consideration for the circumstances of businessmen but concedes nothing to artists, whose means of production are individual. The United States makes a big unearned profit; it might think a bit about the way in which the art is made which makes the money for the weapons no artist wants. It's quite possible to drive the American artists out of America for these reasons.'

April 1981

Due to Judd's increasing scepticism about Dia's commitment and ability to finish the project, new contracts are prepared by his lawyer John Jerome. Dia commits to the creation of the 100 works in mill aluminium, the fifteen outdoor concrete works, a large installation of works by Chamberlain, a six-barrack installation by Flavin, and Newman's prints. All works are to be completed by the end of 1984. Of great concern to Judd is the guarantee of permanence for the installations. Clauses are written into the contract binding Dia to perpetual ownership and maintenance of the work. The aluminium works are to be installed in the two former artillery sheds, redesigned by Judd. The dimensions of these works will be determined by the size of the interior space and will be in direct proportional relationship to the windows.

August 1981

Judd begins reworking the flat-roofed artillery sheds at Fort Russell. Interior partitions are removed, roofs are repaired and garage doors, which predominate on two sides of the buildings, are replaced with large, cross-framed, aluminium windows. Eventually galvanised iron roofs similar to Quonset huts (sheep-shed structures indigenous to the area) will be added to the tops of the walls, doubling their height. Plans for the ends of the huts to be constructed of glass, thereby allowing light to

penetrate the buildings along two perpendicular axes, a[re] scrapped due to engineering and budgeting problems.

Autumn 1981

Writes 'On Russian art and its relation to my work', published in *Art Journal*. Judd admits that, as a young artist, his knowledge of Malevich and the Constructivists was limited, and that his admiration for the work of Newman, Reinhardt, Davis and Piet Mondrian was slow to form due to his bias against geometry. He blames the lack of critic interest in Russian art on the primacy of Western European art, complaining that 'we had a guy who found a snow shovel and who talked for decades, producing talking artists' and that 'Picasso, who produced junk for foxt years, and not much before, is hailed' and, in reference t[o] the lack of interest in his own work, he alludes to both Johns and Rauschenberg: 'I've lived in the shade of a coa[t] hanger and bedspread. These household goods can't be a[n] advance on Newman and Pollock.'

September 1981

Shows in New York for the first time in two and a half years at Leo Castelli's ground-floor gallery on Greene Street. The work is a massive plywood wall construction measuring $3.5 \times 24.5 \times 1$ m ($12 \times 80 \times 4$ ft) that consists of grid of three vertical sections and ten horizontal section each defined by horizontal and diagonal planes. Writing in the *Village Voice*, Roberta Smith calls the work a master piece. It is purchased by English collector Charles Saatch[i] who initially refuses to allow Judd to oversee its installation. Ultimately Saatchi allows fabricator Peter Ballant[i]r[e] to install the work in London, but, contrary to Judd's insistence, an outside crew is used to de-install the work. Judd declares the work destroyed.

16 October 1981

Trisha Brown Dance Company's *Son of Gone Fishin'* premieres at the Brooklyn Academy of Music. Judd's first stage design consists of three coloured backdrops. At regular intervals these are first slowly raised, first 2 m (6ft), and then out of sight, revealing a progression of divided and undivided planes of colour, and then the sequence is repeated in reverse.

1982

Begins commercial production of limited editions of furniture with New York-based fabricators Jim Cooper and Ichiro Kato.

Spring 1982

Begins the renovation of the Arena at Fort Russell.

Writes 'On Installation', in which he complains 'the installation and context for the art being done now is poor and unsuitable. The correction is a permanent

installation of a good portion of the work of each of the best artists ... [this is] crucial to the autonomy and integrity of art to its defense, especially now when so many people want to use it for something else.'

December 1982

Donates a work for a benefit exhibition/auction *Art for a Nuclear Weapons Freeze*.

February 1983

Although Flavin has visited Marfa and begun to plan his installation, Heiner Friedrich informs Judd that the Flavin project must be postponed due to a shortage of funding. Judd writes a formal objection to Friedrich. Friedrich responds in March, stating that an independent foundation must be created to continue the Marfa project.

April 1983

John Chamberlain arrives in Marfa and installs nineteen works in the Wool and Mohair Building, including a large work in foam, *Barge Marfa*, created on-site. The Chamberlain works open to the public on 13 April.

Summer 1983

Begins the purchase of several significant ranches in southern Presidio County, close to the Mexican border.
    Invited to make a work in a rectangular public plaza in Providence, Rhode Island, Judd collaborates with architect Lauretta Vinciarelli. They expand the proposal into a sequence of six circular concrete structures, occupy-

ing the entire site. The proposed structures include a bus station, two gardens and a work of art. The project is stalled in 1984 by the urban planning team responsible for the plaza, who, according to Judd, 'had planned for three years and were not about to un-think what they hadn't thought about'.

20 September 1983

At Yale University Judd lectures for the first time on the relationship between art and architecture, a subject that will absorb him for the rest of his life. He uses the occasion to defend his own work and to attack postmodernist trends in both disciplines:
    'I've always disliked the division between form and content ... this unreal and uninformative division is just part of the larger division between thought and feeling ... Everything happens together and exists together and does not divide because of a meaningless dichotomy ... My work has the appearance it has, wrongly called "objective" and "impersonal", because my first and largest interest is in my relation to the natural world, all of it, all the way out.'
    'The many derivative artists and architects of the moment don't know that they can't begin to understand the forms they try to revive ... It's more important to understand why a work is very good, especially now when quality is considered undemocratic and vague generality and trite derivation are considered thought and tolerance ... art has been declining for fifteen years, following architecture which has already sunk into musical comedy ... We are starting a new era while suffering increasing mediocrity ... even the ideas of quality and knowledge are disappearing.'

November 1983

Donald Judd: Eight Works in Three Dimensions inaugurates the Knight Gallery of the Spirit Square Arts Center in Charlotte, North Carolina.

19 January 1984

In an effort to prepare Judd for the Dia Art Foundation's eventual removal of funding for Marfa, Heiner Friedrich writes to Judd: 'we are now intensifying our research to found a new institution which would have as its sole intention to carry the "Transpecos Museum" into the future'.

Summer 1984

Travels for the first time to the Soviet Union.

September – October 1984

Publishes 'A long discussion not about masterpieces but why there are so few of them' in two parts in *Art in America*. Judd's dismay at contemporary practice is evident from

Chamberlain Building.
Architectural adaptation
by Donald Judd.
Permanent Collection
the Chinati Foundation,
Marfa, Texas

the beginning: 'The quality of new art has been declining for 15 years.' He continues with denunciations aimed at a wide array of targets, including the governments of the US and the Soviet Union ('a carnivorous eagle and an omnivorous bear'), second-generation Abstract Expressionism ('radical ideas are adopted and then toned down, to be incorporated into the conservatism they denied'), contemporary Expressionist painting (Baselitz's brushwork is 'thoughtless, passionless, flaccid, and is a parody of Expressionism') and postmodernism as a whole ('Postmodern is being used to obscure the issue of quality ... it's hypocrisy to seem to criticize the work of the recent past, especially by ascribing spurious purposes and meaning to it, while indiscriminately mining the greater past'). Once again he renounces the tendentious categorisation of his work: 'I've said and written many times that the label "minimal" is meaningless in all ways ... that my work is definitely not impersonal – whatever that might be in art – and no one listens.'

In 1984 he begins making works in enamel-painted aluminium, fabricated by Doris Quarella of the Swiss company Lehni AG. Soon after, Judd begins the production of metal desks, chairs, tables and bookcases in fifteen colours of painted aluminium, as well as in anodised aluminium, galvanised iron and copper.

29 November 1984

Participates in 'Criticism at the Crossroads', a round-table symposium with Lucy Lippard, Donald Kuspit, Clement Greenberg, Carter Ratcliff and Leon Golub, moderated by Susan Sontag.

February 1985

Dia announces that it is cutting its funding due to the decline of Schlumberger stock. Several projects are in danger of being abandoned, including Judd's in Marfa and, in New York, installations by John Chamberlain and Walter de Maria and performance spaces devoted to the work of La Monte Young and Robert Whitman. Eventually, the Chamberlain and Whitman projects, along with a planned installation of Flavin's work in Garrison, New York, are cancelled. Heiner Friedrich resigns, and a new Board of Directors is formed.

10–11 April 1985

Judd lectures at the Detroit Institute of the Arts, Michigan, and participates in a panel discussion with Trisha Brown and Robert Ashley about their collaboration on *Son of Gone Fishin'*.

Aerial view of the Chinati Foundation and Marfa, Texas

14 April 1985

Participates in 'Making Shelter', a symposium hosted by *The Harvard Architecture Review* at the Graduate School of Design. Other panellists include Siah Armajani, Mary Alice Dixon, Mario Gandelsonas and Adele Santos.

1985

Leaves Leo Castelli for the Paula Cooper Gallery, where he will have three solo shows.

9 July 1985

John Jerome, Judd's lawyer, threatens Dia with a lawsuit concerning the contracts that guaranteed the permanency of the installations in Marfa.

November 1985

Writes to several members of Dia's board, reiterating that he is preparing to file suit against Dia, claiming breach of contract.

The Mansana's west building is completed by the end of 1985. Several of the earliest three-dimensional works are installed in the south room; the north room is used as a studio; the middle room contains Judd's library.

December 1985

Begins negotiations with Dia's new director Charles Wright for the reorganisation of the Marfa installations and their eventual transfer to an independent, non-profit organisation.

1986

Meets the artist Roni Horn, for whose work Judd is full of praise. The two remain friends throughout his life. Judd eventually acquires Horn's work *Things that Happen Again*, two identical, solid-copper rounded objects, the shorter ends of which are concave and the larger ends of which are flat. Although the work was originally shown in two rooms, Judd later installs the work with Horn's permission in an abandoned building at the Chinati Foundation in Marfa (see entry for October 1987).

July 1986

Premiere of Trisha Brown Dance Company's *Newark*, for which Judd designs the set and also develops the sound concept, which consists of extended bagpipe tones, played separately by musician Peter Zummo.

November 1986

Judd attempts to collaborate with Carl Andre, Peter Eisenman, Frank Gehry, Oldenburg and van Bruggen

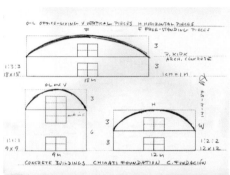 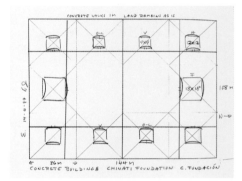

and Serra on the development of a large tract of land between Lake Erie and downtown Cleveland, Ohio. As in Providence, Judd is invited to make a work of art, but attempts to make architecture in its place. Judd proposes a 'prone skyscraper' so as not to obscure the lake from the city centre. Judd's proposal, as well as those of the other collaborators, is rejected.

Winter 1986 to Spring 1987

Designs a series of ten concrete, barrel-vaulted buildings for the south-west corner of the Chinati property. The buildings are to be arranged on an existing rectangular grid of sidewalks constructed amid the former prisoner-of-war buildings and are to contain free-standing works by Judd. Construction is halted with only two of the buildings partially completed.

January 1987

Judd discontinues fabrication of painted aluminium works with Lehni AG in Switzerland, and moves the

Concrete buildings. The Chinati Foundation, Marfa, Texas

Architectural drawings for complex of concrete buildings. Collection of Judd Foundation

production of art first to Studer Ag in Switzerland, and
then to Lascaux Conservation Materials in Brooklyn.
Furniture production is moved to the Janssen factory in
the Netherlands.

28 April 1987

Receives the Skowhegan Medal for sculpture, along with
Ryman for painting and Robert Wilson for design.

29 April 1987

Receives the Brandeis University Creative Arts Award for
sculpture.

October 1987

Dia transfers the ownership of the property and artworks
in Marfa to a new, public foundation, The Chinati Founda-
tion/La Fundación Chinati. Named after a nearby mountain that abuts Judd's ranch, the word is derived from the
Aztec word for blackbird, *Xantl*. Initial board members
include William C. Agee, Judd, Annalee Newman (widow
of Barnett Newman), El Paso-based attorney Carl Ryan,
Jane Shurley (a local businesswoman) and Brydon Smith.
    Oldenburg and van Bruggen visit Judd in Marfa.
While touring the Foundation grounds, Judd points out
and explains the crumbling concrete funeral marker of
Louie, the oldest horse of the US First Cavalry formerly
stationed at the base. Being too old to travel when the
cavalry disbanded in 1932, Louie was ceremonially shot
and buried at the site. Inspired by the story, the artists
begin to develop a work for permanent installation
at Chinati.

10 October 1987

Judd holds the first Chinati Foundation Open House,
an event conceived to bring the local community to
the project. Temporary exhibitions include prints by
Newman and Josef Albers (the former a gift of Annalee
Newman, the latter from Judd's personal collection)
and drawings by Robert Tiemann of San Antonio. In the
first catalogue for The Chinati Foundation/La Fundación
Chinati, Judd reiterates his ideas of installation and
permanence: 'The enterprise in Marfa was meant to be
constructive. The art was meant to be, and now will be,
permanently installed and maintained in a space suitabl
to it ... Somewhere a portion of contemporary art has to
exist as an example of what the art and its context were
meant to be. Somewhere, just as the platinum-iridium
meter guarantees the tape measure, a strict measure
must exist for the art of this time and place. Otherwise
art is just show and monkey business.'

1988

Paul Gredinger, a Swiss advertising executive and art co-
lector, agrees to give Judd life-time use of Eichholteren,
an inn built in the 1940s sited on Lake Lucerne on the ou
skirts of Küssnacht am Rigi, Switzerland, in exchange for
Judd's renovation and installation of the building and its
grounds. Judd collaborates with Zurich-based architect
Adrian Jolles. Their aim, as stated by Jolles, is to 'reveal
the building's inherent qualities, and to create spaces,
which, thanks to their neutrality, are equally suited to
living, working and exhibiting art'.

Summer 1988

An exhibition by the Swiss painter Richard Paul Lohse, organised by Rudi Fuchs and Judd, opens at the Chinati Foundation. The first exhibition of Lohse's work in America, it is later installed at 101 Spring Street, and then travels to the Haags Gemeentemuseum in Holland.

September 1988

An exhibition of Giuseppe Panza's collection at the Reina Sofía Museum in Madrid includes four plywood pieces attributed to Judd. Constructed without the artist's consent, the works are poorly fabricated with inferior material, improper fastenings and incorrect measurements. Judd writes a furious letter of protest to Panza.

October 1988

A retrospective curated by Barbara Haskell opens at the Whitney Museum of American Art in New York.

21–22 January 1989

Judd participates in a workshop on the relationship between art and architecture sponsored by the Frederick R. Weisman Art Foundation in Santa Monica, California. Other participants include Daniel Buren, Chamberlain, Henry Cobb, Eisenman, Gehry, Michael Graves and Irwin. Responding to Eisenman's claim that good architecture is by necessity hostile to art, thus forcing artists to contend with the building, Judd calls his logic 'pure sophistry', insisting that architecture should serve art.

Spring 1989

Writes 'Ausstellungsleitungsstreit' for the exhibition catalogue of *Bilderstreit* in Cologne. Judd reiterates and expands his complaints against museums and his perception that their activities are detrimental to art. Despite an agreement between the organisers and Judd, the essay is not included in the catalogue and is eventually published in the April/May 1989 issue of the German magazine *Kunstforum*.

Interior at Eichholteren. Architecture and furniture by Donald Judd

Brigitte Huck, opens at the Österreichisches Museum für angewandte Kunst in Vienna during the Gulf War. Judd supplies the essay 'Nie Wieder Krieg' for the exhibition catalogue, writing, 'War is failure ... War is rich, lazy, simple and easy'. He attacks both the US and Soviet Union governments, noting the destructive nature of military-based economies in which bureaucracy grows and art and architecture shrink. Judd also contributes three anti-war posters for the exhibition. While in Vienna he meets Russian artist Ilya Kabakov.

June 1991

Discontinues fabrication of wood furniture in limited editions with James Cooper and Ichiro Kato. Fabrication continues in the sub-basement of 101 Spring Street by Rupert Deese and Jeff Jamieson.

July 1991

Designs new floors for the Paleis Lange Voorhout in The Hague. The idea for the design is derived from several recent print editions.

September 1991

First exhibition at the Pace Gallery in New York.

October 1991

Claes Oldenburg and Coosje van Bruggen's gift to the Chinati Foundation, *Monument to the Last Horse*, an aluminium polyurethane foam and polyurethane enamel sculpture 6 × 5 × 3.5 m (19 ft 8 in × 17 ft × 12 ft 4 in), is installed and inaugurated at the Chinati Foundation Open House.

Judd and Marianne Stockebrand establish an independent publishing company, Der Zweite Pfeil, and produce their first book for the Albers exhibition at the Chinati Open House, with essays by Judd and Brenda Danilowitz of the Josef and Anni Albers Foundation.

1992

With curator Christian Witt-Döring, Judd redesigns the installation of Vienna's Museum für angewandte Kunst' collection of eighteenth-century furniture, including the re-creation of the Dubsky Room, a space originally located in the Dubsky Palace in Brno. Of this room, Judd writes, 'This is a small, uneasy room uneasily placed in a large, doubly uneasy room. I think it should be in the basement. But Witt-Döring and I did our best, uneasily.'

6–7 March 1992

Participates in the American Society of Landscape Architects' symposium 'The Texas Landscape'. His argument to the society is a radically simple one: leave the land alone

Donald Judd and Claes Oldenburg at the dedication of Claes Oldenburg and Coosje van Bruggen's *Monument to the Last Horse* in 1991

May 1992

Participates in a Barnett Newman Symposium at Harvard University.

13 June – 26 July 1992

Travels to Japan for the opening of a retrospective at the Shizuoka Prefectural Museum of Art. The exhibition tours to the Kitakyushu Municipal Museum of Art in 1993. Judd gives lectures at the openings of both shows.

October 1992

Ingólfur Arnarsson installs thirty-six graphite drawings on

Paintings and works
on paper by Ingólfur
Arnarsson 1991–2.
The Chinati Foundation,
Marfa, Texas

paper and two watercolour on poured concrete paintings made during his summer's residency at Chinati; they remain on permanent display.

Moves production of lightweight wood furniture from Yorkshire to Galway, Ireland.

March 1993

Shows two large floor works in Cor-ten steel and two large vertical wall works at the Pace Gallery. In an essay for the catalogue, '21 February 93', Judd discusses the historical placement of art in public spaces and provides a chronology of his work's spatial development. 'Any work of art ... is harmed or helped by where it is placed ... Further, any work of art is harmed or helped, almost always harmed, by the meaning of the situation in which it is placed. There is no neutral space, since space is made, indifferently or intentionally, and since meaning is made, ignorantly or knowledgeably.' Judd stresses the fundamental difference between his work and the European sculpture that preceded it: 'the development of space in past work, from Greek sculpture through the Italian Renaissance to Giacometti and David Smith does not expand space, it is always a solid, thereby totemic, monolithic, and the space surrounding the work is pictorial'. Judd writes that the placement of his work, and the divisions between units, has allowed for the creation and the clear articulation of the space surrounding the work. 'Space is new in art and is still not a concern of more than a few artists.'

April 1993

Opening of a furniture retrospective at the Museum Boijmans Van Beuningen in Rotterdam, Holland. A catalogue

of the furniture is published by the museum for which Judd contributes the essay, 'It's hard to find a good lamp'.

September 1993

Donates a print to ACES (Alert Citizens for Environmental Safety), an El Paso-based activist group fighting the nuclear waste dump in Sierra Blanca.

October 1993

Permanent installation of Ilya Kabakov's gift to the Chinati Foundation, *School No.6*, is inaugurated at the Chinati Foundation's annual Open House. Fully occupying one of the U-shaped barrack buildings at the foundation, the work is an evocation of an abandoned, Soviet-era schoolhouse.

November 1993

Feeling ill, Judd visits a doctor in Texas before leaving for several major exhibitions in Europe. The doctor diagnoses the flu. Still feeling ill, Judd travels to Europe and sees a doctor in Cologne, who diagnoses advanced non-Hodgkins lymphatic cancer. The prognosis is pessimistic. Judd is hospitalised in Cologne from 29 November to 10 December.

Donald Judd, a retrospective curated by Volker Ratte-meyer and Renate Petzinger, opens at the Museum Wiesbaden, Germany, on the occasion of Judd's receipt of the Stankowski Prize, given for career achievement in art and design. The exhibition features prints, early sculpture, furniture, architecture models and plans, and poster designs. Judd is too ill to travel for the opening. An extensive catalogue, *Donald Judd: Räume – Spaces*, is published.

An exhibition at Amsterdam's Stedelijk Museum, curated and installed by Rudi Fuchs, accompanies Judd's receipt of the Sikkens Prize, given by Dutch company Akzo for the use of colour in art. Although Judd feels well enough to visit and approve of the installation, he is too ill to attend the opening and award ceremony. His last essay, 'Some Aspects of Color in General and Red and Black in Particular', in which Judd discusses both his use of space and colour, is published on the occasion of the exhibition.

A print retrospective, with an accompanying catalogue raisonné of prints published by Edition Schellmann, opens at the Haags Gemeentemuseum, curated by Mariette Josephus Jitta.

December 1993

Judd returns to New York for treatment at New York Hospital/Cornell Medical Center.

12 February 1994

Donald Judd dies at New York Hospital in Manhattan. He is buried at his ranch house at Ayala de Chinati, Las Casas.

Ilya Kabakov
School No.6 1993.
The Chinati Foundation
Marfa, Texas

Selected Reading

Collected Writings by the Artist

Donald Judd Complete Writings, 1959–1975, Gallery Reviews, Book Reviews, Articles, Letters to the Editor, Reports, Statements, Complaints, Halifax and New York 1975.
Donald Judd Complete Writings 1975–1986, Eindhoven 1987.
Donald Judd, Architektur, exh. cat., Westfälischer Kunstverein, Münster 1989. Introduction by Marianne Stockebrand.

Donald Judd: Écrits 1963–1990, Galerie Lelong, Paris 1991.

The Chinati Foundation Newsletter, Marfa, 1995 to present, regularly publishes writings by Donald Judd.

Monographs

William C. Agee, *Don Judd*, exh. cat., The Whitney Museum of American Art, New York 1968. Notes by Dan Flavin and selected writings by Donald Judd.
Donald Judd: Structures, exh. cat., Galerie Sonnabend, Paris 1969.
Don Judd, exh. cat., Van Abbemuseum, Eindhoven, Museum Folkwang, Essen, and Whitechapel Art Gallery, London 1970. Essay by Jean Leering, selected writings by Donald Judd and republication of interview 'Questions to Stella and Judd' by Bruce Glaser, edited by Lucy Lippard.
Don Judd, exh. cat., Kunstverein Hannover 1970. Essays by Manfred de la Motte, Martin Friedmann, Emily Wassermann, Philip Leider, interview 'Questions to Stella and Judd' by Bruce Glaser and 'Complaints: Part I' and selected writings by Donald Judd.
Don Judd, Retrospective Exhibition of Works, exh. cat., Pasadena Art Museum 1971. Essay and interview with Donald Judd by John Coplans.
Don Judd: 18 Skulpturen aus galvanisiertem Eisenblech 1972/73, exh. cat., Galerie Heiner Friedrich, Cologne, Galerie Heiner Friedrich, Munich, and Annemarie Verna, Zurich 1973.
Brydon Smith (ed.), *Donald Judd*, exh. cat., National Gallery of Canada, Ottawa 1975. Essay by Roberta Smith and catalogue raisonné of paintings, objects and wood-blocks 1960–1974 by Dudley Del Balso, Roberta Smith and Brydon Smith.
Donald Judd: Skulpturen, exh. cat., Kunsthalle Bern 1976. Essay by Johannes Gachnang and republication of essays on Jackson Pollock, Barnett Newman and Kasimir Malevich by Donald Judd.
Dieter Koepplin, *Donald Judd: Zeichnungen/Drawings 1556–1976*, exh. cat., Kunstmuseum Basel 1976.

Donald Judd für Josef Albers, exh. cat., Moderne Galerie Bottrop 1977. Interview with Donald Judd by Kasper König.
The Sculpture of Donald Judd, exh. cat., Art Museum of South Texas, Corpus Christi 1977. Essay by William C. Agee.
Donald Judd, exh. cat., National Gallery of Canada, Ottawa and The Vancouver Art Gallery, Vancouver 1975. Essay by Brydon Smith and 'Imperialism, Nationalism and Regionalism' by Donald Judd.
Rudi Fuchs (ed.), *Donald Judd*, exh. cat., Stedelijk van Abbemuseum, Eindhoven 1979.
Brian Wallis, *Donald Judd: Eight Works In Three Dimensions*, exh. cat., Knight Gallery/Spirit Square Arts Center, Charlotte, North Carolina 1983. Essay 'On Installation' by Donald Judd.
Donald Judd: Möbel Furniture, Zurich 1986. Essay by Donald Judd.
Donald Judd, exh. cat., Stedelijk van Abbemuseum, Eindhoven, Städtische Kunsthalle, Düsseldorf, ARC/Musée d'Art Moderne de la Ville de Paris, Fundació Joan Miró, Barcelona 1987. Essays by Rainer Crone and Rudi Fuchs.
Donald Judd, exh. cat., Galerie Lelong, Paris 1987. Text by Donald Judd.
Donald Judd, exh. cat., Lawrence Oliver Gallery, Philadelphia 1987. Essay by Ronald Jones.
Barbara Haskell, *Donald Judd*, exh. cat., The Whitney Museum of American Art, New York 1988.
Donald Judd, exh. cat., Waddington Galleries, London 1988. Essay by Lynne Cooke.
Jochen Poetter (ed.), *Donald Judd*, exh. cat., Staatliche Kunsthalle Baden-Baden 1989. Essay by Franz Meyer and interview with Donald Judd by Jochen Poetter.

Donald Judd, exh. cat., Kunstverein St Gallen 1990. Introduction by Roland Wäspe and discussion with Donald Judd by Angeli Janhsen.

Yve-Alain Bois, *Donald Judd: New Sculpture*, exh. cat., The Pace Gallery, New York, and Galerie Lelong, Paris 1991.

Donald Judd: Architektur, exh. cat., Österreichisches Museum für angewandte Kunst, Vienna 1991. Essays by Peter Noever, Brigitte Huck, Rudi Fuchs and 'Nie Wieder Krieg' by Donald Judd. Second edition published 2003.

Donald Judd: Large-Scale Works, exh. cat., The Pace Gallery, New York 1993. Essays by Rudi Fuchs and Donald Judd.

Mariette Josephus Jitta and Jörg Schellmann (eds.), *Donald Judd: Prints and Works in Editions, A Catalogue Raisonné*, exh. cat., Haags Gemeentemuseum, The Hague, and Edition Schellmann, Cologne and New York 1993. Essays by Mariette Josephus Jitta and Rudi Fuchs.

Donald Judd: Räume – Spaces. Kunst + Design: Donald Judd – Preisträger der Stankowski-Stiftung 1993 (Art + Design: Donald Judd – Recipient of the Stankowski Prize 1993), exh. cat., Museum Wiesbaden 1993. Texts by Rudi Fuchs, Franz Meyer, Renate Petzinger, Volker Rattemeyer and '101 Spring Street' by Donald Judd.

Donald Judd Furniture Retrospective, exh. cat., Museum Boijmans Van Beuningen, Rotterdam, and Villa Stuck, Munich 1993. Essay by Brigitte Huck and 'It's hard to find a good lamp', 'Eichholteren, Switzerland', 'Marfa, Texas: Concrete Buildings' and '101 Spring Street' by Donald Judd.

Donald Judd: Sculpture, exh. cat., PaceWildenstein, New York 1994. Essay by William C. Agee.

Donald Judd: The Moscow Installation, exh. cat., Galerie Gmurzynska, Cologne 1994. Essay by Rudi Fuchs and 'Russian Art in Regard to Myself' by Donald Judd.

Brydon E. Smith, *Donald Judd*, exh. cat., Paula Cooper Gallery, New York 1995.

Donald Judd: Escultura, Gravura, Mobiliário (Sculpture, Prints, Furniture), Centro Cultural de Belém, Lisbon 1997. Essays by Hal Foster and Prudence Carlson. Includes selected writings by Donald Judd and 1971 interview by John Coplans.

Donald Judd: Early Fabricated Work, exh. cat., PaceWildenstein, New York 1998. Essay by Rosalind E. Krauss and excerpts from Robert Smithson's writings.

Donald Judd 1960–1991, exh. cat., The Museum of Modern Art, Saitama, and The Museum of Modern Art, Shiga 1999. Essays by Gen Umezu, Sachiko Osaki, Marianne Stockebrand, interview by John Coplans and selected writings by Donald Judd.

Dietmar Elger (ed.), *Donald Judd: Colorist*, exh. cat., Sprengel Museum, Hanover 2000. Essays by William C. Agee, Martin Engler and 'Some Aspects of Color in General and Red and Black in Particular' by Donald Judd.

Donald Judd: Late Work, exh. cat., PaceWildenstein, New York 2000. Essay by Richard Shiff.

Thomas Kellein, *Donald Judd: Early Work 1955–1968*, exh. cat., Kunsthalle Bielefeld and The Menil Collection, Houston 2002. Essays 'The Student of Painting' and 'Specific Objects' by Donald Judd.

Donald Judd: 50 x 100 x 50, 100 x 100 x 50: anodized aluminum: brass: copper: stainless steel: plexiglass: plywood: Cor-ten steel, exh. cat., PaceWildenstein, New York 2002. Essay by Richard Shiff.

Selected Exhibitions

Green Gallery, New York, 17 December 1963 – 11 January 1964.

Leo Castelli Gallery, New York, 5 February – 2 March 1966.

Primary Structures: Younger American and British Sculptors, Jewish Museum, New York, 27 April – 12 June 1966.

Whitney Museum of American Art, 27 February – 14 April 1968.

Galerie Sonnabend, Paris, 6 – 29 May 1969.

Galerie Bischofberger, Zurich, May – June 1969.

Galerie Rudolf Zwirner, Cologne, 4 – 30 June 1969.

New York Painting and Sculpture: 1940–1970, The Metropolitan Museum of Art, New York, 18 October 1969 – 1 February 1970.

Van Abbemuseum, Eindhoven, 16 January – 1 March 1970; travelled to the Folkwang Museum, Essen, 11 April – 10 May 1970; Kunstverein Hannover, 20 June – 2 August 1970; Whitechapel Art Gallery, London, 29 September – 1 November 1970.

Leo Castelli Gallery and Warehouse, New York. 11 April – 9 May 1970.

Guggenheim International Exhibition 1971, The Solomon R. Guggenheim Museum, New York, 12 February – 25 April 1971.

Pasadena Art Museum, California, 11 May – 4 July 1971.

Sonsbeek 71, Park Sonsbeek, Arnhem, 19 June – 15 August 1971.

Documenta 5, Kassel, 30 June – 8 October 1972.

Contemporanea, Parcheggio di Villa Borghese, Rome, 30 November 1973 – 17 March 1974.

Lisson Gallery, London, 22 January – 23 February 1974.

The National Gallery of Canada, Ottawa, 24 May – 6 July 1975.

Drawing Now, The Museum of Modern Art, New York, 23 January – 9 March 1976.

Galerie Annemarie Verna, Zurich, 8 April – 13 May 1976.

Donald Judd: Skulpturen, Kunsthalle Bern, 14 April – 30 May 1976.

Donald Judd: Zeichnungen/Drawings 1956–1976, Kunstmuseum Basel, 14 April – 23 June 1976; travelled to the Kunsthalle Tübingen; Museum des 20. Jahrhunderts, Vienna; Musée d'Art et d'Histoire, Geneva.

Art Museum of South Texas, Corpus Christi, January – March 1977.

Donald Judd für Josef Albers, Moderne Galerie Bottrop, 8 May – 12 June 1977.

Donald Judd: Drawings 1956–76, Rijkmuseum Kröller-Müller, Otterlo, 25 March – 16 May 1978.

Vancouver Art Gallery, British Columbia, 5 May – 4 June 1978.

Stedelijk van Abbemuseum, Eindhoven, 26 April – 2 June 1979.

Leo Castelli Gallery, New York, 10 September – 31 October 1981.

Donald Judd: Eight Works in Three Dimensions, Knight Gallery, Charlotte, North Carolina, 5 November 1983 – 6 January 1984.

Furniture by Donald Judd, 101 Spring Street, New York, 1984.

Donald Judd Furniture, Max Protetch Gallery, New York, December 1984.

Donald Judd, Brice Marden, Cy Twombly, Andy Warhol, The Saatchi Collection, London, March – October 1985.

Art Minimal, Musée d'Art Contemporain, Bordeaux, 2 February – 21 April 1985.

Donald Judd: Furniture, Doris Lehni-Quarella and Galerie Annemarie Verna, Zurich, 27 February – 16 March 1985.

Qu'est-ce que la sculpture moderne?, Musée National d'Art Moderne, Centre Georges Pompidou, Paris, 3 July – 13 October 1986.

Stedelijk van Abbemuseum, Eindhoven, 26 April – 2 June 1987; travelled to the Städtische Kunsthalle, Düsseldorf, 27 June – 9 August 1987; Musée d'Art Moderne de la Ville de Paris, 8 December 1987 – 7 February 1988; Fundació Joan Miró, Barcelona, 25 February – 24 April 1988; Castello di Rivoli, Turin, 1988.

The Whitney Museum of American Art, New York, 20 October – 31 December 1988; travelled to Dallas Museum of Art, Texas, 12 February – 16 April 1989.

Donald Judd, Architektur, Westfälisher Kunstverein, Münster, 16 April – 4 June 1989.

Waddington Galleries, London, 22 May – 17 June 1989.

Staatliche Kunsthalle Baden-Baden, 27 August – 15 October 1989.

Kunstverein St Gallen, 21 April – 29 July 1990.

Donald Judd: Architektur, Österreichisches Museum für angewandte Kunst, Vienna, 14 February – 8 April 1991.

Donald Judd: New Sculpture, The Pace Gallery, New York, 13 September – 19 October 1991.

This selection includes one-person and group museum and gallery exhibitions, accompanied by significant catalogues, and early one-person exhibitions in Europe and America.

Donald Judd: Furniture, Kasseler Kunstverein, Kassel,
 11 June – 20 September 1992.

Donald Judd: Large-Scale Works, The Pace Gallery, 142
 Greene Street, New York, 27 March – 24 April 1993.

Donald Judd Furniture Retrospective, Museum Boijmans Van
 Beuningen, Rotterdam, 25 April – 20 June 1993;
 travelled to Villa Stuck, Munich, 29 July – 3 October
 1993.

*American Art in the Twentieth Century: Painting and Sculpture
 1913–1993*, Martin-Gropius-Bau, Berlin, 8 May –
 25 July 1993; travelled to Royal Academy of Arts,
 London, 16 September – 12 December 1993.

*Donald Judd: werken uit Nederlandse openbare collecties en een
 Belgische privé-verzameling t.g.v. de Sikkensprijs 1993*,
 Stedelijk Museum, Amsterdam, 28 November 1993
 – 23 January 1994.

Don Judd: Prints 1951–1993, Haags Gemeentemuseum,
 The Hague, 26 November 1993 – 31 January 1994;
 travelled to Haus für konstruktive und konkrete
 Kunst, Zurich, 3 September – 6 November 1994;
 Österreichisches Museum für angewandte Kunst,
 Vienna, 16 November 1994 – 22 January 1995; Insti-
 tut Valencià d'Art Modern, Valencia, 23 February –
 16 April 1995.

Museum Wiesbaden, 12 December 1993 – 6 March 1994;
 travelled to Städtische Kunstammlungen
 Chemnitz, 19 June – 31 July 1994; Badisches
 Landesmuseum, Karlsruhe, 27 August – 20
 November 1994; The Museum of Modern Art,
 Oxford, 15 January – 26 March 1995;
 Kunsthallen Brandts Klaedefabrik, Odense,
 30 June – 1 October 1995.

Donald Judd: The Moscow Installation, Galerie Gmurzynska,
 Cologne, 5 March – 21 May 1994.

Donald Judd: The Last Editions, Brooke Alexander Editions,
 New York, 10 September – 29 October 1994.

Centro Cultural de Bélem, Lisbon, 16 May – 10 August 1996.

Wall Pieces by Donald Judd, The Chinati Foundation, Marfa,
 29 September 1995 – September 1996.

Donald Judd: Retrospective der Druckgraphik, Museum Wiesbaden, 8 September – 24 November 1996.

Donald Judd: Early Fabricated Work, PaceWildenstein, New
 York, 3 February – 14 March 1998.

Dan Flavin/Donald Judd: Aspects of Color, The Menil Collection, Houston, 30 October 1998 – 24 January 1999.

Donald Judd 1960–1991, The Museum of Modern Art,
 Saitama, 23 January – 22 March 1999; travelled to
 The Museum of Modern Art, Shiga, 22 May – 11 July
 1999.

Donald Judd: Colorist, Sprengel Museum, Hanover,
 16 January – 30 April 2000; travelled to Kunsthaus
 Bregenz, 12 May – 9 July 2000; Musée d'Art Moderne et d'Art Contemporain, Nice, 8 October 2000 –
 21 January 2001.

Donald Judd: Late Work, PaceWildenstein, 142 Greene Street,
 New York, 13 October – 11 November 2000 and 32
 East 57th Street, 27 October – 25 November 2000.

Donald Judd: Prints 1961–1994, Susan Sheehan Gallery, New
 York, 10 January – 31 March 2001.

Untitled (Slant Piece), Paula Cooper Gallery, New York,
 31 March – 28 April 2001.

Donald Judd: Early Work 1955–1968, Kunsthalle Bielefeld,
 5 May – 21 July 2002; travelled to The Menil Collection,
 Houston, 31 January – 27 April 2003.

*Donald Judd: 50 x 100 x 50, 100 x 100 x 50: anodized aluminum:
 brass: copper: stainless steel: plexiglass: plywood: Cor-ten
 steel*, PaceWildenstein, New York, 18 October –
 16 November 2002.

List of Works

1   *Untitled* 1961
Liquitex on canvas
171.4 × 123.2 (67 $^1/_2$ × 48 $^1/_2$)
DSS 15
Private Collection, Courtesy PaceWildenstein, New York

2   *Untitled* 1961
Liquitex and sand on masonite
122 × 243.8 (48 × 96)
DSS 19
Solomon R. Guggenheim Museum, New York.
Gift of Mr and Mrs Leo Castelli, 1972

3   *Untitled* 1961
Oil on masonite and wood with aluminium baking pan
122.2 × 91.8 × 10.2 (48 $^1/_8$ × 36 $^1/_8$ × 4)
DSS 23
The Museum of Modern Art, New York.
Gift of Barbara Rose

4   *Untitled* 1962
Light cadmium red oil on liquitex and sand
on masonite with yellow Plexiglas
122 × 243.8 × 7 (48 × 96 × 2 $^3/_4$)
DSS 30
San Francisco Museum of Modern Art.
Bequest of Phyllis Wattis

5   *Untitled* 1962
    exhibited example fabricated 1988
Light cadmium red oil on wood with iron pipe
122 × 84 × 54.6 (48 $^1/_{16}$ × 33 $^1/_{16}$ × 21 $^1/_2$)
DSS 33
Collection of Judd Foundation

6   *Untitled* 1962
Light cadmium red oil on striated plywood, black oil
on wood with galvanised iron and aluminium
193 × 244.5 × 30 (76 × 96 $^1/_4$ × 12)
DSS 34
Öffentliche Kunstsammlung Basel, Kunstmuseum

7   *Untitled* 1963
    exhibited example fabricated 1975
Light cadmium red oil on wood and purple lacquer
on aluminium
122 × 210.8 × 122 (48 $^1/_{16}$ × 83 × 48 $^1/_{16}$)
DSS 35
National Gallery of Canada, Ottawa. Purchased 1975

8   *Untitled* 1963
Light cadmium red oil on wood with purple Plexiglas
49.5 × 123.2 × 123.2 (19 $^1/_2$ × 48 $^1/_2$ × 48 $^1/_2$)
DSS 38
Estate of Dan Flavin

9   *Untitled* 1963
Light cadmium red oil on wood with iron pipe
56.2 × 115.1 × 77.5 (22 $^1/_8$ × 45 $^3/_8$ × 30 $^1/_2$)
DSS 39
Hirshhorn Museum and Sculpture Garden,
Smithsonian Institution. Joseph H. Hirshhorn
Purchase Fund, 1991

10   *Untitled* 1964
Chartreuse oil on wood and yellow enamel on iron
49.5 × 122 × 86.4 (19 $^1/_2$ × 48 $^1/_{16}$ × 34)
DSS 46
The Helman Collection

11   *To Susan Buckwalter* 1964
    exhibited example fabricated 1965
Galvanised iron and blue lacquer on aluminium
76.2 × 358.2 × 76.2 (30 × 141 × 30)
DSS 56
Addison Gallery of American Art, Phillips Academy,
Andover, Massachusetts (Gift of Frank Stella [PA 1954])

12   *Untitled* 1965
    exhibited example fabricated 1968
Red lacquer on galvanised iron
12.7 × 175.3 × 21.6 (5 × 69 × 8 $^1/_2$)
DSS 70
Froehlich Collection, Stuttgart

13 *Untitled* 1966
Amber Plexiglas and stainless steel
50.8 × 122 × 86.4 (20 × 48 × 34)
DSS 82
Froehlich Collection, Stuttgart

14 *Untitled* 1966
Stainless steel
36.8 × 194.3 × 64.8 (14 $^1/_2$ × 76 $^1/_2$ × 25 $^1/_2$)
DSS 117
Museum Ludwig (Donation Ludwig 1976)

15 *Untitled* 1968
Stainless steel and yellow Plexiglas
10 units, each 23 × 101.6 × 78.7 (9 $^1/_{16}$ × 40 × 31)
DSS 123
Froehlich Collection, Stuttgart

16 *Untitled* 1969
Clear anodised aluminium and brushed aluminium
21 × 642.6 × 20.3 (8 $^1/_4$ × 253 × 8)
DSS 175
Van Abbemuseum, Eindhoven

17 *Untitled* 1969
Clear anodised aluminium and purple Plexiglas
83.8 × 172.7 × 122 (33 × 68 × 48)
DSS 179
Thomas and Cristina Bechtler, Switzerland

18 *Untitled* 1969
    exhibited example fabricated 1970
Cold-rolled steel
6 units, each 100 × 100 × 100 (39 $^3/_8$ × 39 $^3/_8$ × 39 $^3/_8$),
with 25 (9 $^3/_4$) intervals
DSS 186
Öffentliche Kunstsammlung Basel, Kunstmuseum

19 *Untitled* 1969
Copper
10 units, each 23 × 101.6 × 78.7 (9 $^1/_{16}$ × 40 × 31)
DSS 204
Solomon R. Guggenheim Museum, New York.
Panza Collection, 1991

20 *Untitled* 1970
Clear anodised and purple anodised aluminium
20.5 × 644 × 21 (8 $^1/_{16}$ × 253 $^9/_{16}$ × 8 $^1/_4$)
DSS 224
Moderna Museet, Stockholm. New York Collection 1973

21 *Untitled* 1970
Clear anodised aluminium
10 units, each 23 × 101.5 × 79 (9 $^1/_{16}$ × 39 $^{15}/_{16}$ × 31 $^1/_8$)
DSS 239
Öffentliche Kunstsammlung Basel, Kunstmuseum

22 *Untitled* 1972
Copper and light cadmium red enamel on aluminium
91.6 × 155.5 × 178.2 (36 × 61 $^1/_4$ × 70 $^3/_{16}$)
DSS 271
Tate. Presented by the American Fund for
the Tate Gallery 1992

23 *Untitled* 1973
Plywood
7 units, each 195.6 × 195.6 × 195.6 (77 × 77 × 77),
with 10.2 (4) intervals
DSS 279
Museum Wiesbaden

24 *Untitled* 1973
Brass and red fluorescent Plexiglas
6 units, each 86.4 × 86.4 × 86.4 (34 × 34 × 34),
with 20.3 (8) intervals
DSS 282
Solomon R. Guggenheim Museum, New York.
Panza Collection, 1991

25 *Untitled* 1978
Plywood
16 units, each 50 × 100 × 50 (19 $^{11}/_{16}$ × 39 $^3/_8$ × 19 $^{11}/_{16}$)
The Chinati Foundation

26 *Untitled* 1982
Aluminium and purple Plexiglas
3 units, each 100 × 100 × 37 (39 $^3/_8$ × 39 $^3/_8$ × 14 $^9/_{16}$),
with 32 (12 $^5/_8$) intervals
82-12
Annemarie and Gianfranco Verna

27 *Untitled* 1984
Enamelled aluminium
30 × 180 × 30 (11 $^{13}/_{16}$ × 70 $^7/_8$ × 11 $^{13}/_{16}$)
84-21
Giuseppe Guizzetti

28 *Untitled* 1984
Enamelled aluminium
30 × 180 × 30 (11 $^{13}/_{16}$ × 70 $^7/_8$ × 11 $^{13}/_{16}$)
84-46
Private Collection

29 *Untitled* 1985
Enamelled aluminium
30 × 300 × 30 (11 $^{13}/_{16}$ × 118 $^1/_8$ × 11 $^{13}/_{16}$)
85-51
Tate. Presented by Janet Wolfson de Botton 1996

30 *Untitled* 1986
Douglas Fir plywood and orange, amber, alizarin, brown,
purple and yellow over black Plexiglas
30 units, each 100 × 100 × 50 (39 $^3/_8$ × 39 $^3/_8$ × 19 $^{11}/_{16}$)
86-25
Collection of Judd Foundation

31 *Untitled* 1987
Enamelled aluminium
2 units, each 30 × 360 × 30 (11 ¹³/₁₆ × 141 ³/₄ × 11 ¹²/₁₆)
87-30
Jamileh Weber Gallery, Zurich

32 *Untitled* 1989
Clear anodised aluminium and black anodised
aluminium
100 × 200 × 200 (39 ³/₈ × 78 ³/₄ × 78 ³/₄)
89-1
Musée d'Art Moderne, Saint-Etienne Métropole

33 *Untitled* 1989
Clear anodised aluminium with amber and black
Plexiglas
100 × 200 × 200 (39 ³/₈ × 78 ³/₄ × 78 ³/₄)
89-2
Bernier/Eliades Gallery and Tanit Gallery

34 *Untitled* 1989
Clear anodised aluminium and blue Plexiglas
100 × 200 × 200 (39 ³/₈ × 78 ³/₄ × 78 ³/₄)
89-4
Collection of Judd Foundation

35 *Untitled* 1989
Clear anodised aluminium
100 × 200 × 200 (39 ³/₈ × 78 ³/₄ × 78 ³/₄)
89-11
Collection of Judd Foundation

36 *Untitled* 1989
Galvanised iron
150 × 750 × 165 (59 × 295 ¹/₄ × 64 ¹⁵/₁₆)
89-40
Tate. Presented by the American Fund for
the Tate Gallery 2000

37 *Untitled* 1989–90
Enamelled aluminium and galvanised iron
150 × 750 × 165 (59 × 295 ¹/₄ × 64 ¹⁵/₁₆)
Kunstsammlung Nordrhein-Westfalen, Düsseldorf

38 *Untitled* 1990
Blue anodised aluminium and clear Plexiglas
10 units, each 23 × 101.6 × 78.7 (9 ¹/₁₆ × 40 × 31)
90-3
Tate. Presented by the American Fund for
the Tate Gallery 2002

39 *Untitled* 1992
Cor-ten steel
3 units, each 150 × 150 × 150 (59 ¹/₁₆ × 59 ¹/₁₆ × 59 ¹/₁₆),
with 50 (19 ¹¹/₁₆) intervals
92-3
Museo Nacional Centro de Arte Reina Sofía, Madrid

40 *Untitled* 1992
Cor-ten steel with green, yellow, purple, ivory, orange
and black Plexiglas
6 units, each 50 × 100 × 50 (19 ¹¹/₁₆ × 39 ³/₈ × 19 ¹¹/₁₆),
with 50 (19 ¹¹/₁₆) intervals
92-5
Collection of Judd Foundation

41 *Untitled* 1993
Douglas Fir plywood with grey, yellow, brown, blue,
orange and green transparent Plexiglas
6 units, each 50 × 100 × 50 (19 ¹¹/₁₆ × 39 ³/₈ × 19 ¹¹/₁₆),
with 50 (19 ¹¹/₁₆) intervals
93-1
Collection of Judd Foundation

Lenders

PRIVATE COLLECTIONS

Thomas and Cristina Bechtler, Switzerland
Bernier/Eliades Gallery and Tanit Gallery
Estate of Dan Flavin
Giuseppe Guizzetti
The Helman Collection
Private Collection
Private Collection, Courtesy PaceWildenstein, New York
Jamileh Weber Gallery, Zurich
Judd Foundation
Annemarie and Gianfranco Verna

PUBLIC COLLECTIONS

Addison Gallery of American Art, Phillips Academy, Andover, Massachusetts
Öffentliche Kunstsammlung Basel, Kunstmuseum
Museum Ludwig, Cologne
Kunstsammlung Nordrhein-Westfalen, Düsseldorf
Van Abbemuseum, Eindhoven
Tate, London
Museo Nacional Centro de Arte Reina Sofía, Madrid
The Chinati Foundation, Marfa
Solomon R. Guggenheim Museum, New York
The Museum of Modern Art, New York
National Gallery of Canada, Ottawa
Musée d'Art Moderne, Saint-Etienne Métropole
San Francisco Museum of Modern Art
Moderna Museet, Stockholm
Froehlich Collection, Stuttgart
Hirshhorn Museum and Sculpture Garden, Smithsonian Institution
Museum Wiesbaden

Photographic Credits

Index